INFORMING AND CONSULTING EMPLOYEES

The New Law

INFORMING AND CONSULTING EMPLOYEES

The New Law

NICHOLAS SQUIRE
KATHLEEN HEALY
JOANNA BROADBENT

OXFORD
UNIVERSITY PRESS

This book has been printed digitally and produced in a standard specification in order to ensure its continuing availability

OXFORD
UNIVERSITY PRESS

Great Clarendon Street, Oxford OX2 6DP

Oxford University Press is a department of the University of Oxford.
It furthers the University's objective of excellence in research, scholarship,
and education by publishing worldwide in

Oxford New York

Auckland Cape Town Dar es Salaam Hong Kong Karachi
Kuala Lumpur Madrid Melbourne Mexico City Nairobi
New Delhi Shanghai Taipei Toronto

With offices in

Argentina Austria Brazil Chile Czech Republic France Greece
Guatemala Hungary Italy Japan South Korea Poland Portugal
Singapore Switzerland Thailand Turkey Ukraine Vietnam

Oxford is a registered trade mark of Oxford University Press
in the UK and in certain other countries

Published in the United States
by Oxford University Press Inc., New York

Reprinted 2009

ISBN 978-0-19-928364-4

Preface

The purpose of this book is to analyse the Information and Consultation of Employees Regulations 2004 (*ICE Regulations*), which came into force on 6 April 2005 and represent a potentially highly significant development in the UK employee consultation landscape.

The ICE Regulations implement the EU Information and Consultation Directive (2002/14/EC) of 2002. The Directive's impact has been limited in a number of European Member States, where it was little more than restatement of practices already firmly enshrined in their existing domestic law. Not so for the UK, where the ICE Regulations herald what may be a fundamental shift in UK employee relations.

Before the advent of the ICE Regulations, employers were required to inform and consult with their employees or employee representatives in only a limited range of circumstances, broadly on collective redundancies or on the transfer of a business. Under the ICE Regulations, employees now have the right to request that their employer enters into negotiations with employee representatives to put in place an information and consultation agreement, giving the employees or their representatives the right to be notified, and to have their views taken into account, in a wide range of different situations and circumstances.

The ICE Regulations already apply to employers who have at least 150 staff. By April 2008, the right to request information and consultation bodies will have been extended to employees in companies with at least 50 employees.

The Government views the ICE Regulations as giving rise to a range of benefits, including increased employee loyalty and employee motivation, and as a key component in development of the "high-performance" workplace. However the jury is out on whether this will in fact be the case.

From an employer perspective, the ICE Regulations have been seen as a threat in some quarters and an opportunity in others. There has generally been a more uniformly positive reaction from employee bodies, although trade unions, while hopeful that the ICE Regulations will encourage the emergence of a new consultation and participation culture in the UK, will nevertheless be anxious to ensure that information and consultation bodies do not adversely affect their own position within the employer organisation.

At the time of writing, the ICE Regulations are still brand new, and in a number of areas remain unclear. The ICE Regulations operate by reference to "undertakings" and it is regrettable that there is already some doubt in relation to the core issue of what actually amounts to an undertaking for these purposes. Another source of potential uncertainty is the fact that in a number of respects the ICE Regulations simply reproduce the wording in the Directive without trying to clarify what it means. This is particularly the case with the default procedure that applies if the parties cannot agree information and consultation rules. The language used is difficult to interpret. We offer our views on what the correct approach should be to some of these questions, and wait with interest to see how employers, employees and trade unions (as well as legal practitioners) approach these rights and duties.

Our European neighbours will no doubt be looking at how the UK gets to grips with the ICE Regulations with some interest. Indeed, multinational employers and trade union organisations may already be looking to the European experience for a steer on what they should be doing in the UK. With this in mind, we have sought at the end of the book to give a flavour of the obligations existing in a number of other European countries.

The book has been written with the aim of giving practical guidance on how we believe the ICE Regulations are likely to operate. We hope we have anticipated some of the key questions arising and drawn together the themes in the key guidance documentation supporting the ICE Regulations, in particular the DTI Guidance and the guidance issued by ACAS.

Special thanks to our colleagues David Pollard and Louise Taylor for their comments and input and to Brechje Nollen, Laurence Harvey Wood, Andrew Murphy and Mark Lembke for their input on Chapter 11.

The law is stated as at 31 July 2005.

Summary Contents

Contents

Table of Cases

Table of Legislation

Paragraph numbers in **bold** indicate that the regulation is reproduced in full.

UK Statutes

Statutory Instruments

European Legislation

Directives

Germany

Netherlands

Treaties

1

Introduction

1.01 This book explores the impact and effect of the Information and Consultation of Employees Regulations 2004 (SI 2004/3426) (the *ICE Regulations*). The Regulations, made under powers in section 42 of the Employment Relations Act 2004, implement in Great Britain the EU Information and Consultation (European Parliament and Council) Directive 2002/14/EC (the *Information and Consultation Directive*). Equivalent legislation has been implemented in Northern Ireland by the Information and Consultation of Employees Regulations (Northern Ireland) 2005 (Statutory Rule 2005/47).

1.02 The ICE Regulations came into force on 6 April 2005. They are likely to extend considerably the circumstances in which larger and medium-sized employers are obliged to inform and consult with employee representatives in relation to matters affecting the workforce. As a result, the ICE Regulations may have a significant impact on the nature and structure of employment and industrial relations within workplaces in the United Kingdom. Some employment relations analysts have suggested that over time the ICE Regulations will herald a cultural shift towards a much more participative role for employee representatives within UK business generally, along the model of structures currently in place within other European countries, such as France, Germany, and the Netherlands.

1.03 The ICE Regulations may also have implications for existing workplace arrangements with other employee representatives. One question is how consultative bodies set up under the ICE Regulations will interact with existing trade union arrangements and the extent to which trade unions will be prepared to participate in consultative bodies involving non-union representatives.

1.04 The purpose of this book is fourfold:

(1) to set the ICE Regulations in the context of employee participation rights within the UK;
(2) to analyse the contents of the ICE Regulations;
(3) to give guidance on the practical implications of the ICE Regulations for employers, employees and their representatives; and
(4) to contrast the UK position with that of certain other countries in the European Union that have long-standing experience of domestic works councils.

1.05 The need for clear practical guidance arises both because the ICE Regulations introduce a number of new concepts and also because of the way in which the Government has chosen to implement the Information and Consultation Directive. In a number of areas (perhaps most notably in relation to the standard information and consultation provisions that apply if parties cannot agree on negotiated information and consultation arrangements) the ICE Regulations have simply incorporated verbatim the wording used by the Information and Consultation Directive. Understanding what this may mean or require in practice is not straightforward because the language used is imprecise and also because a number of the principles are unfamiliar in a UK context.

1.06 More importantly, the ICE Regulations have been drawn in such a way as to give employers significant flexibility to devise and negotiate arrangements that are relevant and appropriate to their particular business structures. There is no black-and-white 'right answer' as to how the ICE Regulations should be approached. Employers, trade unions, and others therefore need to understand the scope and purpose of the ICE Regulations in order to appreciate the practical flexibilities that may be open to them.

1.07 To assist all parties in the practical application of the ICE Regulations, the Department of Trade and Industry (*DTI*) has published an Explanatory Memorandum and Regulatory Impact Assessment, along with full guidance (a copy of which is set out at Appendix 3 to this book). The Advisory,

Conciliation and Arbitration Service (*ACAS*) also published good-practice advice on information and consultation in October 2004 (available on the ACAS website[1]). Where relevant, this book cross-references recommendations made by the DTI Guidance and ACAS good-practice advice.

A. THE BACKGROUND TO THE INFORMATION AND CONSULTATION DIRECTIVE

The possibility of introducing a framework at European Union level for **1.08** information and consultation on matters affecting workers was raised in the European Commission's 1995 medium-term Social Action Programme. Demands for legislation then intensified following the controversial announcement in February 1997 by Renault, the French car manufacturer, of the closure of its manufacturing plan at Vilvoorde in Belgium. The Vilvoorde controversy caused various interested parties to suggest that existing legal frameworks intended to ensure employee involvement in the affairs of the undertaking employing them afforded insufficient protection to workers (although, subject to the limited specific circumstances summarised at paragraphs 1.31 to 1.34 below, there were of course no such arrangements in the UK anyway). This point was subsequently specifically identified at Recital 6 to the Information and Consultation Directive which noted that pre-existing structures have 'not always prevented serious decisions affecting employees from being taken and made public without adequate procedures having been implemented beforehand to inform and consult them'.

In July 1997, the European Commission commenced a first round of con- **1.09** sultations with the European-based social partners on whether further legislation was necessary. Following various discussions with the social partners, on 11 November 1998 the Commission tabled a proposal for a Directive establishing a general framework for informing and consulting employees in the European Community. The proposal appears to have been at least in part prompted and almost certainly hastened by the refusal of the Union of Industrial and Employer's Confederations of Europe (UNICE), one of the European-level social partners representing business interests, to enter negotiations with the other social partners. UNICE's opposition stemmed from its member organizations in Germany, Greece, Portugal, and the UK, which regarded EU action to require the introduction of information and consultation obligation at a national level as a breach of the principle of subsidiarity. UNICE also took the view that

[1] http://www.acas.org.uk/services/ic.html.

the European Works Council Directive would be sufficient to protect worker interests where European-level intervention was justified, in other words where employer proposals had transnational implications. Consequently, UNICE rejected the draft Directive as unnecessary and called it a 'harmful ... attack on companies' capacity to make decisions'. It particularly objected to the provisions on sanctions, which it regarded as overprescriptive. The draft Directive proposed the cancellation of the legal effects of management decisions on labour contracts (although, as will be seen in Chapter 8, this proposal was removed from the final version of the Information and Consultation Directive). This was subsequently described by UNICE as 'an extreme and disproportionate sanction'.

1.10 On the other hand, the European Trade Union Confederation (*ETUC*), one of the European social partners representing employee interests, welcomed the draft Directive but thought it did not go far enough. It set out its concerns in a position paper published in 1998. Its suggested amendments included:

(a) the extension of the draft Directive to all undertakings (as opposed to undertakings above a specified size) and clarification of the definition of 'undertaking';
(b) extension of the draft Directive to ensure that information and consultation rights applied to all employees, regardless of their type of employment contract;
(c) the incorporation of a wider definition of 'information and consultation', allowing information to be given at the planning stage of a decision, as well as on an ongoing basis; and
(d) provision for a broader range of required subjects for information and consultation, such as mergers, transfer of production, and cutbacks.

No specific changes were made to the draft Directive to reflect these concerns, although as outlined in Chapter 7, in practice, information and consultation about the matters outlined in (d) are likely to be required at the planning stage under the standard information and consultation requirements.

1.11 During negotiations, several key changes were introduced to the draft Directive. Perhaps most significant amongst these was the removal of the provisions relating to sanctions (referred to in paragraph 1.09 above), which would have suspended the legal effect of a decision until information and consultation was completed (see also Chapter 8). The changes also saw the introduction of a two-tier application procedure, allowing Member States to choose between imposing the information and consultation obligation on undertakings or establishments. Prior to this change, the draft Directive referred only to undertakings. Another change, of particular note to the UK, was the introduction of staggered introduction dates for those Member States in which companies were not legally obliged to have any permanent body of employee representatives.

The Information and Consultation Directive was finally agreed by the Council of Ministers on 11 March 2002. **1.12**

EU Member States had three years to implement the Information and Consultation Directive. The ICE Regulations are designed to implement the Information and Consultation Directive in Great Britain. They came into force for undertakings with 150 or more employees in the UK on 6 April 2005. They comprise 43 separate Regulations and two brief schedules. The ICE Regulations are divided into nine parts. **1.13**

The Government prepared the ground for the introduction of the ICE Regulations with considerable care. It issued a discussion paper, *High Performance Workplaces: The Role of Employee Involvement in a Modern Economy*, in July 2002. Consultations then took place and the Government agreed a framework with the Confederation of British Industry (*CBI*) and the Trades Union Congress (*TUC*) for implementing the Information and Consultation Directive. Once the framework had been agreed, a consultation paper and draft regulations were published on 7 July 2003. Consultation closed on 7 November 2003. Following the first round of consultation, a further draft of the ICE Regulations was published on 7 July 2004. The final form of the ICE Regulations was published in December 2004. **1.14**

The impact of the Information and Consultation Directive is likely to be more significant in countries like the UK and Ireland where the culture of employee participation is less well-established than in many other EU countries. **1.15**

B. THE PURPOSE OF THE INFORMATION AND CONSULTATION DIRECTIVE

The purpose of the Information and Consultation Directive is set out in its recitals. Recital 7 notes that 'there is a need to strengthen dialogue and promote mutual trust within undertakings in order to improve risk anticipation, make work organisation more flexible and facilitate employee access to training within the undertaking while retaining security, make employees more aware of adaptation needs, increase employees' availability to undertake measures and activities to increase their employability, **1.16** promote investment in the operation and future of the undertaking and increase its competitiveness.'

1.17 Further, 'there is a need, in particular, to promote and enhance information and consultation on the situation and likely development of employment within the undertaking and, where the employer's evaluation suggests that employment within the undertaking may be under threat, the possible anticipatory measures envisaged . . . with a view to offsetting the negative developments or their consequences and increasing the employability and adaptability of the employees likely to be affected.'[2]

1.18 This was particularly the case given that, in the opinion of the European Commission, existing legal frameworks for employee information and consultation at community and national level have tended to adopt 'an excessively *a posteriori* approach to the process of change, neglect the economic aspects of decisions taken and do not contribute either to genuine anticipation of employment developments within the undertaking or to risk prevention'.

1.19 The key principles underlying the Information and Consultation Directive are therefore clear: a significantly enhanced and participative role for employee representatives in relation to a range of matters affecting the employing business, and at a sufficiently early stage in the process to ensure that there is proper involvement before final business decisions affecting employees are taken.

1.20 The Government anticipates that the new information and consultation arrangements will deliver substantial economic and social benefits over time. According to the DTI's Regulatory Impact Assessment, 'effective employee information and consultation systems are a key enabler of higher performance workforces—they can help staff feel more involved and valued by their employer, and make them better aware of the business climate in which the organisation is operating and help them be more responsive to and better prepared for change.'

1.21 The Regulatory Impact Assessment goes on to consider the benefits of information-sharing and consultation from three different perspectives: those of the employee, the employer, and the economy at large.

1.22 In terms of employees, the logic is that they will have the right to be consulted on important decisions and have access to information that could directly impact on their working lives. As a result of improved information and consultation the DTI considers that they are more likely

[2] Information and Consultation Directive, Recital 8.

to be committed to their job and more likely to participate in training measures that will in turn improve their employability/skills.

As far as employers are concerned, the DTI argues that productivity of enterprises should increase as a result of more highly-skilled workers (due to greater motivation and willingness to participate in training measures). Employees are likely to be more committed to their job, and more prepared to be flexible. A more committed workforce should lead to lower staff turnover. **1.23**

In terms of the economy more generally, the DTI believes that increased productivity and lower labour turnover should enhance the competitiveness of the UK economy. Further, if employees become more willing to undertake training as a result of greater information and consultation, the result would be a more skilled workforce. **1.24**

It remains to be seen whether any or all of these perceived benefits will emerge. In practice, much is likely to depend on the attitude of employers. Where the employer's approach is a reactive one, focussed on doing the minimum possible to comply with legal requirements, it is questionable whether many of the benefits described in the Regulatory Impact Assessment will accrue. By contrast, employers who fully embrace the principles of the high-performance workplace may be better placed to use those bodies to drive social and economic benefits within the workplace. However the true picture will only become clear over time. **1.25**

C. PUTTING THE REGULATIONS IN CONTEXT: EXISTING UK INFORMATION AND CONSULTATION STRUCTURES

As described in greater detail in Chapter 2, the principal effect of the ICE Regulations is that from 6 April 2005, any undertaking that employs 150 or more employees in the UK can be required to set up an employee representative body that must be informed and, in specified circumstances, consulted with over a broad range of business issues. Undertakings employing 100 or more employees but fewer than 150 employees can be required to do the same from 6 April 2007, with a further extension of the ICE Regulations from 6 April 2008, so that all undertakings employing 50 or more employees can be required to set up employee representative bodies from that date. **1.26**

The coming into force of the ICE Regulations does not automatically mean that new information and consultation structures will need to be set in **1.27** place within all employers of the requisite size. (As will be explained in more detail in Chapter 4, there is no requirement on an employer to take steps to set up an employee representative body in the absence of a valid employee request to negotiate information and consultation arrangements.) Nevertheless, for many organizations, the ICE Regulations are likely to herald a significant change to any existing arrangements for employee information and consultation.

1.28 One of the principal reasons for this is that at present information and consultation structures within many UK companies are far less extensive than can be required under the ICE Regulations.

1.29 Indeed non-unionized employers may not have any pre-existing framework for the provision of information to and consultation with employees or their representatives.

1.30 Paragraphs 1.31 to 1.45 summarize the existing circumstances in which employers may be required to inform and consult or negotiate with trade unions or other employee representatives.

D. EXISTING REQUIREMENTS TO INFORM AND CONSULT

1.31 At present, subject to certain industry specific requirements, formal collective information and consultation processes with employees or employee representatives only apply in three circumstances: on collective redundancies, on business sales, and in relation to health and safety matters. Various information and consultation obligations in relation to pensions are expected to be introduced shortly.

1. Collective Redundancies

1.32 In relation to collective redundancies, Section 188 of the Trade Union and Labour Relations (Consolidation) Act 1992 (*TULRCA*) requires an employer who is proposing to dismiss as redundant 20 or more employees at one establishment within a period of 90 days or less to consult appropriate representatives of affected employees about the dismissals. Where the affected employees are of a description in respect of which an independent trade union is recognized by their employer, consultation takes place with representatives of the trade union. Otherwise, consultation is required to take place with employee representatives elected by the affected employees for the purposes of consultation, or elected or appointed by the affected employees for other purposes but who have authority to receive information and be consulted about the proposed dismissals on behalf of the effected employees.

2. TUPE

An information and, depending on the circumstances, a consultation obligation will also arise in relation to business sales under the Transfer of Undertakings (Protection of Employment) Regulations 1981 (*TUPE*). Regulation 10 of TUPE imposes an obligation on an employer of employees affected by a relevant transfer to provide appropriate representatives of such employees with specified information and to consult about 'measures' the employer envisages taking in relation to such employees in connection with the relevant transfer. Appropriate representative for these purposes has the same meaning as in the collective redundancy legislation. **1.33**

3. Health and Safety

Information and consultation obligations also arise in relation to health and safety matters. The Health and Safety at Work etc. Act 1974 imposes an obligation on employers to consult safety representatives regarding arrangements for the safety and health of employees at work. There are also a number of specific information and consultation obligations in relation to health and safety legislation set out in the Safety Representatives and Safety Committees Regulations 1977 (SI 1977/500) and the Health and Safety (Consultation with Employees) Regulations 1996 (SI 1996/1513). **1.34**

4. Pensions

On 6 June 2005 the Department for Work and Pensions published a consultation document and two sets of draft regulations to be made under sections 259–261 of the Pensions Act 2004. These sections require consultation to be carried out where employers or trustees are proposing major or significant changes to affected members' future pension arrangements. The Department for Work and Pensions is also planning to publish (in January 2006) draft non-statutory guidance to support these regulations. **1.35**

The draft Occupational and Personal Pension Schemes (Consultation by Employers) Regulations 2006 envisage requiring most employers in relation to occupational or personal pension schemes to consult on proposals to make 'listed changes' before any decision (or series of decisions) to make those changes is made (see Table 1.1). If the proposal to make a 'listed change' is made by a person other than the employer, that person must notify each employer. The requirements will have a phased **1.36** implementation, with employers of more than 150, 100, and 50 employees having to implement them from 6 April in 2006, 2007, and 2008 respectively. These requirements are in addition to existing requirements to consult in relation to additional specified matters, such as stakeholder pensions, member-nominated trustees, and pension scheme contracting-out.

Table 1.1 Listed changes

Occupational pension schemes
General
(i) Increase in normal retirement age for active or prospective members
(ii) Closure of scheme to new members or for future accrual
(iii) Removal of employer's liability to contribute
(iv) Introduction of member contributions in a previously non-contributory scheme

Money purchase benefits
(i) Reduction in employer contributions/increase in member contributions towards the scheme by 2% or more; or
(ii) Reduction in employer contributions to below a level of 3%

Non-money purchase benefits
(i) Change of some or all benefits to money purchase benefits
(ii) Reduction of future accrual rate
(iii) Increase in member contributions by 2% or more

Personal pension schemes
(i) Reduction (by 2% or more or to below 3%) or cessation of employer contributions payable under direct payment arrangements; or
(ii) Increase in member contributions by 2% or more

Excluded changes
Changes required by legislation or by a determination by The Pensions Regulator or having no lasting effect on eligibility or benefits.

1.37 Specified written information must be given to affected members at least two months before the proposed effective date of the change and consultation undertaken with at least one of any members' representatives or, in certain circumstances, directly with the members. Consultation may be with:

(1) trade union representatives; or
(2) information and consultation representatives under the ICE Regulations; or
(3) nominated member representatives elected for the purpose of the regulations.

The choice rests with the employer. In practice it seems likely that if there are established information and consultation representatives under the

ICE Regulations, there will usually be little reason for the employer to choose to go down the election option.

The employer must then consider the responses received. A complaint may be made to the Pensions Regulator of failure to comply with the consultation obligations.

E. COLLECTIVE BARGAINING

Employers who are unionized may have existing recognition arrangements with trade unions. Those arrangements may be voluntary or, since the implementation of the Employment Relations Act 1999, imposed. Under the statutory recognition procedure contained in Schedule A1 to TULRCA, trade unions will have collective bargaining rights where recognition arrangements are in place. Under voluntary recognition arrangements, employers and trade unions may negotiate over any one or more of terms and conditions of employment or the physical conditions in which workers are required to work; engagement or non-engagement or termination or suspension of employment or the duties of employment of one or more workers; allocation of work or the duties of employment between workers or groups of workers; matters of discipline; a worker's membership or non-membership of a trade union; facilities for trade union officials; and the machinery for negotiation and consultation (see section 178 TULRCA). Under the statutory recognition arrangements, collective bargaining is defined as negotiations relating to pay, hours and holidays subject to the parties agreeing that additional matters may also be the subject of collective bargaining. Paragraph 171A of Schedule A1 (inserted by section 20 of the Employment Relations Act 2004) gives the Secretary of State power to add pensions to the matters to which negotiations may relate. **1.38**

The information and consultation requirements introduced by the ICE Regulations will in many cases be more wide-ranging than collective bargaining arrangements, but there may well be an element of overlap. For example, matters relating to hours and holidays, which fall within the scope of the statutory recognition arrangements, would also fall within the scope of the ICE Regulations. Collective bargaining agreements entered into under voluntary recognition arrangements will often be even broader in scope. **1.39**

However, unlike collective bargaining, the ICE Regulations require consultation rather than negotiation to take place with employee representatives. Having said that, under the standard information and consultation provisions employers are required to consult 'with a view to reaching agreement' on decisions likely to lead to substantial changes in work organization or in contractual relations. It is likely that this is akin to a **1.40** negotiation obligation (see for example the decision of the European Court of Justice in *Junk v Kühnel*,[3] in relation to similar information and consultation obligations in the context of collective redundancies). In practice, an employer that is negotiating an information and consultation arrangement may wish specifically to exclude from the scope of the negotiated agreement any matter that is covered by an existing collective bargaining agreement (see further Chapter 5). In any event, the ICE Regulations will open up the possibility of a more wide-ranging exchange of information about the relevant undertaking than is traditionally the case with collective bargaining, and will require consultation in relation to many (but not all) of those matters.

1.41 As mentioned above, tripartite discussions between the DTI, the CBI, and the TUC prior to the publication of the draft ICE Regulations resulted in broad agreement on the framework for the ICE Regulations. This meant that reaction to the final form of the ICE Regulations has, to date, been relatively muted. The main focus of the tripartite discussions had been over the procedure for triggering negotiations over information and consultation arrangements. The CBI was in favour of preserving the status quo and wanted to ensure that companies which had pre-existing arrangements for information and consultation could retain them, whilst the TUC wished to ensure incorporation of a procedure to enable challenges to arrangements that were not based on general agreement with the workforce. As explained in more detail in Chapter 4, where 10% of the workforce want to hold negotiations on new arrangements, qualifying existing arrangements can be maintained unless at least 40% of the workforce endorses the request for new negotiations in a ballot. In the TUC's view, anything less onerous would have exposed existing agreements (including trade union agreements) to 'easy challenge'.

1.42 Notwithstanding concerns in certain union quarters (largely because of a perceived risk that the ICE Regulations could dilute existing collective bargaining arrangements or lead to the creation of rival non-union structures within the workplace), the TUC has largely welcomed the opportunities offered by the ICE Regulations. The TUC describes the ICE Regulations as 'a golden opportunity to increase [union] presence in workplaces, particularly those where there are union members but where the boss has until now been refusing to engage collectively with staff'.[4] This reflects the fact that, in the absence of a pre-existing agreement, employees will only need to show support from 10% of the workforce to

[3] [2005] IRLR 310.

[4] TUC press release 'New information and consultation rights should mean no more "bolts from the blue" ', 5 April 2005.

require an employer to negotiate an information and consultation agreement, as opposed to the 40% support needed under TULRCA to obtain statutory union recognition. This enthusiasm for the new procedures is notwithstanding the fact that the ICE Regulations do not require information and consultation to take place with union representatives. The TUC had argued that this should be the approach to implementation taken in the UK.[5]

More specifically, the TUC assumes that the ICE Regulations will assist trade unions in addressing issues beyond those of pay and conditions that have been their traditional preserve. In a paper published in August 2004,[6] the TUC also expressed its hope that the ICE Regulations would, in particular, make it easier for trade unions to have rights to be consulted over training. This may in any event eventually be achieved through the statutory recognition route. In March 2005 the DTI issued a request for information about the extent to which training is covered in voluntary collective bargaining arrangements, with a view to keeping collective bargaining under the statutory procedure in line with voluntary arrangements. **1.43**

Finally, the TUC welcomes the fact that the ICE Regulations will cover those trade union members who are not covered by collective agreements. According to 2004 TUC statistics, only 7% of the UK workforce is covered by collective bargaining arrangements. **1.44**

Indications from the CBI are that it expects the impact of the ICE Regulations to be markedly less significant than that envisaged by the TUC. Throughout the consultation process the CBI stressed that the ICE Regulations needed to allow employers maximum flexibility to consult at an appropriate business level. The final version of the ICE Regulations meets the concern expressed that the original drafting did not always make this sufficiently clear. When the ICE Regulations came into force, the CBI Director-General commented that 'These new rules will be irrelevant to most companies because they already have systems that employees are happy with for discussing developments with them.'[7] As discussed in Chapter 3, it is not necessarily clear that such agreements will meet the requirements for pre-existing arrangements set out in the ICE Regulations, and it therefore remains to be seen whether the CBI takes too **1.45**

[5] TUC discussion document 'EU Directive on Information and Consultation: How will it affect employment relations in the UK?'.

[6] *Negotiating Skills and Learning*.

[7] CBI news release 'New worker consultation law will rarely be needed—CBI chief', 5 April 2005.

sanguine a view of the effect of the ICE Regulations, particularly given the comments of the TUC.

1.46 Whatever the CBI's view, one of the key issues that employers with existing trade union arrangements will need to address is how to run their information and consultation arrangements under the ICE Regulations alongside those union arrangements. This question is considered in more detail in Chapters 5 and 6, but it is likely that dual arrangements will operate in a number of organizations. This will mean that an employer will inform and consult under the ICE Regulations with a consultative body comprising information and consultation representatives (who may but will not necessarily be trade union representatives) and will separately bargain collectively with recognized trade unions in respect of pay and other matters.

F. EUROPEAN WORKS COUNCILS

1.47 On a cross-border basis, pan-European companies (that is, community-scale undertakings or groups of undertakings with at least 1,000 employees within the European Union, including at least 150 employees in each of two separate European Union Member States) will also be subject to the provisions of the European Works Council Directive 94/45/EC, implemented in the UK in the Transnational Information and Consultation of Employees Regulations 1999 (SI 1999/3323) (*TICE* Regulations). The TICE Regulations are also of significant interest in the context of the ICE Regulations because the approach taken in the drafting of the ICE Regulations is, in a number of respects, identical to that taken in the earlier regulations and the Government has clearly used a number of the provisions of the TICE Regulations as a model for the ICE Regulations.

G. VOLUNTARY ARRANGEMENTS

1.48 Outside the processes summarized above there are no other statutory requirements in the UK for an employer to engage collectively with its employees or anyone representing them. Many employers have set up voluntary bodies for the exchange of information about matters relevant to the organization, but there are few arrangements that are as broad in scope as the ICE Regulations. The Regulatory Impact Assessment to the ICE Regulations estimates that approximately half of all establishments in the UK with over 25 employees have a formal means of communication and consultation between employers and employees. The fact that the

DTI's Workplace Employee Regulations Survey 1998 (quoted in the Regulatory Impact Assessment) suggests that 35% of employees rate the way management involve employees as poor or very poor is indicative of the limited scope of many such arrangements. Frequently, arrangements provide only for the dissemination of information and do not extend to consultation.

H. SUPPORTING THE STRUCTURE OF THE ICE REGULATIONS: THE ROLE OF THE CENTRAL ARBITRATION COMMITTEE

As a general point it is worth noting that the ICE Regulations give the Central Arbitration Committee (*CAC*) a key role to play in supporting the effective operation of the Regulations. Specific detail is set out in the various chapters of this book but an overview of its function and role is set out below. **1.49**

The CAC is a permanent arbitration body. It is governed by the provisions of sections 259–64 of TULRCA. **1.50**

All members of the CAC are appointed by the Secretary of State. Only persons experienced in industrial relations may be appointed, and the Secretary of State is statutorily required to ensure that the members include some persons whose experience is as representatives of employers and some whose experience is as representatives of workers (section 260(3) TULRCA). **1.51**

After a period when its profile was very low, the role of the CAC has been expanded materially since the Labour Party came into power in 1997. It plays a significant role in relation to the statutory procedures for trade union recognition set out in Schedule A1 to TULRCA. It was also vested with powers and obligations in relation to European Works Councils by TICE that are similar to those it has now been given under the ICE Regulations. **1.52**

The CAC's role under the Regulations is both administrative and determinative. **1.53**

In terms of administration, the CAC has a role as an independent third party to whom employees of an undertaking can submit a request for negotiating an information and consultation procedure if they prefer not to issue such request direct to the undertaking itself (see further Chapter 4). **1.54**

In its role as a determinative body, the CAC is empowered to adjudicate **1.55** on a broad range of different grounds of application or complaint under the ICE Regulations. Regulation 24 makes clear that the only remedy for infringement of the rights conferred by the ICE Regulations (save in relation to certain of the provisions relating to confidential information and protections for information and consultation representatives and others) is by way of complaint to the CAC. The scope of the CAC's role in this respect is considered in more detail in Chapter 8. The types of application and complaint that the CAC has power to determine include:

- the determination of a complaint by an employee or employee's representative in relation to data (or the non-disclosure of data) for the purpose of determining the number of people employed by the employing undertaking (Regulation 6);
- the determination of a complaint by an employee or employee's representative that an employer with a pre-existing agreement in place who has announced its intention to hold a ballot for employee endorsement of an employee request for an information and consultation procedure has not arranged for the ballot to be held within the requisite time period (Regulation 8(8)) or that the ballot fails to comply with the requirements of the ICE Regulations (Regulation 10(2));
- the determination of a complaint by an employee or employee's representative that no valid pre-existing agreement is in place (Regulation 10(1));
- the determination of an application by an employer, an employee or an employee's representative in relation to the validity of an employee request, an employer notification or whether an obligation to initiate negotiations for an information and consultation arrangement exists (Regulation 13);
- the determination of a complaint by an employee or employee's representative about the election or appointment of negotiating representatives (Regulation 15(1));
- the determination of a complaint by an employee or employee's representative about any ballot held for employee approval of a negotiated agreement (Regulation 17(1));
- the determination of a complaint by an employee or employee's representative that a ballot has not been held for the election of information and consultation representatives (Regulation 19(4));
- the determination of a complaint about the operation of a negotiated agreement or the standard information and consultation provisions (Regulation 22(1));
- the determination of an application as to the reasonableness of a

requirement by the employer that information or documents must be held in confidence or as to whether the non-disclosure of information or documents is permitted on the grounds that disclosure would seriously damage the functioning of, or be prejudicial to, the employer (Regulations 25(6) and 26(2)).

The CAC has issued general guidance about its role in relation to such complaints and applications, which indicates the general approach that the CAC is likely to take. **1.56**

I. THE STRUCTURE OF THIS BOOK

Each chapter in this book considers a different aspect of the ICE Regulations. In the remaining chapters of this book: **1.57**

- Chapter 2 looks at when, and to which entities, the ICE Regulations apply;
- Chapter 3 explores the extent to which employees may be able to rely on pre-existing agreements as an alternative to the mechanisms prescribed by the ICE Regulations;
- Chapter 4 examines the process under which negotiations for information and consultation arrangements are initiated under the ICE Regulations;
- Chapter 5 considers the procedure for negotiating information and consultation arrangements;
- Chapter 6 discusses the possible contents of a pre-existing or negotiated agreement and the extent to which these are likely to mirror existing arrangements;
- Chapter 7 analyses the standard information and consultation provisions that will apply within an organization if a voluntary information and consultation procedure cannot be agreed;
- Chapter 8 focusses on the sanctions that may apply if an employer fails to comply with a negotiated or standard information and consultation procedure;
- Chapter 9 addresses the question of whether confidential documents or information need to be disclosed to relevant representatives, whether they can be disclosed subject to obligations of confidentiality, and whether, in certain circumstances, they can be withheld altogether;
- Chapter 10 outlines the protections accorded to employee representatives and other employees participating in the information and

consultation process from being dismissed or subject to a detriment, and the remedies available in the event of a breach; and

- Chapter 11 considers how other European countries with a more established tradition of information and consultation approach some of these questions and explores whether a similar approach could be taken in the UK.

2

When Do the ICE Regulations Apply?

The ICE Regulations apply to 'undertakings' with a specified number of employees. **2.01**

This chapter considers: **2.02**

(1) what will constitute an undertaking for these purposes;

(2) consequently which organizations will be caught by the ICE Regulations, either from 6 April 2005 if the undertaking has 150 or more employees, or subsequently for smaller undertakings with 50 or more employees;

(3) how to calculate whether the undertaking has the relevant number of employees to trigger the application of the ICE Regulations; and

(4) how the ICE Regulations will affect corporate groups, which may have a significant number of employees engaged across different group companies.

A. WHAT IS AN UNDERTAKING?

The Information and Consultation Directive gave Member States the choice to implement the Directive either in relation to 'undertakings employing at least 50 employees in any one Member State' or 'establishments employing at least 20 employees in any one Member State'. **2.03**

2.04 The Information and Consultation Directive defines an undertaking as a 'public or private undertaking carrying out an economic activity, whether or not operating for gain, which is located within the territory of the Member States' (Article 2). An 'establishment' is a 'unit of business defined in accordance with national law and practice, and located within the territory of a Member State, where an economic activity is carried out on an ongoing basis with human and material resources' (Article 2).

2.05 The Government has opted to structure the ICE Regulations so that they apply to 'undertakings'. The Government's view on what constitutes an 'undertaking' is set out in the DTI Guidance on the ICE Regulations. The Guidance suggests that an undertaking is a 'separately incorporated legal entity . . . as distinct from say an organizational entity such as an establishment, division or business unit of a company. It would also include partnerships, co-operatives, mutuals, building societies, friendly societies, associations, trade unions, charities and individuals who are employers—if they carry out an economic activity. It may also include schools, colleges, universities and NHS trusts and government bodies (both central and local), again if they carry out an economic activity.'

2.06 The DTI's interpretation of what constitutes an undertaking may well be subject to challenge. Certainly, the definition of undertaking in the Information and Consultation Directive is not materially different from the concept of an undertaking for the purposes of the Acquired Rights Directive (Council Directive 2001/23/EC) (*ARD*). The ARD does not formally define an undertaking but the provisions of the ARD apply 'where there is a transfer of an economic entity which retains its identity, meaning an organised grouping of resources which has the object of pursuing an economic activity, whether or not that activity is central or "ancillary" '.[1]

2.07 Case-law on the ARD and the English regulations implementing it (TUPE) will clearly be relevant to the interpretation of the ICE Regulations. Indeed, this is specifically acknowledged in the DTI Guidance, which states that established case-law on the ARD and TUPE is likely to be relevant to the question of what constitutes an 'economic activity' for the purposes of the Regulations. In terms of what constitutes an 'undertaking', decisions on TUPE appear to take a broader view than the DTI suggests is the case under the ICE Regulations. For example, an autonomous division of a company will not be an undertaking under the ICE Regulations, according to the DTI's interpretation. Yet there is little doubt that it will fall within the scope of the ARD and TUPE. Does this mean that the concept of an undertaking may, in fact, have a wider meaning

[1] ARD art. 1(b).

than suggested by the DTI Guidance? Conceptually, it may be that the distinction can be justified on the basis that an autonomous division forms 'part of an undertaking'—both ARD and TUPE apply to the transfer of an undertaking 'or part of an undertaking', but the distinction between an undertaking and part of an undertaking is not readily apparent from the case-law.

Turning to the question of what constitutes an 'economic activity', the concept of 'economic activity' tends to be construed relatively widely for the purposes of both the ARD and TUPE. For example, the following have been held to involve 'economic activity': a doctor's practice (in *Jeetle v Elster*[2]), a charitable foundation which provided assistance to drug addicts (in *Dr Sophie Redmond Stichting v Bartol*[3]), and a local authority's refuse collection service which was subsequently transferred to a commercial company which operated for a profit (in *Alderson v Secretary of State for Trade and Industry*[4]). **2.08**

The principal exception to this line of cases can be found in the decision of the European Court of Justice in *Henke v Gemeinde Schierke*[5] in which it was found that the transfer of purely administrative functions between two local government bodies did not amount to the transfer of an 'economic activity'. *Henke* is in many respects the low-water mark in terms of a finding that there is no economic activity, and several subsequent decisions have sought to read *Henke* as restricted to a restructuring of public administrative functions (for example, the subsequent decision by the European Court of Justice in *Mayeur v Association Promotion de L'Information Messine*[6]). **2.09**

However, even on this narrow interpretation of *Henke*, there are a number of public authority activities that may not satisfy the 'economic activity' test. The DTI Guidance for example doubts that central government departments, whose main activities concern the exercise of public authority, would be covered by the ICE Regulations. This reflects the view taken in the July 2003 Consultation paper *High Performance Workplaces: Informing and Consulting Employees*, which indicated that a majority of central and local government employees would not be covered, and invited views on how the principles in the Regulations could be extended to such employees. **2.10**

Not surprisingly, the Government considers it inappropriate that the information and consultation principles set out in the ICE Regulations may not apply to certain public bodies. It has therefore produced a code of **2.11**

[2] [1985] ICR 389.
[3] [1992] IRLR 366.
[4] [2004] ICR 5120.
[5] [1997] ICR 764.
[6] [2002] ICR 1316.

practice, which is intended to apply the principles of the ICE Regulations to central government departments. Local authorities will be encouraged to adhere to its principles.

B. UNDERTAKINGS OR ESTABLISHMENTS

2.12 It is apparent that the ICE Regulations might have applied more widely had the Government decided to implement them on the basis of the 'establishment' definition.

2.13 Regardless of arguments as to what an undertaking means for these purposes, there appears to have been broad agreement between the DTI, the CBI, and the TUC that the ICE Regulations should apply to undertakings rather than establishments. The TUC's approach to implementation was outlined, in a discussion document published in June 2002.[7] It took the view that operating the ICE Regulations at the 'undertaking' rather than the 'establishment' level would be more straightforward because it would:

(1) help ensure equal treatment for employees within multi-establishment undertakings;
(2) help provide for consultation with higher-level management who are more likely to have responsibility for decision-making; and
(3) be more in keeping with the existing pattern of consultation arrangements in the UK.

2.14 According to the leading decision of the European Court of Justice in relation to the meaning of establishment, *Rockfon A/S v Specialarbejderforbundet i Danmark*,[8] a case on the Collective Redundancies Directive (Directive 98/59), the term establishment 'must be understood as meaning, depending on the circumstances, the unit to which the workers made redundant are assigned to carry out their duties'. Further, the European Court of Justice found that it was not necessary for there to be an establishment for there to be a unit endowed with a management which could independently effect collective redundancies.

2.15 Although *Rockfon* obviously concerns a different EU Directive from the Information and Consultation Directive, 'establishment' will almost certainly be given the same meaning. Therefore, if the Government had

[7] *EU Directive on Information and Consultation: How Will It Affect Employee Relations in the UK?*, TUC discussion document prepared by Mark Hall, Industrial Relations Research Unit, University of Warwick.

[8] [1996] ICR 673.

chosen to adopt the 'establishment' approach, the ICE Regulations would have applied separately to most work locations.

The consequence of this is that multi-site employers would (subject to their ability to agree voluntary arrangements on a different basis) potentially have had to set in place a broad number of separate information and consultation arrangements across their workforce regardless of how appropriate this would in fact have been in relation to their overall employment and industrial relations structures. **2.16**

C. WHEN THE ICE REGULATIONS APPLY: THE BASIC PRINCIPLES

Regulation 3 provides that the ICE Regulations apply to undertakings employing the requisite number of employees in the UK (as to which see further paragraph 2.23) and whose registered office, head office, or principal place of business is situated in Great Britain (i.e. the United Kingdom, excluding Northern Ireland). Undertakings whose registered office, head office, or principal place of business is situated in Northern Ireland are covered by equivalent regulations relating to Northern Ireland made by the Department of Employment and Learning Northern Ireland (DELNI). **2.17**

A registered office for the purposes of the ICE Regulations will have the meaning given to it by section 297 of the Companies Act 1985, being the registered office a company is required to establish to which all communications and notices may be addressed. **2.18**

Head office is not a term with any technical meaning and will presumably be given its natural meaning so as to apply to an undertaking's administrative and operational headquarters. **2.19**

According to the DTI Guidance on the ICE Regulations, the reference to a principal place of business is intended to capture organizations that unlike companies, do not have a registered or head office (for example, partnerships or co-operatives). **2.20**

An interesting question arises as to the position of UK branches of overseas companies. A UK branch will not have a registered office in Great Britain, nor will it technically have a head office or principal place of business in this country. Operations with a large number of employees in the UK may be structured as branches of overseas companies (for example, overseas banks). On the face of it, it would appear that the ICE Regulations may not apply in respect of such operations. In practice, it **2.21** is probable that (consistent with the principles summarized at paragraphs 2.07, 2.08 and 2.09 above) the UK operation will be viewed as a separate undertaking with its centre of operation in Great Britain being characterized as a head office or principal place of business for the purposes of the ICE Regulations.

2.22 Where the registered office is situated in Great Britain and the principal place of business is situated in Northern Ireland or vice versa, the ICE Regulations only apply where the majority of employees are employed to work in Great Britain (Regulation 3(2)). Otherwise the Northern Ireland regulations apply.

2.23 In terms of employee numbers, the ICE Regulations have a staggered impact. They apply to undertakings with at least 150 employees in the UK with effect from 6 April 2005. They will apply to undertakings with at least 100 employees with effect from 6 April 2007, and to undertakings with at least 50 employees with effect from 6 April 2008. Medium-sized undertakings therefore have a longer lead-in time before the ICE Regulations take effect. There are no plans to extend the ICE Regulations to smaller undertakings (although the operation of the Information and Consultation Directive is due to be reviewed by the European Commission, Member States, and the Social Partners by 23 March 2007, and it is possible that the question of extending the scope of the Directive may be raised at that time).

2.24 The DTI has estimated that because the ICE Regulations only apply to undertakings with 50 employees or more, only just over 3% of enterprises in the UK will be affected. However, according to the DTI, those enterprises employ some 75% of employees in the UK.

2.25 Of those enterprises to which the ICE Regulations do apply, enterprises with 50 to 99 employees are by some way the largest group. According to the DTI Regulatory Impact Assessment published with the ICE Regulations some 49% of enterprises with 50 or more full-time equivalent employees have between 50 and 99 employees. Around 13,000 UK enterprises are estimated to have 150 or more employees, and therefore became subject to the ICE Regulations from April 2005.

2.26 Even where an undertaking does have a sufficient number of employees for the ICE Regulations to apply to that undertaking, the undertaking in question will not automatically be required to set in place an information and consultation arrangement. The position is described in greater detail in Chapter 4, but in the absence of a valid employee request, the undertaking is not required to take any positive action.

D. APPLICATION OF THESE PRINCIPLES TO CORPORATE BODIES

It will be clear from the above that, as a minimum, every individual corporate entity will amount to a separate undertaking. In other words, where an enterprise has a large number of different group companies, the ICE Regulations will apply by reference to each individual group company and not by reference to overall group structures. **2.27**

For a single corporate entity divided into a number of autonomous operating divisions, (subject to the possible arguments summarized at paragraph 2.7), it is the entity that is the undertaking for the purposes of the ICE Regulations. **2.28**

That said, as explained below, the ICE Regulations also permit a different approach (either group wide or by reference to more than one arrangement within a single company) to be adopted by agreement. **2.29**

Example 2.1
Company A has a divisionalized structure. It employs some 1,500 employees in the UK in seven different divisions at some 25 different sites. Applying the undertaking definition at least it is currently interpreted by the DTI, the divisionalized structure and the fact that there are a number of different sites are irrelevant considerations. Assuming that an employee request is triggered (or Company A voluntarily decides to initiate negotiations), the ICE Regulations will require a single information and consultation arrangement to be put in place within Company A rather than a series of different information and consultation arrangements on a divisional basis. However, as explained below, it would be possible to negotiate differently structured arrangements (for example, a different information and consultation procedure for each division) if these were considered by all parties to be more appropriate.

Example 2.2
Group B has four different subsidiaries. Company B1 has 200 employees, Company B2 120 employees, Company B3 80 employees, and Company B4 40 employees. All employees perform exactly the same work at the same location. Assuming it cannot be shown that the employees are in reality employed by a single group company (as to which see further paragraph 2.32), the application of the ICE Regulations means that each company will need to be considered separately. The Regulations will therefore apply in respect of Company B1 with effect from 6 April 2005, in respect of Company B2 with effect from 6 April 2007, and to Company B3 with effect from 6 April 2008. The Regulations will not apply in respect of Company B4 if it continues to have fewer than 50 employees.

The ICE Regulations do not explicitly prevent employers from seeking to arrange their employment structures so as to avoid the application of the **2.30**

ICE Regulations, for example, by ensuring that no subsidiary employs more than 49 employees (but see further paragraph 2.39 for possible timing implications). Draft DTI Guidance had indicated that 'courts would look at the reality of the situation and where a person actually works rather than simply at what the employment contract says' and implied that employee numbers could be calculated by reference to where employees actually worked rather than the strict legal position. This comment does not appear in the final guidance, which expressly states that employees of a subsidiary, parent or fellow subsidiary of a common parent will not be relevant to the number of employees engaged in the undertaking.

2.31 Quite apart from whether it would make sense from an administrative or industrial relations perspective to structure employment arrangements to try to avoid the application of the ICE Regulations, and despite the changes to the DTI Guidance, if in reality it is clear that, notwithstanding the label attached to the employment relationship by the employer, the employees in fact all work for the same group entity, there must be a significant risk that the CAC would nonetheless find that those individuals were in fact all employed by that single group company.

2.32 It is increasingly common in some industry sectors (for example, for regulatory reasons in financial services companies) for employees to be employed not by group operating companies but by associated service companies (i.e. in genuine arrangements which have not been designed specifically to seek to circumvent the application of the ICE Regulations). On the face of the ICE Regulations, there does not appear to be any basis to 'pierce the corporate veil' and to attribute the employees to the operating undertakings for whom they perform their services. This would mean that under the standard information and consultation provisions, any information and consultation would technically operate on the level of the service company itself, although the CAC may again strain to take a commercial approach in line with underlying realities.[9] Of course, it would almost certainly be agreed as part of any negotiated agreement that information and consultation would operate at operating company level.

[9] There is precedent for this in other legislation. For example, in *Graphical, Paper and Media Union v Derry Print* [2002] IRLR 380, a decision relating to the statutory recognition procedures in Schedule A1 of TULRCA, the CAC concluded that in an exceptional case two or more employers could be regarded as a single employer if in reality is there is overwhelming evidence that, in all relevant respects, they are actually one.

E. DO INFORMATION AND CONSULTATION STRUCTURES HAVE TO OPERATE BY REFERENCE TO UNDERTAKINGS?

Employees can only initiate negotiations for an information and consultation agreement under the ICE Regulations if their employing company has a sufficient number of employees (with employees of other group companies not counting towards the threshold, subject to the comments in paragraphs 2.30 to 2.32). If negotiations do not result in an agreed arrangement and the standard information and consultation provisions apply (as to which see further Chapter 7), then these can only operate at the level of the undertaking. **2.33**

However, throughout the consultation process prior to the implementation of the ICE Regulations, the DTI recognized the importance to both employers and employees (and their representatives) of a flexible approach to information and consultation. Different arrangements will be appropriate to different organizations, depending on their corporate structure, existing employee representation mechanisms, and a range of different factors. As the DTI puts it in the Explanatory Memorandum to the ICE Regulations, 'there should be no single, static model for information and consultation—a "one size fits all" approach would not be appropriate'. **2.34**

The ICE Regulations are therefore structured to allow a single information and consultation mechanism to operate across a series of different undertakings or for there to be a number of different information and consultation arrangements within a single undertaking, provided in each case that this is agreed to by the employees and the arrangements, taken together, cover all employees within the undertaking. As indicated at paragraph 2.33, following an employee request it is only if arrangements cannot be agreed and the standard information and consultation provisions apply that these have to operate at the level of each individual undertaking. Additionally, the ICE Regulations may not require further steps to be taken at all following an employee request if a pre-existing agreement is in place which satisfies various requirements specified in Regulations 8.1(a) to (d), the employer elects to hold a ballot and there is insufficient support in a ballot for an information and consultation arrangement. **2.35**

F. CALCULATING WHETHER THE UNDERTAKING EMPLOYS SUFFICIENT EMPLOYEES TO TRIGGER THE APPLICATION OF THE ICE REGULATIONS

2.36 In determining whether the number of employees employed by an undertaking is sufficient to trigger the application of the ICE Regulations, the calculation is made by reference to the average number of employees employed in the previous 12 months (Regulation 4(1)).

2.37 The average number of employees is calculated by working out the average number of employees employed in each month in the previous 12 months (whether they were employed throughout the month or not, so starters and leavers will count in respect of the month of joining and departure, as the case may be), adding together those monthly figures and dividing the number by 12 (Regulation 4(2)).

2.38 If the undertaking has been in existence for less than 12 months, the average is taken over the number of months the undertaking has been in existence (Regulation 4(4)).

Example 2.3
Company C has 160 employees on 30 April 2005. Its employee numbers have stayed constant since 1 December 2004. Between the end of April 2004 and 30 June 2004, Company C employed 110 employees. During the summer it took on an extra 60 employees during July and August, but between the beginning of September and the end of November the numbers dropped once again to 110 employees. In determining whether the ICE Regulations apply to Company C at 30 April 2005, the following calculation would be required:

5 months with 110 employees
2 months with 170 employees
5 months with 160 employees

Total number of employees 1690 ÷ 12 = 140.83.

Accordingly, the Regulations do not apply at 30 April 2005. Assuming numbers remained constant, the Regulations would apply if the calculation was made at the end of June 2005.

2.39 The requirement for averaging over a 12-month period may mean that the ICE Regulations could technically apply at a time when the actual employee number is materially below the relevant threshold. So, for example, the ICE Regulations might apply from 6 April 2005 to an undertaking with materially fewer than 150 employees at that time, if it has in the recent past had a significantly larger workforce but where, perhaps as a result of a divestiture, those numbers have reduced to a significant degree. Each situation would need to be considered on its own facts.

Example 2.4
Employer D's workforce has historically been approximately 400. However, in March 2005 a substantial business sale resulted in the divestiture of a large proportion of Employer D's operations, and with it three-quarters of its workforce. Even though employee numbers are now less than 150, the Regulations would apply in relation to Employer D as at 6 April 2005 because under the averaging process required by Regulation 4 the average workforce over the year exceeds 150 employees.

G. WHO IS AN EMPLOYEE?

The ICE Regulations define an employee as 'an individual who has entered into or works under a contract of employment'. In other words, the broader definition of a 'worker' (typically defined so as to catch not just someone working under a contract of employment but also an individual who has undertaken to do or perform personally any work or services for another party to the contract) that has been adopted in a range of other recent employment legislation does not apply for the purposes of the Regulations. **2.40**

On the issue of which workers will amount to employees for the purpose of the ICE Regulations, the DTI Guidance broadly reflects the approach taken to the issue by the Court of Appeal in *Ready Mixed Concrete (South East) Ltd v Minister of Pensions and National Insurance* and *Montgomery v Johnson Underwood Ltd.*[10] To establish that he is an employee, a worker will need to show: **2.41**

(1) a requirement personally to provide services in consideration for remuneration (*mutuality of obligation*);
(2) that he is subject to the client's control in the performance of those services; and
(3) that all other provisions of the arrangements are consistent with a contract of service.

Although the guidance suggests that no one of these factors is conclusive, cases indicate that a worker will fail in his claim if he cannot show mutuality of obligation or the necessary degree of control, without further consideration of the surrounding circumstances. **2.42**

Having said that, this area is constantly developing and particular issues are likely to arise in relation to certain categories of atypical worker. A topical current example concerns the status of agency workers. Recent **2.43**

[10] [1968] 2 QB 497 and [2001] ICR 819.

case-law has considerably extended the circumstances in which an individual whose services are made available through an agency may in fact be treated as an employee of the recipient. In *Dacas v Brook Street Bureau (UK) Limited,*[11] the Court of Appeal indicated that an individual made available by an agency but who had worked for the recipient for a period of some four years under its control could be an employee of the recipient because of the possibility of an implied contract of service, regardless of the ongoing involvement of the employment agency (see also *Franks v Reuters Limited*[12] and the Court of Appeal's judgment in May 2005 in *Bunce v Postworth Ltd t/a Skyblue*[13]). Other categories of individual who might seek to argue that they are employees include independent contractors, particularly those engaged through service companies, but who in practice provide services to a single client. The DTI guidance indicates that *temporary* agency workers would not be employees, but is silent on the wider issues surrounding agency workers.

2.44 From a practical perspective, an employer is likely to want to take the view that agency workers and other similar categories of individual are not employees, and then to defend any challenge that is made. The DTI Guidance suggests that the safest course in cases of doubt is to assume that workers whose status is dubious are employees. But this is unlikely to prove attractive to many employers. While this would avoid any challenge about a failure to implement the ICE Regulations, employers are in practice going to be unwilling to concede issues of employment status so readily. It could have knock-on implications in other areas, e.g. tax, working time.

2.45 However, the ICE Regulations give some flexibility to employers as to how they count part-time employees (but only for the purposes of determining the number of employees within an undertaking over the 12-month averaging period). Under Regulation 4(3), the employer may decide (but is not required) to count certain part-time employees as half of a full-time employee for a relevant month.

2.46 A part-time employee may be so counted if, for the whole of a month within the 12-month averaging period, the employee works under a contract by virtue of which he would have worked for 75 hours or less in that month:

(1) were the month to have contained 21 working days;
(2) were the employee to have had no absences from work; and
(3) were the employee to have worked no overtime.

[11] [2004] ICR 1437. [12] [2003] ICR 1166. [13] [2005] IRLR 5570.

It is apparent from Regulation 4(3) that if an employee so qualifies for part of a month only (for example, because his or her hours of work are adjusted during the month), he or she may not be counted as half of a full-time employee for that month. **2.47**

As mentioned above, if the undertaking has been in existence for less than 12 months, the relevant period is the number of months the undertaking has been in existence (Regulation 4(4)). **2.48**

One point that is unclear from the ICE Regulations is what happens when an undertaking which already has in place a negotiated agreement, or in relation to which the standard information and consultation provisions apply, permanently reduces its workforce below 50 employees. There is no reason in principle why a negotiated agreement could not incorporate a term providing that the agreement would fall away in those circumstances (or possibly be suspended pending a subsequent increase in employee numbers). Otherwise the agreement would appear to remain in force, as would the standard information and consultation provisions. There is, for example, nothing in the ICE Regulations similar to the provisions that operate in respect of trade union statutory recognition arrangements and which enable bargaining arrangements to be terminated where the employer employs fewer than 21 employees, averaged over a 13-week period (see paragraph 11, Schedule A1 of TULRCA). **2.49**

H. VERIFICATION OF RELEVANT INFORMATION

Regulation 5 gives an employee or an employees' representative the right to request data from the employer for the purpose of enabling the employee or employees' representative: **2.50**

(1) to make the calculation of the numbers of employees employed by the undertaking (Regulation 5(3)(a)); and
(2) to determine what number of employees constitutes 10% of the employees in the undertaking (Regulation 5(3)(b)).

It is possible that different data will be required for these two calculations (given that certain part-time employees can be counted as half an employee for the purposes of calculating the number of employees employed by the undertaking, but that part-timers count as single employees for the purposes of calculating the 10% threshold). **2.51**

Where such a request has been made, the employer must provide the relevant information within one month of the request. The only requirement for the request is that it must be in writing and dated (Regulation **2.52**

5(2)). The employer is required to provide the employee or employees' representative who made the request with data to enable him to make the calculation of the relevant numbers of employees. Although no specific detail is given in the ICE Regulations of what data must be provided, it would be prudent for the employer to set out details of the total number of employees within the undertaking over much of the past 12 months, including details of those who are counted as half of a full-time employee in accordance with Regulation 4(3). There is no strict requirement to do so, but a full explanation may help to stave off a challenge that the data provided are false or incomplete.

2.53 Any employee or employees' representative who makes such a request but fails to receive any (or an adequate) response may present a complaint to the CAC that the employer has failed to provide the data or that they are false or incomplete in a material particular (Regulation 6(1)). Such a complaint may not be made until one month has elapsed from the date of the employee request for details of numbers (Regulation 6(3)). However, there appears to be no time limit within which the complaint must be brought, so theoretically a complaint could validly be made some considerable time after the event, although there is no obvious reason why an employee would want to delay making a complaint.

2.54 If the CAC finds the complaint to be well founded, it is required to make an order requiring disclosure to be made (Regulation 6(2)). That order must specify the data in respect of which the complaint has been found to be well founded and which must be disclosed, the date (or, if more than one, the earliest date) on which the employer refused or failed to disclose data, or disclosed false or incomplete information, and the date (being at least one week from the date of the order) within which the employer must disclose the relevant data.

I. TESTING WHETHER THE ICE REGULATIONS APPLY

2.55 It is worth bearing in mind that the ICE Regulations do not permit an employer, employee, or employee representative to seek a pre-emptive determination as to whether an undertaking has a sufficient number of employees for the ICE Regulations to apply or indeed whether an atypical organizational entity constitutes an undertaking. Instead, it will be necessary for an employee request or employer notification to be made to initiate negotiations for an information and consultation arrangement (as to which, see further Chapter 4). At that point a declaration can be sought from the CAC as to the validity of the request or, as the case may be, notification. The process is explored in detail in Chapter 4.

3

Pre-Existing Agreements

3.01 This chapter examines the circumstances in which pre-existing agreements may be relied upon as an alternative to the other mechanisms prescribed by the ICE Regulations. It covers the following areas:

- whether pre-existing agreements should be put in place;
- the requirements for an agreement to qualify as a pre-existing agreement;
- the types of agreement that will not qualify;
- what adjustments might need to be made to ensure that an existing arrangement qualifies as a pre-existing agreement for the purposes of the ICE Regulations; and
- the circumstances in which a pre-existing agreement may cease to be valid.

A. BACKGROUND

3.02 One of the key features of the ICE Regulations is that in certain circumstances existing information and consultation arrangements can be used to engage with employee representatives, rather than agreements formally negotiated under the ICE Regulations (see Chapter 5) or imposed under the standard information and consultation provisions (see Chapter 7) (see Table 3.1).

3.03 The possibility of relying on existing arrangements derives from the Information and Consultation Directive. Recital 23 of the Information and Consultation Directive states that in achieving the objective of the Directive, Member States are to ensure: 'where appropriate, that management and labour have a leading role by allowing them to define freely, by agreement, the arrangements for informing and consulting employees which they consider to be best suited to their needs and wishes'.

3.04 Article 5 further provides that: 'Member States may entrust management and labour at the appropriate level . . . with defining freely and at any time through negotiated agreement the practical arrangements for informing and consulting employees.'

3.05 Regulation 8 of the ICE Regulations provides that where an employer receives an employee request to negotiate an information and consultation agreement, if that employer already has a valid 'pre-existing agreement', the employer can choose to test support for the employee request by balloting the employees. If there is insufficient support for the employee request—that is, if fewer than 40% of employees in the undertaking vote in the ballot (or where at least 40% have voted, if the majority do not vote in

Table 3.1 Comparison of pre-existing/negotiated/standard information and consultation requirements as specified in the ICE Regulations

Requirement	Pre-existing agreement	Negotiated agreement	Standard information and consultation procedures
In writing?	Yes	Yes	No, although any agreement varying standard information and consultation procedures must be in writing
Dated?	No	Yes	No, although any agreement varying standard information and consultation procedures must be dated
Cover all employees of the undertaking?	Yes	Yes	No, although any agreement varying standard information and consultation procedures must cover all employees in the undertaking
Approved by the employees/employee representatives?	Yes, but method of approval not stated in ICE Regulations. DTI Guidance suggests support can be demonstrated by (1) simple majority of those voting in a ballot; (2) the majority of the workforce expressing support through signatures; or (3) the agreement of employee representatives representing the majority of the workforce	Yes. A negotiated agreement is deemed approved if (1) all the negotiating representatives sign it; or (2) a majority of the negotiating representatives sign it and either (i) at least 50% of employees in the undertaking approve it in writing; or (ii) at least 50% of employees who vote in a ballot (satisfying the requirements of Regulation 16(3)) approve the agreement	No, although any agreement varying standard information and consultation procedures must be signed by a majority of the information and consultation representatives

Requirement	Pre-existing agreement	Negotiated agreement	Standard information and consultation procedures
Signed by or on behalf of the employer?	No	Yes	No, although any agreement varying standard information and consultation procedures must be signed by or on behalf of the employer
Set out how the information must be given?	Yes, although no requirement for representatives to be elected	Yes: either the agreement must provide for the appointment or election of representatives to whom the employer must provide the information (and with whom the employer must consult); or provide that the employer must provide information directly to the employees of the undertaking and consult the employees directly	No, although any agreement varying standard information and consultation procedures must set out how information must be given, as per requirements for negotiated agreements
Obligation to 'consult'?	No, but agreement must set out 'how the employer is to give information to the employees and seek their views on such information'	Yes: agreement it must 'set out the circumstances in which the employer must inform and consult his employees'	Yes: employer must consult on information set out in Regulation 20(1)(b) (situation, structure and probable development of employment within the undertaking and on any anticipatory measures envisaged, in particular where there is a threat to employment within the undertaking) and 20(1)(c) (decisions likely to lead to substantial changes in work organization or in contractual relations)

favour) then the request may be rejected, and (subject to certain exceptions) there is then a three-year moratorium from the date on which the request was made (or if multiple requests have been made, from the date on which the request, which results in the 10% threshold being reached, is sent to the employer or, of the request is sent to the CAC, the date on which the CAC notifies the employer of the number of employees making the request) before a further request can be submitted (see Chapter 4). Note that this route is only open where the employee request is from fewer than 40% of the employees in the undertaking; if the employee request has the support of 40% or more of the relevant workforce then the employer is required to enter into negotiations for an information and consultation agreement.

Although the ICE Regulations do set out certain requirements in order for **3.06** arrangements to qualify as a pre-existing agreement, they contain very little detail as to what should be covered by such an agreement once it qualifies. For example, the ICE Regulations are not prescriptive as to the frequency of meetings, subject matter of consultation, etc. This contrasts with the more prescriptive requirements relating to the standard information and consultation arrangements which apply to parties who have tried and failed to reach agreement with negotiating representatives on the appropriate form of consultation (see Chapter 7).

There is some debate as to whether it is possible to enter into pre-existing **3.07** agreements for undertakings with 150 or more employees, after 6 April 2005. Regulation 8(1) states that the relevant date on which any pre-existing agreement needs to satisfy the various limbs of the qualifying test is 'the date that [valid employee] request was made'. This seems to suggest that a valid pre-existing agreement can be entered into at any time prior to receipt of a valid employee request.

Employers may therefore wish to consider putting in place a pre-existing **3.08** agreement. If the employer, in an undertaking to which the ICE Regulations already apply, does initiate negotiations for a pre-existing agreement, it is possible that doing so may amount to an employer notification under Regulation 11 (the employer notification route being available for those employers who wish to take the initiative to begin the process of putting in place a negotiated agreement with employee representatives (see further Chapter 4)).

One way to reduce the risk of a decision by an employer to initiate discus- **3.09** sions on a pre-existing agreement being found to be an employer notification is for the employer to make it clear that the action it is taking is *not* in accordance with Regulation 11. This could be unattractive—employee representatives in receipt of such a notice may look to the ICE Regulations and decide that they are better off rallying support for an employee request for a negotiated agreement.

B. WHY WOULD AN EMPLOYER CONSIDER IMPLEMENTING A PRE-EXISTING AGREEMENT?

3.10 In general terms, most employers are likely to consider putting in place a pre-existing agreement for one of two main reasons: either as a 'protective' step to minimize the likelihood of an employee request (and the possibility of having to put in place an agreement under the ICE Regulations) or as a 'positive' step because of perceived workplace benefits flowing from appropriately structured employee representation arrangements.

3.11 The employer's reasoning will probably not only govern whether taking such a step is appropriate, but will also shape the structure and content of such an agreement.

3.12 The following are likely to be the principal reasons why an employer may wish to consider implementing a pre-existing agreement.

1. To Secure More Flexible Employee Representation Arrangements than under the ICE Regulations

3.13 Pre-existing agreements have an advantage over the standard information and consultation procedures for the employer, in that there are no statutory requirements as to what must be covered. The parties therefore have complete flexibility to agree terms that are best suited to the organization.

3.14 If the employer is concluding a pre-existing agreement as a 'protective' measure, its aim is likely to be to secure an agreement which is less onerous than the requirements of the standard information and consultation requirements. However this point should not be overstated. Employees are unlikely to agree to arrangements that are materially different from those which may be achieved via a negotiated agreement or through the standard information and consultation procedures.

3.15 Pre-existing agreements have an advantage over negotiated agreements, in that a number of the requirements of the ICE Regulations, including in particular the dispute procedures in Regulation 22 and the confidential information obligations in Regulation 25, do not apply to pre-existing agreements. There is therefore less prescription as to what pre-existing agreements should contain and how they should operate. This lack of prescription cuts both ways so that, for example, the protections in the

ICE Regulations for the employer, with regard to information in respect of which employee representatives are subject to an obligation of confidentiality, will not apply.

2. To Improve/Develop Communication between the Employer and the Workforce

The decision as to whether to initiate discussions to conclude a pre-existing agreement will depend also on the existing relationship between employees and the employer. Would introducing an employee consultative body be a positive and pro-active step by the employer towards achieving a better and more effective relationship with staff? Could it also be an opportunity to resolve ongoing matters that might be outstanding within the organization, e.g. any collective disputes with staff? **3.16**

Consideration will need to be given to the structure of the employer's organization and the scope and influence of any existing employee representative body. Does the employer already recognize trade unions for the purposes of collective bargaining? If so, what percentage of the workforce is covered by such arrangements? What is the likely reaction of the unions to a new pre-existing agreement? **3.17**

Generally trade unions have welcomed the introduction of the ICE Regulations, seeing them as giving an opportunity to unions potentially to extend their influence. However the relationship between the employer and the union will be damaged if the union's view is not sought on this matter. Without advance warning, the union may view a move to implement a pre-existing agreement with suspicion, and may have concerns that such a step could erode its influence and authority. **3.18**

If the employer already has a collective bargaining agreement covering part of the workforce and is considering implementing a pre-existing agreement separate from those collective bargaining arrangements, he may then be faced with a 'mixed constituency', i.e. two sets of employee representatives, to whom different and possibly overlapping obligations are owed. Consideration needs to be given to the practicalities of handling information and consultation with the two sets of employee representatives bodies going forward before proceeding with discussions on implementing a pre-existing agreement. **3.19**

3. To Reflect/Change the Culture within the Organization

For some organizations, putting in place an agreement for collective information and consultation may be merely a matter of formalizing **3.20** arrangements which are already in place. For other organizations, the decision to introduce such an agreement might result in significant culture change. How willing is the employer in practice to embrace such a change? What is management's view? Is the employer willing and able to devote sufficient resource to the operation of such an agreement? If an employer is not prepared to support the process, then it is clearly unwise to initiate a process to put a pre-existing agreement in place.

3.21 Employers who have operations outside the UK may wish to consider what employee consultation mechanisms exist elsewhere within their organization, and may wish to consult with local management to assess what lessons can be learned from their experience.

3.22 Consider also the likely reaction of the workforce. Employees may be uninterested in a collective information and consultation process. This may not be a reason for doing nothing, however. If the employer is keen to develop a 'high-performance' workplace, there could be real value in the employer taking pro-active steps to establish a pre-existing agreement.

C. THE CONTENT OF A PRE-EXISTING AGREEMENT

3.23 Having considered the relative merits of seeking to put a pre-existing agreement in place, the other key consideration for the parties will be what the agreement should cover.

3.24 If the employer already has arrangements in place with which the workforce are broadly happy, then it may be easy enough to enshrine those arrangements within a pre-existing agreement.

3.25 If not, then in considering what matters should be covered by a pre-existing agreement, employees or their representatives are likely to want arrangements that broadly mirror the standard information and consultation procedures—in other words, arrangements they could secure by submitting an employee request and effectively 'waiting out' the negotiation period. Anything offered by the employer which is materially less than the standard procedure is likely to be more difficult to agree.

3.26 The ICE Regulations do not specify what could or should be contained in a pre-existing agreement. Chapter 6 analyses the content of Annex 1 of the DTI Guidance and its suggestions for the contents of pre-existing and negotiated agreements and looks at what the parties might wish to cover in such agreements.

D. THE REQUIREMENTS FOR A VALID PRE-EXISTING AGREEMENT

A 'pre-existing agreement' is defined in the ICE Regulations as: **3.27**

an agreement between an employer and his employees or their representatives which—
(a) is made prior to the making of an employee request; *and*
(b) satisfies the conditions set out in regulation 8(1)(a) to (d).

Regulation 8(1) provides that a pre-existing agreement is an agreement which is:

- in writing;
- covers all the employees of the undertaking;
- has been approved by the employees; and
- sets out how the employer is to give information to the employees or their representatives and seek their views on such information.

1. Multiple Agreements

Regulation 8 expressly contemplates that there may be more than one agreement in existence. Provided the conditions above are satisfied by each of the agreements, if one undertaking has multiple agreements which, taken together, cover all of the employees in the undertaking, then the agreements will qualify (in other words, there is no requirement that all employees be covered by a single 'umbrella' agreement). **3.28**

Example 3.1
An employer has 300 employees of whom 50% are covered by a historical arrangement known as the 'Employee Forum'. The employee representatives who sit on the Employee Forum meet with management twice yearly, when the employer's interim and final results are announced. The Employee Forum has a written constitution which confirms the rights of the Employee Forum to meet with management twice a year and discuss matters affecting the employees.

The remaining 50% of the workforce is covered by an agreement which was drafted and circulated by the employer following discussions with representatives of this section of the workforce. The agreement is similar to the constitution of the Employee Forum.

Provided the employer can show that the Employee Forum and the newer agreement both have the approval of the employees (see below for what constitutes approval), they should together qualify as a pre-existing agreement. However if the information process for either arrangement is in fact only a 'one-way' exchange of information, the agreements will not qualify.

Example 3.2

An employer has 200 employees. They are represented by four representatives who were elected recently to sit as a working party set up by the employer to look at staff turnover and conduct discussions with the employer on this issue.

Unless the working party arrangement is covered by a written agreement which has the approval of the employees and which sets out how information will be given and views sought, the working party arrangement will not amount to a pre-existing agreement.

3.29 Regulation 9 deals with pre-existing agreements covering groups of undertakings. In the same way as an undertaking may be covered by more than one agreement (split e.g. by business sector/employee grade/department), so a pre-existing agreement may cover employees in more than one undertaking. Therefore one or more agreements covering employees across a number of different undertakings may also together constitute valid arrangements in relation to those undertakings for the purposes of the ICE Regulations.

E. THE ELEMENTS OF THE DEFINITION IN REGULATION 8(1)

3.30 This section covers the conditions set out in Regulation 8.

1. Agreement Must Be in Writing

3.31 To be valid, a pre-existing agreement must be in writing. Regardless of how established arrangements for informing and consulting are within an organization, or how accepted a custom and practice of engaging in a process of information/consultation might be, if that arrangement or practice has not been reduced to writing then it will not count as a valid pre-existing agreement.

3.32 If an employer already has an established custom and practice of informing and consulting with staff, then it may be sensible for the parties to agree to record that arrangement in writing if they wish to be able to rely on those arrangements going forward.

2. All Employees in the Undertaking Must Be Covered

3.33 Whether an employer has one agreement or multiple agreements, the arrangements in existence must singly or together cover 'all the employees of the undertaking'. The definitions of 'undertaking' and 'employees' have been covered in Chapter 2.

Example 3.3
A group employer has an employee body which covers all of the subsidiary group companies (group companies A, B, and C). The employee body meets annually with a representative of the parent company prior to the shareholder annual general meeting. However head office staff members are employed by the parent company and are not covered by the employee body.

The agreement will not count as a pre-existing agreement in respect of the employees of the parent company unless the parent company employees are either added to the agreement, or a new agreement is put in place covering them. It will, however, qualify as a pre-existing agreement for the employees of group companies A, B, and C (provided all employees, including management and any directors of these subsidiaries, are covered).

The DTI Guidance makes the point that several different methods of **3.34** providing information may exist within an organization, which may be recorded either in a single agreement or in multiple agreements which together cover the entire workforce. These agreements, when taken together, may amount to a pre-existing agreement.

Example 3.4
Within an employer's organization those employees who work on the shop floor have regular monthly lunchtime sessions to which all employees are invited and at which information is given and there is an opportunity to ask questions and contribute views.

The employees who do not work on the shop floor (i.e. the remaining office staff) are represented by two individuals. A representative of management meets with the two individuals from time to time to inform them of any issues affecting employees. The individuals are expected to collate the views of those employees they represent and feed back any material issues.

Provided the two sets of arrangements are recorded in writing and have the approval of staff, they will together constitute a valid pre-existing agreement.

The requirement that an agreement covers *all* employees of the undertak- **3.35** ing is in practice likely to be one which will mean many agreements will not qualify. It is rare for such agreements to cover the higher echelons of an organization—notably management, including, for example, executive board directors (who are also employees and therefore would need to be covered). Agreements which have been structured other than with Regulation 8 expressly in mind are therefore likely to fall foul of this requirement.

Example 3.5
A company has a written agreement setting out an information and consultation process which covers 'all the employees of the Company'. It is not clear from the face of the document whether management, including the directors of the company, are covered. In fact management have tended to take turns at being responsible for meeting with employee representatives annually to discuss matters. Does the agreement qualify as a pre-existing agreement?

Possibly not. Although Regulation 8(1) states simply that a pre-existing agreement must cover 'all the employees of the undertaking', in practice the company's arrangements may not be seen as 'covering' management, even though in practice they involve management. The extent to which pre-existing agreements will be open to challenge on this point will be of particular interest.

3. The Agreement Must Set Out How Information Is to Be Given and Views Sought

3.36 In order to qualify as a pre-existing agreement, the arrangement in place must encompass a process whereby information is provided and 'views sought'.

Example 3.5

A company has a written agreement with its employee representatives which provides that information relating to the company, its business activities, and any important changes will be provided in the form of a quarterly newsletter.

Unless the agreement with the employees provides for a mechanism whereby employers or their representatives can provide views to the company on the information disseminated through the newsletter, this agreement will not be sufficient to qualify as a pre-existing agreement, as there is no method provided by which the employer can seek views from the employees or their representatives on the information provided.

3.37 There is no express reference to 'consultation' in this context. Consultation is defined in the Information and Consultation Directive as 'the exchange of views and establishment of dialogue between the employees' representatives and the employer'. Further, Article 5 of the Information and Consultation Directive which provides for the parties to be able to use pre-existing agreements, expressly refers to 'informing and consulting employees'.

3.38 However, rather than referring to 'consultation' (as is referred to in Regulation 16(1) in relation to the requirements for negotiated agreements), or even to the 'exchange of views' and establishment of dialogue (as per the Information and Consultation Directive), Regulation 8 instead requires that a pre-existing agreement must set out how 'views [are] sought'.

3.39 Is there is a difference between the 'exchange of views' and the 'seeking of views'? The former would seem to imply more of a two-way street, with the onus on the employer to respond to any views put forward by the employee. The latter may amount to a lesser obligation, with an obligation only to ask the representatives for their views, without necessarily needing to respond to them. It is possible therefore that the legal obligations in respect of pre-existing agreements are less than those contemplated by the Information and Consultation Directive because of the different language used.

In practice, however, if the arrangements in place are not meaningful, an employee request for a new information and consultation procedure is far more likely (although such a request would still need to be supported by the requisite percentage of employees). **3.40**

4. The Agreement Must Be Approved

In order to be valid, the employer will need to be able to demonstrate that the agreement has the approval of the employees it purports to cover. **3.41**

In practice the requirement for approval may mean that many existing information and consultation arrangements (even if they can be shown to apply to all employees within the undertaking) do not qualify as pre-existing agreements. **3.42**

Those organizations that already have arrangements in place for informing and consulting with employees may not necessarily be able to demonstrate employee approval for those arrangements. For example, management within the employer's organization may have put the procedures in place for workforce information and consultation on its own initiative and may not have sought to test the level of support for those procedures. **3.43**

The inclusion of the requirement for employers to be able to show support for pre-existing arrangements is to ensure that where an employer wishes to continue to use existing information and consultation procedures, it can be demonstrated that those procedures genuinely do have the support of the workforce. **3.44**

F. WHAT CONSTITUTES APPROVAL UNDER THE ICE REGULATIONS?

The ICE Regulations themselves do not contain a definition of what constitutes 'approval'. However, an indication of what is likely to constitute approval is to be found in the DTI Guidance. **3.45**

The DTI Guidance states that in the DTI's view, approval would include: **3.46**

(a) support indicated through a simple majority among those voting in a ballot of the workforce; or
(b) a majority of the workforce expressing support through signatures; or
(c) the agreement of representatives who represent a majority of the workforce.

3.47 The approval requirements applicable to pre-existing agreements are similar but slightly less onerous than those suggested by the DTI Guidance for negotiated agreements. Under Regulation 16(3) a negotiated agreement must be signed by *all* the negotiating representatives and if it is not, then a majority must sign it *and* 50% of employees (or if a ballot is held, 50% of employees voting in a ballot) must also approve it in writing.

3.48 Organizations that have multiple agreements can demonstrate support for each of those agreements in different ways—there is no requirement for the method of support to be uniform.

3.49 The requirement for an agreement to be approved in order to qualify as a pre-existing agreement is one which may be relatively straightforward where there are already employee representatives in place, or for smaller organizations, where getting the majority of the workforce to sign may be possible. However for larger organizations the need to obtain approval (which may involve the employer holding a ballot or getting the signatures of at least 50% of the employees) is likely to be a more onerous prospect.

3.50 The DTI Guidance encourages employers who believe they have support for existing arrangements to consider getting approval for those arrangements e.g. by discussing the agreement and the requirements of the ICE Regulations with existing representatives to see if formal approval can be obtained. This may, however, prove difficult in practice where such a request could prompt employee representatives to take a fresh look at existing arrangements to see if more could be achieved under a new information and consultation arrangement.

3.51 One point employees will need to bear in mind when they seek approval from employee representatives is that those individuals must genuinely be representatives of the employees. The ICE Regulations do not define who will constitute employee representatives for these purposes. Clearly, trade unions will be representatives in respect of those categories of employee in relation to which they are recognised by the employer. Representatives elected by a ballot of employees are likely to be employee representatives. But employers will need to be alive to the possibility of a challenge if there is any basis for arguing that the individuals in question are not genuinely representatives.

G. WILL OTHER TYPES OF AGREEMENTS QUALIFY AS PRE-EXISTING AGREEMENTS?

Many organizations will have a variety of agreements already in place which provide for the involvement of employees in the decisions made or contemplated by the employer which impact on staff. **3.52**

1. European Works Council Agreements

The definition of a pre-existing agreement in Regulation 2 expressly excludes European Works Council (EWC) agreements concluded in accordance with the TICE Regulations. **3.53**

EWCs have a different function to national works councils and one is not a substitute for the other. In explaining why an EWC agreement is expressly excluded from the definition of a valid pre-existing agreement, the DTI Guidance highlights the fact that EWCs have the right to be informed about 'transnational questions which significantly affect workers' interests'. An EWC does not have the right to be informed about matters that only impact on one particular country within a multinational's organization (although many companies would usually inform the EWC of significant national matters in the ordinary course). **3.54**

In contrast, the focus of domestic works councils is very much on issues which affect employees within their country, e.g. changes to terms and conditions, redundancies, and other such matters. So, for example, a redundancy exercise which proposed closures in e.g. France, Germany, and Italy would be a matter in respect of which an EWC would have the right to be informed. However, a redundancy exercise affecting e.g. employees in France only, would not be something in respect of which the EWC would have the right to be informed, however large the single redundancy exercise might be. **3.55**

The timing of the information and consultation process (where a proposal impacts on more than one European jurisdiction) and the interaction of the requirements to inform and consult domestic works councils with the requirements to inform the EWC have given rise to litigation in recent years. In particular courts in France have recently been asked to consider which body should be informed and consulted first: the EWC or the domestic works council? **3.56**

The announcement by Marks & Spencer of its decision to close its European retail outlets gave rise to much publicity and also to litigation in **3.57** the French civil courts as to the correct timing of consultation with both the EWC and with the domestic French works councils. The civil court of Paris found that the French works council should have been informed and consulted as soon as the detail of a proposed project was sufficiently precise to allow the information/consultation process to begin. The failure to fulfil this obligation could not be justified by arguing that the employer was first obliged to consult the EWC (in this case Marks & Spencer had not, in fact, consulted with the EWC and this was therefore not a valid argument).[1]

3.58 More recently, two other French civil courts have held that the EWC should be informed and consulted *before* the French works' council in relation to matters that have a transnational effect.[2]

2. Redundancy and TUPE Consultation Bodies

3.59 A number of employers may already have employee representation arrangements in place to deal with redundancy exercises where collective consultation obligations are triggered under section 188 of TULRCA.

3.60 Employers may also have arrangements in place to handle the information and consultation exercise required on the transfer of a business where TUPE applies.

3.61 Whilst such bodies are normally set up for specific redundancy/reorganization exercises, some employers who anticipate change over a number of months or years may ask employees to elect a body of representatives with whom they can consult over such issues in the medium to longer term. This is particularly so for an employer who may be engaged in a series of transactions or a significant internal reorganization exercise, where having a standing employee representative committee may be an advantage.

3.62 If there are written agreements in place in respect of such bodies, then those bodies, provided the agreements satisfy the requirements set out in Regulation 8, are capable of amounting to a pre-existing agreement. However in practice such arrangements are likely to be narrow in scope (particularly in relation to the remit of the employee representatives and the subject matters covered) and this may therefore not satisfy employees wanting something more akin to the standard information and consultation procedures.

[1] TGI Paris, 9 April 2001, Marks & Spencer.
[2] TGI Nanterre, 1 August 2003, ALSTOM and TGI Paris, 10 October 2003, ALTADIS.

3. Collective Agreements with Trade Unions

A collective agreement may qualify as a pre-existing agreement if it is in writing, sets out how the employer will inform and consult with the trade union representatives, and if it has been approved. The DTI Guidance highlights the fact that a collective agreement could qualify as a pre-existing agreement, as even if all employees are not union members, those in the bargaining unit will be covered by the collective agreement (and therefore presumably will be deemed to be covered by the collective bargaining agreement for the purposes of the requirement in Regulation 8(1)(b)). **3.63**

If within an undertaking there is a collective agreement covering one section of the workforce, the remaining employees would need to be covered by a separate pre-existing agreement, so that taken together, all of the employees in the undertaking are covered. **3.64**

H. CAN AN EXISTING AGREEMENT BE AMENDED TO ENSURE THAT IT QUALIFIES?

It is only when faced with an employee request (which, once made, starts the time running on what is a fairly tight timetable for the parties to initiate and conclude negotiations—see Chapter 5) that an employer needs to be able to demonstrate that any pre-existing agreement qualifies (because if it does, he can elect to ballot the workforce on levels of support for the arrangement already in existence). Note, however, that, if a valid employee request has been made by 40% or more of the employees within the undertaking on the date on which the request is made, the employer will be required to enter into negotiations for an information and consultation agreement regardless of whether there is a valid pre-existing agreement within the undertaking. This may not mean, however, that the pre-existing agreement falls away (see further paragraphs 4.35 and 4.36). If the arrangement does not qualify as at the date the request is received assuming less than 40% of the workforce has made the request, then it will be too late for the employer at that stage to take steps to remedy any defects that prevent the arrangement qualifying as a pre-existing agreement. For those employers who already have arrangements in place but have not yet received an employee request, the question is whether those arrangements need to be amended to ensure compliance with Regulation 8. See, however, paragraphs 3.8 and 3.9 for a discussion as to whether a decision by an employer to introduce or vary a pre-existing agreement could amount to an employer notification. **3.65**

3.66 Employees or their representatives who make a valid employee request and who do not accept that an employer's existing arrangement validly constitutes a pre-existing agreement may present a complaint to the CAC. The process by which the CAC may be approached to make a determination on the validity of a pre-existing agreement is explored in more detail in Chapter 4.

I. KEY AREAS FOR CONSIDERATION IN EXISTING AGREEMENTS

3.67 Employers who wish to rely on an existing agreement, need to give thought to the following key elements of the existing arrangement to see if a challenge to its validity could be made:

1. Does the Agreement Cover All of the Employees in the Undertaking?

3.68 Consider the terms of any existing agreement. Assuming the agreement or agreements are in writing, do they genuinely cover all employees within the undertaking? For the reasons discussed in paragraphs 3.33 to 3.35, the answer to this question may be no. The scope of arrangements may therefore require adjustment.

2. Has the Agreement Been Approved?

3.69 As already discussed, it is unlikely in practice that existing agreements will have formal employee approval. Assuming the employer believes that there is widespread support for the pre-existing arrangements, he may wish to consider putting that support to the test, e.g. by asking for signatures of either the employee representatives or of the employees themselves. An employer will not be able to take advantage of the ability to test the strength of support for his existing procedures by balloting his workforce (Regulation 9(2)) if those procedures are not ones which can be shown to have workforce support.

3.70 If the agreement was previously approved, consider whether any changes in the workforce which have taken place since the agreement was created impact on the validity of the agreement's approval. Have there been any significant disposals or acquisitions since the agreement was created? If so, are the incoming employees covered by the existing agreement? If not, then the agreement may need to be amended/expanded to cover the new staff. The employer should also check whether any incoming staff are themselves covered by a separate agreement. As mentioned earlier in this chapter, the ICE Regulations expressly contemplate that more than one agreement may together satisfy the requirements for pre-existing agreements.

3. What Is Covered by the Pre-Existing Agreement: Is the Arrangement a 'One-Way Street'?

Existing arrangements may provide for information to be given to employee representatives on a regular basis, but may not encompass consultation with the employee representatives. Listed companies may, for example, be used to meeting with employee representatives around the time of interim and final results announcements, as this provides a good opportunity to give employees information on the financial well-being of the company and provide details of any material plans or developments. Most of the information may, however, already be in the public domain by that stage. **3.71**

For many companies who already have arrangements in place, the concept of a 'two-way' exchange of information and views may come as a change. The standard information and consultation provisions which apply to those who find themselves unable to reach agreement on the scope of information and consultation contemplate that representatives will be able to genuinely influence the decision-making process on matters that will impact on the workforce. Employers whose existing arrangements are only a one-way information channel will not be able to show that those existing arrangements qualify as a pre-existing agreement for the purposes of the ICE Regulations (although as discussed above, there may be a subtle distinction between 'consultation' and 'seeking views' and therefore an agreement which does not expressly refer to consultation may nevertheless qualify). **3.72**

J. WHEN A PRE-EXISTING AGREEMENT CEASES TO BE VALID

Regulation 12(1)(c) provides that where an employer has received an employee request and has successfully balloted the workforce on the basis of having an existing agreement in place, such that he is not obliged to begin negotiations for a new information and consultation arrangement, the employer has a three-year moratorium before a further employee request can be made. **3.73**

The ICE Regulations recognize, however, that changes to an employer's organization may occur over time, which may in turn impact on the **3.74** validity of any pre-existing agreements, in that they may no longer satisfy the requirements set out in Regulation 8.

3.75 Employees may submit a request for a new information and consultation procedure to be established where there are 'material changes in the undertaking' during the applicable period (i.e. during what is otherwise a three-year moratorium) where those changes result in there no longer being an agreement which satisfies the requirements in Regulation 8(1)(b) and (c) (that is, one which covers all the employees in the undertaking and has been approved by the employees: Regulation 12(2)).

3.76 There is no definition of what constitutes material changes in the undertaking. The use of the word 'material' is clearly included to restrict any arguments that minor changes in the workforce could constitute grounds for submitting an employee request for a new information and consultation procedure. It is submitted that the use of the word 'material' therefore excludes hiring and firing in the ordinary course. However, it is unclear at what point natural attrition or 'churn' within an employer's organization may amount to a material change.

3.77 A corporate reorganization (intra-group or otherwise), or a takeover, acquisition, divestiture, or joint venture may well amount to a 'material change' to the undertaking, such that the validity of a pre-existing agreement can be challenged.

K. IMPACT OF CORPORATE TRANSACTIONS ON PRE-EXISTING AGREEMENTS

3.78 As a result of the introduction of the ICE Regulations, one of the areas of interest for prospective purchasers will be the nature of any arrangements within a target business or company.

3.79 Prospective purchasers will want to know (1) what arrangements (if any) exist (so that the expectation of the incoming workforce can be gauged), and (2) if they do exist, what is the nature of those arrangements. Can the purchaser expect incoming employees to be dissatisfied with any pre-existing agreement? What if the purchaser has standard information and consultation procedures or a negotiated agreement in place and does not wish to be bound by the different procedures applying to incoming staff?

3.80 If the incoming staff members are covered by a pre-existing agreement then the purchaser will need to consider whether such arrangements will survive following completion of the transaction and how any such arrangements may impact on existing arrangements that the employer may have in place.

L. INTERACTION BETWEEN THE ICE REGULATIONS AND REGULATION 6 OF TUPE

The Government published draft revised TUPE Regulations on 15 March 2005, which will come into force on 1 April 2006. The current draft makes no amendments to the current drafting of Regulation 6 of TUPE (Regulation 5 of the new draft Regulations), which broadly provides that any collective agreements made with a trade union will transfer. **3.81**

This means that the extent to which other forms of 'collective' agreements (such as pre-existing agreements) will transfer on a TUPE transfer is unclear. **3.82**

Where a pre-existing agreement covers a single undertaking, which then transfers under TUPE, it is safe to assume that the employees will expect the agreement also to transfer (and may seek confirmation of the position during TUPE consultation). However there is no legal obligation under either TUPE or the ICE Regulations on the transferee to continue to operate the pre-existing agreement post transfer. However if the transferee chooses not to continue to operate such an agreement, this may prompt employees to make an employee request. **3.83**

More complex will be the status of a pre-existing agreement which covers more than one undertaking, where one of those undertakings is transferred. Presumably the agreement remains behind to cover the remaining undertakings. But do the staff members who transfer have the right to the continued benefit of those terms? As a matter of law, the answer is likely to be no, and the transferee will need to give consideration therefore to either voluntarily agreeing to maintain those arrangements (ensuring he had obtained a sufficient description of the arrangements during the due diligence process) or covering the incoming employees within the transferee's own arrangements if he has them (and in any event the transferee may need to cover them to ensure his pre-existing agreement does not, following the TUPE transfer, fall foul of the requirement in Regulation 8 that it cover all employees in the undertaking). Or he can do nothing, although again the loss of the benefit of a pre-existing agreement might then be more likely to prompt an employee request for a negotiated agreement to be put in place. **3.84**

One way to address such concerns may be to use the TUPE consultation process to explain what procedures exist and seek the agreement of the **3.85** incoming workforce to those arrangements. Depending on the number of staff to be inherited, there may be real value in the purchaser reaching agreement with incoming staff to avoid being faced with a request for a new information and consultation procedure to be established, a request which may be valid if there has been a 'material change'. Of course, if the transaction is one governed by TUPE, then the seller and purchaser will be obliged to undertake information and consultation with representatives of affected employees in any event. There is no reason why as part of the TUPE consultation process, those employees whom the purchaser is inheriting could not be familiarized with any information and consultation procedures which the purchaser may have in place.

3.86 The way in which the CAC approaches the validity of pre-existing agreements is an area that will be of keen interest to employers and practitioners alike. The powers of the CAC are dealt with in Chapter 4.

M. CONCLUSION

3.87 The requirements set out in Regulation 8 may, in practice, mean that only a small number of pre-existing agreements will comply. Nevertheless employers may wish to give consideration to whether and to what extent it might be appropriate to seek to introduce a new agreement, or amend an agreement, so as to take advantage of the provisions of Regulation 8.

3.88 Although Regulation 8 gives the employer and the employees scope to agree arrangements best tailored to their particular needs, in practice employees who are asked either to agree to new arrangements to satisfy Regulation 8, or to agree changes to an existing agreement to ensure that it qualifies, are likely to want what the standard information and consultation procedures offer at least as a starting point.

3.89 The extent to which pre-existing agreements will be relevant for practical purposes therefore remains to be seen.

4

Requesting Information and Consultation

This chapter examines the process set out in the ICE Regulations for initiating negotiations on information and consultation arrangements. It covers the following principal areas: **4.01**

(1) the right of employees to request and receive information about staff numbers to confirm whether there is a sufficient number of employees within the undertaking to trigger the right to information and consultation;

(2) the making of a request by employees or their representatives to commence negotiations on information and consultation arrangements;

(3) how the employer can/should respond to the making of a request;

(4) the employer's right to initiate negotiations on information and consultation arrangements by making a formal notification; and

(5) the role the CAC has in supporting these arrangements.

As explained in Chapter 2 above, the employer is not bound to take any positive steps under the ICE Regulations in the absence of action by the employees or their representatives. **4.02**

The requirement for an employer to take action will therefore normally be triggered as a result of an approach made to the employer or to the CAC **4.03** by the employees or their representatives (in the form of what is referred to in the ICE Regulations as a 'request'). Provided the request satisfies various requirements stipulated by the ICE Regulations, the employer will have to respond, either by entering into negotiations or, if a valid pre-existing agreement or agreements are in place (see further Chapter 3 on the requirements for a valid pre-existing agreement) and less than 40% of the employees in the undertaking have made the request, by choosing to call a ballot to gauge the level of support for the request.

4.04 Alternatively, if he wishes to do so, the employer is free to initiate negotiations on information and consultation arrangements regardless of any action taken by the employees or their representatives.

A. EMPLOYEES' RIGHT TO INFORMATION

4.05 The ICE Regulations only apply to undertakings with a specified number of employees (see further Chapter 2). Although it will normally be relatively clear whether the undertaking employs a sufficient number of employees for the ICE Regulations to apply, the ICE Regulations give any employee within the undertaking (or a representative of such an employee) the right to request data from the employer for the purpose of determining the number of people employed by the undertaking within the UK (Regulation 5). In addition to establishing details of the precise number of employees in the undertaking, a request will also be of assistance to employees or their representatives in confirming the precise number of employees who will be required to support a valid request (see paragraphs 4.8 to 4.10 for further details on the employee thresholds that need to be satisfied in these circumstances).

4.06 Full details of the rights of employees or employee representatives to data for these purposes are set out in Chapter 2.

B. THE THRESHOLD FOR INITIATING AN EMPLOYEE REQUEST TO NEGOTIATE AN AGREEMENT

4.07 As indicated above, the employer is only obliged to initiate negotiations to reach an information and consultation agreement under the ICE Regulations where a valid employee request has been received.

4.08 In order to be valid, the employee request must:

(1) fulfil certain criteria set out in Regulation 7(4) (see further paragraph 4.13); and

(2) be made by at least 10% of the employees in the undertaking (Regulation 7(2)).

It will be apparent, therefore, that depending on the size of the undertaking in question, a relatively small group of employees may be able to trigger a requirement on the employer to initiate negotiations on information and consultation arrangements. The 10% threshold can either be satisfied in a single request or by aggregating a number of different requests made on the same or different days by employees which when taken together mean that the 10% threshold has been satisfied (Regulation 7(2)). Requests can only be aggregated within any six-month period. Once six months has passed after the making of a request that does not satisfy the 10% threshold, the request will become stale and cannot be aggregated with a subsequent request. This is a change from the previous draft of the ICE Regulations, which did not impose any time limit for the aggregation of requests, so that theoretically a request could have been valid on a permanent basis. **4.09**

Example 4.1
Undertaking A has 500 employees. A valid employee request is received from 30 employees on 20 April 2005. A subsequent valid request is received from 25 employees (including 15 who signed the original request on 30 August 2005). Finally, a third request is received from 20 employees (who have not signed either of the first two requests) on 15 November 2005.

Although a total of 55 signatures have been obtained on employee requests within six months of 20 April 2005, the relevant 10% threshold has not been satisfied. This is because the same employees cannot be counted twice. However, if none of the signatories of the second request had previously signed the first request, then the 10% threshold would have been satisfied when the second request was made.

The 10% threshold is not satisfied when the third request is made on 15 November 2005 because that is more than six months from the date of the initial request and the first request therefore cannot be aggregated. When the third request is received, 45 employees have made a current request, which does not satisfy the percentage threshold.

One issue that is not clear in connection with aggregated requests is whether employees must still be in employment at the date the 'triggering request' is made (see paragraphs 4.22 to 4.25). The definition of employee is someone 'who has entered into or works under a contract of employment'. Former employees are only expressly included within this definition for the purposes of Part VIII and Regulation 40 (which deals with protections for employees and restrictions on contracting-out and are not relevant to aggregation). This implies that requests made by employees who have subsequently left employment should not be aggregated. This **4.10** would accord with the objective of showing sufficient current support for an information and consultation procedure before an employer is required to enter into negotiations.

4.11 The 10% threshold does not apply if it would result in fewer than 15 employees or more than 2,500 employees being required to make a valid employee request. In these circumstances, the figures of 15 and 2,500 will constitute the minimum and maximum number of employees required to make a valid request (Regulation 7(3)).

4.12 It should be noted that each part-time employee will be counted as a single employee for the purposes of determining whether a valid employee request has been made. This is so even if those part-time employees had been counted as representing only half of a full-time equivalent for the purposes of assessing whether the ICE Regulations apply to the undertaking in accordance with Regulation 4(3) (see further Chapter 2).

4.13 In addition to satisfying the 10% threshold, in order to be valid an employee request must:

(a) be in writing;
(b) be sent to the registered office, head office or principal place of business of the employer or the CAC;
(c) specify the names of the employees making the request; and
(d) specify the date on which it was sent (Regulation 7(4)).

4.14 Although there is no formal requirement to do so, it would seem prudent for employees to ensure that any request is sent by recorded delivery/ registered post. Equally, although Regulation 7(4) only requires the employees making the request to be listed, it would be sensible to ask employees physically to sign the request to confirm their agreement to it, to avoid any dispute about whether they have in fact agreed to the request. This is particularly the case where the list is being submitted by employee representatives on behalf of the employees.

C. TO WHOM MUST THE REQUEST BE MADE?

4.15 It will normally be the case that an employee request will be made direct to the employer. However, if the employees/their representatives do not wish to submit a request to the employer (for example, because they wish to retain anonymity), they may instead channel a request through the CAC (Regulation 7(4)(b)(ii)).

4.16 The requirements of Regulation 7(4), summarized at paragraph 4.13 above, apply equally in relation to a request submitted to the CAC, so requesting employees will still need to provide their names to the CAC. However, the CAC will not then forward those names to the employer.

The DTI Guidance on the ICE Regulations recommends that employees submitting their request via the CAC should also give details of a person to act as a point of contact (perhaps a trade union representative or one of the employees) and to assist in liaison between employer and employees. **4.17**

Where the request is made to the CAC, it is required to: **4.18**

(1) notify the employer of the request as soon as is reasonably practicable;
(2) request from the employer such information as it needs to verify the number and names of the employees who have made the request; and
(3) inform the employer and the employees who have made the request how many employees have made the request, on the basis of the information provided by the employees and the employer (Regulation 7(5)).

The employer is required to provide to the CAC any information the latter has requested in order to verify the number and names of the employees who have made the request as soon as reasonably practicable (Regulation 7(6)). **4.19**

It will then presumably be up to the employer to determine whether the number of employees making the request has satisfied the 10% threshold (although see further paragraphs 4.65 and 4.66 on the employer's right to seek a declaration from the CAC as to the validity of an employee request). **4.20**

Where more than one employee request is made over a six-month period and numbers have to be aggregated to determine the validity of a request, it is possible that the request may be made in part to the employer and in part to the CAC. This may complicate the aggregation mechanics but should not affect the underlying principles. The DTI Guidance recommends that in these circumstances, the employer should provide the CAC with the names of those employees who have made their request directly to the employer, so that the CAC can check to ensure there is no double-counting (but see also paragraphs 4.28 and 4.29). **4.21**

D. WHEN IS A VALID REQUEST DEEMED TO HAVE BEEN MADE?

It is important to be able to identify when a valid request has been made because there are a number of consequential timing implications. For example, if the employer is required to elect negotiating representatives and fails to do so, the standard information and consultation provisions **4.22** will apply six months after the date of the employee request. Other timing consequences that flow from the making of a request include the triggering of a one-month period to dispute the request (see paragraph 4.66); the triggering of the one-month period within which an employer with a pre-existing agreement must notify employees of their intention to hold a ballot to test endorsement of the employee request (see paragraph 4.41); and the start of the three-year moratorium on further employee requests if a ballot does not endorse the employee request (see paragraph 4.58).

4.23 If

(1) there is a single valid request by the requisite number of employees; or
(2) more than one valid request (which when taken together are made by the requisite number of employees) is made on the same day,

the request is deemed to be made on the date on which the request is or the requests are sent to the employer by the employees or (if the request has been made through the CAC) the date on which the CAC informs the employer and employees of how many employees have made the request (Regulation 7(7)(a)).

4.24 Because the request is deemed to have been made on the day it is sent rather than the day received, at least where the request is sent to the employer rather than the CAC, it would appear that time will start to run for the purpose of negotiating information and consultation arrangements even if the request is, for example, mislaid by the postal services. Hence the importance of being able to demonstrate that the request has actually been sent.

4.25 If more than one valid request (which taken together are made by the requisite number of employees) is made on separate days, the request is deemed to have been made on the date on which the request which results in the threshold being satisfied is sent to the employer by the employees. If the request has been made through the CAC, the request is treated as made on the date on which the CAC notifies the employer and employees of how many employees have made the request where that request results in the 10% threshold being satisfied (Regulation 7(7)(b)).

E. THE EMPLOYER'S RESPONSE TO A REQUEST

4.26 The most important thing for an employer to do on receipt of an employee request is to take prompt action. In particular, it is important to set a mechanism in place under which the personnel/human resources department (who may not necessarily have been sent the employee request) is notified immediately upon receipt. Failure to take action may mean the employer loses the opportunity to take certain steps, for example to call for a ballot where a pre-existing agreement or agreements are in place.

Following this, the first steps should be to review the request to confirm: **4.27**

- that all those listed are employed by the same group entity (as explained in detail in Chapter 2 above, the ICE Regulations operate by reference to undertakings; an undertaking is a single corporate entity);
- where more than one request is being aggregated, the timing of such requests, and whether those have been made within six months of each other;
- whether the request or requests have been made by the requisite number of employees;
- whether those making the request are all employees (as opposed to, for example, agency workers or independent contractors); and
- that all duplicate employee signatures have been discounted.

Where the request has been submitted to the CAC, the CAC will undertake the necessary confirmations. It is not entirely clear how this process will work if those making the request include a number of individuals whom the employer would not characterize as employees. When providing information to the CAC, the employer should therefore list all those working for the organization whom it does not consider as employees, and request that the CAC excludes them from the count. It is unclear whether the CAC would be prepared to do this. **4.28**

Ultimately, in the event of a dispute it will be for the CAC to determine the validity of an employee request (see paragraph 4.65), for example where the validity of a request hinges on the question of whether the individuals making the request are employees. Given the uncertain state of the law in this area, this is unsatisfactory from an employer's perspective, particularly given that there is no formal requirement on the CAC to hold a hearing before determining issues of this type (although it has power to hold a hearing if it believes it necessary). In practice if the validity of a request is being challenged, employers will want to ask the CAC to convene a hearing to determine the issue to make sure that it has a chance fully to argue why particular individuals should not be regarded as employees. **4.29**

If it is clear that the request is a valid one and the relevant statutory requirements have been met, the employer will be required to enter into **4.30** negotiations unless it is able to rely on valid pre-existing agreements and call a ballot to judge whether the request has the necessary level of support.

4.31 Even if the employer does not believe the request to be a valid one, the DTI Guidance recommends that employers should acknowledge receipt of any request, informing the workforce as a whole and indicating how they intend to respond to it. This is to ensure that there is no confusion as to the employer's position.

4.32 If there is any doubt about whether a request is valid, the employer should take professional advice or make an application to the CAC (see further paragraphs 4.65 and 4.66).

F. EMPLOYER'S RESPONSE TO A REQUEST WHERE VALID PRE-EXISTING AGREEMENTS ARE IN PLACE

4.33 The concept of a pre-existing agreement has been examined in detail in Chapter 3. In summary, a valid pre-existing agreement is an agreement that:

(a) is in writing;
(b) covers all the employees of the undertaking;
(c) has been approved by the employees; and
(d) sets out how the employer is to give information to the employees or their representatives and to seek their views on such information (Regulation 8(1)).

4.34 If the valid employee request has been made by 40% or more of the employees employed in the undertaking on the date on which the request is made, the employer will be required to enter into negotiations for an information and consultation agreement regardless of whether there is a valid pre-existing agreement within the undertaking. In other words, a valid employee request with at least 40% support will always trump a pre-existing agreement.

4.35 It should however be borne in mind that even if a pre-existing agreement is trumped by an employee request with at least 40% support it will not fall away unless there is an express provision in the agreement stipulating that the pre-existing agreement would cease to have effect where negotiations for an information and consultation arrangement have been initiated. In practice, it may be that as part of the process for negotiating an information and consultation agreement the parties will agree that any duplicate provisions in a pre-existing agreement should lapse.

Example 4.2
Company C has a valid pre-existing agreement in place. A valid request is received from 200 employees. At the date such a request is received, Company C employs 500 people. As the employee request has been made by 40% of Company's C workforce, Company C will not be able to test support for the request, and will need to enter into negotiations for a new agreement.

If however the valid employee request was made by fewer than 40% of the employees employed in the undertaking on the date on which the request is made, the employer is not obliged to enter into negotiations for an information and consultation agreement (although it may choose to do so). Instead the employer may elect to hold a ballot to verify whether there is sufficient support for the employee request to enter into negotiations for an information and consultation agreement. **4.36**

There is no requirement for pre-existing agreements to operate by reference to a single undertaking only. This point is explored in detail in Chapter 3 but in summary, if a pre-existing agreement or agreements cover employees in more than one undertaking (for example, where it extends to a number of different group companies), the 40% threshold is calculated by reference to the number of employees covered by the agreement or agreements. It is not calculated simply by reference to a percentage of employees making the request as a percentage of the workforce within any one undertaking (Regulation 9). **4.37**

In other words, although the 10% threshold for a valid request can still be triggered by 10% of the employees in any one undertaking, the 40% threshold is calculated on an aggregated basis counting all the relevant undertakings. **4.38**

This provision therefore prevents 40% of the employees employed within a single undertaking that is part of a number of undertakings covered by a pre-existing agreement or agreements from being able to require negotiations for an information and consultation arrangement in the absence of support from employees in the other undertakings. However, a request by as few as 10% of the employees in one of the undertakings could trigger a ballot across all the affected undertakings if the employer wanted to be able to maintain the status quo (see further paragraph 4.40). **4.39**

Example 4.3
Sister companies D, E, F, and G have a valid joint pre-existing agreement. The companies employ, respectively, 150, 200, 250, and 350 employees. A valid request is received by Company D from 15 of its employees. Even though the request has been made by less than 2% of the employees covered by the pre-existing agreement, the employer will be required to hold a ballot to gauge support for the employee request if it does not wish to enter into negotiations for an information and consultation arrangement within Company D.

Example 4.4

Sister companies H, I, and J have a joint valid pre-existing agreement. Company H has 300 employees, Company I has 250 employees, and Company J 500 employees. A valid request is made by 200 employees of Company H. None of the employees in Company I or Company J is party to the request. Under Regulation 9, even though more than 40% of the employees of Company H have made the request, Company H is under no obligation to enter into negotiations for an information and consultation arrangement, because less than 40% of the employees covered by the pre-existing agreement have made the request. Instead, Companies H, I, and J may jointly decide to hold a ballot for employee endorsement of the employee request.

4.40 Alternatively, in example 4.3 the undertaking that has received the valid employee request (Company D) may choose to hold the ballot for endorsement of the employee request as a ballot within that undertaking alone (Regulation 9(3)). In those circumstances, if the ballot showed the requisite level of support within that undertaking it will be required to enter into negotiations for an information and consultation arrangement. The other undertakings covered by the pre-existing agreement will be unaffected. This option would not be available to Company H (in example 4.4), where there was already 40% support for the request. Company H would either have to hold a group-wide ballot or start negotiations for an information and consultation procedure within the individual undertaking.

G. THE BALLOTING PROCESS

4.41 If an employer with a pre-existing agreement in place is so permitted and elects to hold a ballot it must:

- inform all employees in writing within one month of the date of the employee request of the intention to hold a ballot (Regulation 8(3)(a)). If there is a combined ballot in relation to a pre-existing agreement or agreements covering a number of undertakings, all employees within each undertaking must be so notified (Regulation 9(2)); and
- arrange for the ballot to be held as soon as reasonably practicable thereafter, provided the ballot does not take place before 21 days has passed after the employer has so informed the employees (Regulation 8(3)(b)).

4.42 Timing is therefore extremely important. If the employer fails to notify the employees of its intention to hold the ballot within the one-month time limit, it will lose the opportunity to do so, and will instead be obliged to enter into negotiations for an information and consultation arrangement under the ICE Regulations.

The balloting requirements prescribed by the ICE Regulations are relatively flexible. The ballot must satisfy the three following principal requirements: **4.43**

- that the employer makes such arrangements as are reasonably practicable to ensure that the ballot is fair;
- all employees of the undertaking on the date of the ballot must be entitled to vote in the ballot (or, where the ballot takes place over more than one day, all employees employed in the undertaking on the first day of those days—so that new hires engaged after the first day of the ballot do not have to be given an opportunity to vote); and
- the ballot must be conducted so as to secure that
  (1) so far as is reasonably practicable there is a secret ballot; and
  (2) the votes given at the ballot are accurately counted (Regulation 8(4)).

To ensure fairness, the employer may seek to involve an independent person to supervise the ballot, but is not obliged to do so. **4.44**

There appears to be nothing in the ICE Regulations that would formally prevent the employer from 'campaigning' for a particular vote. Query whether if an employer actively campaigns, while at the same time seeking to restrict a trade union's access to the employees, that would be sufficient to call into question the fairness of the ballot. A further point of contention that may arise in practice could relate to the precise phrasing of the question employees will be asked to vote on, and the latitude that may be available to the employer here to frame the question in a particular way. **4.45**

Where a ballot has been held, the employer is required to notify the employees of the result as soon as reasonably practicable after the holding of the ballot (Regulation 8(5)). **4.46**

The workforce is deemed to have endorsed the employee request if both (1) 40% of the employers employed in the undertaking and (2) the majority of those voting in the ballot endorse the request (Regulation 8(6)). In other words, the employees need to surmount a double hurdle before the request is endorsed. The test is the same as currently applies in relation to a statutory ballot for trade union recognition. **4.47**

If the employee request is deemed to have been endorsed by the workforce ballot, the employer is required to initiate negotiations under the ICE Regulations to set in place new information and consultation arrangements (Regulation 8(5)(b)). As discussed at paragraph 4.35, the pre-existing agreement does not automatically fall away once the employer is requested to enter into negotiations. **4.48**

4.49 However, if the workforce ballot does not endorse the employee request, the employer does not have to proceed with further negotiations to set in place information and consultation arrangements and may continue to rely on the relevant pre-existing agreement (Regulation 8(5)(c)).

H. EMPLOYER-INITIATED ACTION

4.50 It is not just employees or employee representatives who can initiate negotiations for an information and consultation arrangement. The ICE Regulations also give employers the right to start the process. In practice this is only likely to happen infrequently, but it may be that, even in the absence of any indication that employees are anxious for such arrangements to be set in place, the employer sees commercial benefits in setting in place information and consultation arrangements. It may also be attractive for employers to pre-empt an employee request on strategic grounds. An employer in receipt of an employee request from within a group company might, for example, choose to issue a written notification to employees within other group companies if it wants to negotiate a group-wide information and consultation procedure.

4.51 To initiate negotiations, the employer is required to issue a written notification saying that it intends to start the negotiating process which:

(1) states that it is made for the purpose of the ICE Regulations;
(2) states the date on which it is issued; and
(3) is published in such a manner as to bring it to the attention of, so far as reasonably practicable, all the employees of the undertaking (Regulation 11(2)).

4.52 The safest approach to comply with the notification requirement is likely to be to issue a memorandum to all employees, although in certain circumstances other alternatives, such as posting notification on employee message-boards may be sufficient.

4.53 There is nothing to prevent a group that wishes to do so from making notifications across a number of undertakings with a view to negotiating a single information and consultation arrangement covering all those undertakings.

4.54 Once the notification has been issued, the employer must then proceed with the negotiation of an information and consultation procedure. Negotiations must be initiated as soon as reasonably practicable, and within three months (see further Chapter 5).

I. RESTRICTIONS ON EMPLOYEE REQUESTS

4.55 To allow for continuity and certainty within the workforce and to prevent repeated requests from being made, the ICE Regulations also place certain timing restrictions on the validity of employee requests or employer notifications.

4.56 Consequently, if a negotiated agreement is already in place (see further Chapter 5), no employee request for a further negotiated agreement will be valid if made within three years from the date of the existing negotiated agreement (or, if the negotiated agreement is terminated, prior to the date on which termination takes effect—Regulation 12(1)(a)). A similar restriction applies in respect of employer notifications.

4.57 A similar three-year restriction applies where the standard information and consultation provisions apply, and runs from the date on which those provisions start to apply (Regulation 12(1)(b)). See Chapter 7 for an analysis of when the standard provisions will apply in a range of different circumstances.

4.58 If a workforce ballot as described in paragraph 4.41 has not endorsed a prior employee request, no further employee request or employer notification will be valid for a further three years from the date of the employee request giving rise to the ballot (or, if more than one request was aggregated, from the date on which the request, which results in the 10% threshold being reached, is sent to the employer or, if the request is sent to the CAC, the date on which the CAC notifies the employer of the number of employees making the request—Regulation 12(1) (c)).

4.59 There are certain exceptions to the three-year moratorium. There is for example no restriction on the parties voluntarily agreeing to fresh arrangements during this period.

4.60 The moratorium period will also not apply where 'there are material changes in the undertaking during the relevant period' and as a result any pre-existing agreement or agreements no longer cover all the employees of the undertaking or have not been approved by the employees. This is also the case if the material change in the undertaking means that a negotiated agreement no longer covers all the employees of the undertaking (Regulation 12(2)).

4.61 Circumstances where there may be a material change in the undertaking include where an employer has undergone a substantial internal reorganization or restructuring or as a result of acquisitions (and possibly disposals). In itself, there is no reason why a substantial transaction will mean that an existing arrangement no longer covers all the employees of the undertaking. Provided the arrangement is carefully drafted, it should be capable of being broad enough to encompass subsequent joiners.

4.62 One issue that is not clear is the point at which changes in the composition of the workforce would have an impact on the approval of pre-existing arrangements. DTI Guidance indicates that approval could be demonstrated by a simple majority of the workforce voting in a ballot or the agreement of representatives of a majority of the workforce. This implies that if the undertaking has grown substantially since the approval was initially given, the validity of the pre-existing agreement will be open to challenge. In practice, employers will want to keep the approval issue under review and reaffirm the approval periodically if necessary. As indicated in Chapter 3, major changes such as reorganizations or acquisitions are more likely to give rise to a 'material change in the undertaking' than hirings and firings in the ordinary course of business.

J. THE ROLE OF THE CAC

4.63 In addition to its administrative role as a possible recipient of an employee request (see paragraph 4.15), the CAC also has a power of determination in relation to a range of disputes relevant to the initiation of negotiations on information and consultation arrangements.

4.64 These include disputes in relation to:

- the validity of an employee request;
- the validity of a pre-existing agreement or agreements;
- the balloting process to gauge support for an employee request; or
- the validity of an employer notification.

4.65 An employer may consider that an employee request is invalid on one or more of a number of grounds. This may be because the relevant 10% threshold has not been satisfied, the request itself is in the wrong form, the three-year moratorium applies, or the ICE Regulations do not apply to the undertaking in question (for example, because the number of employees within the undertaking is fewer than the requisite threshold). In any of these circumstances, an employer may apply for a declaration that the employee request was invalid (Regulation 13(1)).

4.66 The CAC is only empowered to consider such an application if it is made within one month of the date of the employee request (Regulation 13(3)). Provided the application is made within this time limit, the CAC is required to make a declaration as to whether the employee request was valid. If the CAC decides that it was not valid, the employer will be under no obligation to initiate negotiations on an information and consultation arrangement or take any other steps.

Given the one-month time limit, it is therefore extremely important from an employer's perspective that it responds speedily to receipt of a request. Any delay may mean that even if the employee request is defective, the employer may be too late to make a complaint to the CAC. However, in practice, this is still unlikely to mean that the employer could be forced to inform and consult even where it has received an invalid employee request. If the employer ignores the (ineffective) request, the employees or their representatives will presumably seek to argue that the standard information and consultation provisions apply under Regulation 18(1). If the standard provisions apply, the employer would then be under a duty under Regulation 19(1) to arrange for the election of information and consultation representatives. When it fails to do so, the employees or their representatives could complain about the failure to the CAC under Regulation 19(4). **4.67**

However, Regulation 18(1) states that the standard procedure applies only where 'the employer is under a duty, following the making of a valid employee request'. The CAC would presumably therefore not be able to find that the standard procedure applied (because there had been no valid employee request) and the complaint under Regulation 19(4) would not be upheld. **4.68**

This is however a high-risk strategy for an employer. Should the employee request turn out to be valid, the complaint under Regulation 19(4) would be upheld, exposing the employer to a financial penalty in accordance with Regulation 19(6). Further, it would have lost the opportunity to negotiate an appropriate information and consultation procedure, and would instead have to comply with the standard arrangements.

If any employee of an undertaking or the representative of any such employee does not believe that an existing arrangement of an employer qualifies as a valid pre-existing agreement under Regulation 8(1), it may present a complaint to the CAC (Regulation 10(1)). The complaint must be made within 21 days of the date on which the employer informing the employees that it intends to hold a ballot to gauge support for an employee request. A similar right (which must be exercised within the same 21-day time-frame) arises where a group of undertakings announce an intention to hold a ballot across those undertakings in circumstances where any employees of the undertakings (or their representatives) do not believe that a requirement has been satisfied for such an aggregated ballot to be valid. **4.69**

4.70 If the CAC finds that there is no valid pre-existing agreement, it is required to make an order requiring the employer to initiate negotiations on information and consultation arrangements (Regulation 10(3)(a)). If it finds that the preconditions for a valid combined ballot have not been satisfied, it is required to make an order requiring the employer either to initiate negotiations on information and consultation arrangements or hold a ballot within a single undertaking (Regulation 10(3)(b)).

4.71 An application to the CAC may also be made where the employer would have been entitled to call a ballot but has been dilatory in doing so. If any employee within an undertaking (or any employee representative) believes that an employer who wishes to hold a ballot to gauge support for a pre-existing agreement has not so notified employees within one month of the date of the employee request, he may apply to the CAC for a declaration that an employer is under a duty to commence negotiations for an information and consultation procedure (Regulation 8(7)).

4.72 Similarly, where the employer has notified an intention to hold a ballot but an employee or employee representative believes that the employer has not taken steps to hold a ballot as soon as reasonably practicable after making notification of its intention to hold the ballot, a complaint may be presented to the CAC (Regulation 8(8)). If in these circumstances a complaint is found to be well founded, the CAC is required to make an order requiring the employer to hold the ballot within such period as the order may specify (Regulation 8(9)).

4.73 A complaint may also arise in relation to the ballot process. Under Regulation 10(2), any employee or employees' representative who believes that:

(1) the employer has not made such arrangements as are reasonably practicable to ensure that the ballot is fair;

(2) not all employees of the undertaking have been given an entitlement to vote in the ballot; or

(3) the ballot has not been conducted so as to ensure that so far as is reasonably practicable those voting do so in secret and that the votes given in the ballot are accurately counted

may present a complaint to the CAC within 21 days of the date of the ballot.

4.74 If the complaint is held to be well founded, the CAC will order the employer (or, where the complaint is in relation to a combined ballot, the employers) to hold the ballot again within such period as the order may specify (unless the employer has previously made representations that instead of reholding the ballot he would prefer to initiate negotiations for an information and consultation arrangement, in which case an order will be made to that effect—Regulation 10(3)(c)).

If there is a dispute in relation to the validity of an employer notification, either because it is not in the right form or the three-year moratorium applies, an employee or an employees' representative may apply to the CAC for a declaration as to whether the notification was valid (Regulation 13(2)). **4.75**

An application must be made within one month of the date of the employer notification. Provided the application is made within this time limit, the CAC is required to make a declaration as to the validity of the employer notification. If it is found to be invalid, it will have no force or effect. **4.76**

5

Negotiating an Information and Consultation Procedure

5.01 Once a request has been received from the requisite percentage of staff (normally at least 10% of the workforce within the undertaking—see further Chapter 4), and assuming that request is valid or has been validated (by a ballot, where there is a pre-existing agreement), the employer should then set about initiating negotiations with employee representatives to reach a negotiated agreement on the method of information and consultation which will apply to the parties. If the employer chooses not to initiate negotiations, there is no penalty under the ICE Regulations, but the parties will become subject to the standard information and consultation procedures (detailed in Chapter 7).

This chapter sets out the requirements of the ICE Regulations in relation to the negotiation process. It analyses: **5.02**

- what the goals of the respective parties might be in negotiating an agreement;
- the process of appointing or electing negotiating representatives;
- the complaint process in relation to the election of negotiating representatives;
- the period the parties have to negotiate an agreement;
- the procedures which apply to negotiate a group-wide procedure; and
- once negotiated, how the agreement must be approved.

A. WHAT ARE THE GOALS OF THE PARTIES?

Before embarking on the negotiation process, each party will want to **5.03** consider its objectives. For the employer's part, a failure to reach agreement will result in the application of the standard information and consultation procedures. If the employer is hoping to agree a process with greater flexibility than that contemplated by the standard information and consultation procedures, he will need to consider what might need to be offered in order to achieve this aim.

Given that the employee representatives can 'sit out' the negotiation **5.04** period if they believe that more can be achieved by having the standard procedures apply, the employer will need to give early consideration to the strategy which should be followed, taking into account what particular concerns employee representatives may have and what can be done to meet those concerns.

From the employees' perspective, the negotiation process may be the **5.05** opportunity to agree an information and consultation process which begins to build a real partnership between the employer and the employees. There may also be existing arrangements which work well and which the employees are keen to safeguard or build upon going forward. Trade union representatives may be concerned to ensure that any negotiated agreement does not undermine any existing collective bargaining arrangements or weaken their representation structures. Such contrasting objectives will need to be taken into account by employees and their representatives before they embark on the negotiation process.

B. GETTING THE NEGOTIATION PROCESS STARTED

5.06 Regulation 14 sets out a three-step process which employers must follow to get negotiations for an agreement under way, which is as follows:

1 make arrangements for the election/appointment of negotiating representatives;
2 inform the employees who the negotiated representatives are; and
3 invite the negotiating representatives to enter into negotiations.

1. Appointing Negotiating Representatives

5.07 The role of the negotiating representatives is an important one. They will be responsible for negotiating the agreement information and consultation which is likely to apply to the employees whom they represent for at least the next three years.

5.08 The DTI Guidance states that the negotiated representatives will need to ensure that the arrangements are what employees want, for example in terms of:

- methods of informing and consulting (whether through representatives, directly with the workforce, or a combination of the two);
- how any information and consultation representatives are to be chosen, how many of them, and how they may be replaced;
- the types of subjects on which information and consultation will take place;
- the information to be provided;
- the timing and frequency of information provision and consultation;
- who will represent the employer at any meetings for information and consultation;
- the way in which the employer will respond to the views of employees or their representatives; and
- the circumstances in which the arrangements can be modified or terminated.

5.09 Regulation 14(1) provides that the employer must 'as soon as reasonably practicable' make arrangements for the employees in the undertaking to elect or appoint negotiating representatives. In practice unless an employer has good reason for delaying the appointment or election process (e.g. because he wishes to challenge the validity of the employee request (Regulation 13) (see further paragraphs 4.65 and 4.66), the employer would normally be advised to start the process of appointment or election of representatives as soon as possible after receipt of a valid request having been made. This is because the employer can then maximize the initial three-month period allocated for electing negotiating representatives (see further paragraph 5.39). If the initial three-month period is wasted, then the parties have only six months to reach agreement (unless an extension is agreed). The six-month timetable which is prescribed for the negotiation process is fairly short and time wasted at the outset might cause difficulties later in the process if the parties are not able to agree an extension to the timetable (see paragraphs 5.49 and 5.50).

Before initiating an appointment or election process, it will be prudent for the employer to explain to the workforce what is likely to be involved in being a negotiating representative. The employer may be able to call on existing representatives, or local or regional union representatives to explain to employees what the job is likely to entail. The expected time commitment should also be explained. **5.10**

It should also be explained to the negotiating representatives that they will not automatically become the information and consultation representatives for the organization going forward, particularly given that it is open to the parties to agree during negotiations for the information and consulation agreement that direct forms of information consultation will be relied on and therefore no representation will exist (see the DTI Guidance). In practice the negotiating representatives may be the most sensible choice for the information and consultation representatives, at least for the period immediately following introduction of the new agreement, as they will understand and be familiar with what has been agreed. However there is no requirement under the ICE Regulations that they be elected or appointed for this job once the agreement has been negotiated. **5.11**

Regulation 14(2) sets out the requirements which apply to the appointment or election of negotiating representatives. The requirements are that: **5.12**

(a) the election or appointment is arranged so that all employees of the undertaking are represented by one or more representatives; and
(b) all the employees in the undertaking are entitled to take part in the election or appointment.

Regulation 14 provides that there can either be an 'election' or an 'appointment'. An employer with relatively small numbers of employees, or one who is negotiating for a single undertaking with limited numbers of staff, may choose not to hold a formal election, but instead to have a more informal appointment process. An election would normally involve a formal ballot process, possibly run by an external body. With an appointment, the employer could simply ask for volunteers, put the names of the volunteers to the employees, and if no objections are raised, treat those **5.13** volunteers as appointed. Provided all employees can take part in the appointment process and one or more negotiating representatives, representing all the employees in the undertaking are appointed, this will be acceptable under the ICE Regulations. However the employer may prefer to hold an election instead. Unless care is exercised there is likely to be a greater risk with an appointment process that the negotiating representatives might not be truly representative and therefore the process might be open to challenge under Regulation 15(1) (see paragraphs 5.35 to 5.37).

5.14 Care will need to be taken to ensure that all employees in the undertaking have been given the opportunity to take part in the appointment or election process. The employer will need to factor in those employees who may be on holiday, absent on sick leave or maternity leave, or who are absent for any other reason (e.g. external secondments, travelling overseas on business, etc). Regulation 14(2)(b) makes it clear that *all* employees in the undertaking must be entitled to take part in the election or appointment. Employers will therefore need to notify any absentees in advance, to ensure they have the right to participate in the appointment or election process.

5.15 It is for the employer to choose whether to go down the appointment route or the election route. For larger organizations a combination of both might be appropriate to ensure that the entire workforce is covered. The process may also be driven by the number of volunteers who come forward. The more volunteers there are, the more sensible it may be to have an election. The process must also be one which the employees 'buy into', otherwise the employees could apply to the CAC and challenge the process (see paragraph 5.35).

5.16 The DTI Guidance suggests that the employer should explain to the employees what he is proposing in the way of either an appointment or an election process and seek views on the proposals before proceeding though this is not a requirement of the legislation.

5.17 Where there is to be an election, Regulation 14(2)(b) states that if the election is to be held on one day, then all the employees in the undertaking 'on the day on which the votes may be cast in the ballot' must be entitled to take part. If the ballot is to take place over more than one day, then all those employed on the first of those days must be entitled to vote in the ballot.

Will Omitting to Include One or More Employees in the Election/ Appointment Process Invalidate It?

Not necessarily. However under Regulation 15 if an employee or a representative considers that one or both of the requirements in Regulation 14 has not been complied with, then a complaint can be presented to the CAC. If the CAC finds the complaint well founded, it can order a re-election or appointment and can specify the period in which such re-election or reappointment must take place (Regulation 15(2)). **5.18**

How Many Negotiating Representatives Should be Elected?

The ICE Regulations do not state how many representatives should be elected or appointed. Thus the employer has a fair degree of latitude in deciding how many negotiating representatives it wishes to appoint, but will need to ensure that all the employees of the undertaking are represented by one or more representatives (Regulation 14(2)(a)) and should also bear in mind that employees can complain to the CAC if they are unhappy with the election/appointment process. **5.19**

The employer may wish to have representatives elected either by reference to grade of employee, or to represent different parts of the business, or to represent employees in the location in which they are based. The goals of the employer will be relevant to this issue. Does the employer envisage one collective information and consultation process, with one single body of representatives? Or will the employer be putting in place multiple agreements to deal with different categories of staff? In deciding how many negotiating representatives are needed, the employer will also want to have one eye on the actual process of negotiation. How logistically difficult will it be to arrange negotiating meetings if there are a large number of representatives? What if the representatives are located across a wide variety of sites across the country, thereby making meetings more difficult and costly? To avoid any claims by employees that there has been a breach of the employer's obligations, the employer will be keen to ensure that what is put in place is suitable and effective. **5.20**

The DTI Guidance makes the practical point that in deciding how many representatives should be elected or appointed, a balance needs to be struck, taking into account on the one hand the need to ensure that all of the relevant employees are represented, and on the other hand making sure that the numbers of representatives are manageable when it comes to the process of actually negotiating the agreement. **5.21**

What About 'Understudy' Representatives?

5.22 In deciding how many negotiating representatives an employer wishes to have, it may be sensible to ensure that for each area/group of employees to be represented, there is, if at all possible, a back-up negotiating representative nominated who can stand in for the main representative if that representative falls ill or is absent for any other reason. Given the requirements of the legislation for the negotiating representatives to represent all of the relevant employees within the workforce, it might cause difficulties if only one representative is appointed or elected for a significant part of the organization and is then absent during negotiations. Electing substitutes may not be necessary for smaller organizations, but should be considered for larger operations where absence might cause particular difficulties during the negotiation process.

Who Should the Negotiating Representatives Be?

5.23 The ICE Regulations do not contain any requirements on who the negotiating representatives should be. The DTI Guidance suggests that where possible, the employer should try to ensure diversity within the representative body. So, for example, an employer who has specific interest groups within the organization (representing the interests of e.g. women in the workplace, ethnic minorities, disabled staff, etc.) may wish to approach those groups to see if members are willing to stand for election or appointment. It is assumed that the DTI Guidance contemplates such representatives as being supernumerary, i.e. additional to/over and above representation generally across the undertaking. Where no such groups exist, it may be prudent to state expressly that the employer is keen for the negotiating representatives to represent the opinions of the entire workforce and that applications from/nominations for those representing minority interests would be actively encouraged.

Can the Employer Impose any Restrictions on Those Standing for Election/Appointment?

5.24 It is not uncommon for employers to impose some restrictions on those employees who stand for election as employee representatives. For example, a minimum service requirement is not uncommon, to ensure that those employees who are standing for election have been with the employer for a sufficiently long time to both demonstrate loyalty and to have a basic understanding of the employer's organization. There is nothing in the ICE Regulations to prevent such an approach in relation to the appointment or election of negotiating representatives.

In addition an employer may want to restrict applications to permanent rather than temporary staff, or staff on fixed-term contracts, to ensure that the population of representatives with which the employer is negotiating remains constant throughout the negotiation process and beyond. Although the employer will need to be mindful of the Fixed Term Employees (Prevention of Less Favourable Treatment) Regulations 2002 (*Fixed Term Workers Regulations*), which prevent fixed-term employees being treated less favourably than their permanent counterparts, the Fixed Term Workers Regulations do provide for an employer to be able to defend any allegation of unfairness by showing that the treatment is objectively justified. It may be difficult to justify the exclusion of fixed-term workers from standing as negotiating representatives, unless it can be shown that the period of negotiation is likely to go beyond the scope of certain fixed-term contracts (although a decision to exclude those individuals on fixed-term contracts of six months or less may be justifiable). **5.25**

What about Trade Union Representatives?

Those organizations that have trade union representation should expect the trade union representatives to stand for appointment or election as negotiating representatives. This might be of real advantage to an employer, as such individuals are likely to bring valuable experience and judgement to the role. The DTI Guidance states that although there is no requirement to have any trade union representatives as the negotiating representatives, they may be 'well-placed' to take on the role. **5.26**

An employer will not be able to exclude trade union representatives from standing for election or appointment as negotiating representatives. Such an exclusion would amount to a detriment under section 146(1) of TULRCA. **5.27**

Other Representatives

Employers who already have information and consultation processes in place, but whose arrangements do not satisfy the requirements set out in the ICE Regulations for those to count as pre-existing agreements, may wish to have existing representatives as negotiating representatives, as they may have experience of representing employees in discussions with the employer. **5.28**

Long-haul Crew Members

5.29 Regulation 43 provides various exemptions and exceptions for members of the merchant navy. Regulation 43(1) provides that no long-haul crew member may be a negotiating representative or an information and consultation representative. Regulation 43(2) defines a long-haul crew member as 'a person who is a member of a merchant navy crew other than a ferry worker or a person who normally works on voyages the duration of which is less than 48 hours'. Such persons may not stand for election as either a negotiating representative or as an information and consultation representative. However under Regulation 43(3) the employer can waive this exemption and permit such a person to put themselves forward for appointment or election. It may be that the employer is willing to waive the exemption, so as to ensure a proper cross-section of representation, but if so, it might be prudent to elect a substitute representative to cover any absences.

2. Notifying Employees of the Identity of the Negotiating Representatives

5.30 Once the election or appointment process has been held, the employer must inform the employees *in writing* of the identity of the negotiating representatives (Regulation 14(1)(b)).

5.31 The requirement in Regulation 14(1)(b) for the notification to be made 'in writing' is not further defined. However it seems unlikely that individual notification is required.

5.32 In practice the employer should use whatever means is appropriate to ensure that the relevant employees know who has been appointed or elected, ensuring that the communication to staff is in writing. A meeting of staff to tell them orally the identity of the negotiating representatives will not satisfy the requirements of Regulation 14(1)(b).

3. Invitation to Enter into Negotiations

5.33 Under Regulation 14(1)(c) the employer must 'invite' the negotiating representatives to enter into negotiations to reach a negotiated agreement.

5.34 The ICE Regulations do not specify what is meant by 'invite', but it can be assumed that what is required is a formal communication to the negotiating representatives inviting them to an initial meeting to 'get the ball rolling'.

C. COMPLAINTS ABOUT THE ELECTION OR APPOINTMENT PROCESS

If an employee or an employee's representative wishes to complain about the process of appointment or election of the negotiating representatives, the employee or representative may within 21 days of the election or appointment present a complaint to the CAC (Regulation 15(1)). **5.35**

If the complaint is upheld, the CAC can make an order requiring the employer to arrange for the election or appointment process to take place again within such period as the order shall specify (Regulation 15(2)). **5.36**

It is unclear whether the CAC has the power to order that the employer change the selected method of appointing representatives. If, for example, the employer has chosen an appointment process, can the employer subsequently be ordered to conduct an election? It seems likely that the power of the CAC under Regulation 15(2) is essentially to remedy defects in the process which has taken place, rather than to dictate what form of appointment or election process should be held. **5.37**

D. THE TIMETABLE FOR NEGOTIATION

Once the negotiating representatives are in place, Regulation 14(3) provides that negotiations: 'shall last for a period not exceeding six months commencing at the end of the period of three months beginning with the date on which the valid employee request was made or the valid employer notification was issued'. **5.38**

This means the employer may have a maximum of nine months from receipt of the original request or from issuing a notification (factoring in the initial three-month period) in which to negotiate and reach agreement, unless agreement is reached between the parties to extend the timetable for negotiations. Note the wording of Regulation 14(3): the nine-month period is expressed to be a maximum period. How long in practice it will take parties to negotiate these types of agreement remains to be seen, but it is clear from the ICE Regulations that once a valid request has been made, the parties should not delay in kicking off the negotiation process (not least because it may be possible to use the initial three-month period to get negotiations started). **5.39**

As indicated above, each party will wish to have a strategy in place before embarking on the negotiation process. The negotiating representatives **5.40** may wish to canvass opinions from the employees they represent as to what the employees are expecting from an information and consultation agreement. In the absence of agreement with the employer, the standard information and consultation procedures will apply. If the negotiated representatives' aim is simply to wait out the negotiation process so that the standard procedures apply, then they may be in no hurry to begin negotiations. Contrast this with the position of an employer who is keen to try and reach agreement on a process which differs from that envisaged by the standard procedures.

1. When the Clock Does Not Start to Tick

5.41 Regulation 14(3) provides that in certain circumstances the timetable for negotiations is 'suspended'. To summarize, the relevant circumstances are:

(1) where the employer wishes to test support for an employee request; because he believes he has a pre-existing agreement satisfying either Regulation 8 or 9 (covering the single undertaking or covering the relevant group of undertakings) and the relevant percentage of staff have not supported the employee request;
(2) where the employer wishes to dispute the validity of an employee request under Regulation 13(1);
(3) where an employee or an employee's representative wishes to challenge the validity of the employer notification (Regulation 13(2); or
(4) where the employees wish to dispute the method of election or appointment of negotiating representatives under Regulation 15.

5.42 In any of these circumstances (analysed in more detail below) then the initial three-month period for electing representatives as specified by the ICE Regulations is effectively suspended until the particular matter is finally resolved.

Where the Employer Has a Pre-Existing Agreement

5.43 Under Regulation 14(3)(a) where an employer has a pre-existing agreement and in response to an employee request, which does not have the support of at least 40% of the employees in the undertaking(s), holds a ballot under Regulations 8 or 9, the period between notifying the employees of the proposed ballot and:

(1) where no complaint about the ballot is made to the CAC under Regulation 10, the date of the ballot;
(2) where a complaint is made to the CAC, and the complaint is

dismissed or dismissed on appeal, the date on which it is finally dismissed; or

(3) where there is a complaint to the CAC under Regulation 10 and the result is an order requiring the employer to initiate negotiations in accordance with Regulation 7(1), the date on which the order is made

will not count towards calculating the initial three-month period.

The effect of Regulation 14(3)(a) is to allow an employer who has or believes he has a valid pre-existing agreement time to test support for the employee request without being concerned that the timetable for negotiating a new agreement (if that is what the employer ultimately has to do) has begun to run. The requirements in relation to pre-existing agreements have been dealt with in Chapter 3. **5.44**

Where the Employer Disputes the Validity of the Employee Request

Regulation 14(3)(b) provides that where an employer is disputing the validity of an employee request: **5.45**

- under Regulation 7(2) to (4) (insufficient support for the request); or
- under Regulation 12 (because the request has been made within three years of a previous request or the date of an existing information and consultation agreement); or
- under Regulation 3 (because the undertaking is not covered by the ICE Regulations as at the date the request was made),

then the period between the date of the application to the CAC and the final decision or appeal will not count towards the initial three-month period. See further paragraphs 4.65 and 4.66.

Where There Is a Dispute as to the Validity of the Employer Notification

Where under Regulation 13(2) the employer has served a notification and either an employee or an employee representative wishes to challenge the validity of that notification, e.g. because it has been made within three years of a negotiated agreement, the time during which the employer applies to the CAC for a declaration in relation to the notification shall not count towards the three-month period (see further paragraph 4.75). **5.46**

Where the Employees Dispute the Process of Electing or Appointing the Negotiating Representatives

Under Regulation 14(3)(c) if employees wish to complain to the CAC, pursuant to Regulation 15, that the election or appointment of negotiating **5.47** representatives has not been conducted in accordance with one or more of the requirements of Regulation 14(2), the period between the date the complaint is presented and its resolution (including if a re-election is ordered, the period ordered by the CAC to carry out this re-election) will not count towards the initial three-month period (see further paragraphs 5.35 and 5.36).

2. How Does the Period of Suspension Operate in Practice?

5.48 In the circumstances set out above the parties have additional time in which to resolve the particular dispute before the timetable for negotiating and concluding an agreement begins to run. Without these provisions, in circumstances in which one party wishes to challenge the other or wishes to raise a matter with the CAC, the timetable for concluding an agreement would then be even shorter.

3. What if the Timetable Slips?

5.49 Regulation 14(5) provides that if before the end of the final six-month period the employer and 'a majority of the negotiating representatives' agree that the period should be extended, it can be further extended and the parties can agree on the length of such further period. Furthermore if the additional period is then due to expire, further extensions can be agreed.

5.50 As mentioned at the start of this chapter, in approaching negotiations with employee representatives, the employer will want to have a clear strategy for achieving agreement. The timetable prescribed by Regulation 14(3) is short, and an employer who does not approach negotiations with a firm plan as to where discussions should end up may be faced with negotiating representatives who are prepared to simply 'wait out' the six-month period. As the timetable can only be extended by agreement, then in the absence of such agreement the parties will be subject to the standard information and consultation procedures from the date which is six months from the date the time limit expires, or the date information and consultation representatives are elected under Regulation 19, whichever is sooner (see further Chapter 7). An employer who is seeking to achieve something different will therefore want (and need) to make the most of the negotiating period to try and reach agreement with the negotiating representatives.

5.51 It is important that all parties keep a careful eye on the timetable for reaching agreement. Employers and negotiating representatives should diarize the date on which the request was made and the date that is nine months following that date. The parties may wish to aim for the negotiated agreement to be finalized and approved by the date which is one month before the expiry of the actual statutory deadline, so as to allow for slippage. The parties should bear in mind that in order to approve the finalized negotiated agreement it may be necessary to hold a ballot and therefore enough time to do so, if required, should be allowed (see further paragraphs 5.85 to 5.92).

4. Negotiating a Group-Wide Procedure

Regulation 14(6) expressly contemplates the situation where one or more **5.52** employers within a group wish to initiate negotiations for an agreement which will cover employees in more than one undertaking. In such circumstances where the employees of only one of the undertakings may have issued a valid request, the employers in the other undertakings must then issue a valid employer notification to their employees (see further Chapter 4).

Once such a notification has been issued, then the provisions set out **5.53** above in relation to the appointment of negotiating representatives and the timetable for concluding negotiations apply equally to those additional employers and employees. Note, however, that the timetable for conclusion of the negotiations will run from the date of the initial employee request (and not the date of any later employer notifications).

This provision will be of use to corporate groups who, once a request has **5.54** been received, want to initiate a combined negotiation so that any agreement reached covers all the employees across the group.

It will be important for a group company which receives a valid request **5.55** from its workforce to consider whether that request may impact on the other companies in the group, and to ensure that the holding or parent company is advised of that request so that consideration can be given to whether it is appropriate to rely on the provisions of Regulation 14(6). Communication between group companies will be key to ensuring that the right approach is taken in each case.

E. PERIOD FOR NEGOTIATIONS

Assuming the employer and negotiating representatives are in place and **5.56** the three-month period (suspended or not) has come to an end, the six-month negotiation period then begins.

1. The Duty of Co-Operation

5.57 At the outset of the negotiation process both the employer and the negotiating representatives should have regard to the duty of co-operation set out in Regulation 21. This applies where the parties are negotiating or implementing a negotiated agreement (and when implementing the standard information and consultation procedures; see further Chapter 7).

5.58 Regulation 21 states that the parties are under a duty: 'to work in a spirit of co-operation and with due regard for their reciprocal rights and obligations, taking into account the interests of both the undertaking and the employees'.

5.59 The wording in Regulation 21 is taken virtually word for word from the Information and Consultation Directive, Article 1(3) of which states that:

> when defining or implementing practical arrangements for information and consultation, the employer and the employees' representatives shall work in a spirit of co-operation, and with due regard for their reciprocal rights and obligations, taking into account the interests both of the undertaking or establishment and of the employees.

5.60 What does the duty of co-operation means in practice? It presumably means that the parties should come to the table with an open mind, willing to listen to the other parties' views and ideas, so that a genuine dialogue can be established. In undertaking negotiations, the parties should take account of the wider interests of the undertaking and the employees and ensure that the views they express have these interests in mind. An employer who has already taken final decisions in relation to the matters under negotiation may not be acting in the spirit of Regulation 21. Similarly it may be that negotiating representatives who decide to 'wait out' the negotiating period, rather than entering into negotiations with the employer (with the aim of having the standard information and consultation procedures apply) would also not be acting as is intended by Regulation 21. In practice, though, it is likely to be difficult to show that there has been non-compliance.

5.61 There is also no specific sanction for a breach of Regulation 21 in relation to the negotiation process. Therefore an employer faced with negotiating representatives who decide to wait out the negotiating period so that the standard information and consultation procedures apply will not have any recourse e.g. to the CAC.

2. Setting Out a Timetable for Negotiations

Given that six months is a short period of time in which to negotiate and conclude an information and consultation agreement, the parties may wish to agree a timetable for negotiation meetings at the outset. **5.62**

Such a timetable could cover how often the parties will meet, what will be done between meetings to record the points on which agreement has been reached, and which particular topics will be covered at each of the meetings. A regular meeting plan involving weekly/fortnightly/ monthly meetings can then be agreed and any difficulties with following such a timetable identified at the outset (e.g. absences because of holidays or factory shutdowns, or whether there are likely to be particularly busy periods in the proposed timetable which may make meetings difficult). **5.63**

It may also be useful to agree that the parties establish sub-groups if necessary during the negotiation process, so that if the parties are unable to reach agreement on a particular issue, that issue is delegated to the sub-group to progress (so that one issue does not delay the whole negotiation process). **5.64**

Although there is no requirement to do so, the employer will probably want to take responsibility for scheduling the meetings and for providing any required resources for the meeting (e.g. a note-taker). **5.65**

As suggested above, at the outset both parties should diarize when the six-month consultation period will come to an end, leaving sufficient time at the end to allow for the approval of the final negotiated agreement as is required by Regulation 16 (see paragraphs 5.82 to 5.92). **5.66**

Chapter 10 analyses the various protections given to representatives under the ICE Regulations and their rights to paid time off to perform their duties as negotiating representatives. **5.67**

3. What about Training for Negotiating Representatives and for Managers?

It is common for employers embarking on consultation with employee representatives (particularly redundancy consultation, or where representatives have been appointed to look after health and safety) to offer some initial training and guidance to both managers and representatives as to what will be involved. **5.68**

The ICE Regulations do not stipulate that any training need be given in advance of the negotiation process. However, as the time for negotiating **5.69** an agreement is relatively short a sensible use of the initial three-month period (assuming agreement is reached in relation to the negotiating representatives early into the initial three-month period) might be to devote time to explaining how the employer ideally sees the negotiating process working, and to agree how best to channel efforts so that the chances of reaching agreement within the time-frame contemplated by the ICE Regulations are maximized.

5.70 ACAS suggests that any training and guidance sessions should be joint (i.e. with managers and employee representatives present), to help improve mutual understanding. ACAS also suggests that training should be 'participative, with people being encouraged to exchange views, take part in discussions, share ideas and experiences', to help develop the behaviour that effective information and consultation require.

5.71 Of course, depending on the identity of the negotiating representatives, training may not be required (e.g. if the negotiating representatives who have been appointed or elected are sufficiently experienced or are trade union representatives).

F. REQUIREMENTS FOR A NEGOTIATED AGREEMENT TO BE VALID

5.72 In initiating the negotiation process, both the employer and the negotiating representatives will be mindful of the requirements of the ICE Regulations in order for a negotiated agreement to be valid.

5.73 Regulation 16 contains the requirements which apply to negotiated agreements. Under Regulation 16 a negotiated agreement must: 'cover all the employees of the undertaking and may consist either of a single agreement, or of different parts . . . which, taken together, cover all the employees of the undertaking'.

5.74 Regulation 16(1) further states that the single agreement or each part must:

(a) set out the circumstances in which the employer must inform and consult the employees to which it relates;
(b) be in writing;
(c) be dated;
(d) be approved in accordance with paragraphs (3) to (5)[of Regulation 16];
(e) be signed by or on behalf of the employer; and
(f) either—

(i) provide for the appointment or election of information and consultation representatives to whom the employer must provide the information and to whom the employer must consult in the circumstances referred to in sub-paragraph (a); or

(ii) provide that the employer must provide information directly to the employees to which it relates and consult those employees directly in the circumstances referred to in sub-paragraph (a).

Regulation 16(2) states that where a negotiated agreement consists of different parts, they may provide differently in relation to the matters referred to in Regulation 16(1)(a) and (f) above. **5.75**

Paragraph 37 of the DTI Guidance makes it clear that the parties are free to negotiate the content of the agreement and paragraph 40 further states that the parties are free to agree on the 'method, frequency, timing and subject matter of information and consultation best suited to their particular circumstances'. **5.76**

There are otherwise no requirements as to the content of a negotiated agreement. **5.77**

Annex 1 to the DTI Guidance makes suggestions for the contents of a pre-existing or negotiated agreement. Chapter 6 looks at Annex 1 to the DTI Guidance in more detail and analyses what a pre-existing and a negotiated agreement might contain. **5.78**

1. Pre-Existing Agreements versus Negotiated Agreements

There are a number of key differences between the requirements for pre-existing agreements and the requirements that apply to negotiated agreements. **5.79**

The Requirement to Consult

Negotiated agreements must set out the circumstances in which the employer will inform and *consult* the employees. Contrast this with Regulation 8, which states that a pre-existing agreement must set out how the employer is to give information to the employees or their representatives and 'seek their views' on such information. The word 'consultation' is not mentioned (although a mechanism for exchanging views is required). **5.80**

The use of the word 'consultation' in Regulation 16 suggests that negotiated agreements require a different level of interaction than is required or contemplated by the ICE Regulations in relation to pre-existing agreements. **5.81**

5.82 There is no definition of 'circumstances' but this is presumably a reference to the types of events that should give rise to an information and consultation obligation.

Negotiated Agreement Must Be Dated

5.83 Unlike a pre-existing agreement, a negotiated agreement must be dated. The reason for this requirement is clear. For the purposes of the ICE Regulations it is irrelevant when a pre-existing agreement was created (provided, of course, that the pre-existing agreement meets the requirements for validity under Regulation 8 and has been entered into before a valid employee request is submitted). However, under Regulation 12, no employee request or employer notification is valid if it is made or issued within a period of three years from the date of a negotiated agreement (Regulation 12(a)), or where a negotiated agreement has been terminated within the three-year period, before the date on which the termination takes effect. For this reason it is important to know the date on which the negotiated agreement was put in place, as any challenges to the negotiated agreement within the three years prescribed by Regulation 12 may be invalid.

The Requirements Relating to Approval

5.84 The ICE Regulations are prescriptive as to what an employer must do to enable him to show that the negotiated agreement has been approved. There are no specified methods of approval in the ICE Regulations in relation to pre-existing agreements, although the DTI Guidance does make some suggestions as to what might amount to approval (see further Chapter 3).

5.85 Regulation 16(3) applies to single negotiated agreements and provides that an agreement shall be treated as being approved if *either*:

- it has been signed by all the negotiating representatives; or
- it has been signed by a majority of the negotiating representatives; and *either* approved in writing by at least 50% of the employees employed in the undertaking; *or* approved by a ballot of those employees, the arrangements for which satisfied the requirements in Regulation 16(5), in which at least 50% of the employees voting voted in favour of approval.

5.86 Regulation 16(4) applies to 'part' negotiated agreements. A part shall be treated as having been approved if the part:

- has been signed by all the negotiating representatives involved in negotiating the part; *or*

approved in writing by at least 50% of employees (employed in the undertaking) to which the part relates; *or*

approved by a ballot of those employees, the arrangements for which satisfied the requirements set out in Regulation 16(5), in which 50% of the employees voting, voted in favour of approving the part.

2. Balloting Requirements for Approval

The requirements for the ballot are set out in Regulation 16(5). There are three conditions which apply to ensure the ballot complies with the provisions of Regulation 16(5): **5.87**

- the employer must make such arrangements as are 'reasonably practicable' to ensure the ballot is fair (Regulation 16(5)(a);
- all employees in the undertaking (or relevant part) on the day on which the votes may be cast in the ballot (or if votes may be cast on more than one day, on the first of those days) must be given an entitlement to vote in the ballot (Regulation 16(5)(b);
- the ballot must be conducted so as to secure that 'as far as reasonably practicable' those voting do so in secret (and the votes given in the ballot are accurately counted).

If the employer decides to hold a ballot to seek approval of the negotiated agreement, the employer must inform the employees entitled to vote of the result 'as soon as reasonably practicable' after the date of the ballot. **5.88**

Under Regulation 17(1) if any negotiating representative is unhappy with the ballot, because he believes one of the requirements set out above has not been complied with, he can complain about the procedure to the CAC. Such a complaint must be lodged within 21 days of the date of the ballot. If the CAC finds that the ballot was flawed in some way, it has the power to order a fresh ballot within such period as the CAC specifies (Regulation 17(2)). The timetable for negotiation is suspended whilst any complaint to the CAC about the balloting process is resolved. **5.89**

Clearly the easiest way of demonstrating approval for a negotiated agreement is to have all of the negotiating representatives sign the agreement. However the requirement that *all* the negotiating representatives must sign the agreement means that one recalcitrant negotiating representative has the power to complain about the process and therefore delay/block approval of the agreement. If all of the negotiating representatives refuse to sign the agreement, then the employer has two choices: **5.90** either to put the agreement to the employees and ask for signatures (an option that is only likely to be practicable for single agreements covering smaller organizations, but which may be of more use for 'part' agreements), or to hold a ballot. The ballot has the advantage of needing only 50% of those voting to vote in favour. If the employer is in doubt about being able to get 50% of the employees to sign the agreement, the employer should hold a ballot, to avoid wasting what at that stage might be fairly limited time.

5.91 What is less clear is what happens if agreement is reached on one part of the agreement but not on other parts. Are the parties able to seek approval for the part which has been agreed? Or is an 'all-or-nothing' approach envisaged for negotiated agreements? Regulation 16(4) clearly contemplates that an employer can seek approval for a 'part' agreement. But can that 'part' be a part of an overall negotiated agreement, or must it be a self-standing agreement which relates to a distinct part of the undertaking? Clearly the latter is contemplated by Regulation 16(4) and it may therefore not be possible for that part of an overall agreement in respect of which there is no dispute to have any force and effect if the overall agreement is not approved.

5.92 If a negotiating representative wishes to complain about the ballot he can do so knowing the timetable for agreement will not expire whilst he does so. However the negotiation timetable is only suspended when a complaint about the balloting process is lodged with the CAC. If the employer is unable to get all of the employee representatives to sign the agreement, is unsuccessful in persuading 50% of the relevant employees to approve the agreement, and decides to hold a ballot instead, he must do so quickly, as the negotiation timetable will continue to run throughout this time.

G. CONCLUSIONS

5.93 The ICE Regulations gives the parties maximum flexibility to negotiate an agreement which suits the needs of the particular business, undertaking, or group. Chapter 6 looks at the recommendations in the DTI Guidance as to what matters could be covered in a negotiated (and pre-existing) agreement. The requirements relating to negotiated agreements are more prescriptive than those which apply to pre-existing agreements, but negotiated agreements also have a number of advantages over pre-existing agreements, not least the provisions of the ICE Regulations relating to the disclosure of confidential information (see Chapter 8) and the ability of the parties to approach the CAC in relation to any failure to follow the negotiated agreement (see Chapter 9). Failure to reach a negotiated agreement will result in the parties being bound by the standard information and consultation procedures. Chapter 7 looks at the content of the standard information and consultation procedures and analyses how their application is likely to affect employers, employees and their representatives.

6

The Content of a Pre-Existing/Negotiated Agreement

Both pre-existing and negotiated agreements give an opportunity for flexibilities that are not available under the standard information and consultation provisions and which may therefore makes them attractive for the employer, employees, and their representatives. These are in addition to other potential benefits (and in some cases disadvantages) described in greater detail in Chapter 3 (in relation to pre-existing agreements) and Chapter 5 (in relation to negotiated agreements). **6.01**

This chapter explores these possibilities in greater detail and analyses the possible content of both pre-existing and negotiated agreements set out in Annex 1 of the DTI Guidance. **6.02**

A. THE STARTING POINT

From the employer's perspective, the starting point will be to identify the context in which the agreement is to be set in place: the structure of the employer, its existing approach to employee relations, the aim of the agreement (i.e. is the employer adopting a positive or protective approach?), and the nature of any other arrangements already in existence within the organization. **6.03**

B. ANNEX 1 OF THE DTI GUIDANCE

In deciding on the content of either a pre-existing or a negotiated agreement, both the employer and the employees or their representatives (or in the case of a negotiated agreement, the negotiating representatives) should have regard to Annex 1 of the DTI Guidance, which makes practical suggestions for the content of both pre-existing and negotiated agreements. In addition ACAS has published useful guidance on drawing up voluntary agreements for information and consultation. **6.04**

6.05 The suggestions in Annex 1 to the DTI Guidance are not intended to be either prescriptive or exhaustive. In agreeing the content of negotiated or pre-existing agreements, employers and employees have a completely free hand to agree to the arrangements or mechanisms that best suit their organization. Larger organizations may conclude that it is both more appropriate and more flexible to have several different arrangements for separate parts of the organization. Smaller entities may be happy to agree one single agreement covering the entire workforce. Either approach is acceptable.

6.06 The following sections look in more detail at each suggestion in Annex 1 of the DTI Guidance (see p. 317). As the recommendations are the same for pre-existing agreements as for negotiated agreements, references in the remainder of this chapter to 'agreement' are to both types of agreement. In certain (relatively limited) areas, different considerations may apply to pre-existing and negotiated agreements. When this is relevant, the point is picked up in the text.

C. COVERAGE

1. The Undertaking/Group of Undertakings to Be Covered

6.07 The agreement must be clear as to which 'undertaking' or 'group of undertakings' will be covered. As explained in Chapter 3, single agreements can cover more than one undertaking. Subdivisions within one undertaking may together either be covered by one agreement, or by multiple agreements.

6.08 For agreements that cover more than one undertaking, it might be sensible to list those undertakings that are covered (for example by company name or division, or by office location depending on how the undertakings are structured). Similarly for agreements which will cover only select groupings of employees within an organization (with the other employees being covered by other agreements) then the ambit and coverage of the agreement should be clearly stated.

2. Which Employees in the Undertaking(s) Are Covered?

6.09 The agreement should state which employees are covered by the agreement. This could be done by listing each undertaking covered, or by reference to grade, business sector, or location of employees. A negotiated agreement must cover all employees in the undertaking, though it could consist of a number of parts, each covering a group of employees within the undertaking. Pre-existing agreements must cover all the employees in the undertaking and if they do not, there must be one or more agreements covering the remaining employees.

Should the agreement provide a breakdown of the categories of employee who are covered (e.g. to make it clear that both full and part-time employees are covered, but to exclude e.g. agency workers and self-employed contractors)? Possibly, if the parties are keen to ensure certainty, or for organizations that are heavily reliant on agency or contractor staff and may wish to make it clear that such workers are not covered by the employer's arrangements. However the employer will want to make sure that the description of the employees that are covered is accurate: if the employer mistakenly excludes a group or category of employees then this may render the agreement ineffective if it then fails to cover all relevant employees. **6.10**

Express provision should be made for those who join the undertaking(s) to be automatically covered by the agreement. See, however, the discussion at paragraphs 3.76 and 3.77 as to the point at which substantial attrition or churn may constitute a material change in the undertaking for the purposes of Regulation 12(2)(a), so as to permit an employee request to be made to replace a pre-existing agreement with new information and consultation procedures. The same considerations apply to negotiated agreements, where under Regulation 12(2)(b) an employee request or employer notification can be issued notwithstanding the existence of a negotiated agreement if that agreement no longer complies with Regulation 16(1)(d)—that is to say, it no longer covers all the employees of the undertaking. **6.11**

3. Will Separate Arrangements Exist in Different Parts of the Undertaking?

Annex 1 of the DTI Guidance suggests that in order for the parties to be clear on the scope of the agreement, the agreement should set out or refer to the arrangements that may exist elsewhere within the undertaking. **6.12**

The parties should consider any other information and consultation arrangements and consider (1) whether they should be specifically referred to in the new agreement; (2) whether the agreement needs to set out how the new procedures will interact with any already in existence; or (3) in the case of pre-existing agreements, whether the intention is that the new arrangements should supersede the previous arrangements. Any such arrangements will *not* be automatically superseded unless the pre-existing agreement specifically provides that this is what is intended.

4. Where the Employer Recognizes Unions, How Will any Collective Agreements Be Affected?

6.13 In determining the scope of the agreement it will be important for those organizations that have any existing collective agreements to consider what the relationship between the agreements will be. Will there be any overlap in coverage e.g. as to the bargaining unit, or as to the scope of the agreements? For example, how will a recognition or other collective agreement impact or overlap with an agreement setting out general information and consultation obligations?

6.14 As the ACAS guidance points out, for those employers who recognize trade unions, complex representation patterns can emerge where more than one representative body is in place. This is particularly the case where there may be trade union membership across a significant section of one bargaining unit, but elsewhere very little trade union coverage, or where multiple unions are involved, or where one section of the workforce is unionized and the other covered by non-union representatives.

6.15 It is therefore important that the parties give consideration to how any new information and consultation agreement will interact with existing arrangements. For example it might be appropriate to agree that there should be a single new agreement incorporating collective bargaining for those employees in respect of whom the trade union is recognized and setting out the different rights which apply to the remaining section of the workforce (i.e. the two processes work under the umbrella of one agreement). Alternatively the parties may wish to keep the two processes separate, in which case it may be appropriate to say simply that the new arrangements are without prejudice to the existing collective bargaining rights that exist within the organization. The union in particular may be keen to keep collective bargaining rights completely separate, so as to preserve their authority in respect of such matters. Similarly the employer may prefer to keep the two sets of obligations separate, so as not to risk an implied extension of the collective bargaining rights to other sections of the workforce.

D. METHODS OF INFORMATION AND CONSULTATION

1. What Type of Arrangement Will Be Established?

The parties are free to agree the mechanism by which employees or their representatives will be given information and the way in which they views on that information will be sought. For negotiated agreements, Regulation 14(1) requires representatives to be appointed or elected to negotiate that agreement (see further Chapter 5). However, once the agreement is in place, there is no requirement for employees to be represented going forward, as information and consultation may take place directly with employees. This may be appropriate where there is a single agreement covering a relatively small undertaking where the group of employees covered is small enough to make a direct information and consultation process feasible or, similarly, where multiple agreements cover a number of such small undertakings. **6.16**

If this is the preferred route, it may be useful for the parties to agree that alternative arrangements, e.g. election of representatives, will apply if the undertaking changes materially in size or number of employees (possibly by reference to a percentage increase of the total workforce within the undertaking or part). **6.17**

Notwithstanding any representation arrangements that are agreed, provision should be made in the agreement to allow the employer to provide information directly to employees if the employer deems this appropriate (or if for any reason it proves difficult to arrange a meeting with the employee representatives). This might be the case if, for example, a story appears in the press on a matter appearing to affect employees which is either false or misleading. In such circumstances the employer will want to preserve the right to be able to act quickly by communicating directly with staff. **6.18**

2. Hierarchy of Structures

For those organizations that have or propose to put in place a structure for the information and consultation arrangements which provide for national, regional, and local levels of employee participation, the parties should consider whether and how such structures will be reflected in the agreement. Will information be provided first at the national level to representatives and then cascaded down? Or will information be given simultaneously to all employee representatives? **6.19**

6.20 It may be sensible for the agreement to distinguish between those types of issues which it is appropriate to discuss with all the employee representatives and those which should be raised at national, regional or local level. For example, any proposed acquisition or disposal of a business or company is likely to be something that would require information and consultation across the whole organization. A health and safety matter at one site may be more appropriate for resolution by a sub-set of representatives or with representatives in one business sector/location only. ACAS recommends that the parties consider whether in some instances, it might be sensible for the agreement to provide the ability to set up a joint working party (that is, a sub-set of representatives) if the parties believe this would be the best way of canvassing opinion on and resolving a particular issue within the organization. A joint working party may be a useful tool where the parties agree a particular issue needs attention, but where the full body of representatives may not be needed to resolve the issue.

6.21 Where confidential information is involved, the employer may wish to have a mechanism in the agreement whereby such information is only provided to representatives at national level in the first instance. The level at which consultation occurs may depend on the issue at hand: an issue affecting the wider workforce may need to be first communicated at the national level, an issue only affecting a smaller group of employees could be communicated at local level or even direct to those concerned.

3. Who Will Represent Management at Any Meeting

6.22 Which member of management should be chosen to take responsibility for meeting the employer's obligations in respect of the information and consultation process? Should it be the person who has led the negotiations on the pre-existing or negotiated agreement? This may of course depend on how smooth the negotiation process has been and the extent to which the parties believe their respective aims have been achieved. It may be that the person best placed to lead the discussions from the management side is the Human Resources Director or one of the Human Resources Director's team. Ideally it should be someone with experience of consulting with employee representatives. In addition, someone with appropriate operational responsibility might be advisable. The management designate will also need to have sufficient time to devote to the information and consultation process. The agreement should avoid referring to a specific individual as this may then cause uncertainty if that individual then leaves the organization.

How many members of management will represent the employer? Presumably it will be sensible to have a deputy if the management designate is unable to attend meetings with the employee representatives for any reason. How will absences, etc., be dealt with? What will the scope of management designate's responsibilities be? Should the agreement state how the management representative will feed back to the rest of management? **6.23**

4. Arrangements for Choosing Employee Representatives

Assuming the parties agree that some form of standing committee/ employee representation is appropriate, how will the representatives be chosen? **6.24**

How Many Representatives are Needed?

The first question will be to agree on how many representatives should be appointed or elected. The parties will want to make sure that all of the various employee groups within the organization are represented. There is no minimum or maximum number of employee representatives that can be elected under the ICE Regulations in relation to pre-existing or negotiated agreements. However, under the standard information and consultation procedures the minimum number of employee representatives is one per 50 employees, provided that there are at least two representatives but not more than 25 representatives in total, and this may therefore be a useful rule of thumb. The number should not be so small as to be unrepresentative, nor so large as to be unwieldy. **6.25**

What Parts of the Organization should be Represented?

The parties will need to decide on the appropriate 'coverage'. Consider where the employees are based. Is it sensible to have representation of staff by geographical location? Or possibly by reference to grade, role, department, or seniority? The appropriate number of representatives per 'unit' should be discussed and agreed. In addition it may make sense for the larger interest groups within the employers' organization to have more than one representative (in the same way as TICE requires those Member States that have the largest number of employees within the overall organization to elect additional representatives). **6.26**

In deciding the right number of representatives and agreeing from which parts of the organization they should be chosen, the parties should consider how difficult it might be, in terms of logistics, to meet if a large **6.27** number of representatives are elected or appointed and those representatives are widely scattered.

Restrictions on Employee Representative Candidates

6.28 Should there be any restrictions on those who may stand for election (e.g. a minimum service requirement)? Often a minimum service requirement for posts (e.g. for health and safety representatives) is stipulated, to ensure that those putting themselves forward as employee representatives have at least a basic understanding of the business in which they work.

5. Election or Appointment?

6.29 Once the numbers and coverage have been agreed, how will employee representatives be chosen? There are no formal requirements in relation to pre-existing agreements, and the only requirement for a negotiated agreement is that representatives must be appointed or elected (assuming it is not agreed that information and consultation will be carried out with the employees directly). Will there be a formal election? If so, how soon after the agreement comes into force will that election take place? What kind of election is appropriate? A formal ballot, perhaps run externally by an independent person? Or a more informal election, organized internally?

6.30 If there is no formal election, then how will representatives be chosen? A vote by internal mail or email? A show of hands at a meeting? Unless an organization is small, a show of hands is unlikely to be sufficiently certain or precise. The advantage of a formal independent ballot is that it minimizes the risk of any challenge that the election was not carried out fairly.

6. Term of Office

6.31 How long will the representatives' term of office be? A standard term of office for an EWC representative is four years, but this may reflect the fact that EWCs are only obliged to meet once a year. It will be sensible for the term of office to be sufficient for the representatives to gain experience and grow into the role. A term of office that is too long may have the disadvantage of allowing representatives to become entrenched in their views and therefore potentially less effective.

6.32 What arrangements will apply if a representative resigns from his employment? What if the representative is suspended from duties (e.g. during a disciplinary investigation)—will he still be able to participate in any meetings? What if the representative is absent on sick leave or on holiday at a critical time? How will absences such as secondments, maternity leave, etc., be covered? It may be sensible to elect a representative and a substitute for each category of staff or location to be represented, to ensure that if the main representative is absent, there will be no delays.

7. Facilities and Time Off for Employee Representatives

Regulation 27 provides that an employee who is a negotiating representative or an information and consultation representative is entitled to be permitted by his employer to take reasonable time off during working hours to perform his function as a representative. Chapter 10 analyses this right in more detail, as well as analysing the other protections for employee representatives (and others) set out in the ICE Regulations. **6.33**

Regulation 27 does not apply to employee representatives under pre-existing agreements; however, it may be appropriate to agree and record the scope of any such rights that are to be given in favour of such representatives. It may also be worth clarifying in both a pre-existing and a negotiated agreement what constitutes reasonable time off. For example, how much time will they be expected/permitted to devote to their duties during working hours? How much paid time off will be permitted? Will preparatory time also be permitted (organizations with union representatives usually allow preparation time for their representatives)? Ideally there should also be a right for managers to refuse to permit time off to be taken or to postpone such time off if taking such time would be detrimental to the business. **6.34**

8. Facilities

What facilities will be made available to representatives? It will be useful for the representatives to have access to stationery and to a meeting room and possibly access to secretarial support for the purpose of writing up minutes of meetings, etc. **6.35**

Employers and employees may want to facilitate a process whereby employee representatives can canvass views from staff on issues affecting the workforce (e.g. by making rooms available over lunch for meetings with staff, or by giving the representatives access to email to enable them to communicate with staff). **6.36**

9. The Obligations of Employee Representatives

How will the employee representatives be expected to report back to management? Within what timescales? Will feedback be in writing or in **6.37** the form of follow-up meetings? The parties will want to ensure that the processes put in place are sufficiently flexible to allow different feedback mechanisms to apply, depending on what issue is under discussion.

6.38 The employer may also want to maintain a degree of control over the process of canvassing employees for their views. During particularly busy times it may cause difficulties if the representatives are canvassing the workforce, and the employer may therefore wish to retain the right to control when the views of the workforce are canvassed.

10. The Nature of any Direct Forms of Information and Consultation with Staff

6.39 As discussed in Chapter 3 and Chapter 5, both negotiated agreements and pre-existing agreements can incorporate a mixture of information and consultation with employee representatives and direct with staff.

6.40 For direct information and consultation, then depending on the size of the workforce it may be difficult to arrange meetings for the entire workforce and this may drive the decision on how often meetings should be held. An alternative form of information and consultation might then be appropriate (e.g. in the form of an email update, with provision made for employees to feed back comments). The mechanism for communicating directly with staff should be set out in the agreement.

11. What the Employer Will Do in Response to Employee Representative Feedback

6.41 Once the employer has received feedback from employees or their representatives, what will be the process of responding to views? Will follow-up information be provided? Or will further meetings be held to review and respond to any questions and queries raised? The employer will be mindful of not agreeing a process which becomes unwieldy due to the length of time it takes to complete.

E. FREQUENCY AND TIMING OF INFORMATION AND CONSULTATION

1. How Often Will Information and Consultation Take Place?

6.42 It will make sense for the parties to agree the number of meetings that will be held each year. Under most EWC agreements, additional 'extraordinary' meetings can be called if circumstances dictate. In a number of EWC agreements the right to call additional meetings is a right of the employer only. The employer may wish to have such a right reserved in the agreement.

2. When Will Information and Consultation Take Place?

The parties might wish to agree at what stage in the organization's year it will be appropriate to meet. For example it may be appropriate to meet around the time of the company's results announcements/AGM/other significant date in the company's calendar. **6.43**

F. SUBJECT MATTER

What information will management provide to the employees or their representatives? Will written documentation be made available? Or will information be presented electronically (e.g. by email, or by means of an intranet site updated regularly)? Or is it preferable for management to present information direct to employees or their representatives and seek views (e.g. by a PowerPoint presentation at a staff or employee representative meeting, with a question and answer session thereafter). **6.44**

1. Types of Subject to Be Covered

Of critical importance to the parties will be what subject matter is to be covered. There is nothing in either the ICE Regulations or the DTI Guidance to say what information should be given to employees or their representatives. Annex 1 of the DTI Guidance suggests that the types of subject to be covered should be agreed between the parties, but it gives no further details as to what those subjects should be. This gives the parties maximum flexibility to agree the subject matter that will be covered. There is clearly a balance to be struck between agreeing an exhaustive list of subjects that will be covered (which will give the parties little or no flexibility) and agreeing a list which is so broad that it is open to constant challenges about what is and isn't within the scope of maters to be considered. For this reason it may be sensible for the parties to agree a non-exhaustive list of subject matters so that the parameters of what it is the parties contemplate should be covered are agreed. This may minimize the rise of challenge by employees as to what should be covered. **6.45**

ACAS make various recommendations in its *Employee Communications and Consultation* booklet as to the subject matter of the information that employers should be communicating to employees. **6.46**

6.47 In considering what matters should be covered by the agreement, employee representatives are likely to be mindful of the three categories of information that employers who are subject to the standard information and consultation procedures must provide to employee representatives (Regulation 20(1)). These categories of information are likely to be seen as the minimum requirements of the employee representatives and if the employer wishes to move away from these categories, he may find himself needing to offer something more comprehensive. These categories are analysed in more detail in Chapter 7 but are as follows:

(a) information on 'the recent and probable development of the undertakings' activities and economic situation';

(b) information on 'the situation, structure, and probable development of employment within the undertaking and on any anticipatory measures envisaged, in particular, where there is a threat to employment within the undertaking'; and

(c) information on 'decisions likely to lead to substantial changes in work organization or in contractual relations'.

6.48 Note that the standard information and consultation procedures only require consultation to take place in respect of categories (b) and (c). In addition, the requirement to consult with a view to reaching agreement is limited to decisions covered by category (c) which are within the employer's control.

6.49 Given the requirements set out in Regulation 20 in relation to the standard information and consultation procedures (discussed in detail in Chapter 7), both employer and the employees/employees representatives may take the view that it is preferable to agree a list of matters to be covered. This is not least because the scope of the standard procedure is unclear and therefore may be open to challenge. However, as a practical matter the employer may have limited scope to press for anything that is materially narrower than the Regulation 20 requirements (at least in the context of a negotiated agreement). Under negotiated agreements, the parties may have a short timetable (a maximum of nine months) to conclude a negotiated agreement (see further Chapter 5) before the standard information and consultation provisions apply. The negotiating representatives may react to an attempt by the employer to narrow down significantly the matters to be the subject of the information and consultation rights by simply sitting out the remainder of the negotiating timetable in order to ensure that the standard information and consultation provisions do apply.

2. Will Pay Be Covered by the Negotiated/Pre-Existing Agreement?

The DTI Guidance on what is covered by the standard information and consultation procedures refers explicitly to the Treaty Base (Article 137) under which the Information and Consultation Directive has been adopted, which states that matters such as pay are *not* covered. The DTI's view is that category (3) ('changes in contractual relations') does not cover changes in pay or benefits that have a monetary value (although the DTI Guidance makes the point that this does not negate the need to get consent to any changes to such terms and conditions of employment in the usual way). **6.50**

There is therefore no obligation on an employer to include pay as part of a pre-existing or negotiated agreement, although it may be something that employee representatives are keen to include. Consider also how including a provision on pay will impact on any existing representation arrangements, particularly any collective bargaining agreements with trade unions. As analysed in Chapter 3, trade unions may be keen to 'ring-fence' any collective bargaining arrangements so that their status is preserved. Where the negotiating representatives are also trade union representatives, they may wish to expand the scope of their influence by requesting that any pre-existing or negotiated agreements do cover pay and remuneration issues. **6.51**

3. Should Pension Matters Be Included?

For the same reasons that pay is not covered by the standard information and consultation procedures, it can be argued that pensions issues are also excluded (as pensions would normally be considered to have a monetary value). **6.52**

On 6 June 2005 the Department for Work and Pensions published a consultation document and two sets of draft Regulations to be made under sections 259–61 of the Pensions Act 2004. The draft Occupational and Personal Pension Schemes (Consultation by Employers) Regulations 2006 envisage requiring most employers, in relation to occupational or personal pension schemes, to consult where employers or trustees are proposing to make "listed changes", before any decision or decisions to make those changes are made (see paragraphs 1.35 to 1.37). **6.53**

The draft Regulations confirm that employers will be able to choose to consult with information and consultation representatives under the ICE Regulations. **6.54**

6.55 Note that significant changes to pensions, such as a change to an occupational pension scheme would, according to the DTI Guidance, be covered by category (3) of the standard information and consultation procedures in any event (see paragraph 7.69).

4. Choosing Subjects and Setting Meeting Agendas

6.56 The agreement should set out how subjects for each meeting should be chosen, how the meetings will be organized, and how they will be conducted.

6.57 Under most EWC agreements a subcommittee is elected, consisting of a chairperson, a secretary, and an administrator. The secretary will usually assume the administrative tasks involved in running the EWC, including collating agendas, circulating meeting details, and finalizing minutes of meetings. If such a subcommittee is elected, the terms of election of the subcommittee should be set out in the agreement.

5. Format and Structure of Meetings

6.58 The parties should consider providing in the agreement for:

- how far in advance a meeting should be called (assuming fixed dates each year have not been specified in the agreement);
- whether representatives have their expenses paid (this is usual for EWC meetings). If so, what types of expense will be covered?
- how the agenda will be agreed: should the employer take responsibility for setting the agenda and then seeking input from the representatives?
- once agreed, how far in advance it will be circulated;
- where the meeting will take place. Will the venue change year on year, or will it be fixed?
- who will chair the meetings? How will the chair be chosen? Will the chair always be a representative of management or will employee representatives also be given the opportunity to chair?
- who will take minutes of the meetings? Following the meeting, will the minutes be circulated to all employee representatives? How will comments be collated? Will the final minutes need to be signed off by all of the representatives? What is the position if agreement cannot be reached on the contents of the minutes?

G. INFORMATION AND CONSULTATION

1. The Type and Nature of Information to Be Provided

What types of documents will be made available (e.g. financial information? Information from actuaries?) At what stage will information be made available, e.g. before any scheduled meeting (and if so, how long in advance)? How much detail will be provided? Will employees have the opportunity to ask for further or more detailed information on specific issues? **6.59**

2. How Views/Opinions of Employees Can Be Given

The parties should discuss and agree how they are expecting employees to feed back their views on the subject matter of any information and consultation exercise. Are views to be channelled only through the employee representatives? Or will employees have a mechanism by which they can express views separately from the employee representation process? How will the employer seek feedback on matters where a direct information and consultation with staff is carried out? **6.60**

3. What the Employer Will Do in Response

How will the employer respond to the views of both the employees and their representatives? Will there be a formal process whereby the views of the employer are reported back to the representatives or staff generally? There may a difference between the approach an employer will want to take to responding to employees who are the subject of a pre-existing agreement, where the requirement is only to 'seek views' (Regulation 8(1)(d)), and the approach in relation to negotiated agreements, where the requirement is specifically to inform 'and consult' (Regulation 16(1)(a)). **6.61**

How many opportunities will employee representatives get to give their views to management? If a particular issue is becoming contentious and the parties have opposing views, will there be any mechanism in the agreement for seeking to resolve such an issue (e.g. by referring it to a sub-committee or working party, as recommended by the ACAS guidance)? **6.62**

4. Who Will Represent Management at Any Meeting?

The representatives of management for the purposes of the information and consultation exercise need not be the same as the representatives **6.63** during the negotiations for either the pre-existing agreement or the negotiated agreement. See paragraphs 6.22 to 6.23 for a discussion of who might be best placed to represent management.

H. STATUTORY CONSULTATION REQUIREMENTS

6.64 The parties to any agreement may already have in place various arrangements for consulting in relation to e.g. health and safety matters, TUPE, or redundancy issues, and may also have an EWC. Any agreement should clarify how those existing obligations fit with those to be covered by the agreement and highlight any potential areas of overlap. Existing consultation mechanisms for these areas may be working effectively and therefore the parties may wish to provide that such matters are expressly excluded from the scope of the agreement. Or it might be possible for both arrangements to work in tandem, involving dual consultation with both sets of representatives. If this is the case, the agreement should set out the order in which consultation takes place (e.g. does one body 'trump' the other?).

6.65 An employer who is subject to the standard information and consultation procedures is able to elect under Regulation 20(5) that he intends to comply with any obligations to consult under TUPE or under collective redundancy consultation separately from the information and consultation procedure by notifying the employee representatives on each such event.

6.66 Parties reviewing any pre-existing agreements or negotiating a new information and consultation agreement may wish expressly to include the flexibility to choose to inform and consult with separate bodies in relation to discreet redundancy exercises or TUPE transfers. In any event, the DTI Guidance states that the process to be followed should be considered, to avoid being subject to two different legal requirements to consult over the same issue.

I. CONFIDENTIAL OR PRICE-SENSITIVE INFORMATION

6.67 Annex 1 of the DTI Guidance suggests that an agreement should expressly address how confidential or price-sensitive information will be dealt with by the parties. Here there is more flexibility for employees who have pre-existing agreements than there is for those with negotiated agreements. In the case of a negotiated agreement, the provisions of Regulations 25 and 26 apply (see further Chapter 9). However, in the case of a pre-existing agreement, if such agreement is silent on how confidential or price-sensitive information should be dealt with, there will be very little protection for the employer wishing to disclose such information, other than those provisions relating to confidentiality in the employment contracts of individual employees, (and equally, little scope for employee representatives to require the disclosure of confidential information). The employer may therefore wish to have a contractually enforceable obligation dealing with the disclosure of such information. In considering what provisions should be included in the agreement the parties will need to define what they mean by 'confidential' and 'price-sensitive' information. How will such information be provided (e.g. orally at meetings or by confidential memo to the employee representatives)? What restrictions will apply on the use of that information? What disciplinary measures will apply to the representatives for breach of any obligations of confidentiality?

J. DISPUTES

1. How Can Disputes Be Resolved?

Provisions should be included for dealing with how disputes between the parties in relation to the operation of the information and consultation procedures will be resolved. Although a negotiated agreement is enforceable via the CAC, Annex 1 of the DTI Guidance recommends that both pre-existing and negotiated agreements contain some form of procedure for resolving disputes internally without the need for formal complaint. It is clearly in the employer's interest to include a disputes mechanism, as the CAC has power to make a fine of £75,000 for any failure on the part of the employer in relation to a negotiated agreement or where the standard information and consultation provisions apply (but not in respect of pre-existing agreements). The parties may also wish to agree that internal dispute resolution procedures must be exhausted before the CAC is approached, and may also wish to agree that ACAS be involved in relation to any dispute that had not been resolved by the internal disputes procedure before the CAC is approached. **6.68**

For information and consultation procedures that are agreed within an undertaking which forms part of a wider group, it may be possible to agree that disputes are referred to e.g. a committee consisting of management and employee representatives at the parent company level. For other smaller organizations, or where the procedures apply across the group, the parties may wish to consider referring any disputes to an external third party, e.g. an organization specializing in mediation/ dispute resolution. **6.69**

2. Will a Pre-Existing Agreement Be Legally Binding?

6.70 In the case of a pre-existing agreement, Annex 1 of the DTI Guidance suggests that a provision be included stating whether the agreement is intended to be legally enforceable. In the absence of an express provision to this effect, a pre-existing agreement will be presumed *not* to be legally enforceable, meaning that either party can decide in its discretion that they are no longer bound by the pre-existing agreement.

6.71 If an employer chooses to treat himself as no longer bound by a pre-existing agreement which is not expressed to be legally binding, then at that point the agreement presumably falls away, leaving the employees free to make an employee request (or the employer to serve an employer notification). The same presumably then applies if the employees or their representatives choose not to be bound by a pre-existing agreement. For this reason, as a minimum, the employer may want some provisions, e.g. relating to confidentiality to have legal force.

K. RESTRUCTURING

6.72 The implications of any restructuring on existing information and consultation structures should be considered and express provision made for what the parties intend to happen in the event of a restructuring. Do the parties wish to provide for the election of further representatives to cover any staff inherited as a result of a transaction? Or should the agreement provide that the agreement is subject to a review in such circumstances? In this area certainty is likely to be helpful. Many existing EWC agreements do not expressly provide for what happens in circumstances where an acquisition or disposal substantially alters the organization to which the information and consultation procedures apply and this has led to uncertainty as to whether the EWC continues to exist, or whether it automatically extends to cover any incoming workforce.

6.73 In considering what provisions should be included in any agreement, the parties should bear in mind the provisions of Regulation 12(2) which apply where there have been material changes in the undertaking and which in such circumstances allow either the employer or the employees to proceed with a notification or a request for a new information and consultation procedure.

L. DURATION AND NOTICE PROVISIONS

The parties should agree on the duration of the agreement (if the agreement is to be limited in time). A three-year moratorium will generally apply to employee requests and employer notifications for an information and consultation procedure where there is a negotiated agreement in place. It will therefore be helpful for the agreement to state the date on which it came into force so that the three-year period can readily be identified. **6.74**

Will the agreement contain a notice provision? If so, what will that notice provision be and in what circumstances can notice be given (and by whom)? **6.75**

M. AMENDMENT PROVISIONS

The parties should consider what scope the agreement will contain for varying/amending its provisions. How will any variations to the agreement be recorded/implemented? **6.76**

7

Standard Information and Consultation Arrangements

7.01 This chapter examines the circumstances in which the standard information and consultation provisions laid down in the ICE Regulations will apply and the extent of the obligations the standard arrangements impose on employers. It covers the following areas:

(1) when the standard information and consultation arrangements apply;
(2) the requirements for the election of information and consultation representatives;
(3) when there will be an obligation to inform and/or consult;
(4) the timing obligations that are likely to attach to any requirement to inform and/or consult; and

(5) the circumstances in which the standard arrangements will cease to apply.

A. WHEN WILL THE STANDARD ARRANGEMENTS APPLY?

As indicated in earlier chapters, the standard information and consultation arrangements will only come into play if: **7.02**

- there has been an employee request to negotiate an information and consultation procedure under Regulation 7, or an employer notification under Regulation 11; and
- where there has been an employee request and the undertaking already had a pre-existing agreement, a ballot has been held in accordance with Regulation 8 or 9, as appropriate, and the employees have supported the request to negotiate; and
- the employer has failed to arrange for the appointment or election of negotiating representatives within the requisite period; or
- following the appointment or election of negotiating representatives, the parties have not succeeded in reaching agreement on the form that an information and consultation procedure should take.

The point at which the standard information and consultation provisions start to apply depends on what steps, if any, the employer has taken to comply with an employee request to negotiate. **7.03**

Figure 7.1 illustrates when the standard provisions may apply in a situation where there has been an employee request to negotiate under Regulation 7 or an employer notification under Regulation 11 and no pre-existing agreement was in place. **7.04**

1. Employee Request, No Pre-Existing Agreement and Negotiating Representatives not Appointed

If there has been an employee request under Regulation 7, and there is no pre-existing agreement in force, the employer should arrange for the appointment or election of negotiating representatives. If it fails to do so, the standard information and consultation provisions apply six months from the date of the employee request (Regulation 18(1)(a)(i)). **7.05**

The same is true in the (unlikely) circumstances that an employer notification has been given under Regulation 11 but the employer has then taken **7.06**

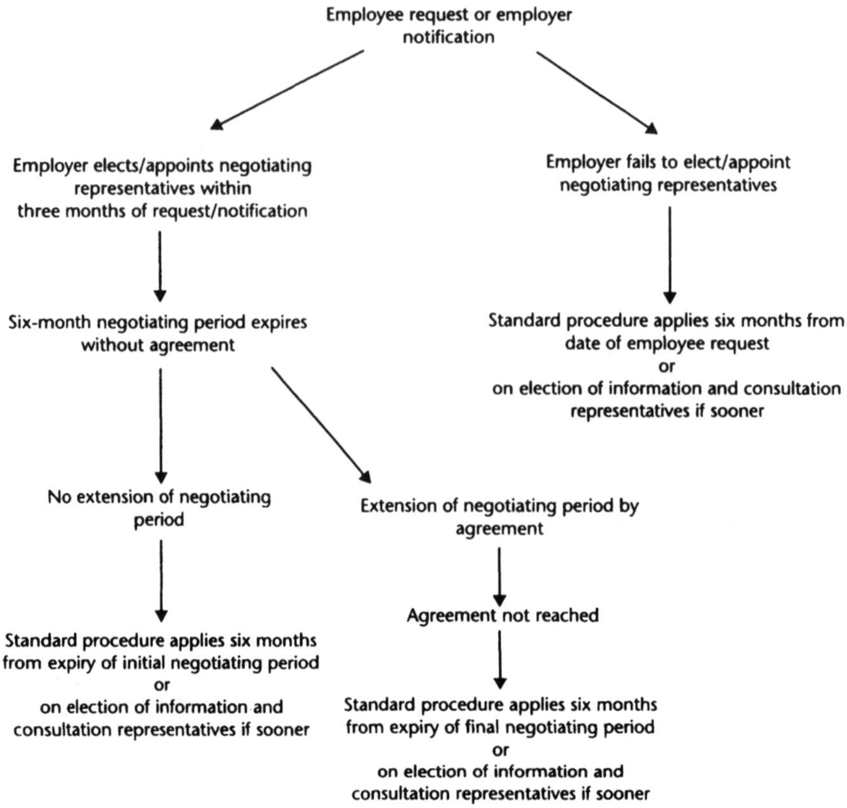

Figure 7.1 Application of standard information and consultation provisions: employee request (no pre-existing agreement) or employer notification.

no further action. The six-month period then runs from the date of the notification (Regulation 18(1)(a)(i)).

7.07 In either case, the standard provisions will apply before the expiry of the six-month period if information and consultation representatives have been elected before that date (Regulation 18(1)(a)(ii)) (and see paragraph 7.14).

2. Employee Request, No Pre-Existing Agreement, Negotiating Representatives Appointed

7.08 If the employer has received an employee request, elected or appointed negotiating representatives, but has been unable to agree on an appropriate information and consultation procedure, the standard procedures will apply six months after the end of the relevant period for negotiations

(Regulation 18(1)(b)(i)). The negotiating period will end after six months (Regulation 14(3)) unless the parties have agreed to an extension.

Again, in either case the standard procedures will apply before the end of the relevant period if information and consultation representatives have been elected sooner than that (Regulation 18(1)(b)(ii)) (and see paragraph 7.14). **7.09**

3. Employee Request, Pre-Existing Agreement

The same basic approach will apply if an employer with a valid pre-existing agreement receives an employee request to negotiate an information and consultation procedure. The only difference in the procedure is that the employer may elect to hold a ballot to gauge the level of support for the request. If the request is supported in the ballot, the employer must then proceed to elect negotiating representatives. The period between notifying the employees of the decision to hold a ballot on the employee request and the date of the ballot itself is not taken into account in calculating the three months within which the employer must elect or appoint negotiating representatives (Regulation 14(3)(a)). Figure 7.2 illustrates the points at which the standard information and consultation provisions will come into force in these circumstances. **7.10**

B. ELECTION OF INFORMATION AND CONSULTATION REPRESENTATIVES

If the standard information and consultation provisions apply, the duty is to inform and consult at the level of the undertaking. This is regardless of whether the employer forms part of a larger corporate group, and whether attempts were made to agree a negotiated agreement covering a number of different undertakings within that group. It is also irrelevant whether the employer attempted to negotiate different agreements for different parts of the undertaking; under the standard provisions the obligation to inform and consult will still apply at the undertaking level. See further Chapter 2 for the meaning of undertaking for these purposes. **7.11**

Under the standard provisions, an employer will be under a duty to inform and consult information and consultation representatives. The standard provisions do not allow an employer to inform and consult directly with employees, as would be possible in the case of either a pre-existing or a negotiated procedure. **7.12**

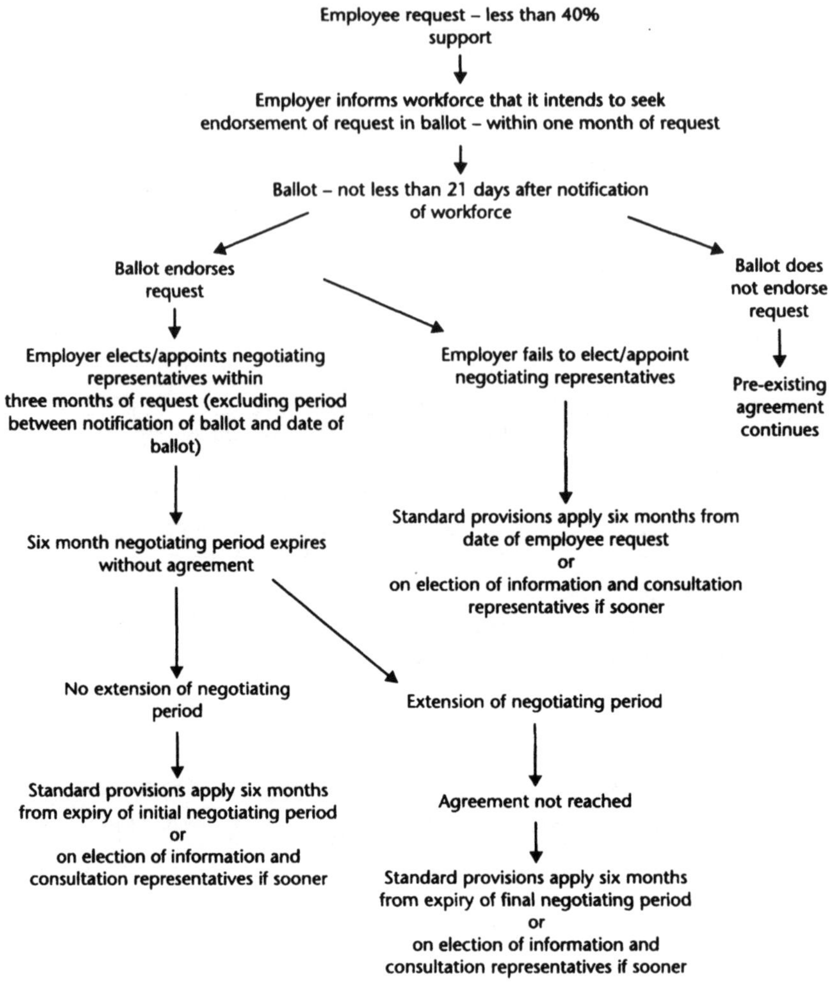

Figure 7.2 Application of standard information and consultation provisions: employee request (and pre-existing agreement).

7.13 If the standard provisions apply, an employer is under a duty to arrange for the election of information and consultation representatives with whom it will consult under the standard provisions. Although negotiating representatives may stand and be elected as information and consultation representatives, they will not automatically become information and consultation representatives if negotiations break down.

7.14 The provisions for the election of information and consultation representatives where the standard provisions apply are set out in some detail in

Regulation 19 and Schedule 2 of the ICE Regulations. The duty to arrange for the election of information and consultation representatives applies before the standard provisions themselves apply: Regulation 19(1) states that where the standard provisions apply, the employer's duty is to 'arrange for the holding of a ballot of its employees to elect . . . information and consultation representatives' before the standard provisions start to apply. The implications of Regulation 19(1) for the time at which representatives need to be elected are explained in paragraphs 7.15 to 7.17.

1. Employer Fails to Elect Negotiating Representatives

If an employer has not responded to an employee request by electing or appointing negotiating representatives within three months, the standard provisions apply six months from the date of the request. The employer must therefore arrange for the election of information and consultation representatives before the end of that six-month period. This will be the case whether or not a ballot has been called to gauge support for an employee request in an undertaking with a pre-existing procedure. Holding such a ballot does not extend the time for the standard provisions to apply except where the employer goes on to elect or appoint negotiating representatives. **7.15**

2. Employer Elects Negotiating Representatives

If the employer has appointed or elected negotiating representatives, but agreement on a negotiated procedure has not been reached, the standard provisions will only come into force 15 months after the initial request, as shown in example 7.1. This assumes that no pre-existing agreement was in force when the request was made, that there has been no extension to the initial negotiating period and that information and consultation representatives have not been elected sooner. **7.16**

Where negotiating representatives have been appointed or elected but negotiations have not succeeded, the employer has six months from the date the negotiating period for an agreement expired (six months, or such longer period as has been agreed with the representatives) to arrange for the election of information and consultation representatives. Again, the time for election of representatives is calculated in this way, whether or not a ballot of support for the request has been called in an undertaking with a pre-existing agreement. The calling of such a ballot is only relevant to the period within which negotiating representatives have to be elected, as discussed in Chapter 5. However, the period for holding a ballot to gauge support for an employee request is not taken into account in calcu- **7.17** lating the three-month period for election of negotiating representatives, effectively extending the timetable by the period it takes to hold the ballot (Regulation 14(3)(a)).

Example 7.1
An employer without a pre-existing agreement receives a valid employee request to negotiate on 1 May 2005. Negotiating representatives are elected by 1 July. The period for negotiations begins on 1 August and ends on 1 February 2006 (Regulation 14(3)). No negotiated agreement is reached. The standard information and consultation provisions apply from 1 August 2006 (or earlier if information and consultation representatives are elected before 1 August 2006).

Example 7.2
An employer with a pre-existing agreement receives a valid employee request to negotiate on 1 May 2005. The employer elects to hold a ballot to gauge support for the request. The ballot is notified to employees on 1 June and takes place on 1 July. The request is supported by the relevant proportion of the workforce. Negotiating representatives are elected on 1 August. The period for negotiations begins on 1 September (three months from the date of the employee request, excluding the one-month period between notification and holding the ballot to test support for the request—Regulation 14(3)) and ends on 1 March 2006. No negotiated agreement is reached. The standard information and consultation provisions apply from 1 September 2006 (or earlier if information and consultation representatives are elected before that date).

3. Numbers of Representatives

7.18 Under Regulation 19(3), the employer must arrange for the election of one information and consultation representative for every 50 employees (or proportion of 50 employees) subject to a minimum of two representatives and a maximum of 25. In other words, organizations with only 50 staff will be required to have two information and consultation representatives, and undertakings with more than 1,250 staff will have 25 information and consultation representatives, regardless of the total number of employees. Although the ICE Regulations do not specify at what date the number of employees is calculated, it seems likely that this will be judged by reference to the number of employees on the date the ballot is held. There is no provision for calculating an average number of employees as there is when determining whether the ICE Regulations apply to a particular undertaking.

Example 7.3
The standard provisions apply to an employer with 175 employees. The employer will be required to arrange for the election of four information and consultation representatives: one representative for every 50 employees or part thereof.

7.19 All the costs of the ballot, including the appointment of an independent ballot supervisor (see paragraph 7.21) are to be met by the employer (Schedule 2, paragraph 15).

If the employer fails to arrange for a ballot to be held in accordance with Regulation 19(1), an employee or employee representative can complain to the CAC (Regulation 19(4)) and the CAC has power to order the employer to arrange a ballot (Regulation 19(5)). This is discussed more fully at paragraphs 7.28 to 7.31. **7.20**

4. Balloting Requirements

The requirements for the ballot to elect information and consultation representatives contained in Schedule 2 are outlined below. A ballot that does not comply with these requirements is defective. **7.21**

- The employer can choose whether to hold a single ballot or a number of separate ballots if that would enable information and consultation representatives to reflect better the interests of the employees as a whole. For example, in an undertaking with one large and four smaller divisions, the employer might take the view that separate ballots should be held in each division to ensure that the interests of all the employees are properly reflected by a representative. This would help avoid a situation in which a single ballot was held and all information and consultation representatives were elected from the large division, effectively meaning that the interests of employees in the smaller divisions were not represented.

  It appears that this is a purely subjective test. The employer only has to consider that the interests of employees would be better reflected by different ballots; it does not need reasonable grounds for this belief (paragraph 2(a)). Therefore, although in theory the employer's election could be challenged, provided the employer can show the logic behind its decision, a challenge would seem unlikely to succeed.
- If fewer employees are standing for election than will be required for there to be one representative per 50 employees, the employer is not required to hold a ballot and can treat those employees who have chosen to stand for election as the information and consultation representatives (paragraph 2(b)). How the standard information and consultation provisions will apply if no employee representatives put themselves forward for election is unclear.
- All employees in the undertaking on the date of the ballot (or the first day if the ballot is spread over a number of days) must be allowed to vote (paragraph 2(c)). This would appear to include all those actually employed (i.e. including employees on notice and on maternity or

sickness absence but excluding new hires who have not yet started work).

- All employees who are employed at the latest date to stand for election as a candidate must be allowed to stand for election. In other words, the employer is not entitled to impose conditions on those standing for election, such as having been employed for a certain period of time (paragraph 2(d)). The only exception to this is in relation to merchant navy long-haul crew members, who are not entitled to be information and consultation representatives in the absence of permission from the employer, presumably on the basis of their frequent long-term unavailability (Regulation 43). A merchant navy long-haul crew member is a person who is a member of a merchant navy crew other than a ferry worker or a person who normally works on voyages the duration of which is less than 48 hours.
- An independent ballot supervisor must be appointed to supervise the ballot (paragraph 2(e)). The employer must have a reasonable belief that the supervisor will carry out his functions competently and have no reason to believe that his independence will be called into question (paragraph 6). The way paragraph 6 is drafted means that independence is judged by reference to the reasonableness of the employer's belief rather than the judgement of a third party such as the CAC (although as indicated below if the employer did not have a reasonable belief in the supervisor's independence and reasonable grounds for that belief the ballot would be defective). This contrasts with the definition of a qualified independent person who is required to conduct ballots for trade union recognition under Schedule A1 of TULRCA, in whose case there must be 'no grounds for believing . . . that his independence in relation to the ballot might reasonably be called into question'.

In practice, an employer is going to have to appoint an external individual or organisation, such as those specified in Regulation 4 of the Recognition and Derecognition Ballots (Qualified Persons) Order 2000,[1] to supervise the ballot. The employer will not be able to leave supervision of the ballot to one of its own employees, as the independence of such a person would clearly be subject to challenge. It may also be possible to appoint third parties such as solicitors with a current practising certificate or an accountant who is eligible for appointment as a company auditor under section 25 of the Companies

[1] Regulation 4 specifies those persons who are recognized as capable of being qualified independent persons for the purposes of conducting a ballot on trade union recognition. There is however no requirement in the ICE Regulations that the ballot supervisor be a qualified independent person.

Act 1989, who would also be recognized as qualified independent persons for the purposes of conducting a trade union recognition ballot. However, in order for the employer to have no reason to believe that their independence would be called into question, they should not be (or be employees of) the company's usual legal advisers or accountants.

- Employee representatives or employees (in the absence of representatives) must be consulted before the final arrangements for the ballot have been published, so far as reasonably practicable (paragraph 2(f)). If there are employee representatives within an undertaking, it would be prudent for an employer to notify them of the proposals, convene a meeting to explain the arrangements, and allow representatives a period of time in which to raise concerns. For organizations without employee representatives, employers should as a minimum publish the proposed arrangements in a way that is accessible to all employees (for example by way of staff noticeboards or a company intranet) and invite them to raise any concerns about the arrangements within a reasonable time. The final arrangements must also be published and brought to the attention of the employees and their representatives (paragraph 2(g)). Again, an obvious way to publish the arrangements would be through notice boards or an intranet.

If the employees or employee representatives believe that the employer **7.22** has failed to comply with any of these requirements, so that the arrangements for the ballot are defective, they can complain to the CAC within 21 days beginning on the date on which the employer's final arrangements were published (paragraph 3). If the complaint is upheld, the CAC must make a declaration to this effect and has power to order the employer to change any of the arrangements required by Schedule 2, specifying what changes the employer is required to make (paragraphs 4 and 5). A ballot that does not meet the requirements of paragraph 2(a) to (f) is defective (paragraph 7).

Presumably the fact that the CAC has power, but is not obliged, to make **7.23** an order requiring an employer to modify its arrangements means that technical breaches of the requirements of paragraph 2 that are not likely to affect the outcome of any ballot will not result in changes to the arrangements being required. This analysis is supported by the fact that the ballot supervisor is only obliged to publish an ineffective ballot report where the paragraph 2 requirements were not satisfied *and* the result of this was that the outcome of the ballot would have been different (see paragraph 7.24).

5. Role of the Ballot Supervisor

7.24 The ballot supervisor is entitled to carry out his role without interference from the employer and an employer must comply with any reasonable request made by the supervisor in relation to the carrying out of his functions (paragraph 8). In particular, the ballot supervisor is required:

- To supervise the conduct of the ballot in accordance with the employer's final arrangements (where necessary as amended by an order of the CAC) (paragraph 9(a)).
- Not to hold the ballot before the employer has published his final arrangements (paragraph 9(b)).
- Not to hold the ballot before the expiry of 21 days beginning with the date of publication of the employer's final arrangements where there has been no complaint to the CAC (paragraph 9(b)(i)). In other words, the ballot supervisor must ensure that the employees and employee representatives have the full 21 day period allowed by the ICE Regulations in which to lodge a complaint with the CAC about the employer's arrangements. The ICE Regulations do not require the ballot to be held within a certain period of the expiry of the 21-day period following publication of the final arrangements. However, if the elections are not held before the standard information and consultation provisions come into force, employees or employee representatives would then be able to present a complaint to the CAC under Regulation 19(4), as discussed further at paragraph 7.28.

  If a complaint about an employer's arrangements is lodged with the CAC, the supervisor must ensure that the ballot is not held before the complaint has been determined and the arrangements modified in accordance with any order made by the CAC (paragraph 9(b)(ii)).
- So far as reasonably practicable, to conduct the ballot to ensure that those entitled to stand as candidates or vote are given the opportunity to do so; ensure that voting takes place in secret; and that votes are fairly and accurately counted (paragraph 9(c)). For example, a ballot supervisor would have to ensure that in the case of an undertaking with shift workers, the ballot was open at times that would give all employees an opportunity to vote.
- Once the ballot has been held, the supervisor must publish the results as soon as reasonably practicable, so that they are available to the employer, and (again so far as reasonably practicable) the employees who were entitled to vote and the candidates who stood for election (paragraph 10).

There will be two circumstances where the ballot supervisor must publish an ineffective-ballot report. The first is if the ballot supervisor believes that any of the balloting requirements have not been complied with *and* that this affected the outcome of the ballot (paragraph 11(a)). An ineffective-ballot report is also required if interference by the employer or a failure by the employer to carry out reasonable requests of the supervisor meant that the supervisor is unable to judge whether the balloting requirements were satisfied (paragraph 11(b)). The report must be published within one month of publication of the results of the ballot and be available to the employer, and so far as reasonably practicable to those entitled to vote in the ballot and those who stood as candidates (paragraphs 12 and 13). **7.25**

If an ineffective-ballot report is published in respect of a single ballot, or in respect of all or a number of separate ballots, the ballot is of no effect and the employer remains under a duty to arrange for the election of information and consultation representatives (paragraph 14(a)). This means that the employer must arrange for another ballot to be held. The employer would therefore need to go through the full process of appointing an independent ballot supervisor and consulting on the arrangements for the ballot again. It would not be possible simply to rerun part of the election (for example in a situation where a substantial number of employees had been prevented from voting, it would not be possible simply to hold an election amongst those employees and combine their votes with those of the rest of the workforce). **7.26**

If separate ballots have been held (for example for different parts of the workforce) and an ineffective-ballot report has been issued in respect of only some of those ballots, the ballots in respect of which the report has been issued have to be reheld. The results of the ballots that have been conducted correctly will stand (paragraph 14(b)(i) and (ii)). **7.27**

6. Role of the CAC

Ballots not conducted in accordance with the requirements of Schedule 2 are a matter for the independent ballot supervisor, as outlined above. In a case where the employer has simply failed to take steps to arrange a ballot at all, the CAC is responsible for enforcement. Under Regulation 19(4), the employees or employee representatives can complain to the CAC that the employer has not arranged for a ballot to be held in accordance with the requirements of Regulation 19(1). If the complaint is upheld, under Regulation 19(5) the CAC must make an order requiring the employer to arrange and hold a ballot. **7.28**

7.29 The time at which a complaint can be made is not specified in the ICE Regulations. The employer's obligation under Regulation 19(1) is to arrange and hold a ballot before the standard information and consultation arrangements apply. As the requirements in Schedule 2 are likely to take at least six weeks to comply with, employees or employee representatives could presumably make a complaint if the employer had not begun to make arrangements within six weeks before the standard arrangements were due to apply, or at any time thereafter.

7.30 Regulation 19(5) also says the CAC can require an employer to 're-arrange' a ballot. Although on the face of it the CAC's jurisdiction under Regulation 19 will only apply where the employer has failed to arrange a ballot, this drafting may be intended to deal with a situation of the sort outlined in paragraph 7.24, in which the employer has published its final ballot arrangements but the ballot has not in fact been held.

7.31 A failure to arrange for a ballot when obliged to do so may have financial consequences for the employer. If the CAC finds the complaint well founded, the employees or employee representatives also have power to apply to the Employment Appeal Tribunal (*EAT*) for a penalty notice to be issued (Regulation 19(6)). The application must be made within three months of the CAC order, in accordance with Regulation 22(6). Unless the employer can show that the failure was due to reasons beyond its control, or that there was some other reasonable excuse for the failure, the EAT must issue a penalty of up to £75,000. For a more detailed discussion of this procedure and the factors the EAT will take into account when setting the level of a penalty, see chapter 8.

C. WHEN WILL THERE BE AN OBLIGATION TO INFORM AND CONSULT?

7.32 As indicated in paragraphs 7.5 to 7.11, the standard information and consultation provisions apply at the level of the undertaking once information and consultation representatives have been elected or, where representatives have not been elected, after a specific period of time has elapsed. The relevant period varies according to the circumstances of the request (see Figures 7.1 and 7.2).

7.33 One of the key features of the standard information and consultation provisions is that they do no more than replicate the provisions of Article 4 of the Information and Consultation Directive. Regulation 20(1) requires employers to give information and consultation representatives information on:

(a) the recent and probable development of the undertaking's activities and economic situation;
(b) the situation, structure and probable development of employment within the undertaking and on any anticipatory measures envisaged, in particular, where there is a threat to employment within the undertaking; and
(c) subject to paragraph (5), decisions likely to lead to substantial changes in work organisation or in contractual relations.

Consultation is required in relation to the matters in (b) and (c) of the standard arrangements (Regulation 20(3)) and consultation in relation to matters in (c) (but not (b)) must be with a view to reaching agreement (Regulation 20(4)(d)).

The decision to replicate Article 4 in Regulation 20(1) means that the **7.34** Government is not at risk of a challenge for having failed properly to implement the provisions of the Directive in this respect. Further, as pointed out in the DTI Guidance, the drafting of the ICE Regulations requires employers to do no more than observe the minimum requirements of the Directive; those requirements have not been 'gold plated'.

However, this approach has some significant disadvantages from the **7.35** perspective of both employers and employee representatives. Most fundamentally, it is not clear from the ICE Regulations exactly what will trigger an information and/or consultation obligation. Not only is the obligation to inform and consult couched in general terms, but the precise scope or meaning of the concepts referred to is unfamiliar in the UK context. For example, it is not immediately obvious what 'the situation, structure and probable development of employment' will encompass.

Until alleged failures to comply with the standard procedures have **7.36** been the subject of complaints to the CAC, it will be difficult for employers, employees or their representatives to establish with any degree of precision in exactly what circumstances a duty to inform and consult will arise. In practice, this is obviously more of a risk for employers, who are at risk of a penalty if the CAC makes a declaration that they have failed to inform and consult, than a problem for employees or their representatives.

Similar criticisms can be made in relation to the requirements surround- **7.37** ing the actual process of consultation, which the ICE Regulations also deal with in very general terms (reflecting the requirements of Article 4(4) of the Directive). Regulation 20(4) requires consultation to take place:

(a) in such a way as to ensure that the timing, method and content of the consultation are appropriate;
(b) on the basis of the information supplied by the employer to the information

and consultation representatives and of any opinion which those representatives express to the employer;

(c) in such a way as to enable the information and consultation representatives to meet the employer at the relevant level of management depending on the subject under discussion and to obtain a reasoned response from the employer to any such opinion.

Again, there is no guidance in the ICE Regulations themselves about what steps an employer needs to take in practice to comply with these requirements. What for example will constitute 'appropriate' timing in any given case? The approach the CAC will take to such issues will only become clear once challenges under the standard procedure are made.

7.38 In the meantime, employers will have to take a pragmatic approach to what is likely to be required. In making this assessment, the recitals to the Directive are likely to be particularly relevant, as giving an indication of the key areas in which the European Commission and Parliament believed information and consultation rights needed to be strengthened. The guidance issued by the DTI Guidance is also likely to be helpful. The remainder of this chapter looks in more detail at the circumstances in which each aspect of Regulation 20(1) may trigger information and/or consultation obligations in practice and at what stage information and/or consultation should in fact take place in each case. It is obviously not possible to provide a definitive list of all the circumstances in which information and consultation will be required.

1. Recent and Probable Development of the Undertaking's Activities and Economic Situation

7.39 The employer only has an obligation to inform, not to consult, about the 'recent and probable development of the undertaking's activities and economic situation'. The use of the words 'recent and probable development' means that information and consultation representatives will need to be told both about what has happened in the business recently, and also about what is likely or expected to happen in the short to medium term. The use of the word 'probable' indicates that the obligation to inform extends only to developments that are reasonably likely to occur. An employer is not obliged to inform staff about all possible developments, however unlikely they may in fact be in practice.

7.40 Regulation 20(1)(a) gives rise to two main issues: what will amount to 'developments of the undertaking's activities and economic situation'; and at what stage the information needs to be provided.

7.41 The sorts of developments referred to in Regulation 20(1)(a) are likely to be found to have two separate dimensions: one relates to what is happening within the company itself (or potentially within a wider corporate group) and one to the wider economic climate in which the business is operating.

From the perspective of the individual undertaking, matters that are likely to be relevant to the provision of information obviously include financial information such as profits or losses. However, the information is not purely related to financial information and will extend to developments in the undertaking's activities. This could encompass decisions in relation to the expansion or reduction of product lines, the gaining or loss of an order or customer where this is significant in the overall business context, or plans for developments of the business (for example by opening a new office or closing an existing one). Possible mergers, acquisitions, or disposals of parts of the business will almost certainly also constitute developments in the undertaking's activities and economic situation. Developments of this sort could overlap with the circumstances that will trigger a consultation obligation under Regulation 20(1)(b) or (c). The DTI Guidance also suggests that changes to senior management or to an undertaking's 'mission statement' or objectives could give rise to an information obligation, although it is not immediately obvious that either represents a change in activities or the economic situation. **7.42**

The broader context within which the business operates may also be relevant to the undertaking's economic situation. Particular economic issues in key markets may be relevant to the development of the undertaking, as will the general trading or business environment. Particularly where the fortunes of a particular organization are closely linked to those of a parent, subsidiary, or a wider corporate group, there may also be an obligation to inform about the activities and economic situation of the group as a whole. **7.43**

On the face of it, therefore, the obligation to inform is wide-reaching and potentially onerous. However, when deciding whether or not a matter is one about which an employer is obliged to inform, the DTI Guidance suggests that regard has to be had to the overall objectives of the Directive. One of these key objectives is the use of information and consultation to promote risk prevention and contribute to 'anticipation of employment developments within the undertaking' (Recital 13). This is the context within which the provision of information has to be considered, even though this is not actually spelled out in the wording of Regulation 20(1)(a). **7.44**

In practice this means that employee representatives are not going to need to be informed about every development of activities or the economic **7.45** situation, however minor. Information and consultation is clearly more geared to ensure that employees and their representatives are aware of 'big picture' issues that are likely to have an impact on the level of employment within the undertaking, or the skills that employees are likely to need in the future to retain employment. The DTI Guidance suggests that in practice employers will need to 'work back' from the issues that would give rise to consultation under Regulation 20(1)(b) or (c) to decide what sort of information needs to be provided under Regulation 20(1)(a). This is likely to be a useful rule of thumb but does not suggest that an employer has an obligation to inform only when a consultation obligation is likely to be triggered.

7.46 This is because the second main issue that is raised by the requirement is at what stage information needs to be provided about relevant developments. As indicated above, the standard provisions do not require information and consultation to take place on a specific basis, such as once or twice a year. Yet the wording of Regulation 20(1)(a) clearly implies that the provision of information is designed to be an ongoing requirement as opposed to something purely ad hoc and in response to a particular event. This interpretation is supported by the provisions of Recital 7 of the Directive, which states that 'there is a need to strengthen dialogue and promote mutual trust'. The ETUC has also stressed its view that information and consultation should be regarded as something that should take place 'on an ongoing, permanent basis'.[2] But Regulation 20(1)(a) would probably not require, for example, the employer to copy its monthly management accounts to the information and consultation body each time they are produced.

7.47 However, in order to comply with the requirement in Regulation 20(1)(a), employers should consider providing information and consultation representatives with information on a regular basis, perhaps to coincide with the publication of final results. (The DTI Guidance suggests that simply providing representatives with publicly available information alone would not necessarily be sufficient and that an employer might be under an obligation to explain the wider context behind the results.)

7.48 Under the default requirements in TICE, an EWC has the right to meet with central management once a year to be informed and consulted about the progress of the business. The requirements in TICE obviously do not in themselves indicate that providing information on an annual basis will mean that the employer is complying with the requirements of the stand-

[2] 'Information and consultation—some arguments from employers' organisations answered by the ETUC', 5 November 2001.

ard provisions under the ICE Regulations. The logistics of a meeting of a domestic body are clearly different from those that apply where a Europe-wide body is concerned. However, giving information and consultation representatives the sort of information outlined above on at least an annual basis makes it less likely that there will be a challenge before the CAC that an employer has failed to fulfil its information obligations. It would also be good practice to agree the frequency of the provision of information with the representatives, and this would reduce the likelihood of a challenge, although the ICE Regulations do not require an employer to seek the representatives' views in this way. The DTI Guidance suggests that an annual meeting would be the minimum necessary to comply with the requirements of the standard procedure.

Taking an 'annual approach' to information and consultation may be **7.49** appropriate where no particularly significant developments in the activities or the economic situation are envisaged. Where this is not the case, employers should not simply assume that they are meeting their obligations under the standard information and consultation provisions by providing information in accordance with a particular timetable. Regulation 20(2) requires information under Regulation 20(1) to be given 'at such time, in such fashion and with such content as are appropriate to enable . . . the information and consultation representatives to conduct an adequate study and, where necessary, to prepare for consultation'. In other words, where a particular event (such as a TUPE transfer, for example) would give rise to both an information and a consultation obligation, the information must be given at a time that will allow the representatives to prepare for consultation with a view to reaching agreement under Regulation 20(1)(c).

This means that if a particular event occurs or is envisaged that is likely to **7.50** have an impact on employees, there is a strong argument that the employer will have failed to comply with Regulation 20(1)(a) if that information is merely passed on to representatives in accordance with the 'usual' timetable. As indicated above, this will particularly be the case where the event in question is something that will trigger consultation obligations under Regulation 20(1)(b) or (c). In such a case, information will be required (depending on the circumstances) either when the event is envisaged or (at the latest) once the particular event has occurred. The DTI Guidance recognizes however that it is not sensible to require information at a stage when there is no degree of certainty about what is likely to happen (i.e. at a stage when a particular event is possible rather than probable). Informing (and subsequently consulting) at too early a stage may be destabilizing.

Example 7.4
An employer loses and acquires customers in the ordinary course of business. No single loss or acquisition of a customer has an impact on how the business is operated, on the number of employees needed, or on the type of work that employees are expected to carry out. There is unlikely to be an obligation to inform employee representatives about individual customers who have been gained or lost, bearing in mind that there is no likely impact on employees. General financial information about the performance of the business would however be required on a regular basis.

Example 7.5
An employer with a limited customer base loses a major order which represents a significant proportion of its turnover. If the order cannot be replaced, this is likely to have a significant impact on the financial profitability of the undertaking and potentially for the employment prospects of staff. This is a matter about which the information and consultation representatives will have a right to be informed, bearing in mind the possible impact on employees. Specific information is likely to need to be provided at the time the order is lost rather than in accordance with a 'regular' pattern, although this may depend on how quickly there will be an impact on employees.

Example 7.6
A financial institution invests heavily in the bonds of a foreign government. The government defaults on its debt, meaning that the institution suffers massive losses, with a corresponding impact on employment prospects within the organization as a whole. This is again a matter about which the information and consultation representatives will need to be informed, representing as it does a recent development of the undertaking's economic situation. The timing of information will again depend on when employees are likely to be affected, but will clearly fall outside the scope of the undertaking's regular information obligations.

2. The Situation, Structure, and Probable Development of Employment

7.51 The next category of information covered by Regulation 20(1) in paragraph (b) refers to 'the situation, structure and probable development of employment within the undertaking and on any anticipatory measures envisaged' in relation to that employment. In this respect, employers have an obligation not only to inform, but also to consult. The DTI Guidance indicates that the obligation emphasizes 'the overall number' of employees within the undertaking, implying that the main focus will be on increasing or decreasing employee numbers and cites the provisions of Recital 8 of the Directive in this respect. However, as outlined below, it seems likely that there could be changes to the situation or structure of employment within an undertaking that would need to be informed or consulted about, even if there was no overall change in employee numbers.

Situation

It appears that the reference to the 'situation' of employment is a geographic test. Therefore, proposed relocations, openings, and closures and the likely impact on employees will all be matters about which the employer has a duty to inform and consult. **7.52**

Structure

The reference to the 'structure' of employment is likely to require information and consultation in two possible respects. The first relates to the way in which employment is organized within an undertaking. If the employer is proposing to adopt a new organizational structure that has an effect on the way in which employees carry out their roles on a day-to-day basis, that is a matter about which the employer will have to consult. Structure is also likely to have a wider reading than a simple reorganization, and could include changes to work practices that do not amount to a wholesale restructuring of the business. It is worth noting that such a change could also give rise to a consultation obligation under Regulation 20(1)(c) as a change in work organization or contractual relations, and the impact of this is addressed in paragraph 7.72. The DTI Guidance indicates that changes to an undertaking's retirement policy or early retirement schemes would also fall within the obligation to inform and consult in Regulation 20(1)(b) (and presumably this would be the case regardless of the impact of such a scheme on overall employee numbers). **7.53**

Example 7.7
An employer has a number of employees engaged on a shift pattern. He is proposing to change the shift pattern to improve productivity. This will affect the times at which work is carried out, without actually changing the nature of the work that any of the employees undertakes. This is likely to be a change to the structure of employment within the undertaking and will therefore be something about which the employer is obliged to inform and consult.

The second aspect of the structure of employment that is likely to be relevant to an employer's obligations to inform and consult relates to changes to the employing entity. Structure therefore has a wider meaning than something that relates purely to organization of work on a day-to-day basis. For example, an employer that is contemplating an asset sale of part or all of its business may have an obligation to inform and consult under Regulation 20(1)(b) as well as 20(1)(c), as the change of **7.54** employer following a sale would amount to a change in the structure of employment within the business. The impact of the overlap between Regulations 20(1)(b) and 20(1)(c) in this respect is dealt with in paragraph 7.76.

7.55 The same analysis would not necessarily apply where the employer is proposing a share sale. In this case there would be no change in employer following the sale; the employing entity would remain the same. The proposed sale would not in itself involve a change in the structure of employment within the undertaking and would not therefore automatically give rise to a consultation obligation (unless there is a pre-sale restructuring in anticipation of the transaction). It is also conceivable that any consequential effect on access to group-wide benefits could be said to relate to the structure of employment and so trigger an obligation under Regulation 20(1)(b). Whatever the position, information and consultation representatives may need to be informed of the sale as a recent or probable development in the undertaking's activities but not necessarily in advance if there is no ongoing effect on employees.

Probable Development

7.56 The other circumstance in which consultation is required under Regulation 20(1)(b) relates to probable developments in employment within the undertaking and on anticipatory measures envisaged. The Regulation goes on to make it clear that the focus of consultation in this respect is where there is a threat to employment within the undertaking. In such circumstances, in accordance with Recital 8 of the Directive, there will need to be consultation about ways of 'offsetting the negative consequences', by way of additional training or skill development. Therefore, although consultation may be required in relation to expansion plans, in practice the consultation obligation will be of most importance where jobs are threatened. The DTI Guidance indicates that it may also be necessary to inform and consult about the status quo even where no changes are proposed by the employer. If, for example, representatives felt that the employer was understaffed, they would be entitled to express that view and be consulted about ways of remedying the situation.

Example 7.8

A company is intending to open a new place of business within the UK to develop a new product line. It will need to recruit new staff. Although this could technically give rise to an obligation to consult under Regulation 20(1)(b), given that the development represents an employment opportunity and will presumably have no impact on existing staff, and that the plans will take some time to develop, the employer will probably choose to inform and consult in accordance with its regular timetable, rather than informing staff as soon as the plan is developed.

Example 7.9
A company is developing plans to transfer its head office function from London to Norwich. Although staff will be given the option of relocating, in practice many will be reluctant to do so. The proposals could give rise to consultation obligations under Regulation 20(1)(b) and/or (c) and clearly represent a threat to employment. The employer will find it difficult to argue that it has met either its information or its consultation requirements if it does not inform and consult staff while the proposals are being developed.

One area in which the threat to employment trigger is likely to be significant is where a proposed share sale will result in a redundancy exercise to eliminate duplication with the purchaser's existing workforce. To date, there have been no statutory requirements to inform and consult staff in relation to a share sale. This position could change for companies with standard information and consultation procedures. Although a share sale will not trigger a consultation obligation in and of itself, a probable post-completion redundancy exercise will be an anticipatory measure envisaged where there is a threat to employment about which the employer is obliged to inform and consult. The fact that the redundancy exercise is not being proposed or carried out by the existing owner does not appear to be relevant to this analysis; the likelihood of a redundancy exercise will make it a 'probable development of employment' and an 'anticipatory measure envisaged' if the current employer is on notice that this is what is proposed, giving rise to the consultation obligation. **7.57**

In practice, this may give an employer an incentive not to know what a buyer's proposals for running the business going forward are: if it does not know what is proposed it cannot be under a duty to inform and consult other than potentially about the fact of the sale itself. It will generally be easier for an employer to adopt a position of 'no knowledge' in a private sale as opposed to a public takeover (at least in the context of a recommended public takeover). This is because the synergy benefits of a takeover, which may include costs savings to be derived from redundancies, will in practice be included in the announcement of a takeover offer, although there is no formal requirement to do so. At least where the offer is to be recommended, these will usually have been discussed in advance with the target's board, putting the employer on notice of the plans. **7.58**

It might be thought that, in practice, such an obligation will give rise to some difficulties, given that the 'current' employer is unlikely to have detailed knowledge about the proposed redundancy exercise. However, Regulation 20(4) requires consultation to be carried out in such a way that **7.59** the timing, method, and content are appropriate, on the basis of the information supplied to the information representatives by the employer and the views that the information representatives express. In relation to matters requiring consultation under Regulation 20(1)(b) there is no requirement that consultation take place with a view to reaching agreement, so it should not be an obstacle to compliance that the final decision will not be taken by the current employer, as long as he makes available to the representatives the information about which he himself is aware. The logic behind this is that the employer is consulting about probable developments rather than actual decisions. Consultation must also take place at the relevant level of management, which will mean someone sufficiently senior to be fully aware of the sale process and its implications. In practice, consultation in this situation is likely to focus on the merits of the proposed sale, bringing the proposed share sale itself within the scope of the consultation exercise by default.

7.60 Bearing this in mind, to be meaningful, consultation in this situation is likely to have to take place before the sale is completed and probably before it is even signed. If consultation only takes place after signing or completion, it is likely that the CAC would find that the consultation had not taken place at an appropriate time, because the consultation can no longer have any influence over the proposed sale. Although consultation can continue in relation to the proposed redundancy exercise, in this situation meaningful consultation cannot take place about the changes to the structure of employment itself in the sense of the share sale as a whole. The impact of Regulation 20(1)(b) is therefore likely to be the imposition of a requirement on a seller to inform and consult about proposed share sales for the first time, at least where the sale is likely to have ongoing consequences for employees within the undertaking. The DTI Guidance recognizes that where confidential information is being disclosed to representatives, the timescale for informing and consulting may be shorter than would otherwise be the case.

7.61 Purchasers may also be affected by the new obligations. In the context of a TUPE transfer, taking on staff by way of an asset sale will amount to a probable development of employment within the undertaking. However, if there is no impact on existing staff the extent of the information and consultation obligation will be limited and employers may in practice take the view that they can inform and consult very shortly before or immediately after the event. As seen in the context of a seller's obligations, the position is more complicated where there will be an impact on existing staff, for example because there will be a redundancy exercise across the combined workforce following the transfer. In this case, earlier information and consultation with the buyer's existing workforce under Regulation 20(1)(b) before the sale agreement is entered into may be required as a probable development of employment (in the sense of being a threat to employment) and an anticipatory measure envisaged.

In the case of a share sale, it is likely that there will be an information and consultation obligation on a buyer only if there will be an impact on its existing workforce after the sale. The purchase should otherwise have no impact on the situation, structure, and probable development of employment within the undertaking. There could of course be an obligation to inform representatives under Regulation 20(1)(a). **7.62**

3. Decisions Likely to Lead to Substantial Changes in Work Organization or Contractual Relations

On the face of it, it appears that it might be easier to predict what is likely to be required by way of information and consultation under Regulation 20(1)(c) than either of the other heads. However, because of the very general way in which the requirement is drafted, difficulties are still likely to arise in certain key respects. It is generally accepted, although this is not expressly stated in the ICE Regulations, that the requirement relates to substantial changes in contractual relations between an employer and its employees, not other third parties. It is crucially important to note that the obligation to inform and consult arises in relation to the decision itself and not just the subsequent changes. **7.63**

Changes to work organization are likely to encompass two main areas: changes to the way in which work is carried out; and changes to the way in which it is organized. For example, a proposal to introduce a new computer system that will have a major impact on the way in which staff carry out their roles is likely to be a substantial change to the way in which work is carried out and require consultation before the new system is implemented. Changes to work patterns (such as a changed shift pattern or alterations to flexible working practices) are likely to amount to changes to the way in which work is organized and again require consultation before the new shift structure, working practices, or other changes are introduced. **7.64**

What will amount to substantial changes in contractual relations may be more problematic. The DTI Guidance suggests that this will only relate to changes that affect a number of employees rather than a single employee. There is, however, nothing in the ICE Regulations to prevent Regulation 20(1)(c) from applying where only a single employee is affected and it is consequently not clear that the DTI Guidance is correct on this point. Even **7.65** if the DTI Guidance is followed, it is not clear whether substantial changes to the contracts of 10 employees (for example) will be enough to trigger a consultation requirement. The Guidance suggests that each case has to be decided on its own merits, so presumably an employer will need to weigh up the extent of the changes being proposed against the number of employees affected and the size of the workforce as a whole. If an undertaking has 2,500 employees and the proposed change affects only 10 employees, it seems strongly arguable that this would not amount to a 'substantial change in contractual arrangements', regardless of the extent of the changes. If however 10 employees were affected out of a workforce of only 50, the same change would be much more likely to be regarded as a substantial change in contractual relations requiring information and consultation.

7.66 Another difficult issue is what exactly is meant by 'contractual relations'. If a narrow approach to the issue is taken, there could be an argument that the employer is only required to inform and consult about those matters that form part of the employment contract itself rather than the wider employment relationship. For example, an employer's disciplinary and grievance procedure will often not be contractual. This implies that changes to the procedure would not constitute substantial changes in contractual relations and the changes would not need to be consulted upon before the policy was amended. If however a wider approach to the question of what amounts to contractual relations is taken, changes to the disciplinary and grievance procedure certainly appear capable of amounting to substantial changes in contractual relations. It will take applications to the CAC to determine the approach likely to be taken to the issue. It is worth noting that the DTI Guidance suggests that changes to disciplinary and grievance procedures would require consultation under Regulation 20(1)(c), and it is probably unlikely that the CAC will take a narrow interpretation of the employer's obligations. In the meantime, employers would be prudent to take a broad view of what constitutes contractual relations, to avoid a claim that they have failed to inform and consult when they should have done so.

7.67 A further question is to what extent issues such as pay will be excluded from consideration as matters of contractual relations. The Government indicated throughout the consultation process on the ICE Regulations that because of the treaty basis on which the Information and Consultation Directive was adopted, it does not extend to pay. The Directive was adopted under Article 137 of the Treaty Establishing the European Community. Article 137(5) provides that the provisions of Article 137 do not apply to pay. This implies that issues surrounding remuneration do not have to be informed and consulted on under the ICE Regulations, although this issue is not addressed expressly in the ICE Regulations themselves.

Example 7.10

An employer operates a contractual bonus scheme. It wants to discontinue its bonus arrangements with effect from the end of the current bonus year. Although the proposals amount to a substantial change in contractual relations, it will not have to inform and consult under the standard procedure because the bonus scheme constitutes pay and therefore falls outside the scope of the ICE Regulations.

Another interesting issue on the same point is the extent to which an employer will have an obligation to inform and consult about proposed changes to a pension scheme under the standard provisions. Pensions would usually be regarded as pay and there should therefore be a strong argument that changes to a pension scheme fall outside the scope of Regulation 20(1)(c). Notwithstanding this, and the DTI's indication in its Guidance that benefits with a monetary value will fall outside the scope of the standard provisions, the Guidance also indicates that an employer will be required to inform and consult about changes to a pension scheme in which an employee has a contractual right to participate. The Guidance does not expand on the reasons why a contractual pension scheme is said to fall within the scope of the standard provisions and this will be a matter for the CAC to decide if an employer's failure to consult is challenged. **7.68**

Ultimately the fact that a pension scheme is contractual should not be relevant to the issue of whether it provides for a monetary benefit and our view is that information and consultation should not be required. The issue may not in fact prove to be of much practical significance, because of the separate information and consultation requirements introduced in relation to changes to occupational pension schemes by sections 259–61 of the Pensions Act 2004 and which are to be set out in regulations. **7.69**

In June 2005, the Department for Work and Pensions issued drafts of the proposed regulations under sections 259–261 of the Pensions Act 2004.[3] These are intended to tie in with the ICE Regulations, and are expected to come into force in April 2006. They are discussed in more detail at paragraphs 1.45 and 1.46. **7.70**

It is important for employers to recognize that complying with information and consultation obligations does not automatically mean that changes to terms and conditions of employment can be made. The **7.71**

[3] See http://www.dwp.gov.uk/publications/dwp/2005/occ_pen_schemes/oppscer06.-pdf.

information and consultation requirements do not override the normal principles about changing terms and conditions of employment, which will require the consent of individual employees in the absence of a clause entitling an employer unilaterally to make the desired variation to terms and conditions. In practice, such a clause is relatively uncommon and strictly interpreted.

7.72 As indicated in paragraph 7.53, in some cases there will be an overlap between the requirements to inform and consult in Regulation 20(1)(b) and (c). In cases where there is such an overlap there will be two main implications. The first relates to the time at which information and consultation should take place; the second to the obligations on the employer when conducting consultation.

7.73 As we have seen, Regulation 20(1)(b) requires information and consultation to take place at an appropriate time about 'the probable development of employment . . . and on any anticipatory measures envisaged'. This implies that the obligation to inform and consult arises at a fairly early stage in an employer's deliberations and certainly before any final decisions have been taken. This interpretation is obviously consistent with the aim of the Information and Consultation Directive to ensure that information and consultation takes place before serious decisions affecting employees are taken (Recital 6).

7.74 In this context it is also worth noting the difference in wording between Directive 98/59/EC (the Collective Redundancies Directive) and the way in which the Collective Redundancies Directive has been implemented in the UK in section 188 of TULRCA. While the Collective Redundancies Directive talks of an employer having a duty to inform and consult when it is 'contemplating' collective redundancies, TULRCA imposes the duty only at a point at which the employer has proposals to dismiss. The EAT decision in *MSF v Refuge Assurance plc*[4] confirmed that the obligation to consult where there is a proposal to dismiss applies at a later stage than where redundancies are merely 'contemplated'. By replicating the wording from the Information and Consultation Directive in the ICE Regulations, the Government has avoided a similar conflict and confirms the fact that consultation will typically have to begin under Regulation 20(1)(b) at a relatively early stage in the employer's deliberations.

7.75 In contrast, Regulation 20(1)(c) imposes an obligation to inform and consult only in relation to 'decisions likely to lead to' the sorts of changes

[4] [2002] ICR 1365.

discussed at paragraphs 7.64 to 7.69. This is much more definite language than that contained in Regulation 20(1)(b) and implies that the obligation under Regulation 20(1)(c) arises at a later stage, once an employer has more concrete proposals about the particular steps that he wishes to take. It is only at that stage that the obligation to inform and consult would arise. The obligation to consult would be with a view to reaching agreement (as to which, see further paragraphs 7.77 and 7.78), so consultation would still have to take place before any final decisions.

This means that where an issue arises that is capable of giving rise to **7.76** obligations under both Regulation 20(1)(b) and (c), the information and consultation process can best be seen as a continuing duty. At the outset, when an employer's deliberations are at an early stage but nonetheless have an impact on the probable development of employment within the undertaking, information and consultation should take place under Regulation 20(1)(b). Subsequently, when the employer's proposals have reached a more formal stage and he is seeking to take a decision that will lead to substantial changes in work organization or contractual relations, the obligation will arise under Regulation 20(1)(c). The employer does not have the right to elect which provision to inform and consult under, but will have to involve the representatives in a dialogue over a period of time to ensure both obligations are complied with.

Example 7.11

An employer is seeking to make efficiency savings and is considering a number of different options, at least some of which will have an impact on the structure of employment within the undertaking. It is likely that these discussions will give rise to an obligation to inform and consult under Regulation 20(1)(b). Subsequently the employer decides that its preferred route would be to implement a complete reorganization of various departments, which will result in some redundancies. This will give rise to information and consultation obligations under Regulation 20(1)(c). The fact that the employer had complied with its information and consultation obligations in relation to the redundancies (under the ICE Regulations or otherwise) would not be a defence to a failure to have consulted under Regulation 20(1)(b) at an earlier stage. Query whether it could have any impact on the level of penalty awarded for failure to comply.

The other issue that arises where consultation obligations overlap in this **7.77** way is the employer's duty to conduct consultation in a particular way. Under both Regulation 20(1)(b) and (c) the obligation is to conduct consultation so that the timing method and content are appropriate. Consultation must take place 'at the relevant level of management', which the DTI Guidance indicates means at a sufficiently senior level that the employer representative has the power to change a decision that is being consulted about. However, in relation to consultations about decisions likely to lead to substantial changes, Regulation 20(4)(d) imposes a further requirement that consultation must also be 'with a view to reaching agreement on decisions within the scope of the employer's powers'.

7.78 In other words, consultation of a higher order is required in relation to matters covered by Regulation 20(1)(c): not only must the employer inform the employee representatives about his proposals, listen to their opinion and provide a reasoned response to that opinion, he must also approach the consultation exercise with a view to reaching agreement, which implies that a degree of negotiation may be required. In a recent decision in the context of the Collective Redundancies Directive, *Junk v Kühnel*,[5] the European Court has confirmed that the words 'with a view to reaching agreement' in effect require negotiations to take place. The employer cannot simply tell the employee representatives what he is going to do and then proceed with that proposal without giving any consideration to their response.

4. Collective Redundancies and TUPE Transfers

7.79 It is clear that both collective redundancies and TUPE transfers are capable of constituting matters about which an employer may be required to inform and consult under the ICE Regulations, either under Regulation 20(1)(b) or (c) or both. Regulation 20(1)(c) expressly states that changes to work organization or contractual relations include those referred to in the collective redundancy provisions of TULRCA and the information and consultation provisions of TUPE. However, the Information and Consultation Directive is expressly without prejudice to the rights of employees to be informed and consulted in the event of a collective redundancy situation under the Collective Redundancies Directive or the Acquired Rights Directive. This led to the prospect of employers being forced to inform and consult about the same set of collective redundancies or TUPE transfer with two separate bodies under two completely separate procedures.

7.80 This is more likely to be a difficulty for a selling employer than for a purchaser. If a purchaser's employees will not be affected by post-transfer measures, it will be unlikely to have information and consultation obligations in respect of its own staff under TUPE. Similarly, a transferee would be unlikely to have to inform and consult its own staff under Regulation 20(1)(c) in the absence of such measures.

7.81 The Government Recognized that it was undesirable to have overlapping information and consultation requirements in this respect and the ICE

[5] [2005] IRLR 310.

Regulations allow an employer to consult under the relevant procedure in TULRCA/ TUPE, rather than under the requirements of Regulation 20(1)(c). The other impact of this is that the priority given to a recognized trade union to be consulted in preference to other types of employee representatives in a collective redundancy or TUPE situation is preserved: the employer cannot choose to consult under the ICE Regulations rather than under TULRCA or TUPE. However, if there is no recognized trade union it would appear that information and consultation representatives elected under the standard information and consultation provisions would constitute appropriate representatives for the purposes of TULRCA and TUPE consultations (the position in relation to a negotiated agreement or a pre-existing agreement is likely to depend on the identity of the representatives).

Regulation 20(5) provides that once a duty to inform and consult arises **7.82**
under section 188 of TULRCA or Regulation 10 of TUPE, the obligations to inform and consult under Regulation 20(1)(c) cease to apply. This is subject to the employer giving the information and consultation representatives written notification that it intends to comply with its obligations under the relevant legislation rather than under the ICE Regulations. In the absence of such a written notification, the employer will continue to be bound by both obligations. An employer can therefore continue to inform and consult with different sets of employee representatives if it chooses to do so.

There are three specific points that it is worth making about this provi- **7.83**
sion. The drafting makes it clear that the opt-out of Regulation 20(1)(c) applies only once the obligation to inform and consult under the relevant legislation has actually arisen. As indicated above, decisions of this nature are more likely to require information and consultation on a continuing basis under both Regulation 20(1)(b) and 20(1)(c). There is nothing in Regulation 20(5) that enables an employer to opt out of his Regulation 20(1)(b) obligation, which as we have seen will typically arise at an earlier stage than under Regulation 20(1)(c). In practice this means that some degree of information and consultation in relation to collective redundancies and TUPE transfers is likely to be required under the ICE Regulations (for example in relation to the actual decision to sell, and to whom) and that this will have to take place at an earlier stage than has been required under TULRCA and TUPE. In this context, it should be borne in mind that a failure to comply with information and consultation obligations in these circumstances would give rise to a liability under the ICE Regulations (a fine of up to £75,000—see paragraphs 8.33–8.37) as well as under TUPE (up to 13 weeks' pay) and/or TULRCA (up to 90 days' pay). It is also the case that there will be circumstances when the provisions of

TULRCA do not apply to proposed redundancies but the ICE Regulations will do. This is most notably the case where fewer than 20 employees (the threshold for collective redundancies under TULRCA) are to be made redundant.

Example 7.12

An employer is considering the transfer of part of its business to a prospective purchaser. The sale will constitute a TUPE transfer and as such is a probable development to the structure of employment as the identity of the employer will change. Information and consultation will probably be required under Regulation 20(1)(b) before the sale agreement is signed. There may also be an obligation to inform and consult under Regulation 20(1)(c) to ensure that the employees have an opportunity to be consulted with a view to reaching agreement. Once the obligation to inform and consult under TUPE has arisen (but only at that point), the employer can notify the information and consultation representatives in writing that it is intending to inform and consult under TUPE rather than the ICE Regulations. Once the notification has been given the obligation to inform and consult under Regulation 20(1)(c) falls away and consultation can take place under TUPE in the usual way.

7.84 Another point for employers to remember when considering how to meet their obligations under the various overlapping pieces of legislation is that a new written notification must be given to representatives 'on each occasion on which the employer has become or is about to become subject to the duty'. This means that the employer will have to think about the issue on each occasion it is proposing to make collective redundancies or sell part of its business. It cannot give a blanket notification to its information and consultation representatives that it will inform and consult under TUPE or TULRCA in preference to the ICE Regulations.

5. Duty of Co-Operation

7.85 It is also worth noting that Part V of the ICE Regulations imposes a duty of co-operation on employer and employee representatives when implementing the standard provisions, as well as when negotiating or implementing a negotiated procedure. Regulation 21 provides that the parties should 'work in a spirit of co-operation and with due regard for their reciprocal rights and obligations, taking into account the interests of both the undertaking and the employees'. This duty mirrors that required by Article 1(3) of the Information and Consultation Directive. This is obviously an extremely difficult obligation to police or enforce, and the ICE Regulations do not contain any sanction for an alleged failure to work in a spirit of co-operation. An employer's duty to consult with a view to reaching agreement in relation to matters falling within Regulation 20(1)(c) is likely to be more important in practice.

D. WHEN WILL THE STANDARD PROVISIONS CEASE TO APPLY?

The ICE Regulations make it clear that the standard information and consultation provisions will not apply indefinitely if the parties subsequently choose to agree to adopt a different procedure. Regulation 18(2) gives the employer and information representatives elected pursuant to the standard procedures the power to agree to a new procedure at any time. To be valid, such a procedure must cover all employees of the undertaking, be signed by a majority of the information and consultation representatives and: **7.86**

- set out the circumstances in which employees will be informed and consulted;
- be in writing and dated;
- be signed on behalf of the employer; and
- either provide for the appointment or election of information and consultation representatives through whom information and consultation will take place, or provide that the employer will inform and consult employees directly.

The difference between this and the requirements for a valid negotiated agreement under Regulation 16(1) is that Regulation 18(2) does not require the agreement to be approved by all negotiating representatives or, in the absence of such approval, by the workforce (either in writing or through a ballot). As indicated above, only a majority of information and consultation representatives need to sign the new procedure (Regulation 18(3)). **7.87**

This is likely to be of value in a situation in which the parties have failed to reach a negotiated agreement because a small number of negotiating representatives have refused to approve a negotiated arrangement and it is impracticable for some reason to obtain approval from a majority of the workforce. In such a case, it would be open to the employer to proceed with election of information and consultation representatives under Regulation 19, and then seek to reach agreement with those representatives on the basis of the earlier (not agreed) negotiated procedure. Assuming that the majority of representatives is willing to agree the negotiated procedure, the employer will once again be taken outside the scope of the default arrangements. Even if such agreement is not possible following **7.88** election of the initial representatives, employers should bear the provisions in mind, as opting out of the standard arrangements in this way is possible at any time.

8

Enforcement

This chapter outlines the enforcement mechanisms adopted in the ICE Regulations and in particular assesses: **8.01**

(1) when the enforcement provisions in the ICE Regulations apply;
(2) the role of the CAC in determining complaints;
(3) the ability of the EAT to issue penalty notices if information and consultation obligations have been breached;
(4) how CAC orders can be enforced; and
(5) limitations on the ability of the CAC to issue orders.

The discussion also focusses on whether the enforcement procedures that have been adopted are likely to be adequate, having regard to the requirements of the Information and Consultation Directive that 'adequate administrative or judicial procedures are available' for the enforcement of rights. A related point is whether the sanctions that apply where information and consultation obligations have not been observed are 'effective, proportionate and dissuasive', also as required by the Information and Consultation Directive. **8.02**

A. INTRODUCTION

Article 8 of the Information and Consultation Directive outlines in general terms how the rights provided by the Information and Consultation Directive are to be protected: **8.03**

1. Member States shall provide for appropriate measures in the event of non-compliance with this Directive by the employer or the employees'

representatives. In particular, they shall ensure that adequate administrative or judicial procedures are available to enable the obligations deriving from this Directive to be enforced.

2. Member States shall provide for adequate sanctions to be applicable in the event of infringement of this Directive by the employer or the employees' representatives. These sanctions must be effective, proportionate and dissuasive.

8.04 In common with most European legislation, the specifics of enforcing information and consultation rights and the sanctions for breaching those rights are therefore a matter for national law rather than being laid down in the Information and Consultation Directive itself. Article 8 was one of the more controversial provisions of the Information and Consultation Directive, with the European Parliament in particular considering that aspects of the Information and Consultation Directive dealing with sanctions for breaches of the information and consultation requirements needed to be strengthened.

8.05 The European Parliament had originally proposed that more stringent sanctions should apply in cases where employers had breached their obligations in the context of decisions that could result in termination of employment, for example a decision to make collective redundancies without informing and consulting about that decision in advance. In such cases it was proposed that an employer's decision should be suspended pending consultation. In other words, the European Parliament wanted to prevent an employer from implementing a decision of this type until the information and consultation process had been completed. The amendment was not ultimately supported by an absolute majority of MEPs and was not adopted. This gives a clear indication that national legislation does not need to invalidate decisions taken in breach of obligations to inform and consult in order for sanctions to be effective, proportionate, and dissuasive.

8.06 The enforcement provisions in the ICE Regulations closely reflect (although do not mirror) those set out in TICE, particularly Regulations 21 and 22. Article 11 of the European Works Council Directive (94/45/EC) requires Member States to provide 'adequate administrative or judicial procedures . . . to enable the obligations deriving from the Directive to be enforced' and 'appropriate measures' in the event that the Directive is not complied with.

8.07 The penalties laid down by the ICE Regulations will not therefore necessarily be accepted as effective, proportionate, and dissuasive simply because they reflect those of TICE, which have not been challenged as a failure properly to implement the provisions of the European Works

Council Directive. It is also worth noting that during the review of the European Works Council Directive that commenced in 2004, ETUC called for sanctions for breaches of that Directive to be tightened, in particular by making decisions taken in breach of the relevant information and consultation procedures invalid.[1]

In itself, this does not have a bearing on the sanctions that the ICE Regulations should provide in order to implement the Information and Consultation Directive. However, ETUC's response is an indication of the importance that employee organizations attach to the sanctions regime. This may make it more likely that the enforcement regime in the ICE Regulations is challenged to assess whether it meets the requirements of the Information and Consultation Directive. Such a challenge would presumably be brought by way of judicial review of the sanctions provisions of the ICE Regulations by an interested trade union and determined either through the English courts or by the European Court of Justice.[2] Alternatively, in the event of union complaints to the European Commission, enforcement proceedings by the Commission could be initiated in the European Court of Justice.[3] **8.08**

B. DO THE ENFORCEMENT PROVISIONS IN THE ICE REGULATIONS APPLY?

Breaches of pre-existing agreements are outside the scope of the enforcement provisions in the ICE Regulations. In the event of a breach of a pre-existing agreement, enforcement would be through whatever process had been agreed by the parties when the agreement was entered into. It is relatively unlikely that an employer would want to agree that such an agreement would be legally enforceable, although employees and their representatives will be reluctant to enter into an agreement that has no effective enforcement procedure. In the absence of a requirement to arbitrate or mediate in the event of a dispute, the main 'sanction' for a failure to comply with the procedure will be the probable employee relations consequences, as well as the risk of an employee request for a negotiated information and consultation procedure under Regulation 7. **8.09**

[1] Resolution 04–05/12/03.

[2] See for example recent challenges to the implementation of the EU Framework for equal treatment in employment and occupation in *R (on the application of Amicus) v Secretary of State for Trade and Industry* [2004] IRLR 430 and of the Working Time Directive in *R v Secretary of State for Trade and Industry ex parte BECTU* [2001] IRLR 559.

[3] See for example enforcement proceedings against the UK in relation to the Collective Redundancies Directive in *EC Commission v United Kingdom* [1994] IRLR 412.

8.10 In relation to negotiated agreements, the enforcement provisions in the ICE Regulations will not automatically come into play whenever there is a breach or alleged breach of the agreement. As outlined in Chapter 6, one of the issues for the parties to decide when seeking to agree a negotiated agreement is what should happen if one of the parties (although in practice this will usually be the employer) fails to comply with aspects of the procedure. It would generally be good practice for the matter initially to be discussed between the employer and employee representatives to see whether the issue can be resolved informally.

8.11 If the dispute cannot be resolved internally, it may be possible to involve third-party assistance through conciliation, mediation, or arbitration. In practice, employers are more likely to favour either conciliation or mediation as a way of resolving disputes than arbitration. An arbitrator would have power actually to determine the dispute, rather than simply helping the parties to reach agreement themselves, which will be unattractive to many employers. Conciliation (through ACAS for example) also has the advantage of being familiar from other industrial relations contexts. In any event, the enforcement provisions in the ICE Regulations will only become relevant if the dispute cannot be resolved between the parties.

8.12 As far as standard information and consultation arrangements are concerned, there will be nothing to prevent the parties seeking to resolve the matter informally before the enforcement provisions under the ICE Regulations are invoked (indeed, the DTI Guidance recommends this course of action). However, this may in practice be less likely, simply because the agreement itself will not lay down a mechanism to be followed in such a case.

C. BREACHES OF NEGOTIATED AND STANDARD ARRANGEMENTS

8.13 Part VI of the ICE Regulations sets out the enforcement regime that applies in cases where disputes in relation to rights under a negotiated agreement or standard arrangement cannot be resolved between the parties.

1. Complaints to the CAC

8.14 Regulation 22(1) provides that where a relevant applicant considers that an employer has failed to comply either with a term of a negotiated agreement, or the standard information and consultation provisions, a complaint can be made to the CAC. The procedure does not apply in reverse; there is no sanction for an information and consultation representative's failure to comply with the provisions of a negotiated agreement and the standard provisions do not impose duties on representatives in this regard.

A relevant applicant is an information and consultation representative where representatives have been elected or appointed, and in other cases either an employee or an employee representative (Regulation 22(3)). Employee representatives are not defined in the ICE Regulations, but in practice are most likely to be trade union representatives. The complaint must be made within three months starting with the alleged failure (Regulation 22(2)). **8.15**

A failure is defined in Regulation 22(3) as either an act or an omission. This is of most significance in relation to negotiated agreements, where the potential for complaints under Regulation 22 is wider than in relation to a standard arrangement. This is because Regulation 22(1) expressly provides that a complaint can be made to the CAC in respect of an employer's failure 'to comply with the terms of the negotiated agreement'. As seen in Chapter 6, in practice the negotiated agreement is likely to deal with a whole range of issues that are not within the scope of the standard arrangements. For example, this could include a failure to elect employee representatives in a particular way or to call an election at a particular time, a failure to provide agreed information or a failure to call an information and consultation meeting when required under the agreement. It is easier to see such failures as omissions rather than acts, hence the importance of the definition in Regulation 22(3). **8.16**

In contrast, most complaints under the standard arrangements are going to arise because an employer has taken some act without having informed or consulted. Here the definition in Regulation 22(3) is unlikely to be of much practical significance, given that taking an act without informing and consulting could be viewed either as an act or an omission. **8.17**

It will be interesting to see how the CAC approaches the concept of when the failure takes place. In some cases this will be easy to establish. For example, if the complaint is that the employer has failed to call a scheduled meeting under a negotiated agreement, the failure will presumably occur on the date that the meeting should have been held. More difficult questions will arise where the CAC is being asked to address more substantive issues, such as a failure to inform and consult about a specific business decision. There is nothing in the ICE Regulations that mirrors the provisions about continuing acts in the discrimination legislation,[4] which **8.18**

[4] See for example s76(6) of the Sex Discrimination Act 1975.

provide that the time limit for complaining about a continuing act only starts running once the act stops.

8.19 It would be logical to see such a failure as continuing over a period of time, rather than occurring on a specific date. For example, negotiations about a possible sale of part of a business are likely to take place over some weeks. Although the obligation to inform and consult under the relevant procedure will probably be triggered at some point during that process before the agreement is actually signed, the obligation to inform and consult once the obligation has been triggered is a continuous one. The three months for bringing a claim under Regulation 22(1) should not be treated as beginning to run at the point at which the obligation would actually have been triggered.

8.20 Otherwise, if a strict approach is taken to the issue of when the complaint has to be made, relevant applicants could theoretically be barred from bringing a complaint before they are even aware that there has been a failure to consult under the relevant procedure. This could be the case if the relevant discussions (about a possible sale in the example given above) continue over a long period of time. In practice the CAC seems likely to take a pragmatic approach to the issue, and find that the time limit begins to run at the date the employees became aware (or could reasonably have been expected to be aware) that there had been a failure to comply with the relevant agreement. This will generally be when the decision is announced. There is however nothing in the ICE Regulations themselves that would indicate that this is the correct approach. The guidance issued by the CAC on its enforcement role under the ICE Regulations does not address how it is likely to approach the issue of time limits.

8.21 The (relatively limited) procedural requirements in relation to CAC applications are set out in Regulation 35. These make it clear that complaints must be made in writing in such form as the CAC requires (Regulation 35(1)). The CAC has indicated in the guidance it has provided about its role in relation to the ICE Regulations that a different form will need to be completed for each application or complaint that can be made. The CAC guidance also indicates that a flexible approach to complaints will be adopted, and that the CAC will try to help parties reach agreements outside the statutory process wherever possible.

8.22 On receipt of a complaint, the CAC will consider whether it is reasonably likely to be settled by conciliation, and if so, refer the complaint to ACAS (Regulation 38(1)). Once the case has been referred, the CAC must notify the complainant and other people with a proper interest in the complaint about the reference. The reference triggers ACAS's power to offer assistance under Regulation 38(2), although Regulation 38(3) gives ACAS the right not to offer its assistance if it is appropriate to do so. If the complaint cannot be settled or withdrawn, ACAS must notify the CAC once it has concluded that further attempts at conciliation are unlikely to result in a settlement (Regulation 38(4)) at which point the CAC must proceed to hear and determine the complaint (Regulation 38(5)).

If the CAC has to determine the complaint, either because the matter is **8.23** not referred to ACAS at all or because conciliation is unsuccessful, it has a duty to ensure that anyone with an interest in the complaint has an opportunity to be heard (Regulation 35(2)). How this is achieved is a matter for the CAC. One of the CBI's comments during the consultation exercise about the proposed role of the CAC was that the lack of detailed procedural rules meant the system 'lacks transparency'.[5] Section 263 of TULRCA governs proceedings of the CAC and section 263(5) allows the CAC to determine its own procedure. The CAC guidance indicates that the procedure that will be adopted will depend on the nature of the complaint made. In some cases the CAC envisages that it will be possible to resolve complaints on the basis of paper submissions. In other cases, it is envisaged that hearings will be required, which will generally be held in public. Proceedings are expected to be informal.

If, having considered the application, the CAC finds it well founded, it **8.24** must make a declaration to this effect and has power (but is not compelled) to order the employer to take steps that are necessary to comply with the relevant procedure (Regulation 22(4)). Under Regulation 35(3) the CAC has power to draw an adverse inference from a party's failure to provide requested information or documents about a complaint. The Regulations do not make it clear whether the request would have to come from the CAC, or could come from the other party.

If the CAC issues a declaration or order, it must be in writing, state the **8.25** reasons for the decision, and specify what steps the employer has to take to remedy the failure and within what period (Regulations 22(5) and 35(5)). For example, if an employer has failed to inform or consult staff about a possible sale or purchase of a business, the CAC has power to require it to provide information and consultation representatives with the relevant information and then consult them about the proposal within a certain period of the order. CAC decisions can be appealed to the EAT on a point of law (Regulation 35(6)).

[5] CBI response to *High Performance Workplaces 'Informing and Consulting Employees'*, paragraph 19.

D. PENALTY NOTICES

8.26 The making of a CAC declaration or order has one immediate consequence for an employer: the prospect of a financial penalty as a result of its failure to comply with the negotiated or standard procedure.

8.27 Article 8.2 of the Information and Consultation Directive requires Member States to ensure that adequate sanctions are in place for dealing with infringements. The ICE Regulations take an approach to this issue that is very similar to that adopted in TICE. Regulation 22(6) provides that where the CAC has made a declaration that a complaint about non-compliance with a relevant procedure is well founded, the relevant applicant can elect to make an application to the Employment Appeal Tribunal (EAT) for the issue of a penalty notice. Unless the applicant to the CAC elects to make an application to the EAT, which it must do within three months of the date of the declaration, there is no financial penalty for a failure to comply with the information and consultation requirements.

8.28 Regulation 22(6) is drafted to apply to any complaint under Regulation 22(1) that has been upheld. This means that a failure to comply with 'administrative' provisions of a negotiated agreement will be subject to a financial penalty in the same way as breaches of more substantive information and consultation provisions, although not necessarily of the same amount.

8.29 If an applicant makes an application to the EAT following a CAC order, imposition of a penalty notice is generally mandatory. Regulation 22(7) provides that in the event of such an application 'the Appeal Tribunal shall issue a written penalty notice to the employer'. The notice must specify the amount of the penalty, the date by which the penalty must be paid and the failure and period covered by the penalty.

8.30 The EAT however does have the ability not to issue a penalty notice where the employer can show that 'the failure resulted from a reason beyond [his] control or that he has some other reasonable excuse for his failure'. In practice it seems likely that an employer is only likely to be able to demonstrate this in exceptional cases akin to the sorts of 'special circumstances' that would potentially excuse a failure to inform and consult in full in a collective redundancy situation or on the transfer of an undertaking.[6] (Employers in such circumstances are still required to take such steps as are reasonably practicable to comply.)

[6] S188(7) of the Trade Union and Labour Relations (Consolidation) Act 1992 and Regulation 11(2) of the Transfer of Undertakings (Protection of Employment) Regulations 1981.

Such special circumstances have been interpreted narrowly and would typically encompass matters such as insolvency situations. However, the fact that an employer is in an insolvency situation will not automatically mean that it is unable to comply with its consultation obligations; this will depend on the facts of the individual case. To be a 'special' circumstance, the Court of Appeal has held that a particular event must be 'something out of the ordinary, something uncommon'.[7] Insolvency is not in and of itself uncommon, so a gradual rundown of a business is unlikely to amount to a special circumstance that would justify a failure to inform and consult. In contrast, a sudden and unforeseen business collapse (perhaps because a key client goes out of business), may well amount to 'special circumstances' within the meaning of section 188(7). **8.31**

It is clear from the ICE Regulations that an employer will not be able to rely on the failure of a parent company to give it the information that would have allowed it to inform and consult in accordance with its obligations under the ICE Regulations. TULRCA expressly provides that an employer cannot rely on the special circumstances defence in such a case in the context of collective redundancies. If it fails to inform and consult because it has not been given the necessary information by a person controlling the employer, the employer is nonetheless liable for a failure to inform and consult.[8] Regulation 20(6) takes a similar approach, specifying that a failure on the part of a person with direct or indirect control of the employer is not 'a valid reason for the employer failing to inform and consult'. **8.32**

If the employer cannot demonstrate that his failure to inform and consult was for reasons outside his control, the EAT can impose a maximum penalty of £75,000 (Regulation 23(2)). The penalty is paid to the Secretary of State rather than to the employees affected by the failure to inform and consult (in contrast to the system of protective awards adopted in the case of a failure to inform and consult under TULRCA or TUPE). The employees and their representatives therefore have no direct financial interest in pursuing an application for a penalty notice. This may make applications less likely other than where the default is especially serious or the application is union-backed, although it should not be overlooked that in many cases the motivation for a complaint may be to ensure compliance. **8.33**

The EAT has to take a range of factors into account when determining the level of penalty to be imposed (Regulation 23(3)). These factors mirror those set out in TICE. The specified factors include (but are not limited to): **8.34**

[7] See for example *Clarks of Hove Ltd v Bakers' Union* [1978] IRLR 366.

[8] S188(7).

- the gravity of the failure;
- the time over which it occurred;
- the reason for it;
- the number of employees affected; and
- the number of employees covered by the relevant agreement in total.

8.35 Common sense suggests that where there has been a serious failure over an extended period that has affected a majority of employees covered by the agreement, the fine is likely to approach the maximum amount. Where the default is less serious, continues for a shorter period or covers a minority of employees, the penalty is likely to be smaller. For example, it is to be expected that a breach of 'administrative' provisions of a negotiated agreement would attract a lower penalty than breaches of more substantive provisions. As yet there have been no EAT decisions under TICE on the way in which it will approach the setting of the relevant penalty.

8.36 There is an outstanding question about whether employee representatives will be able to take a tactical approach to the penalty regime in an attempt to circumvent the £75,000 cap. Regulation 22(1) allows complaints to be presented to the CAC in relation to an employer that has 'failed to comply with the terms of the negotiated agreement or . . . one or more of the standard information and consultation provisions'. It may well be that applicants (especially where there is union backing and the default has been serious) will seek to lodge a number of different complaints arising from what is substantially the same breach, on the basis that an application for a written penalty notice can be made to the EAT as a result of every CAC order.

8.37 For example, if an employer subject to the standard provisions has failed to inform and consult about collective redundancies, there will be an argument that he has failed to comply with the provisions of Regulation 20(1)(a), (b), and (c). Might it also be the case that an 'ongoing' failure by the employer is viewed by the CAC as a series of separate breaches? It may even be possible to separate out different strands of an employer's plans or proposals and to bring a separate claim in respect of each of those. If 'separated' claims are made out in this way, the ultimate penalty could be more than £75,000 in total, notwithstanding the fact that the default stems from a single set of circumstances. It remains to be seen whether the CAC will be willing to entertain such 'overlapping' complaints. The ICE Regulations themselves do not appear to prevent such an approach, and in cases of flagrant failure by employers to comply with the ICE Regulations the CAC may be sympathetic to claims that a number of related but separate breaches have occurred. This is especially so if the £75,000 penalty is seen as an insignificant deterrent for larger employers.

Regulations 23(4) to (7) contain various procedural provisions relating to penalty notices. Regulation 23(4) provides that the EAT must not order a penalty to be paid before the end of the period an employer has to appeal against a CAC declaration or order. (Under the EAT rules of procedure, the relevant period for an appeal will be within 42 days of the date of the declaration or order.) In practice, it seems unlikely that the EAT will be able to consider an application for a penalty notice within that period, regardless of the speed with which the application is lodged. **8.38**

If an employer appeals against the CAC declaration or order, the effect of the penalty notice is suspended until the appeal is determined (Regulations 23(6)). Once the appeal has been determined, or the period for an appeal has expired and no appeal made, the Secretary of State can proceed to recover the amount outstanding under the penalty notice as a civil debt (Regulation 23(5)). Monies payable under penalty notices are paid into the Consolidated Fund (Regulation 23(7)). **8.39**

E. ENFORCING CAC ORDERS

Having looked at the immediate impact of the issue of a CAC declaration or order, a question remains about the sanctions that apply if a CAC order, once made, is not itself complied with. As seen, the CAC has power to order an employer to take specified steps to comply with a negotiated or standard information and consultation procedure. **8.40**

Under Regulation 35(4) a CAC order can be relied upon as a declaration or order of the High Court (in the case of an employer with a registered office, head office, or principal place of business in England and Wales) or as a declaration or order of the Court of Session in the case of a declaration or order made in respect of an employer with its registered office, head office, or principal place of business in Scotland. In contrast with the provisions in Regulation 38(3) and (4) of TICE, Regulation 35(4) does not expressly state that orders of the CAC can be enforced in the same way as an order of the High Court or Court of Session, presumably because such additional wording was felt to be unnecessary. **8.41**

The rules relating to the enforcement of judgments to do or abstain from doing any act in England or Wales are laid down in Schedule 1 of the Civil Procedure Rules, Part 70, Rule 70.5 and in Order 45 of the Rules of the Supreme Court. In Scotland, a CAC order would be enforced as an Order for Interdict or an Order for Specific Implement (as appropriate). The detailed procedure to be followed in Scotland is outside the scope of this work and the remainder of this section focusses on the position in England and Wales. **8.42**

8.43 CPR Rule 70.5 provides for enforcement of awards of bodies other than the High Court and County Courts where it has been provided by statute that they are enforceable as a declaration or order of the High Court. The supporting practice direction (70PD.4) provides that an application for enforcement be made to the High Court specifying the name and address of the person or body corporate against whom enforcement is sought and what is required. A copy of the order or award must be attached to the application notice. If a writ of sequestration is required specific application must be made to the High Court.

8.44 The High Court will then seek to enforce the award or order in accordance with Order 45, Rule 5, which sets out the various ways in which an order for the enforcement of a judgment to do or refrain from doing a particular act can be enforced:

- a writ of sequestration against the property of the person ordered to do or refrain from doing the act;
- where the person ordered to act or refrain from acting is a body corporate, a writ of sequestration against the property of a director or other officer of the company; or
- an order of committal against the person ordered to act or refrain from acting or, in the case of a body corporate, against any director or other officer of the company.

8.45 An individual officer of a company can therefore be personally liable for a failure to comply with a CAC order, notwithstanding the fact that the order was made against the employing entity rather than the director or officer as an individual. In theory a director of a company in breach of a CAC order could be subject to imprisonment or seizure of his personal assets because of the failure to comply.

8.46 Enforcement through sequestration or committal is however subject to a number of important limitations:

- the order must set out the time limit for doing (or not doing) the act in question. As indicated above, a CAC order should include such a time limit as a matter of course;
- a copy of the order must have been personally served on the body corporate before the expiry of that time limit;
- a copy of the order must have been served personally on the director or officer against whom a writ of sequestration or an order for committal is sought before the relevant time limit expires;
- any order for sequestration or committal must contain a penal notice on the face of the document stating that non-compliance with the order may result in the recipient being held in contempt of court and

liable to imprisonment, or, if a body corporate, liable to sequestration of assets.

If any one of these requirements has not been complied with, sequestration or committal will generally not be available.

8.47 Notwithstanding the general need for all these requirements to be complied with, in certain cases the court has power to dispense with the need for the order to be served. The power is most commonly exercised where there is evidence that the individual knows about the order but is evading service. However, the penal notice must be endorsed on the front of the order in any case where an individual is required to do a certain act within a specified time.

8.48 The High Court also has power under Order 45, Rule 6, to extend the time for doing any act required by the original order if necessary, to attach a penal notice, and to personally serve the extended order to ensure that Order 45, Rules 5 and 7, are satisfied but a formal application should be made to the court for this.

8.49 In practice however, there are two steps that employee representatives will want to take to try to ensure that any CAC order is enforceable as an order of the High Court under Regulation 35(4). The first is to make sure that any order issued by the CAC contains a time limit within which the act must be carried out, and the second is to ensure that the order is personally served on the company and its directors, so that in the event of further proceedings to enforce the order there is no doubt that the directors were aware of the order. Further, the employee representatives will want to take steps to ask the CAC to take steps to permit the endorsement of any order with a penal notice when the order is issued.

F. LIMITATIONS ON CAC ORDERS AND EXCLUSIVITY OF REMEDY

8.50 Whether or not a CAC order is capable of enforcement by way of sequestration or committal may in practice be of less importance than at first appears because of limitations in what the CAC can actually order an employer to do to comply with its obligations. On the face of it, the power set out in Regulation 22(4) is very wide, allowing the CAC to make an order to require the employer to take 'such steps as are necessary to comply with the terms of the negotiated agreement or . . . the standard information and consultation provisions'.

8.51 However, this power is in practice substantially modified by the provisions of Regulation 22(9). This states that no order of the CAC can suspend or alter the effect of any act done or of any agreement made by the employer. In other words, the CAC cannot order an employer to rethink or suspend the implementation of a decision that has already been taken simply because the required information and consultation has not taken place in accordance with a negotiated or standard agreement.

8.52 For example, take a situation in which an employer is considering stopping production at a particular site, with a resulting loss of jobs. Information and consultation would be required under the terms of a standard agreement (and in all probability under the terms of a negotiated agreement as well) before a decision to stop production was taken. Regulation 22(9) effectively means that if the decision was in fact taken without the necessary information and consultation having taken place, the CAC would neither be able to order the employer to give further consideration to the decision nor to suspend its implementation pending information and consultation.

8.53 From a UK managerial perspective this is relatively uncontroversial. As indicated in Chapter 1, one of the proposals made by the European Parliament was that the Information and Consultation Directive should be strengthened to allow for the suspension of a decision where it was likely to result in job losses. This proposal was not accepted, which clearly indicates that the Information and Consultation Directive does not require such a suspension of effect, despite the fact that this is a feature of some continental information and consultation structures. For example, when Renault decided to close a plant at Vilvoorde in Belgium in 1997 without informing either the local or the European works councils, courts in Belgium and France suspended the effect of the decision until its information and consultation obligations under the local and European agreements were complied with (although the planned closure ultimately went ahead).

8.54 What is more controversial is what should happen where employee representatives have discovered that the employer is considering steps on which it should be informing and consulting before a final decision has been taken. In this case, would it be open to the employee representatives to complain to the CAC at that stage and for the CAC to make an order compelling the employer to inform and consult before taking a decision? In practice, this would of course depend on whether a CAC hearing could be convened with sufficient speed to allow an order to be made before a decision was taken. (CAC guidance indicates that it will generally ask the other party to comment on an application or complaint within five working days of receipt by the CAC and that the CAC would determine how to proceed with the complaint within a further five working days.)

It is at least arguable that such a power would be consistent with the requirements of Article 8.1 of the Information and Consultation Directive, inasmuch as it would be an adequate procedure enabling the requirements of the Information and Consultation Directive to be enforced. As outlined above (and subject to the limitations outlined in the section on enforcing CAC orders), failure to comply with a CAC order can be treated as a contempt of court. It seems likely that the possibility of imprisonment or sequestration of personal assets would concentrate the minds of an employer's directors and officers and be the most effective way of ensuring compliance with the order and therefore enable employees (by way of an application to the CAC) to enforce their rights under the Information and Consultation Directive. **8.55**

It appears however that it is not intended that the ICE Regulations should give the CAC the power to issue an order which has the effect of suspending managerial prerogative to take decisions relating to the running of a business. Regulation 22(9) goes on to provide that no order of the CAC 'shall have the effect of . . . preventing or delaying any act or agreement which the employer proposes to do or to make'. This appears to mean that the CAC order cannot prevent the employer from taking or implementing business decisions pending information and consultation. **8.56**

For example, assume that in the situation outlined above, the employee representatives discovered that discussions were under way about the possible plant closure before a final decision to close had been taken. In practice, an application to the CAC for an order would be of limited value in terms of enforcing employee rights (as opposed to penalizing a breach) because even once obtained, the order could not force the employer to inform and consult if that would prevent or delay the act that the employer is proposing to take. **8.57**

This appears to mean that although the CAC order could require the employer to inform and consult, the order could not stop it from taking a final decision before that information and consultation had taken place. The employer could apparently still go ahead and take a decision to close without being in breach of the CAC order. Presumably however it would still have an obligation to inform and consult employee representatives after that decision, even though at least part of the consultation obligation could not by definition be complied with because the decision had already been taken. **8.58**

Although the DTI Guidance does not contain any explanation of how it is envisaged Regulation 22(9) will work in practice, this interpretation is supplemented by the provisions of Regulation 24, which provide that the only remedy for complaints about infringement of specified rights **8.59** (particularly rights in relation to when information and consultation should take place) is by way of a complaint to the CAC. This means that it will not be open to employee representatives to seek an injunction from the High Court to prevent an employer from taking or implementing business decisions (whether pending an application to the CAC or subsequently). Such an exclusivity of remedy provision was important to the decision of the High Court in the context of collective redundancies in *Griffin v South West Water Services Limited*[9] and indicates again that the ICE Regulations are not intended to interfere with managerial prerogative to take decisions in the absence of information and consultation.

8.60 There must be an argument that the Government has failed properly to implement Article 8.1 of the Information and Consultation Directive, on the basis that the relevant administrative and judicial procedures are not in place to allow obligations from the Information and Consultation Directive to be enforced. In practice, a CAC order cannot stop a business from either taking or implementing a business decision in the absence of information and consultation. In turn this appears to mean that there is no risk of being found in contempt of court if a business decision is taken or implemented without information and consultation.

8.61 Subject to the financial penalties that can be imposed (see paragraphs 8.26 to 8.39), this gives employers relatively little incentive to comply with the requirements, particularly in relation to the sorts of business situations—such as threats to employment within the undertaking—in which the Information and Consultation Directive specifically aims to improve employee awareness and participation. In fact, CAC orders will be more effective in relation to what might be thought more 'technical' breaches, such as a failure to elect representatives in a particular way. In such a complaint the limitations in Regulation 22(9) would not apply, meaning that contempt of court proceedings are a possibility in the event of a failure to comply with a CAC order in this regard.

[9] [1995] IRLR 15.

9

Confidential Information

This chapter considers: **9.01**

(1) the circumstances in which information or documents can be withheld from information and consultation representatives on grounds of confidentiality;
(2) when such information should be disclosed subject to a confidentiality requirement; and
(3) what happens in the event of a dispute over the confidentiality of information or documents.

A. GENERAL PRINCIPLES

The appropriate treatment of confidential information will be key to the effective operation of information and consultation bodies. It goes without saying that there is a delicate balance to be drawn. On the one hand, there needs to be a sufficient flow of relevant information to allow a meaningful information and consultation process, otherwise the whole purpose of the ICE Regulations would be undermined with potentially **9.02** detrimental consequences for both employer and workforce. On the other, undertakings will clearly be concerned to ensure that highly confidential and often price-sensitive information is kept secure.

9.03 Issues of confidentiality may arise in relation to a whole range of matters potentially covered by the ICE Regulations but are likely to be particularly acute in the context of large-scale transformational issues, such as significant mergers, acquisitions, or disposals.

9.04 Article 6 of the Information and Consultation Directive sets out a framework for how issues relating to confidential information are to be addressed:

> 1. Member States shall provide that, within the conditions and limits laid down by national legislation, the employees' representatives, and any experts who assist them, are not authorised to reveal to employees or to third parties, any information which, in the legitimate interest of the undertaking or establishment, has expressly been provided to them in confidence. This obligation shall continue to apply, wherever the said representatives or experts are, even after expiry of their terms of office. However, a Member State may authorise the employees' representatives and anyone assisting them to pass on confidential information to employees and to third parties bound by an obligation of confidentiality.
> 2. Member States shall provide, in specific cases and within the conditions and limits laid down by national legislation, that the employer is not obliged to communicate information or undertake consultation when the nature of that information or consultation is such that, according to objective criteria, it would seriously harm the functioning of the undertaking or establishment or would be prejudicial to it.
> 3. Without prejudice to existing national procedures, Member States shall provide for administrative or judicial review procedures for the case where the employer requires confidentiality or does not provide the information in accordance with paragraphs 1 and 2. They may also provide for procedures intended to safeguard the confidentiality of the information in question.

9.05 Subject to the confines of the framework set out in Article 6, therefore, the specific detail of issues relating to confidential information is left to be determined by the Member States. In relation to Great Britain this is achieved by Regulations 25 and 26.

9.06 The ICE Regulations approach the question of confidential information on two levels. First, they consider the obligations of confidentiality which may be imposed on information and consultation representatives and other persons in respect of information or documents they receive in their capacity as such (Regulation 25).

9.07 Regulation 26 then goes on to consider the extent to which undertakings may be permitted to withhold information or documents from information and consultation representatives and other persons altogether on the basis that it is confidential.

It is evident, however, that the primary thrust of the ICE Regulations is that information or documents should be disclosed with appropriate confidentiality restrictions attached rather than not disclosed at all and accordingly that non-disclosure is only likely to be permissible in relation to particularly sensitive information, in circumstances where disclosure is likely to cause serious harm or prejudice to the employer. **9.08**

The language of both Regulations 25 and 26 tracks the approach taken in relation to confidential information by Regulations 23 and 24 of TICE, the UK regulations implementing the European Works Council regime. To date, however, the scope of Regulations 23 and 24 of TICE has not been tested. **9.09**

B. WHEN CAN INFORMATION OR DOCUMENTS BE WITHHELD FROM INFORMATION AND CONSULTATION REPRESENTATIVES AND OTHERS?

Regulation 26 addresses the position when an employer seeks to withhold information or documents altogether. Regulation 26 does not apply to pre-existing agreements. The extent to which information or documents can be withheld in circumstances where a pre-existing agreement applies will therefore depend on the terms of the relevant agreement and whether it is legally binding (see further Chapter 3). Employees are also likely to have obligations of confidentiality under their contracts of employment. **9.10**

Regulation 26(1) permits information or documents to be withheld from any person where the nature of the information or document is such that, according to objective criteria, the disclosure of the information or document would seriously harm the functioning of, or would be prejudicial to, the undertaking. **9.11**

Reference to a person in Regulation 26(1) is deliberately drawn as widely as possible and would include, amongst others, information and consultation representatives and (if it was agreed to make use of them under a negotiated agreement[1]) experts or other advisers. **9.12**

[1] There is no provision for experts in the standard information and consultation provisions.

9.13 As a matter of construction, it appears that the concept of seriousness qualifies only the harm criterion and not the prejudice criterion.

9.14 It is clear that Regulation 26(1) does not permit information or documents to be withheld merely on the grounds that they are confidential per se. Given that Regulation 25 permits an employer to impose obligations of confidentiality on recipients of confidential information, employers will normally be expected to disclose information rather than not disclosing it at all. After all, non-disclosure will generally prevent information and consultation from taking place, whereas restricted disclosure will not. To justify total non-disclosure, the 'serious harm' or 'prejudice' tests will need to be satisfied.

9.15 The precise distinction between a disclosure of information or documents that would cause serious harm to the functioning of the undertaking and a disclosure that would be prejudicial to it is unclear. Because the 'seriousness' qualifier does not appear to attach to it, the prejudice test ought in principle to be easier to establish. As a practical matter, though, little may turn on the distinction as both tests are likely to be interpreted restrictively by the CAC. Any other interpretation would be inconsistent with the purpose of the ICE Regulations and the approach set out in Regulation 25, as summarized above.

9.16 It is expected that the scope of the concepts of 'serious harm' and 'prejudice' will be tested before the CAC at a relatively early stage (see paragraph 9.19). In framing the ICE Regulations, a conscious decision was taken by the DTI not to spell out specific circumstances in which serious harm and/or prejudice would be presumed to arise. It had been suggested during consultations over the equivalent provision in TICE (TICE, Regulation 24) that specific circumstances should be identified. A specific example raised in relation to TICE was a situation where disclosure of confidential information would conflict with regulatory obligations to which the employer might be subject (and, as will be seen below, disclosure will often not conflict with regulatory requirements anyway). The proposal to identify specific examples was rejected on the basis that serious harm and/or prejudice would not necessarily always occur in such circumstances and that the test should be applied on a case-by-case basis in the light of the specific facts. This approach will apply equally to Regulation 26.

9.17 If information and consultation representatives and others have failed to keep confidential information or documents disclosed to them on a restricted basis and damage or loss has been suffered as a result, this could be a justification for not disclosing information on a subsequent occasion. Certainly the DTI Guidance takes the view that 'evidence of past leaks might be relevant'. However, a previous breach would not, by itself, justify non-disclosure unless the serious harm or prejudice test is also satisfied. Examples of the consequences of prior leaks may constitute strong evidence to substantiate the decision to withhold.

It should also be borne in mind that the prejudice and serious harm tests operate not on the basis of the employer's subjective view as to what constitutes prejudice or serious harm but on an objective assessment of the position. **9.18**

In the event of a dispute between the employer and information and consultation representatives as to whether the serious harm or prejudice test is made out, the matter can be referred by either of the parties to the CAC for a declaration (Regulation 26(2)). Note that unlike the right to challenge a confidentiality obligation imposed upon recipients of confidential information under Regulation 25 (see paragraphs 9.42–9.48), which is conferred on any person on whom the employer purports to impose an obligation of confidentiality, the right of complaint under Regulation 26(2) is limited to information and consultation representatives. The one exception to this is that where information and consultation representatives have not been elected or appointed (for example, where the standard information and consultation procedure applies but information and consultation representatives have not been elected) a complaint can be made by any employee or employee's representative. **9.19**

In order to make its adjudication, the CAC will normally require the relevant information or documents to be disclosed to it. The CAC acknowledges in its guidance that employers will be concerned that the very information that they seek to retain as confidential may be disclosed as a result of CAC proceedings. In appropriate cases, the CAC may therefore be prepared to conduct a hearing in the absence of another party, or to ensure that the hearing is not held in public, or to defer or prohibit publication of the CAC's decision. If the CAC makes a declaration that the disclosure of the information or document in question would not, according to objective criteria, seriously harm the functioning of or be prejudicial to the undertaking, the CAC must order the employer to disclose the information or documents (Regulation 26(3)). Any such order must specify: **9.20**

- the information or document to be disclosed;
- the recipient or recipients to whom the information or document is to be disclosed;
- any terms on which the information or document is to be disclosed; and
- the date before which the information or document is to be disclosed (Regulation 26(4)).

9.21 If information has been withheld, it may only become clear that the employer is actually in possession of that information at some future point in time (by which time it might no longer be confidential). So an order for disclosure may be of limited value to employees. Even in these circumstances where employee representatives are aware that an employer might be in possession of information that it is refusing to disclose, whether that information can be made available in sufficient time for there to be meaningful information and consultation about it will depend on the speed with which the CAC is able to make its determination. See further below (paragraph 9.64) for discussion of whether financial sanctions attach to the employer in these circumstances.

9.22 It should not be forgotten that an application to the CAC for a declaration as to whether information or documents meet the serious harm or prejudice tests is also available to the employer (Regulation 26(2)).

C. IMPOSING OBLIGATIONS OF CONFIDENTIALITY ON RECIPIENTS OF INFORMATION OR DOCUMENTS

9.23 The overall effect of Regulation 25 (subject to the possibility of intervention by the CAC (discussed at paragraphs 9.43–9.48)) is to permit employers to disclose documents or information that they believe to be confidential on terms restricting their onward disclosure.

9.24 Specifically, Regulation 25 provides that any person to whom the employer, pursuant to his obligations under the ICE Regulations, entrusts any information or document on terms requiring it to be held in confidence shall not disclose that information or document except in accordance with those terms (Regulation 25(1)). The obligation of confidence operates in relation to any person who is in receipt of relevant information or documents, so the employer may impose an obligation of confidentiality not only on information and consultation representatives but also on experts, other advisers, or indeed anyone else to whom the employer permits such information or documents to be disclosed (although, in accordance with Regulation 25(1), such information or documents could be disclosed to information and consultation representatives specifically on the basis that they are not to be shared with experts, or other advisers).

9.25 Regulation 25 only applies to information and consultation pursuant to an employer's obligations under the ICE Regulations. In other words, the provisions of Regulation 25 do not apply in relation to information that is made available to employee representatives pursuant to qualifying pre-existing agreements (see Chapter 3 for further discussion on pre-existing agreements). As a contractual matter, it ought to be possible to incorporate provisions which have a similar effect to Regulation 25 in any pre-existing agreement. Issues relating to confidential information in the context of pre-existing agreements are considered in more detail in paragraphs 9.77–9.80 below.

In order to be able to rely on confidentiality obligations, employers will obviously need to identify which information and consultation documents they believe to be confidential and notify the information and consultation representatives of that fact. From an employer's perspective, clarity is extremely important. It must be sufficiently clear to recipients what information the restriction relates to as well as the scope of the restriction (for example, to whom the information may be passed, the purpose for which it may be used, and any time limit attaching to the restriction). Where employers are vague on these issues, they may find that recipients disclose confidential information inadvertently. In practical terms, identification of relevant categories of information or documents could be built into the terms of a negotiated agreement, with information or documents that the employer believes to be confidential being specifically labelled as such at the point of dissemination. **9.26**

A number of employers already operate systems under which information to be disclosed to other employee representative bodies (such as European Works Councils) is graded according to its sensitivity. So, for example, information that is graded 'company confidential' may be disclosed within the organization but may not be disclosed externally, whereas information that is 'highly confidential' is restricted to the information and consultation representatives themselves. Many employers are likely to find this type of approach an appropriate one to use for the purposes of the ICE Regulations. **9.27**

An employer who is able to show he has undertaken a clear analysis of the types of information that will be confidential and the reason why that is the case (and shared that justification with information and consultation representatives) may also be better placed to justify the confidentiality of particular information and documents to the CAC in the face of a subsequent complaint (see paragraph 9.46). **9.28**

The employer will also want to ensure that the employee representatives and third parties such as experts or advisers sign up to an appropriate form of confidentiality undertaking to confirm their confidentiality obligations. **9.29**

D. BREACHING THE OBLIGATION OF CONFIDENCE

9.30 Regulation 25(3) makes clear that the obligation to maintain the confidentiality of information or documents disclosed to information and consultation representatives or any other person in confidence is a duty owed to the employer, and a breach of the duty is actionable accordingly (subject to the defences and other incidents applying to breaches of statutory duty). In other words, the ICE Regulations specifically provide that a breach of the duty of confidentiality amounts to a breach of statutory duty.

9.31 Breach of statutory duty is an actionable tort. Accordingly, where a breach of statutory duty occurs, the wronged party (i.e. the employer) injured by the breach of duty can sue for damages in respect of loss suffered as a result of the breach of confidentiality.

9.32 In practice, of course, a damages claim will often be problematic for the employer. Issues of quantification of loss are likely to arise and those responsible for any loss will often have limited resources. Furthermore establishing responsibility for a leak may be difficult from an evidential perspective. And finally, there are also industrial relations implications that would need to be considered.

9.33 In principle, an employer would also be able to take injunctive proceedings to restrain a breach of statutory duty or a further breach of such a duty. The reality, however, is that any damage is already likely to have been caused by the time any breach of the requirement of confidentiality comes to the employer's attention.

9.34 Regulation 25(3) also expressly provides that the creation of a liability for breach of statutory duty for failing to comply with an obligation of confidentiality is without prejudice to any other obligation or liability which may arise apart from under Regulation 25(3), for example under common law or equitable principles. An action for breach of confidence may be available where (1) the information disclosed has the necessary quality of confidence; (2) it is communicated in circumstances entailing an obligation of confidence; and (3) there is an unauthorized, unjustified use of that information. However, similar practical obstacles to those described at paragraphs 9.32 and 9.33 above are likely to arise.

9.35 In practical terms, therefore, an employer may have limited recourse in the event of a breach of a requirement of confidentiality. However, as explained at paragraph 9.17 above, a breach may (but will not necessarily) make it easier for an employer not to disclose sensitive information at all on future occasions.

On an individual level, breach of a requirement of confidentiality by an information and consultation representative (or any other person who is employed by the employer) is likely to lead to disciplinary action including, in appropriate circumstances, dismissal. Normal principles will apply in assessing the fairness of any dismissal. Employers are likely to want to include specific provision in negotiated agreements that breach of confidentiality obligations could result in dismissal. **9.36**

An interesting question arises as to what might happen if an employee was dismissed for disclosing confidential information while an application to the CAC was pending as to the reasonableness of the obligation of confidentiality (see further paragraph 9.43) and the CAC subsequently concludes that it was not reasonable to impose that requirement. It seems likely that a dismissal in those circumstances would be unfair. **9.37**

The protection the ICE Regulations give to employees from being dismissed or subjected to other detriment (Regulations 30 and 32—see further Chapter 10) for: **9.38**

- performing functions or activities as a relevant representative or as a candidate in an election for a relevant representative;
- requesting reasonable time off to perform duties as a relevant representative;
- proposing to do either

does not apply if the reason (or principal reason) for the dismissal is that in the performance or purported performance of the employee's functions or activities he has disclosed any information or document in breach of the duty in Regulation 25 (Regulations 30(4) and 32(4)).

E. EXEMPTION FOR WHISTLE-BLOWERS

The provision of information or documents on a confidential basis does not prevent the recipient from disclosing information where he reasonably believes that disclosure to be a protected disclosure under the whistle-blowing provisions incorporated into the Employment Rights Act 1996 (Regulation 25(5)). And the relaxations contained in Regulations 30(4) and 32(4) from liability for dismissal or detriment do not apply if sanctions are applied to the employee in these circumstances. In other words, the employer will not be able to prevent (or otherwise take action against) information and consultation representatives or others who disseminate more widely information or documents that have been disclosed to them subject to an obligation of confidence where that dissemination attracts the protection of the whistle-blowing legislation. **9.39**

A protected disclosure is a disclosure of information which, in the reasonable opinion of the employee making it, shows one or more of the following and in respect of which certain requirements are satisfied (sections 43A to H, Employment Rights Act 1996): **9.40**

(1) criminal offences;
(2) miscarriages of justice;
(3) danger to the health and safety of any individual;
(4) damage to the environment;
(5) breach of any legal obligation; or
(6) the deliberate concealment of information about any of the above.

9.41 Perhaps the most significant point to note here is that the scope of certain of these categories is potentially very wide, in particular the category relating to breach of legal obligation. Recent cases have demonstrated that a breach of the duty of trust and confidence implied into all contracts of employment may be a breach of a legal obligation for these purposes. In *Parkins v Sodexho Ltd*[2] the EAT held that a requirement that an employee report to a supervisor at the end of each shift in order to verify the accuracy of his timesheets could amount to a breach of the implied duty of trust and confidence and that complaints in respect of this could amount to a 'qualified disclosure' for the purposes of whistle-blowing. This was subsequently confirmed in *Fincham v HM Prison Service*[3] where racial harassment and victimization amounted to a breach of the implied term of the contract of employment.

F. CHALLENGES TO THE IMPOSITION OF AN OBLIGATION OF CONFIDENTIALITY ON DISCLOSED INFORMATION OR DOCUMENTS

9.42 The disclosure of information or documents to information and consultation representatives on the basis that it cannot be disclosed to the wider workforce may be unattractive to information and consultation representatives, especially if the employer purports to apply such restrictions too indiscriminately. Representatives may take the view that they should be able to share information with the employees they represent and, where a consultation obligation arises, that proper consultation can only occur where they are in a position to canvass the views of the workforce at large.

9.43 Regulation 25(6) enables a recipient to whom an employer has entrusted any information or document on terms requiring it to be held in confidence to apply to the CAC for a declaration as to whether it was reasonable for the employer to impose such a requirement. Unlike a challenge against the withholding of information or documents altogether under Regulation 26(2), a challenge under Regulation 25(6) is available to

[2] [2002] IRLR 109. [3] [2003] All ER (D) 211 (May).

anyone upon whom the employer has placed an obligation of confidentiality. If the CAC considers that the disclosure of the information or document by the recipient would not, or would not be likely to, harm the legitimate interests of the undertaking, it must make a declaration that it was not reasonable for the employer to require the recipient to hold the information or document in confidence (Regulation 25(7)). Note that the test for the CAC is different to the test that applies when it is adjudicating whether information or documents can be withheld altogether. The test is one of actual or likely harm to the legitimate interests of the undertaking. That is clearly less onerous than the Regulation 26(2) test, but its precise scope is likely only to become clear when the first applications are heard by the CAC.

If the CAC makes a declaration under Regulation 25(7), the information or **9.44** document is not at any time thereafter to be regarded as having been entrusted to the recipient who made the application or to any other recipient on terms requiring it to be held in confidence (Regulation 25(8)). Accordingly, in these circumstances, the information in question can be freely disclosed by the information and consultation representatives to the workforce at large (or, so it would appear, to other third parties, including the press).

An appeal may be made to the EAT on any question of law arising from **9.45** any declaration made by the CAC. In practice, however, it is likely that the majority of determinations made by the CAC in relation to confidential information will be factual ones, so the right to appeal will normally be limited.

Employers may have concerns with a mechanism under which an **9.46** independent third party (albeit one whose members have considerable industrial experience) is given power to make a determination as to the confidentiality of an employer's information. Employers may legitimately feel that they are better placed to make assessments of confidentiality and of the undertaking's legitimate interests. Clearly, in the event of an application being made to the CAC, the employer would need to be able to set out in detail precisely why the information or document in question is considered to be confidential, with a full analysis of the likely implications of any disclosure and why the employer's legitimate interests are likely to be harmed. As suggested above, it is also likely to be helpful if the employer can point to evidence (perhaps in the form of a written risk assessment) that the confidentiality of the relevant information or document was carefully considered at the time—employers who make blanket assertions of confidentiality may find themselves disadvantaged as a result[4].

[4] See also paragraph 9.20 above in relation to the CAC's approach to the public nature of its hearings.

9.47 It is worth noting that employees have a similar right to seek a determination from the CAC in relation to European Works Councils under Regulation 23 of TICE but no application has yet been made to the CAC pursuant to these provisions. The equivalent right under the ICE Regulations will undoubtedly be exercised more frequently.

9.48 As yet, however, it is unclear precisely what approach the CAC is likely to take, and whether it will only be prepared to intervene in the clearest cases in which a confidential label has been inappropriately attached by employers. It is likely however that the CAC will be more favourably disposed towards making an order that information or documents must be disclosed to the wider workforce than an order also permitting disclosure to third parties (although the employer may see the distinction as not being particularly helpful in practice, as once the information in question has been disclosed to the workforce at large it may be hard to prevent its subsequent leak to third parties).

G. HOW DO OBLIGATIONS/DUTIES IN RELATION TO CONFIDENTIAL INFORMATION INTERACT WITH OTHER CONFIDENTIALITY OBLIGATIONS TO WHICH THE EMPLOYER MAY BE SUBJECT?

9.49 Employers may also be subject to other obligations restricting the disclosure of commercially sensitive information, and will need to consider how these interact with their obligations under the ICE Regulations.

9.50 For example, companies whose shares or other securities are listed on a stock exchange will be subject to various obligations relating to the disclosure of market-sensitive information.

9.51 For companies listed on the London Stock Exchange, the relevant requirements are set out in the UK Listing Authority Disclosure Rules. The Disclosure Rules were introduced on 1 July 2005 as part of an overhaul of the UKLA Listing Rules following the implementation of the Market Abuse Directive and the Prospectus Directive and the FSA's review of the listing regime. Under the Disclosure Rules a listed company is required to make a notification as soon as possible of any inside information which directly concerns the company (Rule 2.2).

9.52 Similar requirements are set out in the Alternative Investment Market (AIM) Rules for Companies and the Off Exchange (OFEX) Rules. Companies which are subject to US rules are governed by one or more of the Securities Exchange Commission (SEC) Rules (including Regulation FD

('Fair Disclosure'), New York Stock Exchange Rules, and the National Association of Security Dealers Rules.

Historically, many employers subject to these regimes have been extremely reluctant to disclose price-sensitive information to employee representatives because of concerns about a possible leak. Further, a number of employers have taken the view that the relevant rules do not even permit such disclosures to be made. **9.53**

Such a view appears to be incorrect. The DTI Guidance on the ICE Regulations indicates that neither the UK Listing Rules (as they were drafted at the time the DTI Guidance was issued) nor equivalent US rules prevent a company sharing price-sensitive information with representatives of employees before it is disclosed to the market, as long as those representatives are subject to an obligation of confidentiality. As far as the DTI is concerned, therefore, the approach adopted in Regulation 25 is entirely consistent with regulatory requirements. **9.54**

Specifically, Chapter 9.4 of the now superseded Listing Rules provided that a company need not publicly divulge information about impending developments or matters in the course of negotiation, but may give such information in confidence to various categories of recipient. Amongst those categories of recipient were representatives of the employer's employees or trades unions acting on their behalf, provided the employer was 'satisfied that such recipients of information are aware that they must not deal in the company's securities before the relevant information has been made available to the public'. Similar wording is contained in both the AIM and OFEX rules (see Guidance Note to Rule 10 of the AIM Rules and Chapter 9.6 of the OFEX Rulebook) and in the US, the SEC Rules (specifically, Regulation FD). **9.55**

As mentioned above, Chapter 9.4 of the Listing Rules has now been superseded by the Disclosure Rules. Section 2.5 of the Disclosure Rules provides that a listed company may 'under its own responsibility, delay the public disclosure of inside information, such as not to prejudice its legitimate interests provided that: **9.56**

(1) such omission would not be likely to mislead the public;
(2) any person receiving the information owes [the company] a duty of confidentiality, regardless of whether such duty is based on law, regulations, articles of association or contract; and
(3) [the company] is able to ensure the confidentiality of that information.'

Examples of legitimate interests included in the Disclosure Rules include 'negotiations in course, or related elements where the outcome or normal **9.57** pattern of those negotiations would be likely to be affected by public disclosure' (section 2.5.3, Disclosure Rules).

9.58 Where the company is permitted to delay disclosure of inside information in accordance with section 2.5.3 of the Disclosure Rules, it may selectively disclose that information to persons owing it a duty of confidentiality, if it is in the normal course of that person's employment, profession or duties. Examples of the categories of recipient include 'employee representatives or trade unions acting on their behalf' (section 2.5.7, Disclosure Rules).

9.59 It would appear therefore that the practical effect of the Disclosure Rules is likely to be similar to that under Rule 9.4 of the previous Listing Rules, although the Disclosure Rules are in some respects more qualified—for example, Disclosure Rule 2.5.8 makes the specific point that 'selective disclosure to any or all of the persons referred to in Disclosure Rule 2.5.7 may not be justified in every circumstance where [a company] delays disclosure in accordance with Disclosure Rule 2.5.1'. There may therefore be some circumstances in which it is inappropriate to share price-sensitive information with representatives of employees before it is disclosed to the market.

9.60 One point made in the DTI Guidance is that if a negotiated agreement is in place in relation to an undertaking which provides for the provision of information to and consultation with the workforce as a whole rather than with employee representatives, it will not be possible to make disclosure in accordance with the UKLA rules (now the Disclosure Rules), which only permit disclosure to be made to a limited class of employee representatives. In these circumstances, if the information in question is price-sensitive, it will presumably be possible to justify its non-disclosure under the serious harm or prejudice criteria discussed above.

9.61 A similar approach operates in relation to The City Code on Takeovers and Mergers, the code that governs the acquisition of (listed and unlisted) public companies (and certain private companies) and which is designed to ensure fair and equal treatment of all shareholders in relation to takeovers. Rule 2.1 of the Code requires that all persons privy to confidential information relating to an offer or contemplated offer must treat that information as secret and may only pass it to another person if it is necessary to do so and if that person is made aware of the need for secrecy.

9.62 Disclosure of confidential information may also raise concerns in relation to insider dealing. Under the Criminal Justice Act 1983, it is a criminal offence punishable by seven years' imprisonment for a person to disclose inside information, unless in the proper performance of the functions of an office, employment, or profession whose shares or other securities are listed as a stock exchange. The Criminal Justice Act defines inside information as information which: (1) relates to particular securities or a particular issuer; (2) is specific or precise; (3) has not been made public; and (4) if it were made public, would be likely to have a significant effect on the price of any securities.

Where information is being disclosed by an employer in satisfaction of a legal obligation to inform and consult with employee representatives, such disclosure ought in principle to be 'in the proper performance of the functions of an office, employment or profession'. **9.63**

However, the employer will have an additional responsibility to ensure that information and consultation representatives to whom such information is disclosed are made fully aware that the information in question is inside information and of the implications arising from this. As mentioned above, under the UKLA Disclosure Rules, such information may only be disclosed to employee representatives in circumstances where the employer is satisfied that the representatives are so aware. In all situations, it would be prudent and in the interests of both employer and employee representatives, to provide the employee representatives with a memorandum reminding them of their obligations in relation to inside information and the potential sanctions resulting from non-compliance, and to request them to sign and return it to the employer. **9.64**

Notwithstanding the scope of the disclosure permitted by the Disclosure Rules and the other provisions described above, the authors' experience suggests that, at least in the short term, many employers will continue to be reluctant to make disclosures on this basis. Typically (and especially where the information relates to a sale or acquisition), employers tend to be more concerned about the risk of a leak of price-sensitive information especially if this might occur at a time when it is far from certain that the transaction will proceed, and as a result have chosen not to consult. **9.65**

Whether those concerns are justified or not, it is clear that for the reasons set out above the effect of the ICE Regulations will be that where information and consultation representatives are in place a failure to disclose information to them will normally result in a breach of the ICE Regulations (unless, of course, the serious harm or prejudice defence is, objectively, made out). **9.66**

The question therefore arises as to what sanction, if any, would flow from a failure of the employer to disclose confidential information in these circumstances. As discussed above, the primary remedy for non-disclosure is an application to the CAC for disclosure. If the information **9.67** has been withheld in the first place, the non-disclosure is likely often only to come to the attention of the information and consultation representatives. After a formal public announcement has been made, the employer will presumably be happy to disclose the information at that point.

9.68 The practical risk for the employer in these circumstances is likely to be that failure to disclose the relevant information, in breach of the requirements of Regulations 25 and 26, in itself amounts to a failure to inform and consult properly under the relevant information and consultation arrangements in place within the undertaking, which in turn exposes the employer to financial sanction of up to £75,000 (see Chapter 8). The terms of any negotiated agreement are likely to be relevant here.

H. ANNOUNCEMENTS TO EMPLOYEES INVOLVING PRICE-SENSITIVE INFORMATION

9.69 The DTI has also published, as Annex 2 to the Guidance (see pp. 319 to 322), information on announcements to the workforce at large (as opposed to disclosure to employee representatives only) involving price-sensitive information.

9.70 The key point made in the Annex is that employees should not first be notified of significant news affecting their employment through the media. The Annex emphasizes that (as explained above) the Listing Rules (now the Disclosure Rules) and equivalent rules do allow disclosure of price-sensitive information simultaneously to financial markets and employees.

9.71 The Annex makes the point that the Listing Rules and its equivalents do not prescribe the specific time of day at which announcements should be made, only that they must be made without delay. The Annex indicates that the Government considers it good practice for a company to take such decisions during working hours so that the details can be released at the same time both to the stock market and the employees.

9.72 Whether such an approach is likely to be practicable in all circumstances is open to doubt. The negotiation of transactions can be a very complex process and the timing of announcements can, as a consequence, be difficult to control. As a result, it is often only in the middle of the night that a decision is reached to proceed with a transaction, with the information then being relevant to the financial markets for announcement first thing the next morning. What is clear, however, is that the DTI does expect the impact on employees to be taken into account when considering timing issues, and that every effort should be made to ensure employees and their representatives are notified of significant information at the same time as others.

I. OBLIGATIONS OF CONFIDENTIALITY IN THIRD-PARTY CONTRACTS

A key question in relation to the confidential information provisions contained in the ICE Regulations is the extent to which they impact on and/or override third-party rights. For example, an employer could be in possession of information and documents that may be appropriate for disclosure to information and consultation representatives but in relation to which the employer owes a duty of confidentiality to a third party. It seems (1) that disclosure cannot be avoided on this ground alone and (2) that the provisions of the ICE Regulations may override the third party's rights. **9.73**

This is because Regulation 39 specifies that any provision 'in any agreement' (whether in an employee's contract or not) is void insofar as it purports to exclude or limit the operation of any provision of the ICE Regulations. This would presumably be the case regardless of whether the purported exclusion or limitation is express or indirect. **9.74**

To give a practical example, it is common for sellers of businesses or undertakings to disclose information to prospective purchasers for due diligence purposes. A frequent condition of access to such information is that the purchaser must enter into a confidentiality or non-disclosure agreement. The question arises as to whether a confidentiality agreement is enforceable in circumstances where the prospective purchaser is obliged to disclose such information (or maybe simply to disclose the fact of the intended acquisition) to its own employees in accordance with its own information and consultation obligations under the ICE Regulations. In practice, such a disclosure obligation is only likely to arise for the prospective purchaser at a relatively advanced stage of the sale process, but when it does arise it seems clear that by virtue of Regulation 39 the prospective purchaser will be both empowered and required to disclose that information which is reasonably necessary for its information and consultation obligations, regardless of the terms of the confidentiality/non-disclosure agreement. Because the effect of Regulation 39 is to render void any provision in any agreement that purposes to exclude or limit the operation of any provision of the ICE Regulations, it would appear that the relevant provision of the confidentiality/non-disclosure agreement would not be enforceable as against the prospective purchaser by the **9.75** seller (provided, of course, there is a genuine obligation to disclose the information).

9.76 This may have both legal and practical implications. Legally, given the effect of Regulation 39, it appears that a seller may have no remedy against the prospective purchaser for non-compliance (although a potential buyer may seek to insert a specific carve-out into the confidentiality or non-disclosure agreement permitting disclosure 'as required by law'). From a practical perspective, however, a prospective purchaser is likely to be concerned that onward disclosure of relevant information may result in its exclusion from the transaction. And, from the seller's perspective, the principal practical concern is that it may not be able to control the non-disclosure of sensitive information. In order to secure some control over the possible disclosure of sensitive information, the seller may require that the basis and timing of any disclosure should be decided in consultation with the seller.

J. OBLIGATIONS IN RELATION TO PRE-EXISTING AGREEMENTS

9.77 As explained in paragraphs 9.10 and 9.25 above, Regulations 25 and 26 do not apply in respect of pre-existing agreements. In the absence of any express provision, employers are likely to have limited protection if confidentiality terms in a pre-existing agreement are breached (for example, action against an offending employee for breach of confidentiality obligations in the employment contract).

9.78 Because Regulations 25 and 26 do not apply employer and employee representatives are therefore free to identify and agree between themselves how they will treat confidential information in any pre-existing agreement. In principle, therefore, the employer could take a very broad (and subjective) view as to what information or documents are confidential and can be withheld. However the employer will need to be mindful of practical considerations. If too restrictive an approach is taken and the agreement is consequentially seen by employees as insufficiently balanced there is a greater risk of an employee request for a negotiated agreement (see further Chapter 4 for the implications of this).

9.79 The employer will normally also want to make the confidentiality provisions of a pre-existing agreement legally enforceable (even if the remaining provisions of the pre-existing agreement are not legally binding) so that there is a remedy in the event of a breach.

It is strongly recommended that employers should make very clear in any **9.80**
pre-existing agreement what type of information is to be designed as confidential, when it can be withheld, and the consequences of any breach of confidentiality by information and consultation representatives.

10

Protections for Information and Consultation Representatives and Contracting-Out

10.01 This chapter considers the various protections the ICE Regulations give to negotiating representatives, information and consultation representatives, and others. The scope of the protections is aimed at ensuring that employee representatives and others are able to perform their duties effectively by imposing sanctions on an employer for dismissing them or subjecting them to a detriment for performing their functions, or seeking to do so. The approach is similar to that provided in a range of other employment legislation including TUPE, TULRCA, the Health & Safety (Consultation with Employees) Regulations 1996, TICE, and provisions relating amongst other things to working time, whistle-blowing, flexible working, and a range of other areas.

10.02 This chapter starts by looking at the provisions aimed at facilitating the proper exercise of the employee representative's duties. It then looks at the non-dismissal and non-detriment provisions.

10.03 The chapter also considers the restrictions on contracting out from the provisions of the ICE Regulations (both in relation to protections for information and consultation representatives and others, and more generally).

A. TIME OFF

1. Right to Time Off

Regulation 27 provides that an employee who is either a negotiating representative or an information and consultation representative is entitled to be permitted by his employer to take reasonable time off during the employee's working hours in order to perform his functions as such a representative (Regulation 27(1)). **10.04**

Working hours for the purposes of Regulation 27 are taken to be any time when, in accordance with his contract of employment, the employee is required to be at work (Regulation 27(2)). **10.05**

As described in more detail in Chapter 5 a negotiating representative is a person elected or appointed under Regulation 14(1)(a) for the purpose of negotiating an information and consultation arrangement. An information and consultation representative is a person who has been appointed or elected as such pursuant to a negotiated agreement for information and consultation. Where the standard provisions for information and consultation apply, an information and consultation representative is someone elected as prescribed in Regulation 19. **10.06**

In keeping with the general principle that pre-existing agreements fall substantially outside the scope of the ICE Regulations, representatives under a pre-existing agreement are not given any right to time off, reasonable or otherwise, under the ICE Regulations. Consideration should therefore be given to whether it is appropriate to incorporate suitable provisions relating to time off in a pre-existing agreement. **10.07**

The Regulations do not define 'reasonable time off'. However, case-law relating to equivalent provisions in other legislation indicates that the test of 'reasonableness' is an objective one, taking account of what is reasonable in all the circumstances (*Wignall v British Gas Corporation and Borders Regional Council v Maule*[1]), but having regard in particular to the following factors: **10.08**

- how much time off is required to perform the functions;
- how much time off the employee has already been permitted for this purpose; and

[1] [1984] ICR 716, and [1993] ICR 199.

- the circumstances of the employer's business and the effect of the employee's absence upon it.

10.09 Representatives do not have a right to time off for training purposes (it would seem difficult to argue that, whilst in training, an employee is performing functions as a representative).

2. Right to Be Paid for Time Off

10.10 An employee who is permitted to take time off under Regulation 27 is entitled to be paid remuneration by his employer for the time taken off at the appropriate hourly rate (Regulation 28(1)).

10.11 Regulation 28 effectively replicates the provisions of section 62 of the Employment Rights Act 1996. The provisions of Chapter II of Part XIV of the Employment Rights Act 1996 apply to the calculation of a week's pay for these purposes in the same way as they apply to employee representatives or candidates for employee representatives in relation to collective redundancies or business transfers.

10.12 The appropriate hourly rate, in relation to an employee, is the amount of one week's pay divided by the number of normal working hours in a week for that employee when employed under the contract of employment in force on the day when time off is taken (Regulation 28(3)).

10.13 However, Regulation 28(4) provides that where the number of normal working hours differs from week to week or over a longer period, the amount of one week's pay is divided instead by:

(a) the average number of normal working hours calculated by dividing by 12 the total number of the employee's normal working hours during the period of 12 weeks ending with the last complete week before the day on which the time is taken off; or

(b) where the employee has not been employed for a sufficient period to enable the calculations to be made under sub-paragraph (a), a number which fairly represents the number of normal working hours in a week having regard to such of two relevant considerations as are appropriate in the circumstances.

10.14 The two relevant considerations in question are the average number of normal working hours in a week which the employee could expect in accordance with the terms of his contract, and the average number of normal working hours of other employees engaged in relevant comparable employment with the same employer (Regulation 28(5)).

Example 10.1
Employee A works from 9.30 a.m. to 5.30 p.m. Monday to Friday with one hour for lunch. His annual salary is £20,000. The appropriate hourly rate is determined by dividing his week's pay, £384.62, by 35, i.e. £10.99 per hour.[2]

Example 10.2
Employee B works a variable pattern of hours under which over a 12-week cycle he works 45 hours in the first four weeks, 30 hours in the next 4 weeks, and 45 hours in the last four weeks. His annual salary is £20,000. In accordance with Regulation 28(4), the average number of normal weekly working hours in this 12-week period was 40, i.e. (45 × 4) + (30 × 4) + (45 × 4) ÷ 12. The appropriate hourly rate is determined by dividing his week's pay, £384.62, by 40, i.e. £9.62.

The right of an information and consultation representative or negotiating representative to be paid for reasonable time off in the performance of his duties does not affect any right of that person in relation to remuneration under his contract of employment (Regulation 28(6)). **10.15**

Regulation 28(7) makes clear that any contractual remuneration paid to an employee in respect of a period of time off under Regulation 27 goes towards discharging any liability of the employer to pay remuneration under Regulation 28(1) and that conversely any payment of remuneration under Regulation 28(1) in respect of a period goes towards discharging any liability of the employer to pay contractual remuneration in respect of that period. **10.16**

3. Disputes Relating to Time Off

Any disputes relating to time off fall within the jurisdiction of the employment tribunal. Regulation 29 permits an employee to present a complaint to the employment tribunal that his employer: **10.17**

(a) has unreasonably refused to permit him to take time off as required to perform his functions in accordance with Regulation 27; or
(b) has failed to pay the whole or part of any amount to which the employee is entitled as pay for reasonable time off in accordance with Regulation 28.

A complaint must be made before the end of the period of three months beginning with the day on which the time off was taken or on which it is alleged the time off should have been permitted. There is a residual power **10.18**

[2] Where the employee undertakes overtime, the normal working hours are the fixed number or minimum number of hours as set out in the contract of employment, even if this number exceeds the number of hours without overtime (ss234(2) and (3) Employment Rights Act 1996).

for an employment tribunal to permit an application within such further period as the tribunal considers reasonable in a case where it is satisfied that it was not reasonably practicable for the complaint to be presented before the end of the three-month period (Regulation 29(2))(b). A recent example of a broader approach to the question of reasonable practicability is *Marks & Spencer plc v Williams-Ryan*.[3] This was an unfair dismissal case but the principles ought to be equally applicable to a complaint under the ICE Regulations. In *Ryan*, the applicant was allowed to bring a claim before the employment tribunal, notwithstanding the expiry of the time limit, because she had been advised to exhaust all internal appeal procedures prior to bringing such a claim and she was not aware of the time limit. The allowance was in part made because the applicant brought her claim within a reasonable period of being notified of the outcome of her internal appeal.

10.19 If the employment tribunal finds the complaint to be well- founded it is required to make a declaration to that effect (Regulation 29(3)).

10.20 In addition, if the complaint is that the employer has unreasonably refused to permit the employee to take time off, the employment tribunal shall also order the employer to pay to the employee an amount equal to the remuneration to which he would have been entitled under Regulation 28 if the employer had not refused (Regulation 29(4)). Regulation 29(4) may be contrasted with the broader provision in section 172(2) of TULRCA, which states that 'the amount of the compensation shall be such as the tribunal considers just and equitable in all the circumstances having regard to the employer's default in failing to permit time off to be taken by the employee and to any loss sustained by the employee which is attributable to the matters complained of'.

10.21 If the complaint is that the employer has failed to pay the employee the whole or part of any amount to which he is entitled under Regulation 28, the employment tribunal shall also order the employer to pay to the employee the amount it finds due to him (Regulation 29(5)).

B. PROTECTION AGAINST DETRIMENT AND UNFAIR DISMISSAL

10.22 The ICE Regulations also seek to protect employee representatives and others from being subjected to sanctions for seeking to enforce their rights under the ICE Regulations. These include protection against dismissal

[3] [2005] IRLR 562.

(achieved, in a similar fashion to other recent legislation, by introducing new categories of automatically unfair dismissal) and protection against other detriment short of dismissal.

1. Right Not to Be Unfairly Dismissed

In relation to dismissal, the ICE Regulations provide that the dismissal of a representative is automatically unfair where the reason (or, if more than one, the principal reason) for the dismissal is a reason specified in either Regulation 30(3) or 30(6). 'Principal reason' is undefined, but in a case relating to automatically unfair dismissal that occurred where an employee took time off under section 57A of the Employment Rights Act 1996 in order to assist a dependant who had fallen ill, it has been held that it represents a higher threshold than for discrimination cases, where the discrimination must be a substantial or effective reason for the dismissal (*Hollick v Leonard t/a Leonard Mann & Co.*[4]). **10.23**

The protection provided by Regulation 30(2) applies to: **10.24**

(a) an employees' representative;
(b) a negotiating representative;
(c) an information and consultation representative; or
(d) a candidate in an election in which any person elected will, on being elected, be such a representative (Regulation 30(2)).

As noted elsewhere in this book, an employee representative is not defined in the ICE Regulations. It will include trade union representatives and presumably others elected or appointed for general information and consultation purposes. Employees' representatives are given a number of rights and powers under the ICE Regulations, including the right to request data on the number of employees within the undertaking (see further Chapter 2) and to make various complaints to the CAC (for example in relation to a ballot to endorse an employee representative when there is a pre-existing agreement in place (see further Chapter 4) or in relation to the appointment or election of regulatory representatives (see Chapter 5)). **10.25**

A dismissal will be automatically unfair under Regulation 30(3) where the reason or principal reason for dismissal is that: **10.26**

(a) the employee performed or proposed to perform any functions or activities as such a representative or candidate; or

[4] 2002, ET 3301504 unrep.

(b) the employee exercised or proposed to exercise an entitlement conferred on the employee by Regulation 27 or 28 (i.e. a request to reasonable time off or to be paid in respect of such time off); or

(c) the employee (or a person acting on his behalf) made or proposed to make a request to exercise such an entitlement (Regulation 30(3)).

10.27 There is, however, one narrow exception from the principle that a dismissal in these circumstances will be automatically unfair. The dismissal of an employee for performing or proposing to perform any functions or activities as an employees' representative or candidate (i.e. for a reason specified in Regulation 30(3)(a)) is not automatically unfair if the reason (or principal reason) for the dismissal is that in the performance, or purported performance, of the employee's functions or activities he has disclosed any information or document in breach of a duty of confidentiality imposed in accordance with Regulation 25 (Regulation 30(4)). This is to make clear that an employer can dismiss an employee representative who fails to comply with a duty of confidentiality in relation to information or documents disclosed to him (see further Chapter 9). A dismissal in these circumstances may nevertheless be unfair on normal procedural grounds.

10.28 It should also be noted that a dismissal for disclosing any information or document in breach of the duty in Regulation 25 may still be automatically unfair if the employee reasonably believed the disclosure in question to be a 'protected disclosure' within the meaning given to that expression by section 43A of the Employment Rights Act 1996 (see further Chapter 9).

10.29 In addition to the protection under Regulations 30(2) and (3) mentioned above for employee representatives and candidates, Regulations 30(5) and 30(6) extend in a number of defined situations the application of protection against unfair dismissal to any employee who has been dismissed for specific reasons relating to the exercise or attempted exercise by him of rights in connection with the ICE Regulations, regardless of whether or not he is a representative as defined within Regulation 30(2).

10.30 Under Regulation 30(6), a dismissal will be automatically unfair if the reason (or, if more than one, the principal reason) for the dismissal is that the employee:

(a) took, or proposed to take, any proceedings before an employment tribunal to enforce a right or secure an entitlement conferred on him by the ICE Regulations;

(b) exercised, or proposed to exercise, any entitlement to apply or complain to the CAC or the EAT conferred by the ICE Regulations;

(c) requested, or proposed to request as envisaged in Regulation 5, data on the numbers of employees within the employer's undertaking;

(d) acted with a view to securing that an agreement was or was not negotiated or that the standard information and consultation provisions did or did not become applicable;

(e) indicated that he supported or did not support the coming into existence of a negotiated agreement or the application of the standard information and consultation provisions;

(f) stood as a candidate in an election in which any person elected would, on being elected, be a negotiating representative or an information and consultation representative;

(g) influenced or sought to influence by lawful means the way in which votes would be cast by other employees in a ballot arranged under the ICE Regulations;

(h) voted in such a ballot;

(i) expressed doubts, whether to a ballot supervisor or otherwise, as to whether such a ballot had been properly conducted; or

(j) proposed to do, failed to do, or proposed to decline to do, any of the things mentioned in sub-paragraphs (d) to (i) above.

It will be seen from the above that the protection accorded to employees in **10.31** connection with the operation of the ICE Regulations is wide-ranging and is intended to ensure that rights conferred by the ICF Regulations can be freely exercised.

Furthermore, it is immaterial whether the employee actually has the **10.32** right in question or whether the right has actually been infringed provided that the employee's claim to the right and, if applicable, the claim that it has been infringed must be made by the employee in good faith (Regulation 30(7)).

The Employment Act 2002 (Dispute Resolution) Regulations 2004 (the **10.33** *Dispute Resolution Regulations*) will apply to any claim of unfair dismissal under the ICE Regulations. Accordingly, a failure by an employee to raise and pursue a grievance under the Dispute Resolution Regulations will result in the reduction of any compensation by between 10 and 50%.

Various adjustments have also been made to other statutory provisions **10.34** to bolster the protection given to employees in the circumstances. Thus, by inserting a new section 105(7G) in the Employment Right Act 1996, the ICE Regulations make it automatically unfair to dismiss an employee as redundant if the reason (or, if more than one, the principal reason) for which the employee was selected for dismissal was one of the specified reasons summarized in paragraphs 10.26 and 10.30 above (Regulation 31(1)).

10.35 Similarly, the one-year qualifying period for a claim of unfair dismissal is disapplied in relation to any dismissal that is automatically unfair under the ICE Regulations (by adding a new sub-section (k) to section 108 of the Employment Rights Act 1996). Nor does the upper age limit on bringing a claim apply when the dismissal is automatically unfair under the ICE Regulations (this is achieved by adding a new sub-section (k) to section 109 of the Employment Rights Act 1996).

2. Right Not to Be Subjected to Detriment

10.36 In the same way as with a range of other employment legislation, Regulation 32 also protects employee representatives and others from being subjected to any detrimental act or omission not amounting to dismissal in connection with the exercise or attempted exercise of rights under the ICE Regulations.

10.37 Regulation 32(2) provides that any employee who is:

(a) an employee's representative;
(b) a negotiating representative;
(c) an information and consultation representative; or
(d) a candidate in an election in which any person elected, will, on being elected be such a representative

has the right not to be subjected to any detriment by any act or deliberate failure to act by his employer, done on a specified ground. Regulation 32(5) extends the protection afforded by Regulation 32 to any employee, regardless of whether or not he is a representative as defined within Regulation 32(2).

10.38 The specified grounds referred to in Regulation 32(2) are the same as those that would give rise to automatic unfair dismissal if the employee was dismissed (see paragraphs 10.26 and 10.30). The detriment provisions do not apply where the detriment in question amounts to dismissal (Regulation 32(8)).

10.39 As with automatic unfair dismissal, there is an exception from the requirement not to cause a detriment where the employee being subjected to a detriment has in the performance or the proposed performance of his functions or activities as a representative or candidate disclosed any information or documents in breach of a duty of confidentiality imposed in accordance with Regulation 25 (although as with dismissal the exception does not apply where the employee reasonably believed the disclosure to be a 'protected disclosure' within the meaning given to that expression by section 43A of the Employment Rights Act 1996).

An employee who believes he has been subjected to a detriment in contravention of Regulation 32 may present a complaint to an employment tribunal (Regulation 33(1)). **10.40**

In terms of remedy, the provisions of sections 48(2) to (4) and 49(1) to (5) of the Employment Rights Act 1996 apply to any complaint brought under Regulation 33. **10.41**

A complaint must be made before the end of the period of three months beginning with the date of the act or failure to act to which the complaint relates or, where that act or failure is part of a series of similar acts or failures, the last of them. There is a residual power for an employment tribunal to permit an application within such further period as the tribunal considers reasonable in a case where it is satisfied that it was not reasonably practicable for the complaint to be presented before the end of that period of three months. **10.42**

For these purposes, where an act extends over a period, the 'date of the act' means that the last date of that period, and a deliberate failure to act shall be treated as done when it was decided on. In the absence of evidence establishing the contrary, an employee shall be taken to decide on the failure to act when he does an act inconsistent with doing the failed act or, if he has done no such inconsistent act, when the period expires within which he might reasonably have been expected to do the failed act if it was to be done (section 48(4) Employment Rights Act 1996). **10.43**

As with a complaint for unfair dismissal, the Dispute Resolution Regulations will apply in respect of any claim. This requires a written grievance to be submitted prior to any claim and the employer to be given at least 28 days to respond. **10.44**

In relation to any such complaint, it is for the employer to show the ground on which any act, or deliberate failure to act, was done (section 48(2) Employment Rights Act 1996). In other words, the employer needs to establish that the principal reason for subjecting the employee to a detriment is not one of the reasons specified in Regulation 32. **10.45**

If an employment tribunal finds a complaint to be well founded, it is required to make a declaration to that effect and may make an award of compensation to be paid by the employer to the complainant in respect of the act or failure to act to which the complaint relates. **10.46**

The amount of compensation is such amount as the employment tribunal considers just and equitable in all the circumstances. In assessing what **10.47** is just and equitable, the employment tribunal must have regard to the infringement to which the complaint relates and any loss which is attributable to the act, or failure to act, which infringed the complainant's right. There is no limit on the compensation that can be awarded. This is consistent with the provisions in section 49 of the Employment Rights Act 1996, which apply to complaints of detriment in respect of other types of employee representatives mentioned in section 47 of the Employment Rights Act 1996.

10.48 Such loss shall be taken to include the expenses reasonably incurred by the complainant in consequence of the act or failure to act, to which the complaint relates and loss of any benefits that he might reasonably be expected to have had but for that act or failure to act.

10.49 The employment tribunal will apply the same principles concerning the duty to mitigate as apply in common law to calculation of the loss suffered by a complainant, and compensation may also be reduced by such proportion as the employment tribunal considers just and equitable if the tribunal makes a finding that the act, or failure to act, to which the complaint relates was to any extent caused or contributed to by any action of the complainant (sections 49(4) and (5) Employment Rights Act 1996).

3. Conciliation

10.50 Regulation 34 gives ACAS jurisdiction to conciliate disputes under Regulations 29 or 33 relating to protection against dismissal or detriment by adding a new paragraph (p) to section 18 Employment Tribunals Act 1996.

C. NO CONTRACTING-OUT

10.51 The Regulations further seek to protect employees by limiting the right of the parties to contract out of the provisions of the ICE Regulations.

10.52 In relation to the protections for information and consultation representatives and others summarized in this chapter, Regulation 40 provides as follows:

> Any provision in any agreement (whether an employee's contract or not) is void insofar as it purports:
> (a) to exclude or limit the operation of any provision of Part VIII; or
> (b) to preclude a person from bringing any proceedings before an employment tribunal under that Part.

10.53 Any clause in an employee's contract of employment, or indeed in any other form of agreement (including an agreement with a third party), that purports to exclude the protections for employee representatives and others outlined in this chapter will therefore be void under this provision.

The restriction on contracting-out is subject to two important exceptions. First, it does not apply to any agreement to refrain from instituting or continuing proceedings before an employment tribunal where an ACAS conciliation officer has taken action under section 18 of the Employment Tribunals Act 1996. Secondly, contracting-out is permissible for the purposes of a compromise agreement. **10.54**

The normal conditions must apply for a compromise agreement to be valid, namely: **10.55**

(a) the agreement must be in writing;
(b) the agreement must relate to the particular proceedings;
(c) the employee must have received advice from a relevant independent advisor as to the terms and the effect of the proposed agreement and, in particular, its affect on his ability to pursue his rights before an employment tribunal;
(d) when the adviser gives the advice, either a contract of insurance or an indemnity provided for members of a profession or professional body must be in force covering the risk of a claim by the employee in respect of loss arising in consequence of the advice;
(e) the agreement must identify the advisor; and
(f) the agreement must state that the conditions in sub-paragraphs (a) to (e) are satisfied.

Regulation 39 deals with contracting-out from the provisions of the ICE Regulations more generally (i.e. the provisions apart from those relating specifically to protections for information and consultation representatives and others). The approach is similar to that taken in other employment legislation, such as TUPE. It prevents the employer from disapplying any provision of the ICE Regulations. **10.56**

Regulation 39(1) provides as follows: **10.57**

> Any provision in any agreement (whether an employee's contract or not) is void insofar as it purposes:
> (a) to exclude or limit the operation of any provision of these Regulations other than a provision of Part VIII; or
> (b) to preclude a person from bringing any proceedings before the Central Arbitration Committee or the Employment Appeal Tribunal under any provision of these Regulations other than a provision of Part VIII.

The provisions of Regulation 39(1) do not apply to any agreement to refrain from continuing any proceedings referred to in sub-paragraph **10.58**

(b) above after the proceedings have been instituted. In other words, a claim or complaint can be validly settled by the parties without breaching the no contracting-out rules.

10.59 Again, the restriction against contracting-out applies to a provision in any form of agreement, including an agreement with a third party.

10.60 As the DTI Guidance makes clear, Regulation 39 does not prevent parties from agreeing whatever arrangements they may consider appropriate for information and consultation under a negotiated agreement. That is because the ICE Regulations expressly envisage and permit arrangements other than those specified by the standard information and consultation provisions to be agreed between the parties. However a negotiated agreement would not be able validly to prevent representatives from bringing a complaint for breach of the negotiated agreement or (for example) to exclude access to confidential information on a more limited basis than provided for by Regulations 25 and 26. By contrast, the provisions of Regulation 39 would not apply to a pre-existing agreement in those circumstances because Regulations 25 and 26 do not apply to pre-existing agreements.

11

How Do We Compare?

This chapter analyses information and consultation rights in France, Germany, and the Netherlands. It does not cover the collective representation rights in each country in relation to collective dismissals, which are generally outside the scope of this book. Rather it focusses on the general rights of the domestic works councils in each of these jurisdictions. **11.01**

A. INFORMATION AND CONSULTATION RIGHTS IN FRANCE

1. Overview of Employee Representation in France

The system of employee representation is well established in France and continues to develop, both through case-law and through French legislative intervention. It became a legal obligation in 1936, with legislation on works councils dating from 1945. The system is relatively complex, allowing representation at various levels within an organization and **11.02** with an active part being played by French trade unions. The extent of the domestic legislation already in place meant that no further legislation was required in France to implement the Information and Consultation Directive.

11.03 Under French law, if certain conditions are met, three separate staff representative bodies may need to be established, that is, a staff delegate body, a works council, and a health and safety committee. In addition, trade unions can appoint employees to act as their representatives within an employing entity.

2. Staff Delegates (*Délégués du Personnel*)

11.04 Staff delegates must be elected in all establishments with a workforce of at least 11 people. They are elected by the workforce every two years, and may stand for election more than once.

Rights of Staff Delegates

11.05 Staff delegates may present the employer with collective or individual demands concerning:

- the workforce;
- the application of the French Labour Code and other laws and regulations relating to social benefits and health and safety;
- the application of collective bargaining and other collective agreements.

11.06 The employer must hold monthly meetings with the staff delegates in order to take note of their demands.

11.07 Staff delegates are allowed paid time off to carry out their duties (10 or 15 hours per month, depending on the number of employees at the establishment).

11.08 The role of staff delegates can include the following: discussing dates for paid holidays with the employer; being consulted on collective redundancies (in companies with fewer than 50 employees); receiving information on collective bargaining and collective agreements. They also have access to the staff register (the register containing the names of all employees and information relating to them) and to working time records.

Additional Rights of Staff Delegates

Staff delegates act in place of the works council and the health and safety committee in companies with at least 50 employees, where no such bodies have been set up (e.g. because no candidates stood for election). **11.09**

In a company with fewer than 50 employees, a staff delegate can be appointed by a trade union to serve as a union delegate (see the section on trade unions below). **11.10**

Election of Staff Delegates

Staff delegates are elected according to an electoral process that takes a minimum of one and a half months. It is a relatively complex process. There are precise rules on who can vote and who can be a candidate. In addition, the national unions must be invited at the initial stage of the electoral process (1) to negotiate an agreement regarding the organization of the election; and (2) to nominate candidates. **11.11**

3. Works Councils

A company with at least 50 employees must give its staff the opportunity to elect a works council. **11.12**

Where a company has several autonomous establishments, a works council must be set up in each such establishment, and a central works council must also be set up. The central works council is made up of the head of the company, an elected delegation made up of works council members from the various establishments, and optional representation from trade union organizations. **11.13**

The works council is chaired by the head of the employer (or his/her delegate), and is made up of elected members and of trade union representatives (the latter are not entitled to vote). The works council must meet at least once a month (and at the request of at least half the elected members). Works council members are entitled to take time off (20 hours per month in addition to works council meetings) to conduct their works council duties. **11.14**

In certain situations, the works council is entitled to appoint an expert (e.g. an accountant) to advise it, with the expert's fees being paid by the employer. **11.15**

The works council's role is to ensure that the workforce has a collective voice, and that its views are taken into account on an ongoing basis. The **11.16** employer has to give the works council a range of economic and other information, and must also consult the works council on various matters. This is discussed further below.

11.17 The works council also manages or oversees all social and cultural activities that take place in the company for the benefit of the workforce or their families, such as staff provident and contingency funds, medical services, and leisure and sports activities. The works council has a budget for these purposes, which is funded by the employer.

11.18 The process for electing the works council members is broadly the same as that described above for staff delegates.

11.19 In companies with fewer than 200 employees, the head of the company may decide that the staff delegates should also serve on the works council (Section L. 431–1–1 of the Labour Code). The same elected officials will therefore act both as works council members and as staff delegates.

Group Works Council

11.20 A group works council must be set up within a group of companies where a 'dominant undertaking' controls or exerts a dominant influence over the other members of the group. The role of the group works council is relatively limited. It is merely entitled to receive information, for example about the group's business, financial position, economic perspectives, and employment development and forecasts and does not have the right to be consulted.

4. Trade Unions

11.21 Five trade union confederations are deemed to be representative nationwide in France, no matter what the employer's area of activity. These organizations need not prove that they are representative, and may accordingly take part in collective bargaining as of right, both at company level and industry-wide. Other trade union organizations must prove that they are 'representative'.

11.22 At company level, representative trade unions can play a role in the following ways:

(a) they can set up a 'section'; and
(b) they can then appoint union delegates.

Trade Union Sections

Each representative trade union may set up a 'section' in any company, without any particular formalities. A union section represents the interests of its members. 11.23

Trade Union Delegates

In principle, trade union delegates may be appointed only in companies with a workforce of over 50. However, in companies with a workforce of fewer than 50, staff delegates may be appointed as trade union delegates. 11.24

The number of trade union delegates appointed per establishment (one to five) depends on the size of the workforce. 11.25

The role of trade union delegates is to represent their trade union in dealings with the company's management. They take part in (and indeed have a monopoly over) collective negotiations with the company. Collective agreements made between the company and trade union delegates confer rights and obligations on the entire workforce, not just the members of the trade unions in question. 11.26

Significant changes to the law on collective bargaining were made in May 2004. In particular: 11.27

(1) previously, a collective agreement was valid provided it was signed by a representative trade union. Following the 2004 legislation, a collective agreement will only be valid if it has been signed by one or more trade unions representing a majority (or, if it has not been opposed, by unions representing a majority).
(2) the 2004 law considerably expanded the areas in which collective bargaining within a company can adapt and/or derogate from legal requirements.

The employer must allow trade union delegates paid time off to discharge their duties, between 10 and 20 hours per month depending on the company's size. 11.28

5. Works Council Information/Consultation Rights

Periodic Information Rights

The works council is entitled to receive information about the company, including the following: 11.29

- within one month of its being elected: details of the company's legal structure and organization, its economic position, its position within the group, and the distribution of the company's share capital between shareholders with at least 10% of capital;

- a quarterly report on general trends in production, levels of orders, and the company's financial situation; and
- a quarterly or bi-annual report on the number of employees, with details of fixed-term, part-time, and temporary workers and external contractors' workers present in the company.

It is also given:

- the company's annual report (and other shareholder documents/communications) that are before the general meeting of shareholders;
- an annual report containing a variety of information of concern to the workforce, including turnover, profits/losses, production volumes/values, headcount variations, level of use of subcontractors, level of remuneration for each category of employee, details of occupational accidents. Companies with over 300 employees must provide additional details of productivity and production capacity trends; and
- an annual report comparing the employment conditions and training arrangements applicable to male and female staff.

Companies with over 300 employees must also provide an annual employment report (*bilan social*) containing detailed data covering a number of topics including remuneration, health and safety conditions, other working conditions (such as working time), and training. The works council issues an opinion on this report.

The works council may be advised by an accountant, whose fees must, in some cases, be paid by the employer.

Exceptional Information and Consultation Rights

11.30 As well as having the right to certain information at regular intervals throughout the year, the works council must also be consulted:

(1) on questions concerning the organization, management, and general functioning of the business, including measures liable to affect the volume or structure of the workforce, working time, working and employment conditions, and training arrangements;

(2) on questions affecting the company's structure, notably:
- any major change in production structures, or to the company's economic or legal structure;
- in the event of a merger, transfer, or sale of the company, where subsidiaries are purchased or sold, and where shares in the company change hands;

(3) when a headcount reduction is envisaged (note that onerous consultation procedures must be followed where collective dismissals are planned);

(4) on questions relating to the company's general operations, notably:
- company research and development policy;
- any plans to borrow funds or issue new equity;
- personnel policy (including recruitment and training);
- collection and transfer of personal data relating to employees;
- participation (profit-sharing);
- working time; and
- company rules and regulations;

(5) when the company is faced with possible insolvency; and

(6) where the company is party to a *concentration operation* (i.e. a transaction triggering an obligation to notify French or European competition authorities).

The works council has a statutory right to be informed when a public takeover bid is made for the company, and (if it wishes) may summon the bidder to a meeting in order to make observations to the bidder. If the bidder does not attend, it is barred from exercising voting rights attaching to its shares in the target. **11.31**

Meaning of Consultation

Consultation has a specific meaning. Firstly the company must provide the works council with a written statement of all relevant information. This includes: **11.32**

(1) details of the proposal in question;
(2) the legal, social, economic, and financial implications of the proposal for affected employees;
(3) any envisaged measure(s) and their impact (e.g. on pay, working conditions, relocation, redundancies).

After consultation, the works council gives its opinion on the proposal. The employer is under no obligation to act in accordance with the works council's opinion but it is obliged to obtain the opinion in order for the consultation process to be completed. This means that the works council can prolong the consultation procedure by asking for further information. It can refuse to give an opinion until its questions have been answered. **11.33**

The requirement to obtain an opinion goes beyond the definition of consultation used in the Information and Consultation Directive (which refers to 'the exchange of views and establishment of dialogue'). The **11.34**

Directive did not follow the more onerous definition of 'consultation' that appears in Directive 2001/86 on employee involvement in a European company. That definition is closer to the French notion of consultation, referring to 'the establishment of dialogue and exchange of views . . . at a time, in a manner and with a content which allows the employees' representatives, on the basis of information provided, to express an opinion on measures envisaged by the competent organ which may be taken into account in the decision-making process'.

Timing of Information and Consultation

11.35 The information and consultation process must be completed before the employer makes a decision. The information and consultation process must allow the works council a 'reasonable period' of time to formulate its opinion. Where the works council is consulted on collective dismissals, the timetable varies depending on the number of employees affected.

11.36 A meeting agenda should be agreed with the works council secretary and given to all members of the works council at least three days before the meeting (eight days in the case of a central works council). The documents setting out the information for the works council on the proposed transaction must be circulated in good time before the meeting.

11.37 The works council may, however, require further information during the first meeting. If so, it is advisable to convene another meeting.

11.38 The amount of time needed for the consultation process will depend on the complexity of the proposal and whether the works council agrees or disagrees with it. The works council may claim that it is unhappy with the information provided or that it has not been given sufficient time to consider the information, and can go to court to try to obtain an order for more time or information.

11.39 The works council cannot prevent the employer from implementing the proposal. However, an order from the court for more time or information may mean implementation is delayed until the time has elapsed or more information is given. The company is under no obligation to take account of the works council's views but it must give well-founded, complete answers to any questions raised by the works council before seeking the works council's formal opinion.

Failure to Comply with Information and Consultation Obligations

11.40 Non-compliance with the obligation to consult the works council is a criminal offence. The head of the employer (e.g. the managing director) could be ordered to pay a maximum fine of €3,750 and/or to serve a maximum one-year prison term. For a second offence the penalties are increased to a fine of up to €7,500 and two years' imprisonment.

However, the most common and effective way in which the works council can try to force the employer to comply with its information/consultation obligations is to seek a court order suspending implementation of the proposal until the company fulfils those obligations. The company may incur a daily penalty throughout this suspension period if it fails to comply with the order. **11.41**

B. INFORMATION AND CONSULTATION RIGHTS IN GERMANY

1. Overview of Employee Representation in Germany

Germany has a complex system of employee representation which operates at several levels. **11.42**

Although the Information and Consultation Directive was to have been implemented in Germany by 23 March 2005, a draft bill has yet to be published. However, given the existing comprehensive information and consultation rights of works councils, no substantial amendments or modifications are expected to implement the requirements of the Directive into German law. **11.43**

Those companies which employ 500 or more employees are required to ensure that one-third of the members of the supervisory board (*Aufsichtsrat*) are elected employee representatives (*Drittelbeteiligungsgesetz*). In companies which regularly employ 2000 or more employees, half of the supervisory board must be composed of elected employee representatives (*Mitbestimmungsgesetz*). Employee representation on a supervisory board is outside the scope of this chapter. **11.44**

The main employee representation system in Germany is referred to as the 'works constitution' (*Betriebsverfassung*) system. This is governed by the Works Constitution Act (*Betriebsverfassungsgesetz/BetrVG*). Under this Act, employees have the right to elect a works council (*Betriebsrat*) in establishments/businesses that regularly employ five or more employees.[1] Where a company has several establishments (e.g. several plants in different cities) at least two of which have a works council, the works councils have to establish a company works council (*Gesamtbetriebsrat*) which **11.45**

[1] S1(1) *BetrVG*.

operates at company level.[2] The company works council is responsible for matters that concern the whole undertaking or several of the establishments and which cannot be regulated by the various local works councils at plant level.[3]

11.46 In the case of a group of undertakings, the company works councils or, in their absence, the plant level works councils may establish a group works council (*Konzernbetriebsrat*) provided that certain minimum requirements are met.[4] The group works council is responsible for matters which concern the group of undertakings or several companies in the group and which cannot be regulated by the company works councils. The Works Constitution Act also recognizes employee representative bodies for special groups of employees such as young employees, apprentices, and disabled employees.

11.47 The German works constitution system has a long tradition dating back to the first Works Councils Act (*Betriebsrätegesetz*) of 1920. Notably, in 1946 the Allied powers revived the German works constitution system after the Second World War by enacting Control Council Law No. 22 (*Kontrollratsgesetz Nr. 22*), a precursor to today's *Betriebsverfassungsgesetz*.

2. Participation of Works Councils

11.48 Works councils are elected by, and responsible for, all employees except for members of the managing body representing the company (e.g. the managing director of a *Gesellschaft mit beschränkter Haftung* (*GmbH*) (limited liability company)) and certain other managerial/senior employees (*leitende Angestellte*), i.e. employees with certain managerial powers whom the law regards to be part of management rather than the workforce (a key difference to the scope of the ICE Regulations, which contemplates that all employees, including management, should participate). Management employees do not take part in the election of the works council and are not represented by it. However, in establishments with at least 10 such employees, such employees can establish a speakers' committee (*Sprecherausschuss*).[5]

11.49 The works council or, depending on the issue at stake, the company or group works council has certain participation rights set out in the *Betriebsverfassungsgesetz*. These relate to certain social, personnel, and economic matters and range from the right to be informed, to consultation rights, to the power to veto certain decisions, to the power to have to consent to

[2] S47(1) *BetrVG*. [3] S50(1) *BetrVG*. [4] S54(1) *BetrVG*.
[5] S1(1) Speakers' Committee Act (*Sprecherausschussgesetz*).

actions of the employer. If the works council's consent is required, the usual form in which such consent is given is by way of a written works agreement (*Betriebsvereinbarung*) concluded between the employer and the works council. Such a works agreement is binding upon all employees represented by the works council.[6]

3. Works Councils in Practice

In Germany works councils in the work environment are relatively commonplace. As a general rule, the larger the company, the more likely it is that a works council will have been established. **11.50**

Employee representation within the works constitution system involves substantial financial expenditure on the part of the employer. According to a recent study, in 2003/04 the typical costs of the implementation of the Works Constitution Act for a German company were €650.12 per employee per year.[7] Despite the economic cost, however, a works council can be very beneficial for a company provided there is a relationship of trust between management and the works council. A works council can significantly contribute to effective co-operation between employees and management. In difficult situations (e.g. a redundancy scenario), works councils frequently share the responsibility for the difficult decisions that must be taken. Similar to the duty of co-operation set out in Regulation 21 of the ICE Regulations, the German works council and the employer must also observe their overriding duty to co-operate with each other in a spirit of mutual trust and confidence to the benefit of the employees and the establishment.[8] **11.51**

It should be noted that works councils are not the same as trade unions. Unions provide candidates in works council elections but normally there are other independent candidates as well. Often the employees who are elected are those whom the majority of the workforce regard as being most competent and trustworthy, irrespective of whether they are union members. **11.52**

4. Participation Rights of the Works Council in Matters Covered by the Information and Consultation Directive

The areas covered by the information and consultation duties set out in Article 4(2) of the Information and Consultation Directive relate to **11.53**

[6] Cf. s77(4) *BetrVG*.
[7] *Niedenhoff*, AuA 2004, 24.
[8] See s2(1) *BetrVG*.

economic matters[9] and personnel matters.[10] An outline of the rights of the works council in relation to these matters under the German *Betriebsverfassungsgesetz* (*BetrVG*) is set out below.

Economic Matters

11.54 Economic matters are part of the core tasks of management. Acknowledging this, the Act provides specifically that the works council must not interfere with the management of the establishment by taking unilateral actions.[11] Accordingly, as regards economic issues, the participation rights of the works council are relatively limited in comparison to other matters such as social or personnel matters. The consent of the works council is not required in relation to economic matters except in the event of significant operational changes (see below). In general the works council is entitled only to be informed and consulted about economic matters.

5. Information and Consultation of the Economic Committee

11.55 In all companies that regularly employ 100 or more employees, the company works council or, in the absence of a company works council, the plant level works council must establish an economic committee (*Wirtschaftsausschuss*). The economic committee is an auxiliary body of the works council and must consult with the employer on economic matters and inform the relevant works council about such consultation.[12] The employer must inform the economic committee in full about the economic matters in a timely fashion and provide any necessary documents, provided that this does not put the company's business or trade secrets at risk. The employer must also explain any impact on personnel planning.

Economic Matters

11.56 Section 106(3) *BetrVG* contains the following list of economic matters:

(1) the economic and financial situation of the company;
(2) the position regarding production and sales;
(3) the production and investment programme;
(4) rationalization plans;

[9] See art. 4(2) (a) ('development of the undertaking's or the establishment's activities and economic situation') and (c) ('decisions likely to lead to substantial changes in work organisation or in contractual relations') of the Information and Consultation Directive.

[10] See art. 4(2) (b) ('situation, structure and probable development of employment within the undertaking or establishment and on any anticipatory measures envisaged, in particular where there is a threat to employment') of the Information and Consultation Directive.

[11] S77(1) clause 2 *BetrVG*.

[12] Section 106(1) clause 2 *BetrVG*.

(5) production and working methods, including the introduction of new working methods;
(6) matters concerning occupational environmental protection;
(7) any cutback or closure of an establishment or part of an establishment;
(8) the relocation of an establishment or part of establishments;
(9) the merger or break-up of undertakings or establishments;
(10) the modification of an establishment's organization or of an establishment's purpose; and
(11) any other events or plans that may significantly affect the interests of the company's employees.

The final point on the list is a 'catch-all provision'. It applies, for example, if the company sells assets in an asset deal[13] or if a shareholder sells its shares in the company thereby selling the company. In the latter case, the employer must inform the economic committee of the name of the buyer, any relevant provisions in the purchase agreement, and any intentions of the buyer which may affect the company's employees.[14] However, the sale and purchase agreement itself does not have to be produced to the economic committee (because it relates to an economic matter of the shareholder and not of the company). **11.57**

Confidential Trade and Business Secrets

An exception to the duty to inform and consult the economic committee exists if the company's business or trade secrets are at risk, but this exception is narrowly construed. In practice it is difficult for a company to rely on this exception because the members of the economic committee are subject to a duty of confidentiality in relation to matters which are expressly designated to be confidential trade or business secrets. A breach of this duty of confidentiality is a criminal offence punishable with a fine or imprisonment of up to one year. **11.58**

Timing Issues

The economic committee should have a meeting with the employer once a month.[15] In practice, however, usually around four meetings a year take place unless special circumstances make additional meetings necessary. If, for example, a transaction is proposed which may significantly affect the employees' interests, the employer must inform the economic committee in good time about the proposed transaction. The **11.59**

[13] BAG (Federal Labour Court), 22.1.1991–1 ABR 38/89, AP Nr. 9 zu § 106 BetrVG 1972.
[14] BAG, 22.1.1991–1 ABR 38/89, AP Nr. 9 zu § 106 BetrVG 1972.
[15] S108(1) *BetrVG*.

information must be supplied to the economic committee before a final decision is taken by management to proceed with a particular proposal. In a transaction, this is normally before signing and in any event before closing.

Disputes

11.60 Disputes with works councils about whether the employer has fulfilled its obligations to the economic committee are rare. If the parties disagree as to whether a matter qualifies as an economic matter, as defined in section 106(3) *BetrVG*, either party may bring an action before the labour court for a determination. However, if the dispute is about the scope of the information duty or whether information is correctly classed as a trade or business secret and therefore not within the scope of the disclosure obligation, a hearing must take place before the settlement committee (*Einigungsstelle*) prior to any labour court litigation. The settlement committee is composed of an equal number of designates from the employer and the works council and is chaired by an impartial chairman.

11.61 Proceedings before the labour court or the settlement committee do not prevent a transaction from proceeding. However, if the employer gives false or incomplete information or provides it late, this constitutes an administrative offence punishable with a fine of up to €10,000.[16] If the employer is in material breach of its duties under the Act, the works council or any trade union represented in the establishment can bring an action before the labour court to compel the employer to undertake, or refrain from undertaking, a course of action.[17] This general rule also applies if the employer is in material breach of its duties to the economic committee.

Negotiation of a Reconciliation of Interests and a Social Plan with the Works Council

11.62 One of the most significant areas of works council involvement is where the employer plans to undertake measures which qualify as an operational change within the meaning of section 111 *BetrVG*. In this case, the employer has to inform and consult the works council and negotiate agreements concerning the implementation and consequences of the proposed actions (i.e. a reconciliation of interests (*Interessenausgleich*) and a social plan (*Sozialplan*)).

[16] S121 *BetrVG*. [17] S23(3) *BetrVG*.

Operational Changes

In undertakings that regularly employ more than 20 employees, the employer must comprehensively inform the works council of all proposed operational changes which can have significant disadvantages for the workforce or substantial parts of the workforce on a timely basis, and must consult about them.[18] Section 111 clause 3 *BetrVG* defines the following actions as operational changes within the above meaning: 11.63

- the reduction or closure of the whole establishment or substantial parts thereof;
- the relocation of the whole establishment or substantial parts thereof;
- a merger with other establishments or break-up of establishments;
- fundamental modifications to the establishment's organization, the establishment's purpose, or the establishment's installations;
- the introduction of new working methods and production methods.

The transfer of a business as a whole (section 613a Civil Code/BGB) without any dismissals in connection with the transfer does not qualify as an operational change. In contrast, the transfer of a part of a business often amounts to a break-up of an establishment within the meaning of section 111 clause 3 no. 3 *BetrVG*. 11.64

Information and Consultation

If the proposed change constitutes an operational change, the employer must inform the works council of the proposed measures, the reasons for them, and the consequences for the employees. It is advisable in those circumstances for the employer to prepare a thorough explanation and set this out in a written document which can be handed to the works council. Often the works council requests further information which it needs to be able to consult properly with the employer and prepare for negotiations. This may include, for example, the company's balance sheet or the report from external consultants proposing the restructuring. 11.65

Negotiation about Reconciliation of Interests and Social Plan

The information and consultation phase often merges into the negotiation about a reconciliation of interests and a social plan. The first agreement (i.e. the reconciliation of interests (*Interessenausgleich*)) is a timetable and regulates whether, how, and when the operational change will be implemented. 11.66

[18] S111 clause 1 *BetrVG*.

11.67 The second agreement to be negotiated with the relevant works council (i.e. the social plan (*Sozialplan*)) provides for measures to compensate or mitigate the economic detriment suffered by the affected employees. Such measures may include, for example, early retirement and old-age part-time employment schemes, outplacement counselling, indemnification for relocation expenses or increased commuting expenses, financial support for training measures, and, most typically, severance/termination payments.

11.68 The employer cannot begin to implement the proposed measures (i.e. issue notices of termination) before it has tried to reach an agreement with the works council on the reconciliation of interests.

11.69 In the absence of agreement the prescribed procedure set out below has to be followed, which can take some time to complete. In practice, this gives the works council the opportunity to delay the whole process and provides the works council with significant bargaining power. If the parties cannot agree on the reconciliation of interests, either party may ask the Federal Work Agency (*Bundesagentur für Arbeit*) for conciliation. In the absence of such a request or if the conciliation is unsuccessful, either party can apply for a hearing before the settlement committee (*Einigungsstelle*). With regard to the reconciliation of interests, the settlement committee can only mediate between the parties. If the mediation efforts fail, the employer can proceed with the operational change and implement the proposed measures. However, the whole process can take several months or even a year or more, if every issue is disputed. For example, the works council might disagree with the person proposed by the employer to be chairman of the settlement board and on the number of assessors. In that case, the employer has to ask the labour court to decide these issues. This litigation can require two court hearings. Against this background, employers who are under time pressure often choose to pay higher social-plan benefits in order to obtain the works council's consent and so proceed with the implementation of the operational change.

11.70 If the employer does not observe the procedural requirements, the works council can apply for an injunction against the implementation of the proposed measures. In addition, the employer risks damages claims brought by employees if it does not try to reach agreement on a reconciliation of interests.[19] Moreover, a breach of the duty to properly inform the works council constitutes an administrative offence which can be punished with a fine of up to €10,000.[20]

11.71 In addition to the reconciliation of interests, the employer must also

[19] Cf. s113 *BetrVG*. [20] S121 *BetrVG*.

negotiate a social plan with the works council. The same procedural requirements described above in relation to the reconciliation of interests apply. In practice, both agreements are negotiated together and treated as a 'package'. It should be noted, however, that the works council must consent to the social plan. Therefore, if the works council and the employer cannot agree on a social plan, the settlement committee can issue a binding decision in relation to the social plan which constitutes the parties' agreement.

6. Other Participation Rights in Germany

Quarterly Report to Workforce

Section 110 *BetrVG* provides that the employer is obliged to provide the workforce with a quarterly report about the company's economic situation and development after prior consultation with the economic committee, or, in the absence of an economic committee, the works council. In undertakings that employ between 20 and 1,000 employees, the report can be given verbally (e.g. at a workforce assembly). In undertakings with more than 1,000 employees, the report must be written. Any breach of the obligations to provide the quarterly report can be sanctioned as administrative offence with a fine of up to €10,000.[21] However, in practice, the quarterly report does not play a significant role in German employee relations. **11.72**

Personnel Matters

The German Works Constitution Act provides for a variety of works council rights in regard to personnel matters. For example, prior to the issue of every notice of termination the employer must inform the works council about the termination and reasons for the termination. The works council has one week to provide its opinion on the proposed notice of termination (*ordentliche Kündigung*). If the employer does not follow this procedure, the notice of termination is void.[22] **11.73**

In relation to the personnel matters mentioned in Article 4(2) (b) of the Information and Consultation Directive, the Act contains the following provisions: **11.74**

- The employer has the duty to inform the works council, with the aid of documents, of its personnel planning, especially in relation to present and future personnel requirements as well as personnel

[21] S121 *BetrVG*. [22] S102(1) *BetrVG*.

measures and vocational training measures. The employer must consult with the works council about the manner and scope of the necessary measures and the avoidance of adverse consequences to the affected employees and must do so in a timely manner.[23] Personnel planning includes planning relating to personnel requirements (i.e. how many employees are required, at which location, and when they will be required), personnel coverage (i.e. how can the personnel requirements be covered, e.g. by way of hiring of employees or workforce reduction), workforce allocation (i.e. to which workplaces should available employees be allocated), and planning relating to personnel costs.[24] If the employer acts intuitively and does not carry out personnel planning, there is no duty to inform and consult.[25] However, the works council is entitled to make suggestions relating to the introduction of personnel planning.[26] The duty to inform the works council about personnel planning only arises when concrete plans regarding the above issues are being made.[27]

- Breach by the employer of its duty to inform the works council of its personnel planning constitutes an administrative offence punishable with a fine of up to €10,000.[28] Disputes about personnel planning are relatively rare in practice.
- According to section 92a *BetrVG* the employer must consult with the works council about the works council's proposals regarding securing and promoting employment. The works council has the right to make suggestions dealing with the employer's flexible working time arrangements, promotion of part-time and part-time work for older employees, new forms of work organization, modifications in working methods and processes, qualification of employees, alternatives to outsourcing of work or referral of work to other companies, and a programme of production and investment. If the employer considers the works council's proposals to be unsuitable, it must provide reasons. These reasons must be provided in writing in establishments which employ more than 100 employees.[29] Again, disputes about these consultation rights do not often arise in practice.
- With regard to vocational training, the works council has relatively extensive participation rights. Upon the works council's request, the employer must ascertain the need for vocational training and consult

[23] S92(1) *BetrVG.*

[24] Erfurter Kommentar zum Arbeitsrecht (ErfK)/*Kania*, 5th edn 2005, § 92 *BetrVG* Rn. 5.

[25] Cf. ErfK/*Kania*, 5th edn 2005, § 92 *BetrVG* Rn. 6; *Fitting, BetrVG*, 22nd edn 2004, § 92 Rn. 29.

[26] S92(2) *BetrVG.*

[27] See *Fitting, BetrVG*, 22nd edn 2004, § 92 Rn. 26 et seq.

[28] S121 *BetrVG.*

[29] S92a(2) *BetrVG.*

with the works council about vocational training for employees of the establishment.[30] Moreover, the employer must consult the works council about the establishment and equipping of vocational training facilities, the introduction of vocational training measures in the establishment, and participation in external vocational training.[31] If the employer plans or implements measures that result in a change to the activities of affected employees who lack the necessary professional knowledge and skills to perform their new duties, the works council has to consent to the introduction of vocational training measures. If the employer and the works council cannot reach an agreement, the settlement committee may issue a decision.[32]

The works council's consent is also required in regard to the implementation of vocational training measures in the establishment and in relation to the participation of employees in internal or external training programmes. Again, the settlement committee can deliver a binding decision in the event of a dispute between the parties.[33] **11.75**

C. INFORMATION AND CONSULTATION IN THE NETHERLANDS

1. Overview of Employee Representation in the Netherlands

In the Netherlands the system of employee participation is governed by the Works Council Act (*Wet op de ondernemingsraden*) and the European Works Council Act (*Wet op de Europese ondernemingsraden*). **11.76**

The Works Council Act dates back to 1950[34] when its first version was enacted. Over the past 50 years, the Works Council Act has developed into a comprehensive system of employee participation. The current Works Council Act[35] not only provides for a system of information and consultation, but also provides the works council with a right to give its advice and a right of approval. **11.77**

The Information and Consultation Directive was implemented in the Netherlands by amending the Works Council Act.[36] **11.78**

The implementation of the Directive only required minimal changes to the Act; only the articles providing for the possibility of an exemption **11.79**

[30] S96(1) clause 2 *BetrVG*. [31] S97(1) *BetrVG*. [32] S97(2) *BetrVG*.

[33] See s98(4) *BetrVG*. [34] Act of 4 May 1950, Stb. 1950, K174.

[35] Act of 28 January 1971, Stb 54 as amended lately by the Act of 20 December 2001, Stb. 692.

[36] 29364, Stb. 652/2004.

from the obligation to establish a works council (Article 5 of the Works Council Act) and the duty to observe secrecy (Article 20 of the Works Council Act) needed to be amended.

11.80 The amendments came into force on 22 December 2004.

11.81 On 5 October 2004 a legislative proposal was submitted to the Dutch Parliament to replace the Works Council Act with a new Act called the Employee Consultation Act (*Wet medezeggenschap werknemers*). This Act will not, as currently drafted, materially impact on the current system of employee participation. Indeed, the proposal has encountered resistance and critics have suggested that the proposed changes could just as easily be implemented by way of limited changes to the Works Council Act. Nonetheless at the time of publication it is envisaged that the Employee Consultation Act will come into force at some point in 2006.

2. Works Councils

11.82 A works council is an employee representative body that is elected by and from the employees of an enterprise or a group of enterprises.

11.83 The Works Council Act defines the term 'enterprise' widely to include every organization operating as an independent organization in which work is performed either on the basis of an employment agreement or as a result of an appointment as a civil servant[37]. This means that the Works Council Act covers commercial operations as well as governmental agencies and non-profit organizations. In this summary, any reference to employer, company or business unit assumes that that employer, company, or business unit qualifies as an 'enterprise' for the purposes of the Works Council Act.

11.84 Works councils can be established at the level of a company but also at the level of a business unit. A central works council can be established where two or more companies have a works council. The central works council can be established to cover all companies and therefore also in respect of those companies that do not have a local works council. The central works council has authority over the entire group of companies.

11.85 Regardless of whether a central works council has been established, a group works council may be established for a group of companies.

11.86 Members of the central and group works councils are chosen by the members of the other existing works councils.

[37] Art. 1, s1, subs. c Works Council Act.

The central works councils and group works councils generally have the same powers as the local works councils but only in respect of those issues that are of common interest to all or the majority of the companies for which they have been established. The powers of the local works councils will in such circumstances transfer automatically to the central works council or the group works council. The group works council will not, however, deal with any issues that are dealt with by the central works council. **11.87**

Obligation to Establish a Works Council

The Works Council Act provides that a company or business unit employing 50 or more employees is obliged to establish a works council.[38] For these purposes employees include:[39] **11.88**

(1) all individuals who work on the basis of an employment contract or who have been appointed by a public body (*ambtenaren*). In this regard it is of no relevance whether employees are employed for a fixed or an indefinite period of time, or if they are full-time or part-time;
(2) temporary workers (*uitzendkrachten*) who have been working within the company or business unit for a consecutive period of at least 24 months; and
(3) individuals in respect of whom it has been agreed between the works council and the company or business unit that they will be considered employees within the meaning of the Works Council Act.

The Works Council Act does not impose a sanction on the employer for failing to establish a works council. However, employees can ask the court to order the employer to comply with its obligation to establish a works council. No threshold applies; one employee can file a request. **11.89**

A recent evaluation of the Works Council Act showed that approximately 70% of the employers that meet the threshold have established a works council.[40] **11.90**

The Works Council Act[41] gives the Social Economic Council (*Sociaal Economische Raad*) the authority to exempt an employer from the obligation to establish a works council for a maximum period of five years. However, the Social Economic Council often attaches strict conditions to the exemption requiring some form of employee consultation. Accordingly, in **11.91**

[38] Art. 2 Works Council Act.
[39] Art. 1 ss2 and 3, Works Council Act.
[40] Official Reports Lower House, 2002–2003, Legislative Proposal 28792, No. 1, p. 3.
[41] Art. 5 Works Council Act.

practice, exemptions under this provision are rare. In addition, any trade unions will be given the opportunity to express their views on the request for exemption.

Employee Representation in Companies Employing fewer than 50 Employees

11.92 Companies employing between 10 and 50 employees may elect to establish a works council.[42] However, such companies are obliged to establish an employee representative body (*ERB*) when requested to do so by the majority of the employees. Although an ERB typically has more limited powers than a works council its powers are not insignificant and include a right of approval in respect of proposals regarding working hours, holiday policies or arrangements, working conditions, sick leave, and certain integration issues.

11.93 Companies employing between 10 and 50 employees that have no ERB or works council are nevertheless obliged to hold a personnel meeting at least twice a year. In addition they have a general obligation to consult the employees on any proposals regarding working hours, holiday policies or arrangements, working conditions, sick leave, and certain integration matters.

11.94 Companies employing fewer than 10 employees may elect to hold a personnel meeting on a voluntary basis.

Composition of a Works Council

11.95 The members of the works council are elected by and from the employees of the company by secret ballot. They are usually elected for a period of three years, but can be re-elected after this period. The size of the works council depends on the number of employees in the company, varying from three members in the case of a company employing 50 employees up to a maximum of 25 members for those companies with 7,000 or more employees.

11.96 Only employees who have been employed for at least one year can be elected to the works council. Employees who have been employed for at least six months can, however, vote in the elections for the works council. In both cases this includes temporary workers who are treated as employees for these purposes after they have been working for at least 24 months. Temporary workers, therefore, effectively have the right to vote

[42] Arts. 35(b) to (d) Works Council Act.

and to stand for election to the works council after having worked for the company for two years.

If the number of employees falls below the thresholds referred to above during the term of the works council, this will have no effect on the term or constitution of that works council. Any increase or decrease will, however, be taken into account for the next works council elections. If the number of employees drops below the threshold of 50 employees, the works council will automatically cease to exist after expiration of the current term unless it is continued with the consent of the employer. **11.97**

Committees

The works council has the right to set up committees to the extent that it deems this necessary for the proper performance of its duties.[43] Employees who are not members of the works council can be appointed to these committees. **11.98**

Experts

The works council and its committees have the right to engage an expert to assist in connection with a particular subject.[44] The employer is required to bear the reasonable costs of such an expert. **11.99**

Confidentiality

Members of the works council, members of its committees, and any experts engaged by them are not allowed to disclose any business or trade secrets of the employer or any information in respect of which the employer has imposed a duty of confidentiality.[45] The obligation also applies to the administrative staff of the works council or the committees. **11.100**

Obligations of the Employer

An employer is required to provide the works council with adequate facilities to fulfil its duties, for example, a place where the works council can meet. Members of the works council should be given the opportunity to meet during normal working hours without adverse consequences for their salary or position. Finally, the employer must give the members of the works council sufficient time off each year to consult with each other or third parties. **11.101**

[43] Art. 15 Works Council Act.
[44] Art. 16 Works Council Act.
[45] Art. 20 Works Council Act.

11.102 The costs incurred by a works council in carrying out its duties must be borne by the employer. The employer is also responsible for the costs of experts instructed by the works council and the costs of any legal action brought against the employer by the works council, provided that the works council has informed the employer of these costs in advance.

11.103 Members of the works council, members of any of its committees, or employees who have stood as a candidate in the works council elections cannot be dismissed on the grounds of their membership of the works council, committee, or candidacy. Former members and candidates remain protected for a period of two years after they have ceased to be a works council or committee member and for a period of two years after the election. Their employment can only be terminated with the express permission of the court.

3. Rights and Powers of the Works Council

Mandatory Consultation on Proposed Decisions Outside the Ordinary Course of Business

11.104 The employer is required to consult the works council and give it the opportunity to render its opinion on each proposal in regard to:[46]

(a) a transfer of control of the company, business unit or any part thereof;

(b) the establishment, takeover, or surrender of control of another company or business unit or the commencement, substantial change or cessation of long-term co-operation with another company or business unit; including the entering into, substantial change to, or discontinuance of a substantial financial participation by or on behalf of such company or business unit;

(c) the termination of the activities of the company or business unit or a significant part thereof;

(d) the substantial decrease, expansion, or other change in activities of the company or business unit;

(e) the substantial change in the organization of the company or business unit or in the allocation of responsibilities within the company or business unit;

(f) a change of the location where the company or business unit carries out its activities;

(g) the recruitment or hiring of labour in groups;

[46] Art. 25 Works Council Act.

(h) the making of a significant investment on behalf of the company or business unit;

(i) the taking out of a significant loan on behalf of the company or business unit;

(j) supplying significant credit and/or security for significant debts of another company or business unit, unless in the ordinary course of business;

(k) the introduction or alteration of important technology;

(l) the taking of an important measure regarding the management of the natural environment by the company or business unit, including the taking or changing of policy-related, organizational, or administrative measures relating to the natural environment;

(m) adopting a provision relating to the bearing of financial risks as mentioned in Article 75, paragraph (1) of the Disablement Benefits Act (*Wet op de arbeidsongeschiktheidsverzekering*); and

(n) commissioning an expert from outside the company or business unit to advise on any of the above matters.

No advice needs to be obtained from the works council if the com- **11.105**
pany or business unit is established or is being established abroad and the proposed decision cannot reasonably be expected to lead to a decision referred to in (c) to (f) above concerning a business carried on by the employer in the Netherlands.

Timing

The works council must be consulted by the employer in writing at a time **11.106**
when its opinion could reasonably still have an impact on the proposal.

As part of the consultation process the works council must be provided **11.107**
with an overview of the reasons for the proposal, an explanation of the impact that the decision may have and any consequential measures for the employees. At least one consultative meeting should be held between management and the works council on the relevant issue before the works council can be required to render advice.

Consequences of Decisions by the Employer Contrary to Works Council Opinion

If a decision is taken by the employer contrary to the opinion given by the **11.108**
works council, the employer is obliged to inform the works council and postpone the execution of its decision for one month from the day after

the date on which the employer has notified the works council. The works council may, during that one-month period, take legal action against the employer (see paragraphs 11.117 and 11.118).

Consultation in Respect of the Appointment or Dismissal of a Director

11.109 The employer is required to consult the works council on any proposal to either appoint or dismiss any director[47] of the employer who is ultimately in charge of day-to-day employment issues. Generally, this relates to those directors who are the contact persons for the works councils.

11.110 The advice should be requested at a time when the works council's opinion can still have an impact on the proposed decision. The works council should be provided with the reasons for the decision and in the case of an appointment, with information on the proposed candidate. However, the works council has no legal remedies if the employer does not follow its advice on these matters.

Right of Approval

11.111 Works council approval[48] is required in respect of proposals that concern all or some of the employees as regards the establishment, change, or withdrawal of:

(a) arrangements for pension insurance, profit-sharing, or saving plans;
(b) policies regarding working time or holidays;
(c) a remuneration or job-rating system;
(d) policies regarding safety, health, or benefits in respect of employment or absenteeism due to illness;
(e) policies regarding appointment, dismissal, or promotion;
(f) policies regarding the training of personnel;
(g) policies regarding appraisal;
(h) policies regarding industrial welfare work;
(i) policies regarding direct employee consultation at work;
(j) policies regarding the consideration of complaints;
(k) policies regarding registration and protection of personnel data; and
(l) policies regarding facilities for observation or monitoring of the attendance, behaviour, or performance of employees.

11.112 If the works council refuses to approve the proposed decision, the employer cannot validly implement it. If the employer proceeds without permission, the works council has the power to nullify the decision within

[47] Art. 30 Works Council Act. [48] Art. 27 Works Council Act.

one month after it has become aware of the decision. The employer can, however, seek the alternative approval of the court.

Right to Information

The employer is obliged to supply the works council and any committees appointed by the works council, upon request, with all information in writing reasonably required by the works council or committees for the proper fulfilment of their duties.[49] **11.113**

Furthermore, at the beginning of the term of office of a works council the employer is obliged to provide the works council with information about the employer including: the legal structure of the company or business unit, the articles of association of the employer, and the names and residence of the directors. The employer is also obliged to inform the works council of any changes to this information. **11.114**

Twice a year the employer is obliged to provide the works council with written or oral information in respect of the financial results of the employer, the social policy of the company or business units, and the annual report and accounts of the company. **11.115**

A general meeting must be held twice a year with the works council in which the general affairs of the company or business are discussed. In this meeting the employer is required to inform the works council of any decisions it is proposing that would qualify as decisions that may lead to a right of advice or a right of approval. At the meetings, agreement needs to be reached on when and how the works council will be involved in the decision-making process. **11.116**

Sanctions and Actions

In the event that the employer fails to comply with its obligations under the Works Council Act, the works council may, following the intervention of the Branch Committee (*Bedrijfscommissie*), request that the cantonal court require the employer to comply with its obligations.[50] The cantonal court may, upon the request of the works council or the employees, compel the employer or the works council to perform certain activities or to refrain from performing certain activities. **11.117**

In the case of a failure to observe Article 25 of the Works Council Act (mandatory consultation on proposed decisions outside of the ordinary course of business) or if a decision is made contrary to the opinion given **11.118**

[49] Arts. 24, 31, 31a, 31b, 31c Works Council Act.

[50] Art. 36 Works Council Act.

by the works council, the works council can lodge an appeal against the decision with the Enterprise Chamber (*Ondernemingskamer*) of the Court of Appeal in Amsterdam. The Enterprise Chamber can (depending on the circumstances): (1) oblige the employer to withdraw its decision and cancel any actions taken as a result thereof and/or (2) forbid the employer from performing activities which form part of the decision taken.[51]

[51] Art. 26 Works Council Act.

APPENDIX 1

The Information and Consultation of Employees Regulations 2004

Statutory Instrument 2004 No. 3426

Made	*21st December 2004*
Coming into force	*6th April 2005*

ARRANGEMENT OF REGULATIONS

PART I

GENERAL

PART II

EMPLOYEE NUMBERS AND ENTITLEMENT TO DATA

PART III

NEGOTIATED AGREEMENTS

Whereas a draft of these Regulations was laid before Parliament in accordance with section 42 of the Employment Relations Act 2004[1] and approved by resolution of each House of Parliament.

Now, therefore, the Secretary of State, in exercise of the powers conferred on her by section 42 of that Act, hereby make the following Regulations:

PART 1
GENERAL

Citation, commencement and extent

1.–(1) These Regulations may be cited as the Information and Consultation of Employees Regulations 2004 and shall come into force on 6th April 2005.

[1] 2004 c. 24

(2) These Regulations extend to Great Britain.

Interpretation

2. In these Regulations—

'the 1996 Act' means the Employment Rights Act 1996[2];

'Appeal Tribunal' means the Employment Appeal Tribunal;

'CAC' means the Central Arbitration Committee;

'consultation' means the exchange of views and establishment of a dialogue between—

(a) information and consultation representatives and the employer; or

(b) in the case of a negotiated agreement which provides as mentioned in regulation 16(1)(f)(ii), the employees and the employer;

'contract of employment' means a contract of service or appnlrenticeship, whether express or implied, and (if it is express) whether oral or in writing;

'date of the ballot' means the day or last day on which voting may take place and, where voting in different parts of the ballot is arranged to take place on different days or during periods ending on different days, the last of those days;

'employee' means an individual who has entered into or works under a contract of employment and in Part VIII and regulation 40 includes, where the employment has ceased, an individual who worked under a contract of employment;

'employee request' means a request by employees under regulation 7 for the employer to initiate negotiations to reach an agreement under these Regulations;

'employer notification' means a notification by an employer under regulation 11 that he wishes to initiate negotiations to reach an agreement under these Regulations;

'information' means data transmitted by the employer—

(a) to the information and consultation representatives; or

(b) in the case of a negotiated agreement which provides as mentioned in regulation 16(1)(f)(ii), directly to the employees,

in order to enable those representatives or those employees to examine and to acquaint themselves with the subject matter of the data;

'Information and Consultation Directive' means European Parliament and Council Directive 2002/14/EC of 11 March 2002[3] establishing a general framework for informing and consulting employees in the European Community;

'information and consultation representative' means—

(a) in the case of a negotiated agreement which provides as mentioned in regulation 16(1)(f)(i), a person appnlointed or elected in accordance with that agreement; or

[2] 1996 c. 18.

[3] OJ L 80, 23.3.2002, P29.

(b) a person elected in accordance with regulation 19(1);

'negotiated agreement' means—

(a) an agreement between the employer and the negotiating representatives reached through negotiations as provided for in regulation 14 which satisfies the requirements of regulation 16(1); or

(b) an agreement between the employer and the information and consultation representatives referred to in regulation 18(2);

'negotiating representative' means a person elected or appnlointed pursuant to regulation 14(1)(a);

'parties' means the employer and the negotiating representatives or the information and consultation representatives, as the case may be;

'pre-existing agreement' means an agreement between an employer and his employees or their representatives which—

(a) is made prior to the making of an employee request; and

(b) satisfies the conditions set out in regulation 8(1)(a) to (d),

but does not include an agreement concluded in accordance with regulations 17 or 42 to 45 of the Transnational Information and Consultation of Employees Regulations 1999[4] or a negotiated agreement;

'standard information and consultation provisions' means the provisions set out in regulation 20;

'undertaking' means a public or private undertaking carrying out an economic activity, whether or not operating for gain;

'valid employee request' means an employee request made to their employer by the employees of an undertaking to which these Regulations appnlly (under regulation 3) that satisfies the requirements of regulation 7 and is not prevented from being valid by regulation 12.

Application

3.–(1) These Regulations apply to undertakings—

(a) employing in the United Kingdom, in accordance with the calculation in regulation 4, at least the number of employees in column 1 of the table in Schedule 1 to these Regulations on or after the corresponding date in column 2 of that table; and

(b) subject to paragraph (2), whose registered office, head office or principal place of business is situated in Great Britain.

(2) Where the registered office is situated in Great Britain and the head office or principal place of business is situated in Northern Ireland or vice versa, these Regulations shall only apply where the majority of employees are employed to work in Great Britain.

(3) In these Regulations, an undertaking to which these Regulations apply is referred to, in relation to its employees, as 'the employer'.

[4] S.I. 1999/3323.

PART II
EMPLOYEE NUMBERS AND ENTITLEMENT TO DATA

Calculation of number of employees

4.–(1) Subject to paragraph (4), the number of employees for the purposes of regulation 3(1) shall be determined by ascertaining the average number of employees employed in the previous twelve months, calculated in accordance with paragraph (2).
(2) Subject to paragraph (3), the average number of employees is to be ascertained by determining the number of employees employed in each month in the previous twelve months (whether they were employed throughout the month or not), adding together those monthly figures and dividing the number by 12.
(3) For the purposes of the calculation in paragraph (2) if, for the whole of a month within the twelve month period, an employee works under a contract by virtue of which he would have worked for 75 hours or less in that month—

(i) were the month to have contained 21 working days;
(ii) were the employee to have had no absences from work; and
(iii) were the employee to have worked no overtime,

the employee may be counted as representing half of a full-time employee for the month in question, if the employer so decides.

(4) If the undertaking has been in existence for less than twelve months, the references to twelve months in paragraphs (1), (2) and (3), and the divisor of 12 referred to in paragraph (2), shall be replaced by the number of months the undertaking has been in existence.

Entitlement to data

5.–(1) An employee or an employees' representative may request data from the employer for the purpose of determining the number of people employed by the employer's undertaking in the United Kingdom.
(2) Any request for data made under paragraph (1) must be in writing and be dated.
(3) The employer must provide the employee or the employees' representative who made the request with data to enable him to—

(a) make the calculation of the numbers of employees referred to in regulation 4, and
(b) determine, for the purpose of regulation 7(2), what number of employees constitutes 10% of the employees in the undertaking.

Complaint of failure to provide data

6.–(1) An employee or an employees' representative who has requested data under regulation 5 may present a complaint to the CAC that—

(a) the employer has failed to provide the data referred to in regulation 5(3);

or

(b) the data which has been provided by the employer is false or incomplete in a material particular.

(2) Where the CAC finds the complaint to be well-founded it shall make an order requiring the employer to disclose data to the complainant which order shall specify—

(a) the data in respect of which the CAC finds that the complaint is well-founded and which is to be disclosed to the complainant;

(b) the date (or if more than one, the earliest date) on which the employer refused or failed to disclose data, or disclosed false or incomplete information;

(c) a date, not being less than one week from the date of the order, by which the employer must disclose the data specified in the order.

(3) The CAC shall not consider a complaint presented under this regulation unless it is made after the expiry of a period of one month beginning on the date on which the complainant made his request for data under regulation 5.

PART III
NEGOTIATED AGREEMENTS

Employee request to negotiate an agreement in respect of information and consultation

7.–(1) On receipt of a valid employee request, the employer shall, subject to paragraphs (8) and (9), initiate negotiations by taking the steps set out in regulation 14(1).

(2) Subject to paragraph (3), an employee request is not a valid employee request unless it consists of—

(a) a single request made by at least 10% of the employees in the undertaking; or

(b) a number of separate requests made on the same or different days by employees which when taken together mean that at least 10% of the employees in that undertaking have made requests, provided that the requests are made within a period of six months.

(3) Where the figure of 10% in paragraph (2) would result in less than 15 or more than 2,500 employees being required in order for a valid employee request to be made, that paragraph shall have effect as if, for the figure of 10%, there were substituted the figure of 15, or as the case may be, 2,500.

(4) An employee request is not a valid employee request unless the single request referred to in paragraph (2)(a) or each separate request referred to in paragraph (2)(b)—

(a) is in writing;

(b) is sent to—

(i) the registered office, head office or principal place of business of the employer; or

(iii) the CAC; and

(c) specifies the names of the employees making it and the date on which it is sent.

(5) Where a request is sent to the CAC under paragraph (4)(b)(ii), the CAC shall—

(a) notify the employer that the request has been made as soon as reasonably practicable;

(b) request from the employer such information as it needs to verify the number and names of the employees who have made the request; and

(c) inform the employer and the employees who have made the request how many employees have made the request on the basis of the information provided by the employees and the employer.

(6) Where the CAC requests information from the employer under paragraph (5)(b), the employer shall provide the information requested as soon as reasonably practicable.

(7) The date on which an employee request is made is—

(a) where the request consists of a single request satisfying paragraph (2)(a) or of separate requests made on the same day satisfying paragraph (2)(b), the date on which the request is or requests are sent to the employer by the employees or the date on which the CAC informs the employer and the employees in accordance with paragraph (5)(c) of how many employees have made the request; and

(b) where the request consists of separate requests made on different days, the date on which—

(i) the request which results in paragraph (2)(b) being satisfied is sent to the employer by the employees; or

(ii) the CAC informs the employer and the employees in accordance with paragraph (5)(c) of how many employees have made the request where that request results in paragraph (2)(b) being satisfied.

(8) If the employer decides to hold a ballot under regulation 8 or 9, the employer shall not be required to initiate negotiations unless and until the outcome of the ballot is that in regulation 8(5)(b).

(9) If an application is made to the CAC under regulation 13, the employer shall not be required to initiate negotiations unless and until if the CAC declares that there was a valid employee request or that the employer's notification was valid.

Pre-existing agreements: ballot for endorsement of employee request

8.–(1) Subject to regulation 9, this regulation applies where a valid employee request has been made under regulation 7 by fewer than 40% of employees employed in the undertaking on the date that request was made and where there exists one or more pre-existing agreements which—

(a) are in writing;

(b) cover all the employees of the undertaking;

(c) have been approved by the employees; and

(d) set out how the employer is to give information to the employees or their representatives and seek their views on such information.

(2) Where this regulation applies, the employer may, instead of initiating negotiations in accordance with regulation 7(1), hold a ballot to seek the endorsement of the employees of the undertaking for the employee request in accordance with paragraphs (3) and (4).

(3) The employer must—

(a) inform the employees in writing within one month of the date of the employee request that he intends to hold a ballot under this regulation; and

(b) arrange for the ballot to be held as soon as reasonably practicable thereafter, provided that the ballot does not take place before a period of 21 days has passed since the employer informed the employees under sub-paragraph (a).

(4) A ballot must satisfy the following requirements—

(a) the employer must make such arrangements as are reasonably practicable to ensure that the ballot is fair;

(b) all employees of the undertaking on the day on which the votes may be cast in the ballot, or if the votes may be cast on more than one day, on the first day of those days, must be given an entitlement to vote in the ballot;

(c) the ballot must be conducted so as to secure that—

(i) so far as is reasonably practicable, those voting do so in secret; and

(ii) the votes given in the ballot are accurately counted.

(5) Where the employer holds a ballot under this regulation—

(a) he must, as soon as reasonably practicable after the date of the ballot, inform the employees of the result; and

(b) if the employees endorse the employee request, the employer is under the obligation in regulation 7(1) to initiate negotiations; and

(c) if the employees do not endorse the employee request, the employer is no longer under the obligation in regulation 7(1) to initiate negotiations.

(6) For the purposes of paragraph (5), the employees are to be regarded as having endorsed the employee request if—

(a) at least 40% of the employees employed in the undertaking; and

(b) the majority of the employees who vote in the ballot,

have voted in favour of endorsing the request.

(7) An employee or an employees' representative who believes that an employer has not, pursuant to paragraph (3)(a), informed his employees that he intends to hold a ballot within the period specified in that paragraph may apply to the CAC for a declaration that the employer is under the duty in regulation 7(1) to initiate negotiations.

(8) Where an employer, acting pursuant to paragraph (3)(a), has informed the employees that he intends to hold a ballot, any employee or employees' representative who believes that the employer has not complied with paragraph (3)(b) may present a complaint to the CAC.

(9) Where the CAC finds a complaint under paragraph (8) well-founded it shall make an order requiring the employer to hold the ballot within such period as the order may specify.

Pre-existing agreements covering groups of undertakings

9.–(1) This regulation applies where—

(a) the requirements of regulation 8(1) are satisfied in relation to an undertaking;

(b) the pre-existing agreement or one of the pre-existing agreements covers employees in one or more undertakings other than the undertaking mentioned in sub-paragraph (a); and

(c) the other undertaking or each of the other undertakings mentioned in sub-paragraph (b) is one in respect of which there is an agreement that satisfied, or are agreements that taken together satisfied, the requirements in sub-paragraphs (a) to (d) of regulation 8(1) on the date on which the valid employee request was made in respect of the undertaking mentioned in sub-paragraph (a); and

(d) the valid employee request in relation to the undertaking mentioned in sub-paragraph (a) either—

(i) alone, or

(ii) aggregated with any requests made by employees in the undertakings mentioned in sub-paragraph (b) within the period of six months preceding the date of the valid employee request mentioned in regulation 8(1),

is made by fewer than 40% of the employees in the undertakings mentioned in paragraph (1)(a) and (b).

(2) Where this regulation applies the employers may hold a combined ballot for endorsement of the employee request in accordance with this regulation and in that event regulation 8 shall apply to the ballot with the modification that references to employees shall be treated as referring to the employees employed in all of the undertakings referred to in paragraph (1)(a) and (b).

(3) Notwithstanding paragraph (2), the undertaking mentioned in paragraph (1)(a) may choose to hold the ballot for endorsement of the employee request in accordance with regulation 8 rather than under this regulation.

Complaint about ballot for endorsement of employee request

10.–(1) Any employee in the undertaking referred to in regulation 8(1) or employee in one of the undertakings referred to in regulation 9(1), or representative of such employees, who believes that a requirement has not been satisfied that has to be satisfied in order to entitle either the employer, in accordance with regulation 8(2), to hold a ballot, or the employers, in accordance with regulation 9(2), to hold a combined ballot may, within 21 days of the employer informing the employees of the relevant undertaking under regulation 8(3)(a), present a complaint to the CAC.

(2) Any employee or employees' representative who believes that the arrangements for a ballot held under regulation 8 or 9, as the case may be, did not satisfy one or more of the requirements set out in regulation 8(4) may, within 21 days of the date of the ballot, present a complaint to the CAC.

(3) Where the CAC finds a complaint under paragraph (1) or (2) well-founded it shall—

(a) in the case of a finding on a complaint under paragraph (1) that any requirement set out in sub-paragraphs (a) to (d) of regulation 8(1) was not satisfied in relation to the undertaking referred to in regulation 8(1) or 9(1)(a), make an order requiring the employer to whom regulation 8(1) or 9(1)(a) relates to initiate negotiations in accordance with regulation 7(1);

(b) in the case of a finding on a complaint under paragraph (1) that any requirement set out in sub-paragraphs (b) to (d) of regulation 9(1) has not been satisfied, make an order that no combined ballot shall take place and requiring the employer to whom regulation 9(1)(a) relates, according to the preference he has expressed, to initiate negotiations in accordance with regulation 7(1) or, within such period as the order may specify, to conduct a ballot under regulation 8; and

(c) in the case of a complaint under paragraph (2)—

(i) where prior to the order being made, the employer referred to in regulation 8(1) or 9(1)(a) makes representations to the CAC that he would prefer to initiate negotiations under regulation 7, make an order requiring that employer to do so; or

(ii) in the absence of such representations, order the employer or employers to hold the ballot under regulation 8 or 9, as the case may be, again within such period as the order may specify.

Employer notification of decision to initiate negotiations

11.-(1) The employer may start the negotiation process set out in regulation 14(1) on his own initiative by issuing a written notification satisfying the requirements of paragraph (2), and where the employer issues such a notification regulations 14 to 17 shall apply.

(2) The notification referred to in paragraph (1) must—

(a) state that the employer intends to start the negotiating process and that the notification is given for the purpose of these Regulations;

(b) state the date on which it is issued; and

(c) be published in such a manner as to bring it to the attention of, so far as reasonably practicable, all the employees of the undertaking.

Restrictions on employee request and employer notification

12.—(1) Subject to paragraph (2), no employee request or employer notification is valid if it is made or issued, as the case may be,—

(a) where a negotiated agreement applies, within a period of three years from the date of the agreement or, where the agreement is terminated within that period, before the date on which the termination takes effect;

(b) where the standard information and consultation provisions apply within a period of three years from the date on which they started to apply; and

(c) where the employer has held a ballot under regulation 8, or was one of the employers who held a ballot under regulation 9 and the result was that the employees did not endorse the valid employee request referred to in regulation 8(1), within a period of three years from the date of that request.

(2) Paragraph (1) does not apply where there are material changes in the undertaking during the applicable period having the result—

(a) where a ballot held under regulation 8 or 9 had the result that the employees did not endorse the valid employee request, that there is no longer a pre-existing agreement which satisfies paragraph (1)(b) and (c) of regulation 8 or in the case of a ballot held under regulation 9, that there is no longer an agreement satisfying paragraph (1)(b) of that regulation; or

(b) where a negotiated agreement exists, that the agreement no longer complies with the requirement in regulation 16(1) that it must cover all the employees of the undertaking.

Dispute about employee request, employer notification or whether obligation in regulation 7(1) applies

13.–(1) If the employer considers that there was no valid employee request—

(a) because the employee request did not satisfy any requirement of regulation 7(2) to (4) or was prevented from being valid by regulation 12,

or

(b) because the undertaking was not one to which these Regulations applied (under Regulation 3) on the date on which the employee request was made,

the employer may apply to the CAC for a declaration as to whether there was a valid employee request.

(2) If an employee or an employees' representative considers that an employer notification was not valid because it did not comply with one or more of the requirements in regulation 11(2) or was prevented from being valid by regulation 12, he may apply to the CAC for a declaration as to whether the notification was valid.

(3) The CAC shall only consider an application for a declaration made under paragraph (1) or (2) if the application is made within a one month period beginning on the date of the employee request or the date on which the employer notification is made.

Negotiations to reach an agreement

14.–(1) In order to initiate negotiations to reach an agreement under these Regulations the employer must as soon as reasonably practicable—

(a) make arrangements, satisfying the requirements of paragraph (2), for the employees of the undertaking to elect or appoint negotiating representatives; and thereafter

(b) inform the employees in writing of the identity of the negotiating representatives; and

(c) invite the negotiating representatives to enter into negotiations to reach a negotiated agreement.

(2) The requirements for the election or appointment of negotiating representatives under paragraph (1)(a) are that—

(a) the election or appointment of the representatives must be arranged in such a way that, following their election or appointment, all employees of the undertaking are represented by one or more representatives; and

(b) all employees of the undertaking must be entitled to take part in the election or appointment of the representatives and, where there is an election, all employees of the undertaking on the day on which the votes may be cast in the ballot, or if the votes may be cast on more than one day, on the first day of those days, must be given an entitlement to vote in the ballot.

(3) The negotiations referred to in paragraph (1)(c) shall last for a period not exceeding six months commencing at the end of the period of three months beginning with the date on which the valid employee request was made or the valid employer notification was issued; but the following periods shall not count towards the three month period—

(a) where the employer holds a ballot pursuant to regulation 8 or 9, the period between the employer notifying the employees of his decision to hold such a ballot and whichever of the following dates is applicable—

(i) where there is no complaint to the CAC under regulation 10, the date of the ballot;

(ii) where there is a complaint to the CAC under regulation 10 and the complaint is dismissed by the CAC or on appeal, the date on which it is finally dismissed;

(iii) where there is a complaint to the CAC and the outcome, whether of the complaint or of any appeal from it, is an order to hold the ballot under regulation 8 or 9 again, the date of the ballot that most recently took place;

(iv) where there is a complaint to the CAC under regulation 10 and the outcome, whether of the complaint or of any appeal from it, is an order requiring the employer to initiate negotiations in accordance with regulation 7(1), the date on which the order is made;

(b) where an application for a declaration is made to the CAC pursuant to regulation 13, the period between the date of that application and the final decision of the CAC or any appeal from that decision; and

(c) where a complaint about the election or appointment of negotiating representatives is presented pursuant to regulation 15, the time between the date of the complaint and the determination of the complaint, including any appeal and, where the complaint is upheld, the further period until the negotiating representatives are re-elected or re-appointed.

(4) Where a complaint about the ballot for employee approval of a negotiated agreement is presented pursuant to regulation 17, the time between the date the complaint is presented to the CAC and the determination of the complaint (including any appeal and, where the complaint is upheld, the further period until the re-holding of the ballot) shall not count towards the six month period mentioned in paragraph (3).

(5) If, before the end of the six month period referred to in paragraph (3), the employer and a majority of the negotiating representatives agree that that period should be extended, it may be extended by such period as the parties agree and thereafter may be further extended by such period or periods as the parties agree.

(6) Where one or more employers wish to initiate negotiations to reach an agreement to cover employees in more than one undertaking, any employer whose employees have not made a valid employee request and who has not issued a valid employer notification, shall issue such a notification.

(7) Where paragraph (6) applies, the provisions of paragraphs (1) to (5) of this regulation and regulations 15 and 16 apply with the following modifications—

(a) the references to the employees of the undertaking refer to the employees of all the undertakings to be covered by any agreement negotiated; and

(b) references to employees refer to employees of all the undertakings to be covered by any agreement negotiated.

Complaints about election or appointment of negotiating representatives

15.–(1) If an employee or an employees' representative considers that one or both of the requirements for the appointment or election of negotiating

representatives set out in regulation 14(2) have not been complied with, he may, within 21 days of the election or appointment, present a complaint to the CAC.
(2) Where the CAC finds the complaint well-founded it shall make an order requiring the employer to arrange for the process of election or appointment of negotiating representatives referred to in regulation 14 to take place again within such period as the order shall specify.

Negotiated agreements

16.—(1) A negotiated agreement must cover all employees of the undertaking and may consist either of a single agreement or of different parts (each being approved in accordance with paragraph (4)) which, taken together, cover all the employees of the undertaking. The single agreement or each part must—

(a) set out the circumstances in which the employer must inform and consult the employees to which it relates;
(b) be in writing;
(c) be dated;
(d) be approved in accordance with paragraphs (3) to (5);
(e) be signed by or on behalf of the employer; and
(f) either—
(i) provide for the appointment or election of information and consultation representatives to whom the employer must provide the information and whom the employer must consult in the circumstances referred to in sub-paragraph (a); or
(ii) provide that the employer must provide information directly to the employees to which it relates and consult those employees directly in the circumstances referred to in sub-paragraph (a).

(2) Where a negotiated agreement consist of different parts they may provide differently in relation to the matters referred to in paragraph (1)(a) and (f).
(3) A negotiated agreement consisting of a single agreement shall be treated as being approved for the purpose of paragraph (1)(d) if—

(a) it has been signed by all the negotiating representatives; or
(b) it has been signed by a majority of negotiating representatives and either—
(i) approved in writing by at least 50% of employees employed in the undertaking, or
(ii) approved by a ballot of those employees, the arrangements for which satisfied the requirements set out in paragraph (5), in which at least 50% of the employees voting, voted in favour of approval.

(4) A part shall be treated as being approved for the purpose of paragraph (1)(d) if the part—

(a) has been signed by all the negotiating representatives involved in negotiating the part; or
(b) has been signed by a majority of those negotiating representatives and either—
(i) approved in writing by at least 50% of employees (employed in the undertaking) to which the part relates, or

(ii) approved by a ballot of those employees, the arrangements for which satisfied the requirements set out in paragraph (5), in which at least 50% of the employees voting, voted in favour of approving the part.

(5) The ballots referred to in paragraphs (3) and (4) must satisfy the following requirements—

(a) the employer must make such arrangements as are reasonably practicable to ensure that the ballot is fair;

(b) all employees of the undertaking or, as the case may be, to whom the part of the agreement relates, on the day on which the votes may be cast in the ballot, or if the votes may be cast on more than one day, on the first day of those days, must be given an entitlement to vote in the ballot; and

(c) the ballot must be conducted so as to secure that—

(i) so far as is reasonably practicable, those voting do so in secret; and

(ii) the votes given in the ballot are accurately counted.

(6) Where the employer holds a ballot under this regulation he must, as soon as reasonably practicable after the date of the ballot, inform the employees entitled to vote of the result.

Complaints about ballot for employee approval of negotiated agreement

17.–(1) Any negotiating representative who believes that the arrangements for a ballot held under regulation 16 did not satisfy one or more of the requirements set out in paragraph (5) of that regulation, may, within 21 days of the date of the ballot, present a complaint to the CAC.

(2) Where the CAC finds the complaint well-founded it shall make an order requiring the employer to hold the ballot referred to in regulation 16 again within such period as the order may specify.

PART IV
STANDARD INFORMATION AND CONSULTATION PROVISIONS

Application of standard information and consultation provisions

18.—(1) Subject to paragraph (2)—

(a) where the employer is under a duty, following the making of a valid employee request or issue of a valid employer notification, to initiate negotiations in accordance with regulation 14 but does not do so, the standard information and consultation provisions shall apply from the date—

(i) which is six months from the date on which the valid employee request was made or the valid employer notification was issued, or

(ii) information and consultation representatives are elected under regulation 19,

whichever is the sooner; and

(b) if the parties do not reach a negotiated agreement within the time limit referred to in regulation 14(3) (or that period as extended by agreement under paragraph (5) of that regulation) the standard information and consultation provisions shall apply from the date—

(i) which is six months from the date on which that time limit expires; or

(ii) information and consultation representatives are elected under regulation 19,

whichever is the sooner.

(2) Where the standard information and consultation provisions apply, the employer and the information and consultation representatives elected pursuant to regulation 19 may, at any time, reach an agreement that provisions other than the standard information and consultation provisions shall apply.

(3) An agreement referred to in paragraph (2) shall only have effect if it covers all the employees of the undertaking, complies with the requirements listed in regulation 16(1)(a) to (c), (e) and (f), and is signed by a majority of the information and consultation representatives.

Election of information and consultation representatives

19.–(1) Where the standard information and consultation provisions are to apply, the employer shall, before the standard information and consultation provisions start to apply, arrange for the holding of a ballot of its employees to elect the relevant number of information and consultation representatives.

(2) The provisions in Schedule 2 to these Regulations apply in relation to the arrangements for and conduct of any such ballot.

(3) In this regulation the 'relevant number of information and consultation representatives' means one representative per fifty employees or part thereof, provided that that number is at least 2 and does not exceed 25.

(4) An employee or an employee's representative may complain to the CAC that the employer has not arranged for the holding of a ballot in accordance with paragraph (1).

(5) Where the CAC finds the complaint well-founded, it shall make an order requiring the employer to arrange, or re-arrange, and hold the ballot.

(6) Where the CAC finds a complaint under paragraph (4) well-founded, the employee or the employee's representative may make an application to the Appeal Tribunal under regulation 22(6) and paragraphs (7) and (8) of that regulation shall apply to any such application.

Standard information and consultation provisions

20.–(1) Where the standard information and consultation provisions apply pursuant to regulation 18, the employer must provide the information and consultation representatives with information on—

(a) the recent and probable development of the undertaking's activities and economic situation;

(b) the situation, structure and probable development of employment within the undertaking and on any anticipatory measures envisaged, in particular, where there is a threat to employment within the undertaking; and

(c) subject to paragraph (5), decisions likely to lead to substantial changes in work organisation or in contractual relations, including those referred to in—

(i) sections 188 to 192 of the Trade Union and Labour Relations (Consolidation) Act 1992[5]; and

[5] 1992 c. 52.

(ii) regulations 10 to 12 of the Transfer of Undertakings (Protection of Employment) Regulations 1981[6].

(2) The information referred to in paragraph (1) must be given at such time, in such fashion and with such content as are appropriate to enable, in particular, the information and consultation representatives to conduct an adequate study and, where necessary, to prepare for consultation.

(3) The employer must consult the information and consultation representatives on the matters referred to in paragraph (1)(b) and (c).

(4) The employer must ensure that the consultation referred to in paragraph (3) is conducted—

(a) in such a way as to ensure that the timing, method and content of the consultation are appropriate;

(b) on the basis of the information supplied by the employer to the information and consultation representatives and of any opinion which those representatives express to the employer;

(c) in such a way as to enable the information and consultation representatives to meet the employer at the relevant level of management depending on the subject under discussion and to obtain a reasoned response from the employer to any such opinion; and

(d) in relation to matters falling within paragraph (1)(c), with a view to reaching agreement on decisions within the scope of the employer's powers.

(5) The duties in this regulation to inform and consult the information and consultation representatives on decisions falling within paragraph (1)(c) cease to apply once the employer is under a duty under—

(a) section 188 of the Act referred to in paragraph (1)(c)(i) (duty of employer to consult representatives); or

(b) regulation 10 of the Regulations referred to in paragraph (1)(c)(ii) (duty to inform and consult representatives),

and he has notified the information and consultation representatives in writing that he will be complying with his duty under the legislation referred to in sub-paragraph (a) or (b), as the case may be, instead of under these Regulations, provided that the notification is given on each occasion on which the employer has become or is about to become subject to the duty.

(6) Where there is an obligation in these Regulations on the employer to inform and consult his employees, a failure on the part of a person who controls the employer (either directly or indirectly) to provide information to the employer shall not constitute a valid reason for the employer failing to inform and consult.

[6] S.I. 1981/1794; regulations 10 to 12 have been amended by the Tribunals and Inquiries Act 1992 (1992 c. 53), the Trade Union Reform and Employment Rights Act 1993 (1993 c. 19), the Collective Redundancies and Transfer of Undertakings (Protection of Employment) (Amendment) Regulations 1995 (S.I. 1995/2587), the Employment Rights (Dispute Resolution) Act 1998 (1998 c. 8), the Collective Redundancies and Transfer of Undertakings (Protection of Employment) (Amendment) Regulations 1999 (S.I. 1999/ 1925) and the Transfer of Undertakings (Protection of Employment) (Amendment) Regulations 1999 (S.I. 1999/2402).

PART V
DUTY OF CO-OPERATION

Co-operation

21. The parties are under a duty, when negotiating or implementing a negotiated agreement or when implementing the standard information and consultation provisions, to work in a spirit of co-operation and with due regard for their reciprocal rights and obligations, taking into account the interests of both the undertaking and the employees.

PART VI
COMPLIANCE AND ENFORCEMENT

Disputes about operation of a negotiated agreement or the standard information and consultation provisions

22.–(1) Where—

(a) a negotiated agreement has been agreed; or

(b) the standard information and consultation provisions apply,

a complaint may be presented to the CAC by a relevant applicant who considers that the employer has failed to comply with the terms of the negotiated agreement or, as the case may be, one or more of the standard information and consultation provisions.

(2) A complaint brought under paragraph (1) must be brought within a period of three months commencing with the date of the alleged failure.

(3) In this regulation—

'failure' means an act or omission; and

'prelevant applicant' means—

(a) in a case where information and consultation representatives have been elected or appointed, an information and consultation representative, or

(b) in a case where no information and consultation representatives have been elected or appointed, an employee or an employees' representative.

(4) Where the CAC finds the complaint well-founded it shall make a declaration to that effect and may make an order requiring the employer to take such steps as are necessary to comply with the terms of the negotiated agreement or, as the case may be, the standard information and consultation provisions.

(5) An order made under paragraph (4) shall specify—

(a) the steps which the employer is required to take; and

(b) the period within which the order must be complied with.

(6) If the CAC makes a declaration under paragraph (4) the relevant applicant may, within the period of three months beginning with the date on which the declaration is made, make an application to the Appeal Tribunal for a penalty notice to be issued.

(7) Where such an application is made, the Appeal Tribunal shall issue a written penalty notice to the employer requiring him to pay a penalty to the Secretary of State in respect of the failure unless satisfied, on hearing representations from the employer, that the failure resulted from a reason beyond the employer's control or that he has some other reasonable excuse for his failure.

(8) Regulation 23 shall apply in respect of a penalty notice issued under this regulation.

(9) No order of the CAC under this regulation shall have the effect of suspending or altering the effect of any act done or of any agreement made by the employer or of preventing or delaying any act or agreement which the employer proposes to do or to make.

Penalties

23.–(1) A penalty notice issued under regulation 22 shall specify—

(a) the amount of the penalty which is payable;

(b) the date before which the penalty must be paid; and

(c) the failure and period to which the penalty relates.

(2) No penalty set by the Appeal Tribunal under this regulation may exceed £75,000.

(3) Matters to be taken into account by the Appeal Tribunal when setting the amount of the penalty shall include—

(a) the gravity of the failure;

(b) the period of time over which the failure occurred;

(c) the reason for the failure;

(d) the number of employees affected by the failure; and

(e) the number of employees employed by the undertaking or, where a negotiated agreement covers employees in more than one undertaking, the number of employees employed by both or all of the undertakings.

(4) The date specified under paragraph (1)(b) must not be earlier than the end of the period within which an appeal against a declaration or order made by the CAC under regulation 22 may be made.

(5) If the specified date in a penalty notice has passed and—

(a) the period during which an appeal may be made has expired without an appeal having been made; or

(b) such an appeal has been made and determined,

the Secretary of State may recover from the employer, as a civil debt due to him, any amount payable under the penalty notice which remains outstanding.

(6) The making of an appeal suspends the effect of a penalty notice.

(7) Any sums received by the Secretary of State under regulation 22 or this regulation shall be paid into the Consolidated Fund.

Exclusivity of remedy

24. The remedy for infringement of the rights conferred by Parts I to VI of these Regulations is by way of complaint to the CAC, and not otherwise.

PART VII
CONFIDENTIAL INFORMATION

Breach of statutory duty

25.–(1) A person to whom the employer, pursuant to his obligations under these Regulations, entrusts any information or document on terms requiring it to be held in confidence shall not disclose that information or document except, where the terms permit him to do so, in accordance with those terms.

(2) In this regulation a person referred to in paragraph (1) to whom information or a document is entrusted is referred to as a 'recipient'.

(3) The obligation to comply with paragraph (1) is a duty owed to the employer, and a breach of the duty is actionable accordingly (subject to the defences and other incidents applying to actions for breaches of statutory duty).

(4) Paragraph (3) shall not affect any legal liability which any person may incur by disclosing the information or document, or any right which any person may have in relation to such disclosure otherwise than under this regulation.

(5) No action shall lie under paragraph (3) where the recipient reasonably believed the disclosure to be a 'protected disclosure' within the meaning given to that expression by section 43A of the 1996 Act[7].

(6) A recipient to whom the employer has entrusted any information or document on terms requiring it to be held in confidence may apply to the CAC for a declaration as to whether it was reasonable for the employer to require the recipient to hold the information or document in confidence.

(7) If the CAC considers, on an application under paragraph (6), that the disclosure of the information or document by the recipient would not, or would not be likely to, harm the legitimate interests of the undertaking, it shall make a declaration that it was not reasonable for the employer to require the recipient to hold the information or document in confidence.

(8) If a declaration is made under paragraph (7), the information or document shall not at any time thereafter be regarded as having been entrusted to the recipient who made the application under paragraph (6), or to any other recipient, on terms requiring it to be held in confidence.

Withholding of information by the employer

26.–(1) The employer is not required to disclose any information or document to a person for the purposes of these Regulations where the nature of the information or document is such that, according to objective criteria, the disclosure of the information or document would seriously harm the functioning of, or would be prejudicial to, the undertaking.

(2) If there is a dispute between the employer and—

(a) where information and consultation representatives have been elected or appointed, such a representative; or

(b) where no information and consultation representatives have been elected or appointed, an employee or an employees' representative,

as to whether the nature of the information or document which the employer has failed to provide is such as is described in paragraph (1), the employer or a person referred to in sub-paragraph (a) or (b) may apply to the CAC for a declaration as to whether the information or document is of such a nature.

(3) If the CAC makes a declaration that the disclosure of the information or document in question would not, according to objective criteria, be seriously

[7] Section 43A of the 1996 Act was inserted by the Public Interest Disclosure Act 1998 (c. 23), section 1.

harmful or prejudicial as mentioned in paragraph (1), the CAC shall order the employer to disclose the information or document.

(4) An order under paragraph (3) shall specify—

(a) the information or document to be disclosed;

(b) the person or persons to whom the information or document is to be disclosed;

(c) any terms on which the information or document is to be disclosed; and

(d) the date before which the information or document is to be disclosed.

PART VIII
PROTECTIONS FOR INFORMATION AND CONSULTATION REPRESENTATIVES, ETC.

Right to time off for information and consultation representatives, etc.

27.–(1) An employee who is—

(a) a negotiating representative; or

(b) an information and consultation representative,

is entitled to be permitted by his employer to take reasonable time off during the employee's working hours in order to perform his functions as such a representative.

(2) For the purposes of this regulation, the working hours of an employee shall be taken to be any time when, in accordance with his contract of employment, the employee is required to be at work.

Right to remuneration for time off under regulation 27

28.–(1) An employee who is permitted to take time off under regulation 27 is entitled to be paid remuneration by his employer for the time taken off at the appropriate hourly rate.

(2) Chapter II of Part XIV of the 1996 Act (a week's pay) shall apply in relation to this regulation as it applies in relation to section 62 of the 1996 Act.

(3) The appropriate hourly rate, in relation to an employee, is the amount of one week's pay divided by the number of normal working hours in a week for that employee when employed under the contract of employment in force on the day when time is taken.

(4) But where the number of normal working hours differs from week to week or over a longer period, the amount of one week's pay shall be divided instead by—

(a) the average number of normal working hours calculated by dividing by twelve the total number of the employee's normal working hours during the period of twelve weeks ending with the last complete week before the day on which the time is taken off; or

(b) where the employee has not been employed for a sufficient period to enable the calculations to be made under sub-paragraph (a), a number which fairly represents the number of normal working hours in a week having regard to such of the considerations specified in paragraph (5) as are appropriate in the circumstances.

(5) The considerations referred to in paragraph (4)(b) are—

(a) the average number of normal working hours in a week which the employee could expect in accordance with the terms of his contract; and

(b) the average number of normal working hours of other employees engaged in relevant comparable employment with the same employer.

(6) A right to any amount under paragraph (1) does not affect any right of an employee in relation to remuneration under his contract of employment ('contractual remuneration').

(7) Any contractual remuneration paid to an employee in respect of a period of time off under regulation 27 goes towards discharging any liability of the employer to pay remuneration under paragraph (1) in respect of that period, and, conversely, any payment of remuneration under paragraph (1) in respect of a period goes towards discharging any liability of the employer to pay contractual remuneration in respect of that period.

Right to time off: complaint to tribunals

29.–(1) An employee may present a complaint to an employment tribunal that his employer—

(a) has unreasonably refused to permit him to take time off as required by regulation 27; or

(b) has failed to pay the whole or part of any amount to which the employee is entitled under regulation 28.

(2) A tribunal shall not consider a complaint under this regulation unless it is presented—

(a) before the end of the period of three months beginning with the day on which the time off was taken or on which it is alleged the time off should have been permitted; or

(b) within such further period as the tribunal considers reasonable in a case where it is satisfied that it was not reasonably practicable for the complaint to be presented before the end of that period of three months.

(3) Where a tribunal finds a complaint under this regulation well-founded, the tribunal shall make a declaration to that effect.

(4) If the complaint is that the employer has unreasonably refused to permit the employee to take time off, the tribunal shall also order the employer to pay to the employee an amount equal to the remuneration to which he would have been entitled under regulation 28 if the employer had not refused.

(5) If the complaint is that the employer has failed to pay the employee the whole or part of any amount to which he is entitled under regulation 28, the tribunal shall also order the employer to pay to the employee the amount it finds due to him.

Unfair dismissal

30.–(1) An employee who is dismissed and to whom paragraph (2) or (5) applies shall be regarded, if the reason (or, if more than one, the principal reason) for the dismissal is a reason specified in, respectively, paragraph (3) or (6), as unfairly dismissed for the purposes of Part 10 of the 1996 Act.

(2) This paragraph applies to an employee who is—

(a) an employees' representative;

(b) a negotiating representative;

(c) an information and consultation representative; or

(d) a candidate in an election in which any person elected will, on being elected, be such a representative.

(3) The reasons are that—

(a) the employee performed or proposed to perform any functions or activities as such a representative or candidate;

(b) the employee exercised or proposed to exercise an entitlement conferred on the employee by regulation 27 or 28; or

(c) the employee (or a person acting on his behalf) made or proposed to make a request to exercise such an entitlement.

(4) Paragraph (1) does not apply in the circumstances set out in paragraph (3)(a) where the reason (or principal reason) for the dismissal is that in the performance, or purported performance, of the employee's functions or activities he has disclosed any information or document in breach of the duty in regulation 25, unless the employee reasonably believed the disclosure to be a 'protected disclosure' within the meaning given to that expression by section 43A of the 1996 Act.

(5) This paragraph applies to any employee whether or not he is an employee to whom paragraph (2) applies.

(6) The reasons are that the employee—

(a) took, or proposed to take, any proceedings before an employment tribunal to enforce a right or secure an entitlement conferred on him by these Regulations;

(b) exercised, or proposed to exercise, any entitlement to apply or complain to the CAC or the Appeal Tribunal conferred by these Regulations or to exercise the right to appeal in connection with any rights conferred by these Regulations;

(c) requested, or proposed to request, data in accordance with regulation 5;

(d) acted with a view to securing that an agreement was or was not negotiated or that the standard information and consultation provisions did or did not become applicable;

(e) indicated that he supported or did not support the coming into existence of a negotiated agreement or the application of the standard information and consultation provisions;

(f) stood as a candidate in an election in which any person elected would, on being elected, be a negotiating representative or an information and consultation representative;

(g) influenced or sought to influence by lawful means the way in which votes were to be cast by other employees in a ballot arranged under these Regulations;

(h) voted in such a ballot;

(i) expressed doubts, whether to a ballot supervisor or otherwise, as to whether such a ballot had been properly conducted; or

(j) proposed to do, failed to do, or proposed to decline to do, any of the things mentioned in sub-paragraphs (d) to (i).

(7) It is immaterial for the purpose of paragraph (6)(a)—

(a) whether or not the employee has the right or entitlement; or

(b) whether or not the right has been infringed;

but for that sub-paragraph to apply, the claim to the right and, if applicable, the claim that it has been infringed must be made in good faith.

Subsidiary provisions relating to unfair dismissal

31.–(1) In section 105 of the 1996 Act (redundancy as unfair dismissal)—

(a) in subsection (1)(c) (which requires one of a specified group of subsections to apply for a person to be treated as unfairly dismissed)[8] for '(7F) or (7G)' substitute '(7F), (7G) or (7H)' and

(b) after subsection (7G) insert—

'(7H) This subsection applies if the reason (or, if more than one, the principal reason) for which the employee was selected for dismissal was one specified in paragraph (3) or (6) of regulation 30 of the Information and Consultation of Employees Regulations 2004 (read with paragraphs (4) and (7) of that regulation).'.

(2) In section 108[9] of the 1996 Act (exclusion of right: qualifying period of employment) in subsection (3) (cases where no qualifying period of employment is required)[10]—

(a) the word 'or' at the end of paragraph (j) is repealed; and

(b) after paragraph (k) insert—

'or

(1) paragraph (3) or (6) of regulation 30 of the Information and Consultation of Employees Regulations 2004 (read with paragraphs (4) and (7) of that regulation) applies.'.

(3) In section 109 of the 1996 Act (exclusion of right: upper age limit) in subsection (2) (cases where upper age limit does not apply)[11]—

(a) the word 'or' at the end of paragraph (j) is repealed; and

(b) after paragraph (k) insert—

'or

(1) paragraph (3) or (6) of regulation 30 of the Information and Consultation of Employees Regulations 2004 (read with paragraphs (4) and (7) of that regulation) applies.'.

Detriment

32.—(1) An employee to whom paragraph (2) or (5) applies has the right not to be subjected to any detriment by any act, or deliberate failure to act, by his employer, done on a ground specified in, respectively, paragraph (3) or (6).

(2) This paragraph applies to an employee who is—

(a) an employees' representative;

(b) a negotiating representative;

[8] Section 105 has been amended on a number of occasions to specify additional circumstances in which an employee dismissed by reason of redundancy is to be regarded as unfairly dismissed.

[9] Section 105 has been amended on a number of occasions to specify additional circumstances in which an employee dismissed by reason of redundancy is to be regarded as unfairly dismissed.

[10] Section 108(3) has been amended on a number of occasions to specify additional cases in which no qualifying period of employment is required.

[11] Section 109(2) has been amended on a number of occasions to specify additional cases where the upper age limit does not apply.

(c) an information and consultation representative; or

(d) a candidate in an election in which any person elected will, on being elected, be such a representative.

(3) The ground is that—

(a) the employee performed or proposed to perform any functions or activities as such a representative or candidate;

(b) the employee exercised or proposed to exercise an entitlement conferred on the employee by regulation 27 or 28; or

(c) the employee (or a person acting on his behalf) made or proposed to make a request to exercise such an entitlement.

(4) Paragraph (1) does not apply in the circumstances set out in paragraph (3)(a) where the ground (or principal ground) for the subjection to detriment is that in the performance, or purported performance, of the employee's functions or activities he has disclosed any information or document in breach of the duty in regulation 25, unless the employee reasonably believed the disclosure to be a 'protected disclosure' within the meaning given to that expression by section 43A of the 1996 Act.

(5) This paragraph applies to any employee whether or not he is an employee to whom paragraph (2) applies.

(6) The grounds are that the employee—

(a) took, or proposed to take, any proceedings before an employment tribunal to enforce a right or secure an entitlement conferred on him by these Regulations;

(b) exercised, or proposed to exercise, any entitlement to apply or complain to the CAC or the Appeal Tribunal conferred by these Regulations or to exercise the right to appeal in connection with any rights conferred by these Regulations;

(c) requested, or proposed to request, data in accordance with regulation 5;

(d) acted with a view to securing that an agreement was or was not negotiated or that the standard information and consultation provisions did or did not become applicable;

(e) indicated that he supported or did not support the coming into existence of a negotiated agreement or the application of the standard information and consultation provisions;

(f) stood as a candidate in an election in which any person elected would, on being elected, be a negotiating representative or an information and consultation representative;

(g) influenced or sought to influence by lawful means the way in which votes were to be cast by other employees in a ballot arranged under these Regulations;

(h) voted in such a ballot;

(i) expressed doubts, whether to a ballot supervisor or otherwise, as to whether such a ballot had been properly conducted; or

(j) proposed to do, failed to do, or proposed to decline to do, any of the things mentioned in sub-paragraphs (d) to (i).

(7) It is immaterial for the purpose of paragraph (6)(a)—

(a) whether or not the employee has the right or entitlement; or

(b) whether or not the right has been infringed,

but for that sub-paragraph to apply, the claim to the right and, if applicable, the claim that it has been infringed must be made in good faith.

(8) This regulation does not apply where the detriment in question amounts to dismissal.

Detriment: enforcement and subsidiary provisions

33.–(1) An employee may present a complaint to an employment tribunal that he has been subjected to a detriment in contravention of regulation 32.

(2) The provisions of sections 48(2) to (4) and 49(1) to (5) of the 1996 Act[12] (complaints to employment tribunals and remedies) shall apply in relation to a complaint under this regulation as they apply in relation to a complaint under section 48 of the Act but taking references to the employer as references to the employer within the meaning of regulation 32(1) above.

Conciliation

34. In section 18 of the Employment Tribunals Act 1996 (conciliation) in subsection (1) (which specifies the proceedings and claims to which the section applies)[13]—

(a) the word 'or' at the end of paragraph (m) is repealed;

(b) in the paragraph (n) relating to regulation 19 of the Fishing Vessels (Working Time: Sea-fishermen) Regulations 2004, for '(n)' substitute '(o)'; and

(c) after paragraph (o) insert—

'or

(p) under regulation 29 or 33 of the Information and Consultation of Employees Regulations 2004.'.

PART IX
MISCELLANEOUS

CAC proceedings

35.–(1) Where under these Regulations a person presents a complaint or makes an application to the CAC the complaint or application must be in writing and in such form as the CAC may require.

(2) In its consideration of a complaint or application under these Regulations, the CAC shall make such enquiries as it sees fit and so far as reasonably practicable give any person whom it considers has a proper interest in the complaint or application an opportunity to be heard.

(3) The CAC may draw an adverse inference from a party's failure to comply with any reasonable request to provide information or documents relevant to a complaint presented to it or an application made to it.

[12] Sections 48 and 49 were amended respectively by sections 1(2)(b) and 1(2)(a) of the Employment Rights (Dispute Resolution) Act 1998 (c. 8); there have been other amendments not relevant to these Regulations.

[13] 1996 c. 17. Section 18(1) has been amended on a number of occasions to specify additional proceedings and claims to which the section applies.

(4) A declaration or order made by the CAC under these Regulations may be relied on—

(a) in relation to an employer whose registered office, head office or principal place of business is in England or Wales, as if it were a declaration or order made by the High Court, and

(b) in relation to an employer whose registered office, head office or principal place of business is in Scotland as if it were a declaration or order made by the Court of Session.

(5) A declaration or order made by the CAC under these Regulations must be in writing and state the reasons for the CAC's findings.

(6) An appeal lies to the Appeal Tribunal on any question of law arising from any declaration or order of, or arising in any proceedings before, the CAC under these Regulations.

Appeal Tribunal: location of certain proceedings under these Regulations

36.–(1) Any proceedings before the Appeal Tribunal arising under these Regulations, other than appeals under paragraph (n) of section 21(1) of the Employment Tribunals Act 1996[14] (appeals from employment tribunals on questions of law), shall—

(a) where the registered office or, where there is no registered office, the head office or principal place of business is situated in England and Wales, be held in England and Wales; and

(b) where the registered office or, where there is no registered office, the head office or principal place of business is situated in Scotland, be held in Scotland.

(2) In section 20(4) of the Employment Tribunals Act 1996 (the Appeal Tribunal)—

(a) for '1999 and' substitute '1999,'; and

(b) after '2004' insert 'and regulation 36(1) of the Information and Consultation of Employees Regulations 2004'.

Appeal Tribunal: appeals from employment tribunals

37. In section 21(1) of the Employment Tribunals Act 1996 (circumstances in which an appeal lies to the Appeal Tribunal from an employment tribunal)—

(a) the word 'or' at the end of paragraph (n) is repealed;

(b) in the paragraph (o) relating to the Fishing Vessels (Working Time: Sea-fishermen) Regulations 2004, for '(o)' substitute '(p)'; and

(c) after that paragraph insert—

'or

(q) the Information and Consultation of Employees Regulations 2004.'.

ACAS

38.–(1) If on receipt of an application or complaint under these Regulations the CAC is of the opinion that it is reasonably likely to be settled by conciliation or

[14] Section 21(1) has been amended on a number of occasions to add additional proceedings.

other assistance provided by the Advisory, Conciliation and Arbitration Service ('ACAS') in accordance with paragraph (2), it shall refer the application or complaint to ACAS and shall notify the applicant or complainant and any persons whom it considers have a proper interest in the application or complaint accordingly.

(2) Where the CAC refers an application or complaint to ACAS under paragraph (1), section 210 of the Trade Union and Labour Relations (Consolidation) Act 1992 (power of ACAS to offer assistance to settle disputes) shall apply, and ACAS may offer the parties to the application or complaint its assistance under that section with a view to bringing about a settlement, as if—

(a) the dispute or difference between the parties amounted to a trade dispute as defined in section 218 of that Act; and

(b) the parties to the application or complaint had requested the assistance of ACAS under section 210.

(3) If ACAS does not consider it appropriate to offer its assistance in accordance with paragraph (2) it shall inform the CAC.

(4) If ACAS has offered the parties its assistance in accordance with paragraph (2), the application or complaint referred has not thereafter been settled or withdrawn, and ACAS is of the opinion that no provision or further provision of its assistance is likely to result in a settlement or withdrawal, it shall inform the CAC of its opinion.

(5) If—

(a) an application or complaint is not referred to ACAS, or

(b) it is so referred, but ACAS informs the CAC as mentioned in paragraph (3) or (4),

the CAC shall proceed to hear and determine the application or complaint.

Restrictions on contracting out: general

39.–(1) Any provision in any agreement (whether an employee's contract or not) is void in so far as it purports—

(a) to exclude or limit the operation of any provision of these Regulations other than a provision of Part VIII; or

(b) to preclude a person from bringing any proceedings before the CAC or the Appeal Tribunal under any provision of these Regulations other than a provision of Part VIII.

(2) Paragraph (1) does not apply to any agreement to refrain from continuing any proceedings referred to in sub-paragraph (b) of that paragraph made after the proceedings have been instituted.

Restrictions on contracting out: Part VIII

40.–(1) Any provision in any agreement (whether an employee's contract or not) is void in so far as it purports—

(a) to exclude or limit the operation of any provision of Part VIII; or

(b) to preclude a person from bringing any proceedings before an employment tribunal under that Part.

(2) Paragraph (1) does not apply to any agreement to refrain from instituting or continuing proceedings before an employment tribunal where a conciliation

officer has taken action under section 18 of the Employment Tribunals Act 1996 (conciliation).

(3) Paragraph (1) does not apply to any agreement to refrain from instituting or continuing before an employment tribunal proceedings within section 18(1) of the Employment Tribunals Act 1996 (proceedings under these Regulations where conciliation is available) if the conditions regulating compromise agreements under these Regulations are satisfied in relation to the agreement.

(4) For the purposes of paragraph (3) the conditions regulating compromise agreements are that—

(a) the agreement must be in writing;

(b) the agreement must relate to the particular proceedings;

(c) the employee must have received advice from a relevant independent adviser as to the terms and effect of the proposed agreement and, in particular, its effect on his ability to pursue his rights before an employment tribunal;

(d) there must be in force, when the adviser gives the advice, a contract of insurance, or an indemnity provided for members of a profession or a professional body, covering the risk of a claim by the employee in respect of loss arising in consequence of the advice;

(e) the agreement must identify the adviser; and

(f) the agreement must state that the conditions in sub-paragraphs (a) to (e) are satisfied.

(5) A person is a relevant independent adviser for the purposes of paragraph (4)(c)—

(a) if he is a qualified lawyer;

(b) if he is an officer, official, employee or member of an independent trade union who has been certified in writing by the trade union as competent to give advice and as authorised to do so on behalf of the trade union;

or

(c) if he works at an advice centre (whether as an employee or as a volunteer) and has been certified in writing by the centre as competent to give advice and as authorised to do so on behalf of the centre.

(6) But a person is not a relevant independent adviser for the purposes of paragraph (4)(c)—

(a) if he is, is employed by or is acting in the matter for the employer or an associated employer;

(b) in the case of a person within paragraph (5)(b) or (c), if the trade union or advice centre is the employer or an associated employer; or

(c) in the case of a person within (5)(c), if the employee makes a payment for the advice received from him.

(7) In paragraph (5)(a), 'qualified lawyer' means—

(a) as respects England and Wales, a barrister (whether in practice as such or employed to give legal advice), a solicitor who holds a practising certificate, or a person other than a barrister or a solicitor who is an authorised advocate or authorised litigator (within the meaning of the Courts and Legal Services Act 1990[15]); and

[15] 1990 c. 41.

(b) as respects Scotland, an advocate (whether in practice as such or employed to give legal advice) or a solicitor who holds a practising certificate.

(8) A person shall be treated as being a qualified lawyer within the meaning of paragraph (7)(a) if he is a Fellow of the Institute of Legal Executives employed by a solicitors' practice.

(9) For the purposes of paragraph (6) any two employers shall be treated as associated if—

(a) one is a company of which the other (directly or indirectly) has control; or

(b) both are companies of which a third person (directly or indirectly) has control;

and 'associated employer' shall be construed accordingly.

Amendments to the Employment Appeal Tribunal Rules 1993

41. The Employment Appeal Tribunal Rules 1993[16] shall be amended as follows—

(a) In rule 2(1), after the definition of 'the 2004 Regulations' insert—

' "the Information and Consultation Regulations" means the Information and Consultation of Employees Regulations 2004;';

(b) In rules 3(1)(d), 3(3)(d), 4(1)(e), 5(c) and 7(1)(e), after 'the 2004 Regulations' insert—

'or regulation 35(6) of the Information and Consultation Regulations';

(c) In rule 16AA—

(i) after 'the 2004 Regulations' insert—

'or regulation 22(6) of the Information and Consultation Regulations; and

(ii) for 'those regulations' substitute 'the 2004 Regulations or regulation 22(4) of the Information and Consultation Regulations';

(d) In rules 26 and 31(1)(c)—

(i) omit 'or' before 'regulation 33'; and

(ii) after 'the 2004 Regulations' insert 'or regulation 22 of the Information and Consultation Regulations';

(e) In the Schedule, in the heading to Form 1A—

(i) omit '*or*' before '*regulation* 47(6)'; and

(ii) insert at the end '*or regulation 35(6) of the Information and Consultation of Employees Regulations 2004*'; and

(f) In the Schedule, in Form 4B—

(i) in the heading, after '*Regulations 2004*' insert '*or regulation 22 of the Information and Consultation of Employees Regulations 2004*'; and

(ii) in paragraph 5, after 'Regulations 2004' insert 'or regulation 22 of the Information and Consultation of Employees Regulations 2004 *(delete which does not apply)*.'.

Crown employment

42.—(1) These Regulations have effect in relation to Crown employment and persons in Crown employment as they have effect in relation to other employment and other employees.

[16] S.I. 1993/2854, amended by S.I. 1996/3216, 2001/1128 and 2004/2526.

(2) In these Regulations 'Crown employment' means employment in an undertaking to which these Regulations apply and which is under or for the purposes of a government department or any officer or body exercising on behalf of the Crown functions conferred by a statutory provision.

(3) For the purposes of the application of these Regulations in relation to Crown employment in accordance with paragraph (1)—

(a) references to an employee shall be construed as references to a person in Crown employment; and

(b) references to a contract of employment shall be construed as references to the terms of employment of a person in Crown employment.

Exception for merchant navy

43.–(1) Subject to paragraph (3), no long haul crew member shall be—

(a) a negotiating representative; or

(b) an information and consultation representative.

(2) In paragraph (1), a 'long haul crew member' means a person who is a member of a merchant navy crew other than—

(a) a ferry worker; or

(b) a person who normally works on voyages the duration of which is less than 48 hours.

(3) Paragraph (1) does not apply where the employer decides that the long haul crew member in question shall be permitted to be, as the case may be, a negotiating representative or an information and consultation representative.

(4) Where paragraph (1) applies, no long haul crew member shall—

(a) stand as a candidate for election as a negotiating representative or an information and consultation representative; or

(b) be appointed or elected to be a negotiating representative or an information and consultation representative.

Gerry Sutcliffe

Parliamentary Under Secretary of State for Employment Relations, Postal Services and Consumers, Department of Trade and Industry

21st December 2004

SCHEDULE 1

Regulation 3

APPLICATION OF REGULATIONS

Number of employees	*Date Regulations apply*
At least 150	6 April 2005
At least 100	6 April 2007
At least 50	6 April 2008

SCHEDULE 2

Regulation 19

REQUIREMENTS FOR BALLOTS HELD UNDER REGULATION 19

BALLOT ARRANGEMENTS

1. Ballots held under regulation 19 must comply with the requirements specified in paragraph 2.

2. The requirements referred to in paragraph 1 are that—

(a) the ballot must comprise a single ballot but may instead, if the employer so decides, comprise separate ballots of employees in such constituencies as the employer may decide where the employer considers that if separate ballots were to be held for those constituencies, the information and consultation representatives to be elected would better reflect the interests of the employees as a whole than if a single ballot were held;

(b) if, at any point, it becomes clear that the number of people standing as candidates in the ballot is equal to or fewer than the relevant number of information and consultation representatives (as defined in regulation 19(3)), the obligation on the employer to hold the ballot in regulation 19 will cease and the candidates referred to above will become the information and consultation representatives;

(c) all employees of the undertaking on the day on which the votes may be cast in the ballot, or if the votes may be cast on more than one day, on the first day of those days, must be given an entitlement to vote in the ballot;

(d) any employee who is an employee of the undertaking at the latest time at which a person may become a candidate in the ballot is entitled to stand in the ballot as a candidate as an information and consultation representative;

(e) the employer must, in accordance with paragraph 6, appoint an independent ballot supervisor to supervise the conduct of the ballot;

(f) after the employer has formulated proposals as to the arrangements for the ballot and before he has published the final arrangements under sub-paragraph (g) he must, so far as reasonably practicable, consult with employees' representatives or, if no such representatives exist, the employees, on the proposed arrangements for the ballot; and

(g) the employer must publish the final arrangements for the ballot in such manner as to bring them to the attention of, so far as reasonably practicable, his employees and, where they exist, the employees' representatives.

3. Any employee or an employees' representative who believes that the arrangements for the ballot are defective may, within a period of 21 days beginning on the date on which the employer published the final arrangements under paragraph 2(g), present a complaint to the CAC.

4. Where the CAC finds the complaint well-founded it shall make a declaration to that effect and may make an order requiring the employer to modify the

arrangements he has made for the ballot or to satisfy the requirements in sub-paragraphs (a) to (f) of paragraph 2.

5. An order under paragraph 4 shall specify the modifications to the arrangements which the employer is required to make and the requirements he must satisfy.
6. A person is an independent ballot supervisor for the purposes of paragraph 2(e) if the employer reasonably believes that he will carry out any functions conferred on him in relation to the ballot competently and has no reasonable grounds for believing that his independence might reasonably be called into question.
7. For the purposes of paragraph 3 the arrangements for the ballot are defective if any of the requirements specified in sub-paragraphs (a) to (f) of paragraph 2 is not satisfied.

CONDUCT OF THE BALLOT

8. The employer must—

   (a) ensure that a ballot supervisor appointed under paragraph 2(e) carries out his functions under this Schedule and that there is no interference with his carrying out of those functions; and

   (b) comply with all reasonable requests made by a ballot supervisor for the purposes of or in connection with the carrying out of those functions.

9. A ballot supervisor's appointment shall require that he—

   (a) supervises the conduct of the ballot he is being appointed to supervise, in accordance with the arrangements for the ballot published by the employer under paragraph 2(g) or, where appropriate, in accordance with the arrangements as required to be modified by an order made under paragraph 4;

   (b) does not conduct the ballot before the employer has satisfied the requirement specified in paragraph 2(g) and—

      (i) where no complaint has been presented under paragraph 3, before the expiry of 21 days beginning with the date on which the employer published his arrangements under paragraph 2(g); or

      (ii) where a complaint has been presented under paragraph 3, before the complaint has been determined and, where appropriate, the arrangements have been modified as required by an order made as a result of the complaint;

   (c) conducts the ballot so as to secure that—

      (i) so far as reasonably practicable, those entitled to vote are given the opportunity to do so;

      (ii) so far as reasonably practicable, those entitled to stand as candidates are given the opportunity to stand;

      (iii) so far as reasonably practicable, those voting are able to do so in secret; and

      (iv) the votes given in the ballot are fairly and accurately counted.

10. As soon as reasonably practicable after the date of the ballot, the ballot supervisor must publish the results of the ballot in such manner as to make them available to the employer and, so far as reasonably practicable, the employees entitled to vote in the ballot and the persons who stood as candidates in the ballot.

11. A ballot supervisor shall publish a report ('an ineffective ballot report') where he considers (whether or not on the basis of representations made to him by another person) that—

(a) any of the requirements referred to in paragraph 2 was not satisfied with the result that the outcome of the ballot would have been different; or

(b) there was interference with the carrying out of his functions or a failure by the employer to comply with all reasonable requests made by him with the result that he was unable to form a proper judgement as to whether each of the requirements referred to in paragraph 2 was satisfied in the ballot.

12. Where a ballot supervisor publishes an ineffective ballot report the report must be published within a period of one month commencing on the date on which the ballot supervisor publishes the results of the ballot under paragraph 10.

13. A ballot supervisor must publish an ineffective ballot report in such manner as to make it available to the employer and, so far as reasonably practicable, the employees entitled to vote in the ballot and the persons who stood as candidates in the ballot.

14. Where a ballot supervisor publishes an ineffective ballot report, the outcome of the ballot shall be of no effect and—

(a) if there has been a single ballot or an ineffective ballot report has been published in respect of every separate ballot, the outcome of the ballot or ballots shall be of no effect and the employer shall again be under the obligation in regulation 19;

(b) if there have been separate ballots and sub-paragraph (a) does not apply—

(i) the employer shall arrange for the separate ballot or ballots in respect of which an ineffective ballot report has been issued to be reheld in accordance with regulation 19, and

(ii) no such ballot shall have effect until it has been reheld and no ineffective ballot report has been published in respect of it.

15. All costs relating to the holding of the ballot, including payments made to a ballot supervisor for supervising the conduct of the ballot, shall be borne by the employer (whether or not an ineffective ballot report has been made).

EXPLANATORY NOTE

(THIS NOTE IS NOT PART OF THE REGULATIONS)

These Regulations, made under powers in section 42 of the Employment Relations Act 2004 implement in Great Britain Directive 2002/14/EC establishing a general framework for informing and consulting employees in the European Community ('the Information and Consultation Directive').

The principal provisions of the Regulations provide as follows—

1. Regulation 3 sets out the undertakings to which the Regulations apply.
2. Regulation 4 provides a method of calculating the number of employees in an undertaking, regulation 5 provides the employees of an undertaking with an entitlement to information to make the calculation in regulation 4 and regulation 6 allows a complaint to be made to the Central Arbitration Committee ('the CAC') that the employer has failed to provide such information or has supplied false or incomplete information.
3. Part III deals with negotiated agreements and, in particular, regulation 7 provides that an employer must start negotiations on receipt of a valid employee request. However, the employer does not have to do so if there exists a pre-existing agreement and the request was made by fewer than 40% of employees. In the latter case the employer can choose to seek employee endorsement for the request and, unless at least 40% of employees in the undertaking and the majority of employees who vote do endorse the request, the employer does not have to start negotiations (regulation 8).
4. Regulation 9 allows for combined ballots to be held where there are pre-existing agreements covering groups of undertakings.
5. Regulation 10 covers complaints to the CAC about ballots held under regulation 8 or 9.
6. Negotiations can also be commenced by an employer notification of his intention to start negotiations (regulation 11).
7. Regulation 12 contains certain restrictions on when an employee request or an employer notification can be made.
8. Regulation 13 allows applications to the CAC that an employee request or an employer notification is invalid.
9. Regulation 14 sets out what steps have to be taken to initiate negotiations, including the appointment or election of negotiating representatives and regulation 15 allows a complaint to the CAC in relation to the appointment or election of such representatives.
10. Regulation 16 sets out what a negotiated agreement must contain and how it must be approved and regulation 17 provides for a complaint to the CAC about such approval.
11. Part IV contains provisions relating to the standard information and consultation provisions. Regulation 18 sets out when they apply, regulation 19 obliges the employer to hold a ballot for the appointment of information and consultation representatives to act under the standard provisions and regulation 20 sets out the employer's obligations under the standard provisions.
12. Regulation 21 places the parties under a duty of cooperation.
13. Part VI deals with compliance and enforcement. Regulation 22 provides for complaints to the CAC about the operation of a negotiated agreement or the standard information and consultation provisions and for an application to be made to the Employment Appeal Tribunal for a penalty notice where the CAC finds a failure to comply with the negotiated agreement or the standard provisions by the employer. Regulation 23 deals with penalties under a penalty notice.
14. Regulation 24 provides that the only remedies available are the ones under Parts I to VI of the Regulations and not otherwise.
15. Part VII deals with confidential information and regulation 25 imposes a

statutory duty not to disclose confidential information on anyone to whom such information is given and provides for an application to the CAC to challenge the necessity of information or a document being treated as confidential. Regulation 26 provides that an employer does not have to disclose certain information.

16. Part VIII provides protections to employees taking part in negotiations, information and consultation procedures or elections including protection against unfair dismissal (regulations 30 and 31) and detriment (regulations 32 and 33). Regulation 34 allows ACAS to conciliate in such disputes.

17. Regulations 39 and 40 place restrictions on contracting out of the rights provided by these Regulations.

18. Regulation 42 applies the rights of employees to Crown employees (although the Regulations will only apply if they are employed an undertaking within the meaning of the Directive) and regulation 43 provides an exception for the merchant navy.

A full Regulatory Impact Assessment of the effect that this instrument will have on the costs of business has been prepared and placed in the library of each House. This document can be obtained from the Department of Trade and Industry, Employee Involvement Team, Employment Relations Directorate, 1 Victoria Street, London, SW1H OET. It can also be downloaded from *http://www.dti.gov.uk/access/ria/index.htm.*

APPENDIX 2

Directive 2002/14/EC of the European Parliament and of the Council of 11 March 2002

establishing a general framework for informing and consulting employees in the European Community

THE EUROPEAN PARLIAMENT AND THE COUNCIL OF THE EUROPEAN UNION,

Having regard to the Treaty establishing the European Community, and in particular Article 137(2) thereof,

Having regard to the proposal from the Commission[1],

Having regard to the opinion of the Economic and Social Committee[2],

Having regard to the opinion of the Committee of the Regions[3],

Acting in accordance with the procedure referred to in Article 251[4], and in the light of the joint text approved by the Conciliation Committee on 23 January 2002,

Whereas:

(1) Pursuant to Article 136 of the Treaty, a particular objective of the Community and the Member States is to promote social dialogue between management and labour.

(2) Point 17 of the Community Charter of Fundamental Social Rights of Workers provides, *inter alia*, that information, consultation and participation for workers must be developed along appropriate lines, taking account of the practices in force in different Member States.

(3) The Commission consulted management and labour at Community level on the possible direction of Community action on the information and consultation of employees in undertaking within the Community.

(4) Following this consultation, the Commission considered that Community action was advisable and again consulted management and labour on the contents of the planned proposal; management and labour have presented their opinions to the Commission.

(5) Having completed this second stage of consultation, management and labour

[1] OJ C 2, 5.1.1999, p. 3.

[2] OJ C 258, 10.9.1999, p. 24.

[3] OJ C 144, 16.5.2001, p. 58.

[4] Opinion of the European Parliament of 14 April 1999 (OJ C 219, 30.7.1999, p. 223), confirmed on 16 September 1999 (OJ C 54, 25.2.2000, p. 55), Council Common Position of 27 July 2001 (OJ C 307, 31.10.2001, p. 16) and Decision of the European Parliament of 23 October 2001 (not yet published in the Official Journal). Decision of the European Parliament of 5 February 2002 and Decision of the Council of 18 February 2002.

have not informed the Commission of their wish to initiate the process potentially leading to the conclusion of an agreement.

(6) The existence of legal frameworks at national and Community level intended to ensure that employees are involved in the affairs of the undertaking employing them and in decisions which affect them has not always prevented serious decisions affecting employees from being taken and made public without adequate procedures having been implemented beforehand to inform and consult them.

(7) There is a need to strengthen dialogue and promote mutual trust within undertakings in order to improve risk anticipation, make work organisation more flexible and facilitate employee access to training within the undertaking while maintaining security, make employees aware of adaptation needs, increase employees' availability to undertake measures and activities to increase their employability, promote employee involvement in the operation and future of the undertaking and increase its competitiveness.

(8) There is a need, in particular, to promote and enhance information and consultation on the situation and likely development of employment within the undertaking and, where the employer's evaluation suggests that employment within the undertaking may be under threat, the possible anticipatory measures envisaged, in particular in terms of employee training and skill development, with a view to offsetting the negative developments or their consequences and increasing the employability and adaptability of the employees likely to be affected.

(9) Timely information and consultation is a prerequisite for the success of the restructuring and adaptation of undertakings to the new conditions created by globalisation of the economy, particularly through the development of new forms of organisation of work.

(10) The Community has drawn up and implemented an employment strategy based on the concepts of 'anticipation', 'prevention' and 'employability', which are to be incorporated as key elements into all public policies likely to benefit employment, including the policies of individual undertakings, by strengthening the social dialogue with a view to promoting change compatible with preserving the priority objective of employment.

(11) Further development of the internal market must be properly balanced, maintaining the essential values on which our societies are based and ensuring that all citizens benefit from economic development.

(12) Entry into the third stage of economic and monetary union has extended and accelerated the competitive pressures at European level. This means that more supportive measures are needed at national level.

(13) The existing legal frameworks for employee information and consultation at Community and national level tend to adopt an excessively a posteriori approach to the process of change, neglect the economic aspects of decisions taken and do not contribute either to genuine anticipation of employment developments within the undertaking or to risk prevention.

(14) All of these political, economic, social and legal developments call for changes to the existing legal framework providing for the legal and practical instruments enabling the right to be informed and consulted to be exercised.

(15) This Directive is without prejudice to national systems regarding the exercise of this right in practice where those entitled to exercise it are required to indicate their wishes collectively.

(16) This Directive is without prejudice to those systems which provide for the direct involvement of employees, as long as they are always free to exercise the right to be informed and consulted through their representatives.

(17) Since the objectives of the proposed action, as outlined above, cannot be adequately achieved by the Member States, in that the object is to establish a framework for employee information and consultation appropriate for the new European context described above, and can therefore, in view of the scale and impact of the proposed action, be better achieved at Community level, the Community may adopt measures in accordance with the principle of subsidiarity as set out in Article 5 of the Treaty. In accordance with the principle of proportionality, as set out in that Article, this Directive does not go beyond what is necessary in order to achieve these objectives.

(18) The purpose of this general framework is to establish minimum requirements applicable throughout the Community while not preventing Member States from laying down provisions more favourable to employees.

(19) The purpose of this general framework is also to avoid any administrative, financial or legal constraints which would hinder the creation and development of small and medium-sized undertakings. To this end, the scope of this Directive should be restricted, according to the choice made by Member States, to undertakings with at least 50 employees or establishments employing at least 20 employees.

(20) This takes into account and is without prejudice to other national measures and practices aimed at fostering social dialogue within companies not covered by this Directive and within public administrations.

(21) However, on a transitional basis, Member States in which there is no established statutory system of information and consultation of employees or employee representation should have the possibility of further restricting the scope of the Directive as regards the numbers of employees.

(22) A Community framework for informing and consulting employees should keep to a minimum the burden on undertakings or establishments while ensuring the effective exercise of the rights granted.

(23) The objective of this Directive is to be achieved through the establishment of a general framework comprising the principles, definitions and arrangements for information and consultation, which it will be for the Member States to comply with and adapt to their own national situation, ensuring, where appropriate, that management and labour have a leading role by allowing them to define freely, by agreement, the arrangements for informing and consulting employees which they consider to be best suited to their needs and wishes.

(24) Care should be taken to avoid affecting some specific rules in the field of employee information and consultation existing in some national laws, addressed to undertakings or establishments which pursue political, professional, organisational, religious, charitable, educational, scientific or artistic aims, as well as aims involving information and the expression of opinions.

(25) Undertakings and establishments should be protected against disclosure of certain particularly sensitive information.

(26) The employer should be allowed not to inform and consult where this would seriously damage the undertaking or the establishment or where he has to comply immediately with an order issued to him by a regulatory or supervisory body.

(27) Information and consultation imply both rights and obligations for management and labour at undertaking or establishment level.

(28) Administrative or judicial procedures, as well as sanctions that are effective, dissuasive and proportionate in relation to the seriousness of the offence, should be applicable in cases of infringement of the obligations based on this Directive.

(29) This Directive should not affect the provisions, where these are more specific, of Council Directive 98/59/EC of 20 July 1998 on the approximation of the laws of the Member States relating to collective redundancies[5] and of Council Directive 2001/23/EC of 12 March 2001 on the approximation of the laws of the Member States relating to the safeguarding of employees' rights in the event of transfers of undertakings, businesses or parts of undertakings or businesses[6].

(30) Other rights of information and consultation, including those arising from Council Directive 94/45/EEC of 22 September 1994 on the establishment of a European Works Council or a procedure in Community-scale undertakings and Community-scale groups of undertakings for the purposes of informing and consulting employees[7], should not be affected by this Directive.

(31) Implementation of this Directive should not be sufficient grounds for a reduction in the general level of protection of workers in the areas to which it applies,

HAVE ADOPTED THIS DIRECTIVE:

Article 1

Object and principles

1. The purpose of this Directive is to establish a general framework setting out minimum requirements for the right to information and consultation of employees in undertakings or establishments within the Community.
2. The practical arrangements for information and consultation shall be defined and implemented in accordance with national law and industrial relations practices in individual Member States in such a way as to ensure their effectiveness.
3. When defining or implementing practical arrangements for information and consultation, the employer and the employee's representatives shall work in a spirit of cooperation and with due regard for their reciprocal rights and obliga-

[5] OJ L 225, 12.8.1998, p. 16. [6] OJ L 82, 22.3.2001, p. 16.

[7] OJ L 254, 30.9.1994, p. 64. Directive as amended by Directive 97/74/EC (OJ L 10, 16.1.1998, p. 22).

tions, taking into account the interests both of the undertaking or establishment and of the employees.

Article 2

Definitions

For the purposes of this Directive:

(a) 'undertaking' means a public or private undertaking carrying out an economic activity, whether or not operating for gain, which is located within the territory of the Member States;
(b) 'establishment' means a unit of business defined in accordance with national law and practice, and located within the territory of a Member State, where an economic activity is carried out on an ongoing basis with human and material resources;
(c) 'employer' means the natural or legal person party to employment contracts or employment relationships with employees, in accordance with national law and practice;
(d) 'employee' means any person who, in the Member State concerned, is protected as an employee under national employment law and in accordance with national practice;
(e) 'employees' representatives' means the employees' representatives provided for by national laws and/or practices;
(f) 'information' means transmission by the employer to the employees' representatives of data in order to enable them to acquaint themselves with the subject matter and to examine it;
(g) 'consultation' means the exchange of views and establishment of dialogue between the employees' representatives and the employer.

Article 3

Scope

1. This Directive shall apply, according to the choice made by Member States, to:

(a) undertakings employing at least 50 employees in any one Member State, or
(b) establishments employing at least 20 employees in any one Member State.

Member States shall determine the method for calculating the thresholds of employees employed.

2. In conformity with the principles and objectives of this Directive, Member States may lay down particular provisions applicable to undertakings or establishments which pursue directly and essentially political, professional organisational, religious, charitable, educational, scientific or artistic aims, as well as aims involving information and the expression of opinions, on condition that, at the date of

entry into force of this Directive, provisions of that nature already exist in national legislation.

3. Member States may derogate from this Directive through particular provisions applicable to the crews of vessels plying the high seas.

Article 4

Practical arrangements for information and consultation

1. In accordance with the principles set out in Article 1 and without prejudice to any provisions and/or practices in force more favourable to employees, the Member States shall determine the practical arrangements for exercising the right to information and consultation at the appropriate level in accordance with this Article.

2. Information and consultation shall cover:

(a) information on the recent and probable development of the undertaking's or the establishment's activities and economic situation;
(b) information and consultation on the situation, structure and probable development of employment within the undertaking or establishment and on any anticipatory measures envisaged, in particular where there is a threat to employment;
(c) information and consultation on decisions likely to lead to substantial changes in work organisation or in contractual relations, including those covered by the Community provisions referred to in Article 9(1).

3. Information shall be given at such time, in such fashion and with such content as are appropriate to enable, in particular, employees' representatives to conduct an adequate study and, where necessary, prepare for consultation.

4. Consultation shall take place:

(a) while ensuring that the timing, method and content thereof are appropriate;
(b) at the relevant level of management and representation, depending on the subject under discussion;
(c) on the basis of information supplied by the employer in accordance with Article 2(f) and of the opinion which the employees' representatives are entitled to formulate;
(d) in such a way as to enable employees' representatives to meet the employer and obtain a response, and the reasons for that response, to any opinion they might formulate;
(e) with a view to reaching an agreement on decisions within the scope of the employer's powers referred to in paragraph 2(c).

Article 5

Information and consultation deriving from an agreement

Member States may entrust management and labour at the appropriate level, including at undertaking or establishment level, with defining freely and at any time through negotiated agreement the practical arrangements for informing and consulting employees. These agreements, and agreements existing on the date laid down in Article 11, as well as any subsequent renewals of such agreements, may establish, while respecting the principles set out in Article 1 and subject to conditions and limitations laid down by the Member States, provisions which are different from those referred to in Article 4.

Article 6

Confidential information

1. Member States shall provide that, within the conditions and limits laid down by national legislation, the employees' representatives, and any experts who assist them, are not authorised to reveal to employees or to third parties, any information which, in the legitimate interest of the undertaking or establishment, has expressly been provided to them in confidence. This obligation shall continue to apply, wherever the said representatives or experts are, even after expiry of their terms of office. However, a Member State may authorise the employees' representatives and anyone assisting them to pass on confidential information to employees and to third parties bound by an obligation of confidentiality.

2. Member States shall provide, in specific cases and within the conditions and limits laid down by national legislation, that the employer is not obliged to communicate information or undertake consultation when the nature of that information or consultation is such that, according to objective criteria, it would seriously harm the functioning of the undertaking or establishment or would be prejudicial to it.

3. Without prejudice to existing national procedures, Member States shall provide for administrative or judicial review procedures for the case where the employer requires confidentiality or does not provide the information in accordance with paragraphs 1 and 2. They may also provide for procedures intended to safeguard the confidentiality of the information in question.

Article 7

Protection of employees' representatives

Member States shall ensure that employees' representatives, when carrying out their functions, enjoy adequate protection and guarantees to enable them to perform properly the duties which have been assigned to them.

Article 8

Protection of rights

1. Member States shall provide for appropriate measures in the event of non-compliance with this Directive by the employer or the employees' representatives. In particular, they shall ensure that adequate administrative or judicial procedures are available to enable the obligations deriving from this Directive to be enforced.

2. Member States shall provide for adequate sanctions to be applicable in the event of infringement of this Directive by the employer, or the employees' representatives. These sanctions must be effective, proportionate and dissuasive.

Article 9

Link between this Directive and other Community and national provisions

1. This Directive shall be without prejudice to the specific information and consultation procedures set out in Article 2 of Directive 98/59/EC and Article 7 of Directive 2001/23/EC.

2. This Directive shall be without prejudice to provisions adopted in accordance with Directives 94/45/EC and 97/74/EC.

3. This Directive shall be without prejudice to other rights to information, consultation and participation under national law.

4. Implementation of this Directive shall not be sufficient grounds for any regression in relation to the situation which already prevails in each Member State and in relation to the general level of protection of workers in the areas to which it applies.

Article 10

Transitional provisions

Notwithstanding Article 3, a Member State in which there is, at the date of entry into force of this Directive, no general, permanent and statutory system of information and consultation of employees, nor a general, permanent and statutory system of employee representation at the workplace allowing employees to be represented for that purpose, may limit the application of the national provisions implementing this Directive to:

(a) undertakings employing at least 150 employees or establishments employing at least 100 employees until 23 March 2007, and
(b) undertakings employing at least 100 employees or establishments employing at least 50 employees during the year following the date in point (a).

Article 11

Transposition

1. Member States shall adopt the laws, regulations and administrative provisions necessary to comply with this Directive not later than 23 March 2005 or shall ensure that management and labour introduce by that date the required provisions by way of agreement, the Member States being obliged to take all necessary steps enabling them to guarantee the results imposed by this Directive at all times. They shall forthwith inform the Commission thereof.

2. Where Member States adopt these measures, they shall contain a reference to this Directive or shall be accompanied by such reference on the occasion of their official publication. The methods of making such reference shall be laid down by the Member States.

Article 12

Review by the Commission

Not later than 23 March 2007, the Commission shall, in consultation with the Member States and the social partners at Community level, review the application of this Directive with a view to proposing any necessary amendments.

Article 13

Entry into force

This Directive shall enter into force on the day of its publication in the *Official Journal of the European Communities.*

Article 14

Addresses

This Directive is addressed to the Member States.

Done at Brussels, 11 March 2002.

For the European Parliament	*For the Council*
The President	*The President*
P. COX	J. PIQUÉ I CAMPS

APPENDIX 3

The Information and Consultation of Employees Regulations 2004

DTI Guidance

CONTENTS

SUMMARY OF THE LEGISLATION

- *Coverage*. The legislation applies to 'undertakings' situated in Great Britain that carry out an economic activity and have 50 or more employees. There is equivalent legislation for undertakings situated in Northern Ireland.
- *Trigger*. The requirement to inform and consult employees does not operate automatically. It is triggered either by a formal request from employees for an information and consultation agreement, or by employers choosing to start the process themselves.
- *Negotiated agreements*. Where employees make a request, or employers start the process themselves, there would normally be a period for drawing up and agreeing the on-going information and consultation arrangements to be put in place. Employers and employees are free to agree arrangements and structures tailored to their individual circumstances.
- *Standard provisions*. Where no agreement is reached, certain 'standard' provisions would apply requiring the employer to inform and consult in the way set out in regulation 20.
- *Pre-existing agreements*. There is an important exception for pre-existing agreements. Where the employer already has arrangements in place that have been agreed with employees prior to an employee request being made under the Regulations for new arrangements, the employer may ballot the workforce to determine whether it endorses the employee request, or whether it is happy with what it has. Only if the workforce endorses the request would the employer come under the obligation in the Regulations to negotiate a new agreement, otherwise the pre-existing agreement continues to apply. Pre-existing agreements must be in writing, state how employees or their representatives will be informed and consulted, and cover all the employees in the undertaking.
- *Groups and establishments*. It will be possible to set up arrangements that cover more than one undertaking, and to have different arrangements in different parts of the business, for example, at different establishments (sites), in different business units, or covering different sections of the workforce.
- *Confidential information and employee protections*. Information may be given to employee representatives on a confidential basis to protect the interests of the undertaking, or withheld altogether where disclosure would seriously harm or prejudice the undertaking. There are provisions to protect employees who seek to exercise their legal rights.
- *Enforcement*. Most disputes are to be resolved by the Central Arbitration Committee. Employers may be liable to a financial penalty if they fail to inform and consult as required. The enforcement provisions do not apply to pre-existing agreements.

INTRODUCTION

1. The Information and Consultation of Employees Regulations 2004[1] give employees in larger firms—those with 50 or more employees—rights to be informed and consulted about the business they work for (what this may cover in practice is explained later in the guidance). The Regulations implement an EC Directive[2], and are based on a framework for implementation agreed with the CBI and the TUC[3]. They apply to businesses with 150+ employees from 6 April 2005, to those with 100+ employees from 6 April 2007, and to those with 50+ employees from 6 April 2008. They will not apply to businesses with less than 50 employees.
2. The Government strongly supports the principle of employers informing and consulting their employees on an on-going basis about matters that may affect them. It is good for the employees themselves, and good for the organisations they work for. A wide body of evidence has demonstrated that good practice in human resources, work organisation and employee relations can help raise employee commitment and engagement, helps reduce absenteeism and staff turnover, and leads to higher levels of productivity, performance and customer satisfaction. The legal obligations contained in the Regulations apply to larger undertakings that carry out an economic activity, but the Government would encourage all employers, irrespective of their size and the nature of their activity, to inform and consult their employees in a way suited to their particular circumstances.
3. This guidance is designed to provide a plain explanation of the Information and Consultation Regulations. It aims to help employers comply with their legal obligations. In some places, it offers advice which is not a legal requirement, but which is recommended good practice to help in complying with the law—where this is the case, it is made clear in the text. In practice, the most effective way for employers to meet the legal requirements will be by reaching a voluntary agreement with their employees on how they will inform and consult, and the Government would strongly encourage this. In addition, ACAS provides good practice guidance on how to set up and operate effective arrangements for information and consultation taking account of the legal requirements[4].
4. It is important to bear in mind that this guidance contains the DTI's interpretation of the I&C Regulations and of the EC Directive. Where the Regulations contain provisions not expressly required by the Directive (for example, the provisions on employee requests), this guidance seeks to explain the policy intentions behind them. Ultimately though, it is up to the courts to interpret the legislation—in the first instance, this normally means the Central Arbitration Committee (CAC). In taking decisions, the CAC is not

[1] Statutory Instrument 2004 No. 3426.

[2] Directive 2002/14/EC of the European Parliament and of the Council of 11 March 2002 establishing a general framework for informing and consulting employees in the European Community.

[3] See *High Performance Workplaces—Informing and Consulting Employees* July 2003, chapter 1.

[4] See the ACAS website at http://www.acas.org.uk/

bound to follow this guidance. However, those involved in CAC proceedings, such as employers, employees and their representatives, may bring provisions in the guidance to the attention of the CAC as part of the evidence they submit to support their position. The final say rests with the European Court of Justice.

COVERAGE

5. When it is fully in force, the legislation will apply to undertakings with 50 or more employees in the UK that have their registered or head office, or principal place of business in Great Britain (see regulation 3):

Undertakings

'undertakings'[5]. These are defined in the Directive and the Regulations as 'a public or private undertaking carrying out an economic activity, whether or not operating for gain'. In terms of companies, DTI believes this means a separately incorporated *legal* entity (which would have its own shareholders and, in the case of British companies, a unique registration number at Companies House), as distinct from say an organisational entity such as an establishment, division or business unit of a company. It would also include partnerships, co-operatives, mutuals, building societies, friendly societies, associations, trade unions, charities and individuals who are employers—if they carry out an economic activity. It may also include schools, colleges, universities, NHS trusts, and Government bodies (both central and local), again if they carry out an economic activity. Ultimately it is a matter for the courts to decide (in the first instance, the CAC), on a case-by-case basis, whether an organisation is carrying out an economic activity.

Identifying what constitutes an undertaking determines *whether* the legislation applies. It does not determine *how* it should apply under a pre-existing or a negotiated agreement. It is possible to have an agreement that covers more than one undertaking, or that provides for different arrangements in different parts of the undertaking (see paragraphs 21 and 41 below.

Further guidance on the meaning of the term 'economic activity', including application in the public sector

- The Acquired Rights Directive[6] applies to 'undertakings or parts of undertakings that carry out an economic activity'. It is likely therefore that decisions of the European Court of Justice (ECJ) on the meaning of the term 'economic activity' in the context of that Directive would also be relevant in the context of the Information and Consultation Regulations.
- The ECJ has given a fairly wide interpretation to the term 'economic activity' in the

[5] The EC Directive gives Member States the option to apply the Directive either to 'undertakings' with 50+ employees or to 'establishments' with 20+ employees. The UK has decided to apply it to undertakings.

[6] Council Directive 2001/23/EC on the approximation of the laws of the Member States relating to the safeguarding of employees rights in the event of transfers of undertakings, businesses or parts of undertakings or businesses. Implemented in the UK by the Transfer of Undertakings (Protection of Employees) Regulation 1981 or 'TUPE'.

context of the Acquired Rights Directive. For example, it has held that it covers the provision of healthcare services (*Porter v Queen's Medical Centre (Nottingham University Hospital)* [1993] IRLR 486) and assistance to drug addicts (*Dr Sophie Redmond Stichting v Bartol* [1992] IRLR 366). However, the ECJ has also held that organisations whose principal role is to carry out purely administrative functions, or to exercise public authority, are not carrying out an economic activity where it is merely ancillary to the main purpose (*Henke* [1996] IRLR 701).

- Recent decisions suggest that the *Henke* exception should be construed narrowly[7], but further case law is required to clarify the situation. The main activities of traditional central government departments concern the exercise of public authority (eg legislation, administration and policy development) although they usually have ancillary economic support functions (such as catering and human resources). Accordingly, these departments are thought unlikely to be covered by the Information and Consultation Regulations.
- There may well be difficult cases where a public body both exercises public authority and carries out an economic activity, and it is not clear whether that activity is merely ancillary to its main purpose. Each organisation is unique, and so would have to be looked at on a case-by-case basis. Organisations that are unsure whether they are covered by the Regulations are advised to obtain their own legal advice.
- Leaving aside the issues around the legal definition of 'undertaking' and 'economic activity', the Government fully supports the principle that employees have a right to be informed and consulted about important issues affecting them regardless of the type of organisation they are working in. With this in mind the Government is drawing up a code of practice for central government that will sit alongside the Regulations. It will apply the principles of the legislation to central government departments that are not within the scope of the Regulations. Local Authorities would not be formally covered by the code but, they were not covered by the Regulations themselves, would be encouraged to adhere to its principles by adopting arrangements suitable for their particular circumstances. The Cabinet Office is responsible for developing the code.

undertakings with 50 or more employees in the UK. There are transitional provisions which give smaller employers more time to prepare for the legislation. It applies to:

- undertakings with 150 or more employees from 6 April 2005
- undertakings with 100 or more employees from 6 April 2007
- undertakings with 50 or more employees from 6 April 2008

During these transitional periods, none of the requirements in the legislation would apply to undertakings which fell below the relevant threshold. This means that employees in such undertakings could not make a request for a negotiated agreement, and their employers could not initiate the statutory process themselves by making a notification under regulation 11. However, employers and employees will be free during this period to draw up a pre-existing agreement as referred to in regulation 8, and the Government would encourage them to consider doing so.

The number of employees in an undertaking is averaged out over a twelve month period (see regulation 4). Only 'employees' should be included when

[7] For example, *Mayeur v Association Promotion de l'information Messine* [2000] IRLR 783 and *Collino v Telecom Italia SpA* [2000] IRLR 788.

calculating whether the threshold is met. This would exclude certain categories of workers who are not employees, for example, temporary agency workers and subcontractors. Part-time employees working under a contract for 75 hours or less a month may be counted as representing half a full-time employee.[8] Employees based in Northern Ireland should be included in the calculation, but not those employed overseas.

Further guidance on calculation of employee numbers, including part-time employees and the meaning of the term 'employee'

- To calculate how many employees there are in an undertaking, an average figure over twelve months is used—that is, twelve *completed* calendar months before an employee request under regulation 7 is made. For each of the twelve months, take the number of UK employees employed during the month (whether employed for the whole of the month or only a part of it), add the numbers together and divide by twelve. So for example, if an employee request were made on 30 June, the relevant figure would be the number of employees employed in each month starting with June the previous year and ending with May this year, added together and divided by 12.
- If an undertaking has been in existence for less than twelve months, it is the number of months that it has existed that is used. So for example, if an undertaking has existed for nine completed calendar months, the relevant figure would be the number of employees employed in each of those months, added together and divided by 9.
- An employee who worked in two or more undertakings should be treated as though an employee of each, and so would count towards the 50/100/150 employee threshold in each, and could, for example, put their name to an employee request for an I&C agreement in each.
- ***Part-time employees*** are normally counted as though they were full-time employees. However, for the purpose of the 50/100/150 employee thresholds, the employer *may* (but is not obliged to) count a part-time employee as representing half a full-time employee for any month in which they worked under a contract for 75 hours or less. Absences from work and overtime are ignored when determining whether the contract provides for 75 hours or less during the month, as is the fact that a particular month may have had less than 21 working days.
- Part-time employees could only be counted as representing half a full-time employee for those months in which they were employed part-time throughout the *whole* month. If they were employed full-time during any month (or part of a month), they must be counted as representing a full-time employee for that month. In addition, an employee working under a contract for more than 75 hours a month must also be counted as representing a full-time employee, even though within the organisation they may be regarded as 'part-time' compared with other employees.
- It is important to bear in mind that this provision concerning part-time employees only applies when calculating whether an undertaking has 50, 100 or 150+ employees, and then only if the employer chooses to rely on it. Thereafter, part time employees are treated in exactly the same way as full-time employees. For example, they are counted as representing a full-time employee for the purpose of the 10% threshold for employee requests in regulation 7, or for approving a negotiated or pre-existing agreement, or voting in an election for I&C representatives. They also have the same rights to be negotiating representatives and I&C representatives as full-time employees.

[8] The provision on part-time workers in regulation 4(3) only applies when calculating the number of employees in the undertaking to determine whether it has 50, 100 or 150 employees. It does not apply, for example, to the 10% figure for employee requests in regulation 7.

- ***Meaning of the term 'employee'***. The question of who is an 'employee' has been a difficult area of law for many years and there is no single, conclusive test. The courts have, over the years, devised a number of criteria, some of which have stood the test of time better than others. The key factors to consider are:
  (a) Does the person have to undertake the work personally? The more freedom they have not to do so, and to substitute another person in their place, the less likely they are to be an employee.
  (b) What level of control does the employer have over the person? The greater the degree of control, the more likely they are to be an employee. However, this test can be difficult in the case of skilled or professional people when the employer might not have the necessary expertise to really control the person and they are left to undertake their work as they see fit.
  (c) Are there any other factors in the relationship which would be incompatible with the contract being one of employment? An example of this might be that the person provided all their own tools and materials. While not conclusive, this makes the contract seem less like one of employment as employees usually use equipment provided by their employer.
- No one of these factors will be conclusive but by answering all three it should be possible to reach a decision as to whether most people are employees or not.
- The position of company directors is not straightforward, and depends on the individual circumstances. If a director has entered into a contract of employment with the company he/she would be an employee. If there is no express contract of employment, but he/she nevertheless gets a salary and is expected to work regularly for a certain number of hours, then the courts might find that the director is an employee.
- A partner in a partnership would not be an employee, but there are 'salaried partners' who, depending on the circumstances, could argue that they are controlled by the partnership and are therefore employees.
- An employee who works offshore, or on a fixed-term contract would be an employee for the purpose of the Regulations.
- Where there is doubt about whether someone is an employee, and this is relevant to, for example, whether an undertaking has 50/100/150 employees, or whether 10% of employees have made a request for I&C arrangements, or whether a negotiated or pre-existing agreement covers all employees, the safest option would be to assume the person is an employee. Alternatively, legal advice should be sought.

> ***undertakings with their registered or head office, or principal place of business in Great Britain***. A company with its registered office overseas, but with its head office in Great Britain (or vice versa), would be covered by the Regulations if it has 50+ employees in the UK. In the case of multi-nationals, the Regulations would apply to those companies registered in Great Britain or with their head office here. The reference to 'principal place of business' is intended to capture organisations that, unlike companies, do not have a registered or head office.

Guidance on undertakings with employees in both Great Britain and Northern Ireland

- There is separate legislation implementing the Directive in Northern Ireland. An undertaking with employees in both Great Britain and Northern Ireland should count *all* such employees when calculating whether it has 50+ employees (or 100+ or 150+ employees in the transitional periods), because this threshold applies to employees in the *United Kingdom* (as required by the EC Directive). But the undertaking would only be subject to the Information & Consultation legislation in the country where it has its registered or head office, or principal place of business.

- If a company's registered office was in Great Britain and its head office in Northern Ireland, or vice versa, the legislation of whichever of these countries where it has more employees would apply.
- Once it is determined whether the British or the Northern Ireland Regulations apply, the legislation would then apply in the same way to all employees of the undertaking, whether based in Britain or Northern Ireland. So for example, if the British legislation applied, employees based in Northern Ireland would have the same rights as British-based employees to request data on employee numbers under regulation 5, and would count towards the 10% threshold for employee requests in regulation 7. They would also have the same rights to become negotiating representatives or I&C representatives, and to bring complaints. Enforcement would be through the CAC, an employment tribunal, and the Employment Appeal Tribunal. If the Northern Ireland legislation applied. enforcement would in the main be through the Industrial Court in Northern Ireland.

Groups of companies

6. The fact that an undertaking may be part of a group of companies is *not* relevant for working out whether that undertaking has enough employees to be covered by the legislation. It is the number of employees employed by an individual company that is relevant, not those employed by a subsidiary of the company, a parent company, or a fellow-subsidiary of a common parent company.

Employees' entitlement to data on employee numbers

7. Employees may need data from their employer about the number of employees in an undertaking—to find out whether the undertaking is covered by the legislation at all (including during the transitional periods), and to work out how many employees are needed to make a request under regulation 7 to negotiate an I&C agreement. Regulation 5 gives them a right to this data and requires the employer to provide it within one month. A complaint may be made to the CAC if the employer fails to provide the data, or it is considered false or incomplete in a material way.

Further guidance on requests for data on employee numbers

- A request by employees for data from their employer on the number of employees in the undertaking should be made in writing and dated. The data must be provided within one month of the request. The request may be made by any employee of the undertaking, or anyone on behalf of the employees.[9] If there are part-time employees that the employer intends to count as representing half a full-time employee for the purpose of the calculation, the employer must give the numbers.[10] If there are workers in the undertaking whom the employer considers not to be employees (for example, because they are temporary agency workers), it would be advisable to make this clear in the data provided to employees, to help avoid misunderstanding.

[9] Regulation 5(1) refers to an 'employees' representative' who may make a request for data. The term is not defined. It is intended to allow employees to request data through an intermediary such as a trade union or some other third party, if, for example, they do not want to identify themselves.

[10] A part-time employees as defined in regulation 4(3) may be counted as representing half a full-time employee for the purpose of calculating the number of employees in the undertaking. But they would count as representing a full-time employee for the purpose of calculating the 10% threshold for an employee request under regulation 7.

- Anyone who has requested data from the employer may, after one month of the request, complain to the CAC if the employer fails to provide it. They may also complain if they consider the data to be false or incomplete in a material way, for example, that it does not provide enough information to enable them to work out whether the undertaking is covered by the legislation or how many employees are needed to make a request for an I&C agreement; or that it was incorrect in a way that gave the impression the undertaking was not covered by the legislation. An error or deficiency in the data which had no effect on the outcome would not be material.
- Employees who believe the employer has failed to provide the required data, are advised to consider discussing the matter with the employer to see if a solution can be found before making a formal complaint to the CAC.
- Where the CAC upholds a complaint, it must make an order requiring the employer to provide the necessary data within a given period.

Disputes about coverage

8. Employers who believe they do not come within the scope of the legislation, for example, because they do not have sufficient employees, or because they believe they are not an undertaking carrying out an 'economic activity', may apply to the CAC for a declaration on the matter (see regulation 13). However, they may only do so if they have received an employee request under regulation 7 to negotiate an I&C agreement. Speculative applications where no such request has been made would not be considered by the CAC.

THE PROCESS FOR SETTING UP CONSULTATION AGREEMENTS

Overview of the process

- A valid employee request to negotiate an Information and Consultation (I&C) agreement must be made (or employers may start the process on their own initiative).
- This generally triggers a requirement to negotiate an I&C agreement with representatives of employees.
- However, if an employee request is made and an employer has a valid pre-existing agreement in place, the employer may ballot the workforce to determine whether it endorses the request. If the workforce endorses the request (or the employer decides not to hold a ballot), the requirement to negotiate a new agreement is triggered. If the workforce does not endorse the request in a ballot, the pre-existing agreement continues.
- Where negotiations take place but fail to lead to agreement, standard provisions to inform and consult I&C representatives apply.
- A 3-year moratorium on further employee requests applies where a negotiated agreement is reached, or the standard provisions apply, or a pre-existing agreement has been upheld following a ballot to endorse an employee request.

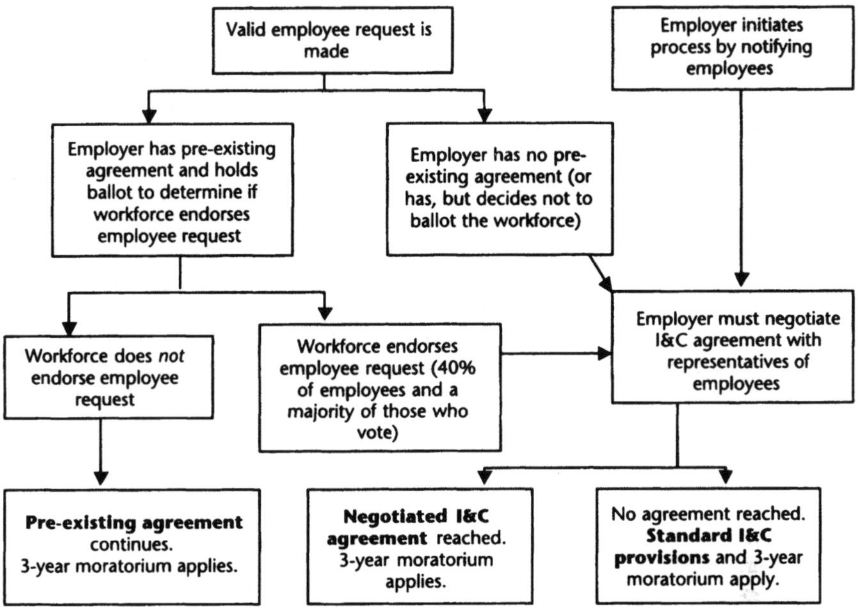

Employee requests to negotiate an I&C agreement

9. The process established by the legislation begins where employees ask to negotiate an I&C agreement (see regulation 7). Employers may also initiate the process themselves without waiting for an employee request (see paragraph 26 below). A request to negotiate an agreement must be made by at least 10% of the employees in the undertaking, subject to a minimum of 15 employees and a maximum of 2,500.[11]

10. Where an undertaking is part of a group of companies, an employee request must still be made by 10% of the employees in the undertaking (ie one of the companies in the group), not 10% of the employees in the group of companies.[12] Similarly, where an undertaking consists of several separate establishments or business units, the request must still be made by 10% of the employees in the undertaking, not 10% of those in one of the establishments or business units.[13]

11. A request must be in writing, and state the names of the employees making it as well as the date on which it is sent. Requests may be sent directly to the employer, or to the CAC which will handle them on their behalf if the employees want to act anonymously.

12. It is possible for different requests to be made from different parts of the

[11] The minimum figure means that a very small number of employees in smaller firms would not be able to start the process; the maximum figure means that a very large number in bigger firms would not be required.

[12] even if there is a pre-existing agreement covering more than one company.

[13] even if there is a pre-existing agreement consisting of several agreements each covering a different establishment/business unit.

workforce, and aggregated over a rolling 6 month period to achieve the 10% threshold.

13. Employers may dispute the validity of an employee request—see paragraph 30 below. There is a three year moratorium on employee requests where there is already a negotiated agreement in force, or the standard I&C provisions apply to the undertaking, or an earlier request was not endorsed by the workforce in a ballot relating to a pre-existing agreement.
14. On receipt of a request from employees to negotiate an I&C agreement, employers are advised to acknowledge receipt of it, to inform the workforce as a whole of the request, and to explain how they intend to respond to it (though these are not requirements of the legislation). Failure to do so could lead to confusion amongst employees as to whether the employer believes the request is valid or believes that enough employees have made it. If an employer wrongly believes that a request is not valid or has been made by too few employees, and fails to act on it, the standard provisions would apply automatically after 6 months—again therefore, employers are advised to inform employees if they believe a request is not valid or has been made by too few employees.

Further guidance on employee requests to negotiate an I&C agreement

- The names of the employees making the request must be given so that the employer can check how many employees are making it (but see below for 'anonymous' requests). Employees are advised to sign the request, and date their signature, to reduce the risk of disputes over whether they really support it. A trade union could collect the names of those wishing to make a request, but it will need to be clear that each individual does indeed support the request.
- Only those who are employees of the undertaking at the time the request is made may put their name to it. A part-time employee is taken to represent a full-time employee for the purpose of an employee request, even if they were counted as representing half a full-time employee for the purpose of the 50/100/150 employee threshold. This means that, in an undertaking with 100 full-time and 100 part-time employees (and therefore 150 full-time equivalent employees), 20 would be required to make a request (10% of the total employees) and these 20 could be full-time or part-time employees.
- ***Aggregated requests.*** A valid employee request *may consist of several separate requests made within a rolling 6-month period which, taken together, meet the 10% threshold. So for example, a request from 8% of the total workforce made by employees based at one site, and another request within 6 months from 5% of the total workforce based at another site would be aggregated.* Where several requests are made from different parts of the workforce, the employer may wish to check that the same employee does not appear on more than one request, in order to avoid double counting. Employers are advised to retain employee requests which do not by themselves achieve the 10% threshold for 6 months in case further requests are made.
- ***'Anonymous' requests.*** Employees who wish to keep their identity secret from their employer may make a request via the CAC. The employees making the request must still give their names to the CAC, and are advised to sign it and date their signature, so that the CAC can check how many employees are making the request. The CAC will *not* forward the names to the employer. When making the request, employees are advised to state the name of their employer and give the registered or head office or principal place of business, together with a contact name and details of someone representing them (for example, one of the employees or a trade union representative), to help the CAC liaise between the employer and employees.

- When the CAC receives a request from employees it must notify the employer of the fact as soon as reasonably practicable, and ask the employer for the information it needs to check the number and names of the employees making the request. The employer must provide this information as soon as reasonably practicable. An employer may have previously received one or more requests directly from employees within the previous 6 months which did not meet the 10% threshold. In that case, the employer is advised to provide the CAC with the names of the employees making the previous request(s), to avoid double counting.
- The CAC would then compare the information provided by the employer (including the names of any employees who had made previous requests within the past 6 months) with the list of employees making the request, and inform both employer and employees how many employees have made the request via the CAC, on the basis of the information provided by each.
- The CAC at this stage in the process is simply carrying out an administrative process on behalf of the employer and employees. It is not exercising any judicial function, for example, in deciding whether the employee request is valid.
- Once the CAC has performed this role of handling an anonymous request, the process would continue in the normal way, with employers required to initiate negotiations for a new agreement, or to hold a ballot of the workforce to endorse the request if they have one or more pre-existing agreements in place, or, if appropriate, challenging the validity of the request or the applicability of the legislation.
- ***Date of employee request.*** The date on which a request is made is normally the date on which it is sent to the employer, but there are two exceptions:
  - *'anonymous' requests made via the CAC.* The date is that on which the CAC informs the employer and employees of how many employees have made the request.
  - *aggregated requests.* The date is that on which the request was sent that achieved the 10% (or 15/2500 employee) threshold.

  The date of an employee request determines:
  - the reference date for calculating the number of employees in the undertaking, averaged over the previous 12 months (regulation 4(1));
  - the start of the one month period in which employers must notify employees if they have a pre-existing agreement and want to hold a ballot to see if the workforce endorses the employee request (regulation 8(3)(a));
  - the start of the three year moratorium on further employee requests where the workforce fails to endorse an employee request in a ballot (regulation 12(1)(c));
  - the start of the one month period in which the employer ay dispute an employee request (regulation 13(3));
  - the start of the three month period for initiating negotiations for an I&C agreement (regulation 14(3));
  - the start of the six month period after which the standard I&C provisions apply by default if an employer fails to act on an employee request (regulation 18(1)).

Pre-existing agreements

15. As a general rule, when a valid employee request is made under regulation 7, the employer will come under an obligation to negotiate an Information and Consultation (I&C) agreement. However, there is an important exception where employers already have in place one or more pre-existing I&C agreements. Instead of negotiating a new agreement, they may ballot the workforce to ascertain whether it endorses the request by employees (see

regulation 8(2)).[14] If they choose not to ballot the workforce, they will come under the obligation to negotiate a new agreement.

16. Where a ballot is held, and 40% of the workforce *plus* a majority of those who vote, endorses the employee request, the employer would come under the obligation to negotiate a new agreement. (This does *not* necessarily mean the pre-existing agreement would no longer stand, particularly if it is a collective agreement with a trade union—see paragraph 25 below).

17. Where fewer than 40% of the workforce or a minority of those voting endorses the employee request, the employer would not come under an obligation to negotiate a new agreement, and a three-year moratorium on further employee requests would begin.

18. Where a pre-existing agreement covers employees in more than one undertaking, employers may hold a single ballot of the employees in all the undertakings covered by the agreement (see regulation 9).

19. ***Requirements for pre-existing agreements.*** Pre-existing agreements must meet the four criteria in regulation 8(1), and must have been agreed before an employee request is made under regulation 7. They can include collective agreements with trade unions that meet the criteria in regulation 8(1)[15], agreements that cover more than one undertaking, agreements that provide for different arrangements in different parts of the undertaking, and multiple agreements (see paragraph 21 below).

20. The criteria for pre-existing agreements are:
    - *they must be in writing.* Where existing arrangements (including collective agreements with trade unions) are not set down in writing, for example because they are based on custom and practice, they would need to be set down in writing if they are to qualify as a valid pre-existing agreement for the purpose of these Regulations;
    - *they must cover all the employees of the undertaking.* An agreement may cover employees in other undertakings as well (for example in a group of companies); or there may be several different agreements each covering different parts of the workforce (such as different establishments), and which between them cover all the employees of the undertaking;
    - *they must set out how the employer is to give information to the employees or their representatives and to seek their views on such information.* The legislation does not impose any requirements or set any restrictions, on the method, frequency, timing or subject-matter of the information and consultation arrangements set up under pre-existing agreements. There may be separate and different arrangements in different parts of the undertaking, such

[14] This exception only applies if fewer than 40% of employees in the undertaking make the request. Where 40% or more of the employees make the request, employers may not hold a ballot to determine whether the workforce endorses it—the obligation to negotiate a new agreement will apply.

[15] the requirement that a pre-existing agreement must cover all the employees in the undertaking does not rule out collective agreements with trade unions even though they may rarely meet this criterion. This is because there may be other pre-existing agreements in place covering the remainder of the employees in the undertaking, such that all the employees are covered by the agreements taken together.

as different establishments or business units, either as a result of a single agreement creating such different arrangements, or as a result of several different agreements within the undertaking; and
- *they must have been approved by the employees*. The legislation does not go into detail on how employee approval could be demonstrated. In DTI's view, it would include support indicated by:
  - a simple majority among those voting in a ballot of the workforce;
  - a majority of the workforce expressing support through signatures. This may be most appropriate in smaller organisations; or
  - the agreement of representatives of employees who represent a majority of the workforce. This would include officials of independent trade unions in workplaces with a recognised union. It would also include other appropriate representatives of employees.

Different agreements covering different parts of the workforce such as different establishments or business units may be approved by employees separately, and in different ways or at different times for each other; agreements covering employees in more than one undertaking may be approved by those employees together, or separately by the employees in each of the undertakings covered.

Further guidance on requirements for pre-existing agreements
- Employers may well find that their existing consultation arrangements do not meet the four criteria for pre-existing agreements set out in regulation 8(1). For example, their arrangements may not cover all the employees in the undertaking, or they may not have been formally approved by the employees.
- Employers wishing to have a valid pre-existing agreement are advised to review the situation in consultation with their employees or representatives of the employees such as trade union representatives or any existing employee consultation forum.
- It may be that existing arrangements do not cover all employees in the undertaking because, for example, they do not extend to management, or they take the form of a collective agreement with a trade union that covers only a part of the workforce. There are a number of options available:
  - Existing arrangements could be extended to cover employees currently outside their scope, eg by giving these employees the right to appoint their own representative(s) to any existing consultation forum, or by broadening the constituencies of existing representatives to cover the currently excluded employees. This extension would need to be approved by the new employees it was designed to cover;
  - Separate consultation arrangements could be put in place just for those employees not covered by the existing arrangements, and which would run in parallel with them. Again, these arrangements would need to be approved by the employees they will cover; or
  - New consultation arrangements could be agreed covering the whole workforce.
- It may be that existing consultation arrangements have not been formally approved by the employees. Employers should not assume that the apparent absence of discontent means employees are happy with existing arrangements. They will need to obtain the express approval of employees for the arrangements in place if they are to meet the requirements of the legislation. This could be achieved by any of the methods set out above. In undertakings with an existing consultation forum, it may be appropriate to review, revamp and agree the arrangements with that forum.
- ***Collective agreements with trade unions.*** A collective agreement could be a valid pre-existing agreement if it is in writing, sets out how the employer will inform and consult

trade union representatives, and has been approved by them. The agreement need not cover all the employees in the undertaking[16], but in that case there would have to be one or more other pre-existing agreements (whether with a union or otherwise) covering the remaining employees.

- ***European Works Council agreements.*** A European Works Council (EWC) agreement would not be a valid pre-existing agreement for the purpose of Regulation 8. EWC agreements are those set up as a result of the EC Directive on European Works Councils[17]. Agreements establishing EWCs might meet the criteria for pre-existing agreements in regulation 8(1) of the I&C Regulations, but they would not be appropriate as such because their focus is on *transnational* issues. The I&C Regulations do not have the same emphasis.

21. ***Pre-existing agreements covering more than one undertaking, or covering different establishments etc, and multiple agreements.*** Although the legislation applies to 'undertakings', it is intended to be flexible enough to allow pre-existing agreements that:
    - cover employees in more than one undertaking;
    - provide for different arrangements in different parts of an undertaking (such as individual establishments, divisions, business units or sections of the workforce); or
    - consist of several agreements each covering only a part of an undertaking.
22. The important point is that, either by themselves, or taken together with other agreements, they meet the criteria in regulation 8(1)—that they are in writing, cover all the employees of an undertaking (and possibly employees in other undertakings as well), set out how employees will be informed and consulted whether through representatives or directly (and they may provide for separate and entirely different arrangements in different parts of the undertaking), and are approved by employees.

Further guidance on pre-existing agreements covering more than one undertaking or covering different establishments etc, and multiple agreements

- ***Pre-existing agreements covering more than one undertaking.*** A pre-existing agreement, including a collective agreement with a trade union, may cover employees in more than one undertaking[18]. For example, in a group of companies, an agreement may establish consultation arrangements that apply to several individual companies within the group, or all of them.
- Where a valid employee request is made by employees in an undertaking with a pre-existing agreement covering more than one undertaking[19], employers may ballot the total

[16] employees in a bargaining unit covered by a collective agreement with a union are taken to be covered by that agreements whether they are members of the union or not.

[17] Council Directive 94/45/EC of 22 September 1994 on the establishment of a European Works Council or a procedure in Community-scale undertakings and Community-scale groups undertakings for the purpose of informing and consulting employees. The exclusion applies to all types of EWC agreement, whether set up under Regulation 17, 42, 43, 44 or 45 of the Transnational Information and Consultation of Employees Regulations 1999 which implement the Directive.

[18] whether the employees have the same or different employers

[19] where a pre-existing agreement covers more than one undertaking, an employee request must still be made by 10% of the employees in one of the undertakings, *not* 10% of the employees in all the undertakings covered by the agreement

workforce in all the undertakings to determine whether it endorses the request (see regulation 9)[20], or just the employees in the undertaking from which the request was made.

- If the workforce endorses[21] the employee request in a ballot, the obligation to negotiate a new I&C agreement would apply in relation to all the undertakings where the ballot was held. However, employers would be free, if they wished, to negotiate either a new agreement applying to all the undertakings covered by the pre-existing agreement, or separate agreements for each (or combinations) of those undertakings.
- If the workforce fails to endorse the employee request in a ballot, employers would not be under any obligation to negotiate a new agreement, and a three-year moratorium on further employee requests would apply to all the undertakings where the ballot was held.
- ***Pre-existing agreements covering different establishments etc.*** A pre-existing agreement may provide for different consultation arrangements in different parts of an undertaking. For example, an undertaking may consist of several (or even hundreds of) establishments such as retail outlets, branches, sites, plants, factories and/or offices. Or it may consist of a number of distinct organisational divisions or business units, or several different groups of workers. Different consultation arrangements may be set up in those different establishments, divisions etc. This could be achieved by a single agreement covering the whole undertaking but providing for different arrangements in the different parts, or by separate agreements for each establishments, division etc.
- Where a valid employee request is made by employees in an undertaking with a pre-existing agreement covering different establishments etc.[22] the employer may ballot the workforce to determine whether it endorses the request. This would be a ballot of all the employees in the undertaking.
- If the workforce endorses the request in a ballot, the obligation to negotiate a new I&C agreement would apply in relation to the whole undertaking. However, employers would be free, if they wished, to negotiate a new agreement again providing for different arrangements in the different parts of the undertaking.
- If the workforce fails to endorse the request in a ballot, the employer would not be under any obligation to negotiate a new I&C agreement, and a three-year moratorium on further employee requests would apply to the whole undertaking.
- ***Multiple pre-existing agreements.*** A pre-existing agreement may consist of several agreements, which when taken together meet the requirement in regulation 8(1) that all the employees in the undertaking are covered. In other words, a single agreement need not by itself cover all the employees in an undertaking, as long as there are one or more other agreements that cover the remaining employees.
- For example, in a multi-establishment undertaking, each establishment may be covered by a separate agreement; or in a multi-divisional undertaking, each division may be covered by a separate agreement. In some undertakings there may be a collective agree-

[20] The combined ballot under regulation 9 may only be held if fewer than 40% of the employees in all the undertakings covered by the agreement make one or more employee requests for an I&C agreement. For this purpose, requests from employees in different undertakings covered by the pre-existing agreement, would be aggregated if made within 6 months of each other. Where 40% or more of the employees in the undertakings covered by the agreement make the request, the employer may not hold a ballot to determine whether the workforce endorses it—the obligation to negotiate a new agreement will apply.

[21] ie the request is supported in the ballot by 40% of employees in all the undertakings covered by the agreement and a majority of those who vote.

[22] where a pre-existing agreement covers different establishments etc., an employee request, to be valid, must still be made by 10% of the employees in the undertaking as a whole, not 10% of the employees in one of the establishments etc.

ment with a trade union covering some of the employees, and another agreement (whether with a union or otherwise) covering the remaining employees.

- In a group of undertakings, there may be multiple agreements each of which covers employees in more than one undertaking in the group. For example, one agreement may cover all the manual employees across the group of undertakings and another all the administrative or managerial employees across the group.
- The legislation gives employers flexibility with regard to the approval of multiple pre-existing agreements. Each agreement may be approved by employees separately, and in different ways and at different times from each other. So for example, one agreement may have been agreed with representatives of a majority of the employees covered by the agreement (it may, for example, be a collective agreement with a trade union), another may have been approved by a majority of the employees it covers voting in a ballot. Alternatively, an employer may decide to seek employee approval of the various agreements all together, for example, in a single ballot of the workforce.
- Where a valid employee request[23] is made by employees in an undertaking with multiple pre-existing agreements, employers may ballot the workforce to determine whether it endorses the request. This would be a ballot of all the employees in the undertaking (or undertakings) covered by the agreements.
- If the workforce endorses the employee request in a ballot, the obligation to negotiate a new I&C agreement would apply in relation to the whole undertaking (or all the undertakings if a combined ballot was held in more than one). If it fails to endorse the request, employers would not be under any obligation to negotiate a new agreement, and a three year moratorium on further employee requests would apply to the whole undertaking (or all the undertakings if a combined ballot was held in more than one).

23. ***Complaints about pre-existing agreements.*** Where employees believe there is no valid pre-existing agreement in place allowing an employer to hold a ballot for endorsing an employee request, a complaint may be made to the CAC (see regulation 10(1)). A complaint may also be made that employers who intend to hold a combined ballot under regulation 9 are not entitled to do so. Where the CAC upholds a complaint, the employer would then come under an obligation to negotiate a new I&C agreement.

Further guidance on complaints about the validity of a pre-existing agreement

- A complaint to the CAC about the validity of a pre-existing agreement, or the ability to hold a combined ballot under regulation 9, must be made within 21 days of the employer informing employees[24] that he/she intends to hold a ballot to see if the workforce endorses an employee request. The employer may not proceed to hold the ballot until this 21 day period for making a complaint has expired. Where a complaint is made, the employer is advised to await the outcome of the CAC case before going ahead with the ballot.
- Complaints may be made by any employee of the undertaking or by a representative of the employees[25]. However, before making a formal complaint to the CAC, employees are

[23] Where multiple pre-existing agreements are in place, an employee request for a new I&C agreement, to be valid, must still be made by 10% of employees in the undertaking as a whole, not 10% of the employees in the part of an undertaking covered by one of the agreements.

[24] as required by regulation 8(3)(a)

[25] Regulation 10(1) refers to an 'employees' representative' who may make a complaint to the CAC about a pre-existing agreement. The term is not defined. It is intended to allow employees to make complaints through an intermediary such as a trade union or some other third party, if, for example, they do not want to identify themselves.

advised to consider discussing the matter with the employer to see if a solution can be found.

- ***The grounds for bringing a complaint are that the requirements for pre-existing agreements set out in regulation 8(1) have not been met, ie that the agreement is not set down in writing, it does not cover all the employees in the undertaking (or where there is more than one, that between them they do not cover all the employees), it does not set out how the employer is to give information to the employees or their representatives and to seek their views on it, or*** it has not been approved by the employees.
- In addition, where employers intend to hold a combined ballot under regulation 9 because they consider they have a pre-existing agreement covering a group of undertakings, a complaint could be brought that:
  - the pre-existing agreement does not in fact cover employees in more than one undertaking;
  - some employees in one or more of the undertakings where the ballot is to be held were not covered by a valid pre-existing agreement on the date when the employee request was made; or
  - 40% or more of the employees in the group of undertakings where the ballot is to be held made a valid employee request for a new I&C agreement.
- In view of the requirement for a pre-existing agreement to be approved by employees, employers are advised (though they are not required by the legislation) to retain some evidence of employee approval
- Where the CAC rejects a complaint about a pre-existing agreement, the employer would be free to go ahead with a ballot for endorsing an employee request.
- Where the CAC upholds a complaint about a pre-existing agreement, the employer would then come under an obligation to negotiate a new I&C agreement.[26] In the case of a complaint about the employer's ability to hold a combined ballot in a group of undertakings, the employer could choose either to hold a single ballot in the undertaking from which a valid employee request had been made (assuming there is a valid pre-existing agreement covering that undertaking), or to start negotiations for a new I&C agreement.
- It should be borne in mind that a complaint about the validity of a pre-existing agreement could only be brought after an employee request to negotiate a new I&C agreement had been made once the Regulations have come into force. Speculative applications to the CAC seeking a ruling on a pre-existing agreement before any such request had been made would not be considered.

24. ***Endorsement ballot.*** Before holding a ballot for endorsement of an employee request, employers must inform the employees that they intend to do so in writing, and within one month of the employee request (see regulation 8(3)).[27] They must then wait 21 days before holding the ballot, in case employees wish to challenge the validity of the pre-existing agreement(s), and arrange for the ballot to be held as soon as reasonably practicable

[26] This would *not* necessarily mean that the pre-existing agreement no longer stood. For example, if the agreement were a collective agreement with a trade union, it would still remain in place. It would simply mean that the agreement would not suffice as a means of fulfilling the employer's obligations under the I&C Regulations following an employee request for an I&C agreement. This is the same as where a workforce ballot had endorsed an employee request for a new I&C agreement.

[27] In the case of a combined ballot under regulation 9 concerning a pre-existing agreement covering a group of undertakings, employers must notify all the employees in the group of undertakings that they intend to hold a ballot.

thereafter. Once the ballot has been held, employers must inform the employees of the result as soon as reasonably practicable.

Further information on the requirements for endorsement ballots

- Employers are required to make such arrangements for the ballot as are reasonably practicable to ensure it is fair. Everyone who is an employee of the undertaking on the date of the ballot[28] must be entitled to vote in it, and so far as reasonably practicable, to do so in secret. Employers must also ensure that votes are accurately counted.
- One way to help ensure the ballot meets these requirements would be to appoint an independent person such as a 'qualified independent person' to supervise it, though this is not a requirement of the legislation. A 'qualified independent person' is defined in the Recognition and Derecognition Ballots (Qualified Persons) Order 2000 (Amendment) Order 2002 (SI 2002/2268), and includes lawyers, auditors, and certain specified organisations[29]. An alternative would be to give employee representatives a role in supervising or scrutinising the ballot and the count.
- An application or complaint may be brought to the CAC by an employee or an employees' representative that:
  - an employer has failed to inform employees within one month of an employee request that he/she intends to hold a ballot for endorsing the request (see regulation 8(7)). If the CAC upholds the application it must make a declaration that the employer is required to negotiate a new I&C agreement;
  - an employer has informed employees that he/she intends to hold a ballot for endorsing an employee request, but has then failed to hold the ballot (see regulation 8(8)). If the CAC upholds the complaint it must make an order requiring the employer to hold the ballot by a given date;
  - one or more of the requirements for a ballot had not been met, for example, that not everyone had been entitled to vote, or that they had not been able to vote in secret, or that the votes had not been accurately counted, or that the ballot had been unfair in some other way (see regulation 10(2)). Any such complaint must be brought within 21 days of the ballot. Where a complaint is upheld, the CAC must make an order requiring the employer either to re-run the ballot or, if the employer prefers, to start negotiations for a new I&C agreement.
- Before making a formal complaint to the CAC, employees are advised to consider discussing the matter with the employer to see if a solution can be found but employees should ensure that they do not miss the 21 day deadline for bringing any complaint in case no resolution with the employer is possible.

25. ***Effect of workforce endorsing an employee request.*** If the workforce endorses an employee request for a new I&C agreement where there is a pre-existing agreement in place, the employer will come under an obligation to negotiate a new I&C agreement. However, this would not necessarily mean that the pre-existing agreement no longer stood. For example, if the pre-existing agreement were a collective agreement with a trade union, it would continue in force. Where the collective agreement provided for collective bargaining, for example, over pay, this would be unaffected. Rather, it would simply mean that the agreement would not suffice as a means of fulfilling the

[28] or if the ballot is to be held on more than one day, an employee on the first of those days

[29] the specified organisations are The Association of Electoral Administrators, Election-.Com Limited, Electoral Reform Services Limited, Popularis Ltd, The Involvement and Participation Association and Twenty-First Century Press Limited. Contact details are available from the Central Arbitration Committee.

employer's obligations under the I&C Regulations following an employee request for a new I&C agreement.

Employer notifications (regulation 11)

26. There is no need to wait for an employee request to start the process for negotiating a new I&C agreement under regulation 14. Employers may initiate the process themselves by notifying employees under regulation 11.[30] Where an employer does so, it would lead on to exactly the same process for negotiations as when employees trigger the process with an employee request. Employers may notify employees in more than one undertaking where they wish to negotiate a single I&C agreement covering more than one undertaking.
27. Following an employer notification to initiate negotiations, there is no possibility of holding a ballot under regulation 8 or 9 since those provisions are about endorsing an employee request to negotiate an I&C agreement. However, employees may dispute the validity of an employer notification at the CAC (see paragraph 30 below), and if a complaint is upheld the employer may not proceed to initiate negotiations for a new agreement.

Further guidance on employer notifications

- An employer notification to initiate negotiations for an I&C agreement must state:
  - that the employer intends to start the negotiating process.
  - that the notification is given for the purpose of the Information and Consultation of Employees Regulations 2004; and
  - the date on which it is issued.
- The notification must be published in such a way as to bring it to the attention of all the employees in the undertaking, so far as reasonably practicable. Where employers wish to negotiate an agreement covering more than one undertaking, they must notify the employees in all the undertakings to be covered.
- Once employees have been notified in this way, the employer must initiate negotiations as soon as reasonably practicable, and within three months at the latest. This means making arrangements for the employees to appoint or elect negotiating representatives, then informing the employees who has been appointed or elected; and inviting the representatives to enter into negotiations (see regulation 14(1))
- Where the CAC upholds a complaint about the validity of an employer notification, the employer may not proceed to initiate negotiations for a new agreement.

Restrictions on employee requests or employer notifications (regulation 12)

28. An employee request for an I&C agreement or an employer notification under regulation 11 would not be valid where it was made within 3 years of:
    - a negotiated agreement being drawn up; or
    - the standard I&C provisions applying; or
    - a ballot having been held under regulation 8 or 9 which failed to endorse

[30] It should be stressed that this is referring to starting the process for a negotiated agreement under regulation 14, where both the negotiation process and the resulting agreement would be subject to the requirements, and enforcement mechanism, in the Regulations. It is not referring to drawing up a pre-existing agreement referred to in regulation 8.

an employee request to negotiate a new I&C agreement, where there was a pre-existing agreement in place.[31]

29. The purpose of this moratorium is to prevent the employer or the employees *unilaterally* overturning a negotiated agreement, or the application of the standard I&C provisions, or a pre-existing agreement where an employee request for a new agreement had not been endorsed by the workforce. However, the employer and employees could *agree* within this 3-year period to terminate a negotiated or pre-existing agreement or to adopt an agreement in place of the standard I&C provisions.

Further guidance on restrictions on employee requests and employer notifications

- This restriction normally applies for three years from:
  - the date of a negotiated agreement (unless the employer and employees or their representatives have agreed to terminate the agreement before the end of three years, in which case the moratorium ends when the agreement terminates); or
  - the date on which the standard rules started to apply. This is 6 months after the period for negotiations ends, or 6 months after a valid employee request where an employer fails to start negotiations (or once I&C representatives have been elected if this is sooner)—see regulation 18(1); or
  - the date of a valid employee request which was not endorsed by the workforce in a ballot under regulation 8 or 9 where there was a pre-existing agreement.
- The 3-year moratorium does not apply where there have been material changes in the undertaking which mean that:
  - in the case of a pre-existing agreement or agreements, they no longer cover all the employees in the undertaking, or they can no longer be considered to be approved by employees; or
  - in the case of a negotiated agreement, that it no longer covers all the employees in the undertaking.
- Examples of situations where this 'material change' clause might be relevant include:
  - where the undertaking has been involved in a merger or acquisition, or there had been an expansion in the business, which resulted in significant numbers of additional employees in the undertaking who would not be covered by a pre-existing or negotiated agreement:
  - where a pre-existing agreement has been terminated such that employees in the undertaking are no longer covered by any agreement.
- If an employee request or an employer notification were made during the moratorium period, its validity could be disputed before the CAC under regulation 13. This might include a dispute over whether there had been material changes in the undertaking. However it would be advisable, if appropriate, to try to settle any such dispute without recourse to the CAC.
- Once the three-year moratorium period has ended, or where there has been a material change in the undertaking, employees are free to make a new request to negotiate an I&C agreement, and employers are free to make a notification under regulation 11 to initiate negotiations for an I&C agreement themselves.

Disputes about employee requests or employer notifications (regulation 13)

30. The employer may dispute the validity of an employee request to negotiate

[31] Where a ballot had been held under regulation 9 because there is a pre-existing agreement covering a group of undertakings, the restriction on employee requests applies to *all* the undertakings.

an I&C agreement, for example, on the grounds that the request was made by insufficient employees, or the undertaking does not have enough employees to be covered by the legislation, or the organisation does not carry out an 'economic activity'. In addition, employees may challenge the validity of an employer notification made under regulation 11, on the grounds that it was covered by the three-year moratorium or was not made in the prescribed way. An application can be made to the CAC for a declaration as to whether a request or notification was valid. Applications must be made within one month of the request or notification.

Further guidance on disputes about employee requests or employer notifications

- An employer may dispute the validity of an employee request for an I&C agreement on the grounds that it:
  - was not made by at least 10% of employees in the undertaking (subject to the minimum of 15 employees and maximum of 2,500), taking account of any other requests made by employees with a 6-month period;[32]
  - was not in writing;
  - was not sent to the employer's registered or head office or principal place of business, or the CAC in the case of an anonymous request by employees;
  - did not specify the date on which it was sent; or
  - was subject to the 3-year moratorium on employee requests.
- An employer may also dispute an employee request on the grounds that:
  - the undertaking did not have sufficient employees to be covered by the Regulations on the date when the request was made.
  - the organisation concerned is not an 'undertaking carrying out an economic activity'.
- An employee, or a representative of the employees[33], may dispute the validity of an employer notification made under regulation 11 on the grounds that it did not comply with the requirements in regulation 11(2) (for example, that it was not dated, or brought to the attention of employees) or that it was covered by the 3-year moratorium on employer notifications.
- There could be misunderstandings on the part of the employer or the employees about an employee request or an employer notification, or about whether the Regulations apply, or how they apply to the specific circumstances of an individual organisation. In view of this, where appropriate, it is advisable for the employer or employees to inform the other if they believe that an employee request or employer notification is not valid, or the Regulations do not apply, before considering bringing a dispute to the CAC.
- For example, the Regulations allow employee requests from different parts of the workforce to be aggregated for the purpose of reaching the 10% threshold, where the requests are made within a 6 month period of each other. A request may be made in the full knowledge that it would not by itself achieve the 10% threshold, and there would therefore be no need to apply to the CAC for a declaration. Or employees might be mistaken as to how many of them need to make a request for a new I&C agreement, or as to whether some of those working in the undertaking are actually 'employees' and can therefore

[32] If the CAC agreed that the request had been made by insufficient employees, the request could still be aggregated with subsequent requests from other employees made within 6 months to achieve the 10% threshold.

[33] Regulation 13(2) refers to an 'employees' representative' who may make a complaint to the CAC about a an employer notification. The term is not defined. It is intended to allow employees to make complaints through an intermediary such as a trade union or some other third party, if, for example, they do not want to identify themselves.

make the request.[34] Rather than making an application to the CAC, it might be possible for the employees simply to obtain additional names for their request so that they do reach the threshold. In such cases; an application to the CAC could be avoided.

Negotiations for an I&C agreement (regulation 14)

31. Following an employee request to negotiate an I&C agreement (if necessary, endorsed by the workforce in a ballot under regulation 8 or 9), or following an employer notification under regulation 11, the employer should initiate negotiations with representatives of the employees as soon as reasonably practicable, and within 3 months at the latest.[35]
32. *Negotiating representatives*. During this 3-month period, the employer must make arrangements for employees to elect or appoint negotiating representatives. The arrangements must ensure that all the employees of the undertaking are entitled to take part in the election or appointment of representatives, and that all employees are represented during the subsequent negotiations. Negotiating representatives do not necessarily have to be the same people as any I&C representatives who will be informed and consulted on an on-going basis under the agreement.
33. Negotiated agreements may cover more than one undertaking, or may provide for different arrangements in different parts of the undertaking (see paragraph 41 below). In the case of agreements covering more than one undertaking, employees in all the undertakings to be covered must be entitled to take part in the election or appointment of negotiating representatives and be represented in the subsequent negotiations. In the case of agreements providing for different arrangements in different parts of the undertaking, separate negotiations may be held with representatives from the various parts.
34. Employers must inform employees in writing of the identity of the representatives who have been elected or appointed, and then invite those representatives to enter into negotiations to reach an I&C agreement. Beyond these requirements, the Regulations give considerable flexibility as to how representatives are appointed or elected, and who they are. However, given the important part they have to play in drawing up the arrangements for information and consultation, it is important that they are *genuine* representatives of the employees.

[34] This is one reason why regulation 5 allows employees to request data from the employer so they can work out how many are needed to make the request.

[35] The 3-month period for starting negotiations is suspended if:
- a ballot to endorse an employee request is held under regulation 8 or 9, or any complaint is brought in relation to this ballot under regulation 10;
- a dispute is brought under regulation 13 about an employee request or an employer notification; or
- a complaint is brought under regulation 15 about the election or appointment of negotiating representatives.

In effect, the 'clock' is stopped for the time it takes to hold a ballot, or to resolve a dispute or complaint (including during any appeal over a CAC decision), or to rehold a defective ballot or election if required by the CAC (see regulation 14(3)).

35. Employees or their representatives may bring a complaint to the CAC if they believe the requirements for negotiating representatives have not been met (see regulation 15). A complaint, must be brought within 21 days of the election or appointment, and the CAC can order the election or appointment to take place again. However, before making a formal complaint to the CAC, employees are advised to consider discussing the matter with the employer to see if a solution can be found.

Further guidance on negotiating representatives

- The role of neqotiating representatives under the legislation is an important one. They must represent the interests of employees in negotiating with the employer the information and consultation arrangements to be put in place within the organisation. They will need to ensure that these arrangements are what employees want, for example, in terms of:
  - methods for informing and consulting (whether through representatives, directly with the workforce, or a combination of the two);
  - how any information and consultation representatives are to be chosen, how many of them, and how they may be replaced;[36]
  - the types of subjects on which information and consultation will take place;
  - the information to be provided:
  - the timing and frequency of information provision and consultation;
  - who will represent the employer at any meetings for information and consultation;
  - the way in which the employer will respond to the views of employees or their representatives;
  - the circumstances in which the arrangements can be modified, or terminated
- ***Elected or appointed.*** Negotiating representatives may be elected in a ballot of the employees, or simply appointed by the employees directly without an election, and it is for the employer to decide which. For example, it would be possible to invite different parts of the workforce to each choose their own representative; or it may be possible simply to invite volunteers to put themselves forward (this may be more appropriate in smaller organisations).
- Different methods of electing or appointing representatives may be used in different parts of the undertaking. For example, in some parts there may be several people interested in being representatives so a ballot may be appropriate, while in other parts there may be only one candidate and no ballot would be needed. Whichever method is used, it is important to ensure that all the employees are entitled to take part in the election or appointment, and that they are all represented during the subsequent negotiations.
- The employer must make the necessary arrangements to ensure that appropriate representatives meeting the legal requirements are elected or appointed by the employees. They could not all be appointed by the employer or by management, although managers who are employees will themselves need to be represented by one or more negotiating representatives, in proportion to their number, since negotiating representatives must represent all employees and a negotiated agreement must cover all employees.
- Where a ballot is held to elect negotiating representatives employers will need to ensure that it is fair and that all employees have the right to vote in it. They may wish to appoint an independent person to supervise the ballot, although this is not a requirement of the legistation.

[36] Negotiating representatives may well themselves become I&C representatives, but do not have to.

- ***Number of negotiating representatives.*** There are no specific requirements as to the number of negotiating representatives, though the employer will need to ensure that sufficient are elected or appointed to represent all the employees. The employer will also need to ensure that representatives from different parts of the undertaking are elected or appointed (for example, different establishments, divisions, or sections of the workforce), so that where there may be differing viewpoints, these are adequately represented. However, in deciding how many negotiating representatives there should be, a balance needs to be struck—if there are too many; it could make it difficult to reach an agreement, or even to find times when everyone can be brought together.
- ***Trade union representatives.*** It is not a requirement of the legislation that trade union representatives within an undertaking where a union is recognised should become negotiating representatives. However, they are likely to be well placed to act as representatives in such workplaces. It should not be assumed though that trade union representatives can automatically represent all the employees in an undertaking, as required by the Regulations.
- It is not a requirement of the legislation that negotiating representatives who draw up an agreement will become Information and Consultation representatives who are informed and consulted under that agreement. The employees, acting through the negotiating representatives, are free to decide to appoint different people to be I&C representatives, or not to have I&C representatives at all but instead to rely on direct forms of information and consultation only.
- Where possible, there would be value in trying to have diversity among negotiating representatives, so that, for example, the views of minority groups within the undertaking are represented in the negotiations.
- No 'long haul crew member' may be a negotiating representative, or stand as a candidate for election as a negotiating representative, unless allowed by their employer (see regulation 43). A long haul crew member is a member of a merchant navy crew other than a ferry worker or someone who normally works on voyages of less than 48 hours[37]. This exclusion recognises the difficulties and disruption shipping companies would face in arranging for crew members to be replaced on ships in order to attend meetings to negotiate an agreement.
- Given the points above, it is advisable (though this is not a requirement of the legislation) to inform employees or their representatives in advance of proposed arrangements for electing or appointing the negotiating representatives, and to give them an opportunity to give their views.

36. ***Conduct and duration of negotiations.*** When negotiating an agreement, the parties (that is, the employer and the negotiating representatives) are required to work in a spirit of co-operation and with due regard for their reciprocal rights and obligations, taking into account the interests of both the undertaking and the employees (see regulation 21). Negotiations between the parties may last for up to 6 months[38], though this period is extendable without limit by agreement between the employer and a majority of the negotiating representatives. They must *agree* to extend this period—it could

[37] it does not include airline staff

[38] the 6 month period begins 3 months after an employee request was made or an employer notification was issued (unless a ballot is held under regulation 8 or 9, or there is a dispute—see footnote 36 above). The 6 month period is suspended while any complaint about a ballot for approval of a negotiated agreement is resolved, and while the ballot is reheld if required by the CAC (see regulation 14(4))

not be unilaterally extended by either the employer or the negotiating representatives. Help is available from ACAS and other organisations to assist in reaching information and consultation agreements.

Negotiated agreements (regulation 16)

37. ***Contents of negotiated agreements.*** The legislation sets only very limited requirements as to the contents of negotiated agreements. It purposely leaves this to the employer and negotiating representatives to decide, giving them considerable flexibility to agree arrangements best suited to their particular circumstances. Agreements must set out the circumstances in which the employees will be informed and consulted, but the legislation does not specify the method, frequency, timing or subject-matter of information and consultation. It will be for the employer and negotiating representatives to agree these points between them. They are free to agree quite different arrangements from those set out in the standard I&C rules in regulation 20 if they wish, though these can be used as a guide.
38. ***Information and Consultation representatives.*** A negotiated agreement may provide for consultation to take place through representatives of the workforce ('I&C representatives'), or it may provide for direct forms of information and consultation with the workforce as a whole. Or it may provide for *both* representative and direct forms of information and consultation. Again, the parties are free to decide. If it is agreed there should be I&C representatives, it is also for the parties to decide how many there will be, how they will be appointed or elected, who they will represent, how long they will serve for, how they may be replaced, and whether anyone other than an employee may be a representative.
39. I&C representatives do not have to be the same people as negotiating representatives. In practice they may be the same, but the legislation does not require it because their role is different—negotiating representatives are those involved in drawing up a negotiated agreement with an employer, I&C representatives are those who may be informed and consulted by the employer under the agreement.
40. ***Requirements for negotiated agreements*** (see regulation 16(1)). Negotiated agreements must:
    - *set out the circumstances in which employers will inform and consult their employees,* though the legislation gives employers and employees freedom to agree on the, method, frequency, timing and subject matter of information and consultation best suited to their particular circumstances;
    - *provide either for the appointment or election of Information and Consultation representatives, or for information and consultation directly with employees* (or both);
    - *be in writing and dated.* It is important that everyone is clear what has been agreed. The date determines the start of the 3 year moratorium on employee requests or employer notifications;
    - *cover all the employees of the undertaking, or group of undertakings if more than one undertaking is to be covered.* In addition, different arrangements in differ-

ent parts of the undertaking may be agreed, for example in different establishments, divisions, business units or sections of the workforce. These separate arrangements may be entirely different from each other, but between them they must cover all the employees of the undertaking;

- *be signed by, or on behalf of, the employer*. It must be clear that the employer has agreed to it. It is for the management of the company to decide who exactly should sign the agreement; and
- *be approved* by the employees. This means it must either:
  (a) be signed by *all* the negotiating representatives; or
  (b) be signed by a *majority* of the negotiating representatives, and either:
    (i) be approved in writing[39] by at least 50% of the employees in the undertaking (or group of undertakings in the case of an agreement covering more than one); or
    (ii) approved by 50% of employees who vote in a ballot.

Further guidance on approval of negotiated agreements.

- It is for the employer to decide how to seek the approval of employees where not all of the negotiating representatives have signed the agreement.
- The provisions on approval of agreements are intended to be as flexible as possible, to give maximum scope for reaching agreements. So for example, if a ballot were held in which insufficient employees approved an agreement, it would still be open to the employer (assuming there was enough time) to negotiate with the representatives modifications to the agreement with a view to seeking employee approval again (or securing the approval of all the negotiating representatives).
- Where employers decide to hold a ballot for the purpose of seeking employee approval for a negotiated agreement, they are required to make such arrangements for the ballot as are reasonably practicable to ensure it is fair (see regulation 16(5)). Everyone who is an employee of the undertaking (or group of undertakings in the case of an agreement covering more than one) on the date of the ballot must be entitled to vote in it, and as far as reasonably practicable, to do so secret. Employers must also ensure that votes are accurately counted. One way to help ensure the ballot meets these requirements would be to appoint an independent person to supervise it, though this is not a requirement of the legislation.
- A complaint may be brought to the CAC by one or more of the negotiating representatives that the requirements concerning the ballot had not been met (see regulation 17). The complaint must be made within 21 days of the ballot. Where a complaint is upheld, the CAC will require the employer to re-hold the ballot.

41. ***Negotiated agreements covering more than one undertaking, or covering different establishments etc.*** Although the legislation applies to 'undertakings', it is intended to be flexible enough to allow negotiated agreements that cover employees in more than one undertaking, or provide for different arrangements in different parts of an undertaking (such as individual establishments, divisions, business units or sections of the workforce). The important point is that such agreements meet the requirements in regulation 16—that they are in writing, dated, signed by the employer, cover all the employees in the undertaking (and possibly employees in other undertakings as well), set

[39] this could include in writing by electronic means

out the circumstances in which employees will be informed and consulted whether through I&C representatives or directly (and they may provide for separate and entirely different arrangements in different parts of the undertaking), and that they are approved by the employees.

Further guidance on negotiated agreements covering more than one undertaking or covering different establishments etc.

- ***Negotiated agreements covering more than one undertaking.*** A negotiated agreement may cover employees in more than one undertaking.[40] For example, in a group of companies, an agreement may establish consultation arrangements that apply to several individual companies within the group, or all of them.
- Where employers receive a valid employee request to negotiate an I&C agreement, and consider that the agreement should cover more than one undertaking, in the first instance they will need to notify the employees in all the undertakings to be covered that they intend to initiate the negotiation process (see paragraph 26 above concerning employer notifications);
- Employers have 3 months to initiate negotiations, during which time they must arrange for the election or appointment of negotiating representatives from the undertakings to be covered.
- It may be appropriate simply to have one negotiating representative from each undertaking to be covered, but not necessarily so. If there were only a few undertakings to be covered, more than one representative may be needed from each to ensure employees are adequately represented in the negotiations, particularly if the interest of employees within an undertaking may diverge significantly. On the other hand, if a large number of undertakings are to be covered, one representative from each may make the negotiations impractical. In that case, some representatives could represent more than one undertaking, or represent distinct groups of employees across the several undertakings. The legislation is intended to give as much flexibility as possible here.
- A negotiated agreement covering more than one undertaking should be signed by the employers concerned and either signed by all the negotiating representatives involved, or by a majority of them and approved by the employees in writing or in a ballot. If a ballot is held, all the employees in the undertakings to be covered by the agreement must be entitled to vote in it.
- Employers could not unilaterally decide that a negotiated agreement will cover more than one undertaking. The agreement will have to be approved by the employees, so this is something that should be discussed with the negotiating representatives at an early stage in the process.
- Where a negotiated agreement covering more than one undertaking is agreed, the 3-year moratorium on employee requests and employer notifications under regulation 11 would apply to all the undertakings covered by the agreement.
- Where negotiations for an agreement to cover more than one undertaking fail employers would become subject to the standard I&C provisions in regulation 20. These will apply separately to each of the undertakings involved in the negotiations.
- **Negotiated agreements covering different establishments etc.** A negotiated agreement may consist of different parts each providing for separate consultation arrangements in different parts of an undertaking. For example, an undertaking may consist of several (or even hundreds of) establishments such as retail outlets, branches, sites, plants, factories, and/or offices. Or it may consist of a number of distinct organisational divisions or, business units, or several different groups of workers. These different parts of an under-

[40] whether the employees have the same or different employers

taking may have relatively little in common with each other—they may be engaged in quite different activities, with few, if any, subjects on which they would all want to be informed and consulted together.

- It may be appropriate for each establishment, division etc to have its own consultation arrangements. Or separate arrangements might cover a number of establishments, for example, on a regional basis. Or there might be different arrangements for different sections of the workforce.
- Where employers receive a valid employee request to negotiate an I&C agreement, and consider that the agreement should provide for separate arrangements in different parts of the undertaking, they must arrange for the election or appointment of negotiating representatives from the various parts of the undertaking where the separate arrangements will exist, and have 3 months to do so.
- It will be possible either to hold a single negotiation in respect of all the separate arrangements (though this could be quite complicated where there is to be a large number of separate arrangements), or separate negotiations in relation to separate arrangements. Again, the legislation is intended to give as much flexibility as possible here, but it will be important that the employees to be covered by these separate arrangements are adequately represented during the negotiations. This means there should be at the very least one representative to negotiate in respect of each separate arrangement, and probably several representatives to ensure that the employees are adequately represented during the negotiations.
- Each part of a negotiated agreement providing for separate arrangements in different parts of an undertaking must be signed either by all the negotiating representatives involved in negotiating that part, or by a majority of them and approved by the employees in writing or in a ballot. The different parts of the agreement could be approved in different ways and at different times. If a ballot is held, all the employees to whom the part of the agreement relates must be entitled to vote in it. However, all parts of the agreement must be approved. It would not be possible for one part to remain unapproved.
- Employers could not unilaterally decide that a negotiated agreement will provide for separate arrangements in different parts of an undertaking. The agreement will have to be approved by the employees, so this is something that should be discussed with the negotiating representatives at an early stage in the process.
- Where a negotiated agreement providing for separate arrangements in different parts of an undertaking is agreed, the 3-year moratorium on employee requests and employer notifications under regulation 12 would apply to the whole undertaking.
- Where negotiations for an agreement providing for separate arrangements in different parts of an undertaking fail, employers would become subject to the standard I&C provisions in regulation 20. These will apply to the undertaking as a whole.

42. ***Enforcement of negotiated agreements***. Negotiated agreements are enforceable through the CAC (see paragraphs 65 and 66 below). Therefore, the more clearly they are worded, the easier it will be for the CAC to understand them correctly and to resolve any disputes as to whether the agreement has been properly followed.

Standard information and consultation provisions

43. ***Applicability of the standard provisions***. The standard information and consultation (I&C) provisions only apply where an employer fails to initiate negotiations for an information and consultation agreement when required

to do so[41], or where negotiations have failed to lead to an agreement (see regulation 18(1)).

44. The standard provisions apply *at the undertaking level*. This means that consultation must take place with information and consultation representatives elected from the undertaking—arrangements may not cover more than one undertaking, and there is no provision for different arrangements in different parts of the undertaking. If there had been negotiations aimed at agreeing arrangements covering more than one undertaking, or providing for separate arrangements in different parts of the undertaking, the standard provisions will nevertheless apply at the individual undertaking level.
45. Where negotiations have taken place but failed to reach an agreement, employers have up to a further 6 months to set up the necessary information and consultation structures. This period is intended to give employers time to arrange the election of I&C representatives, but it is also designed to give a further limited period in which a negotiated agreement might be reached. It should be borne in mind though that if there is still no negotiated agreement by the end of this further 6-month period, and no ballot has been arranged to elect I&C representatives, employers will be liable to a penalty (see paragraph 72 below).
46. Where employers fail to initiate negotiations for an I&C agreement when required to do so, the standard provisions apply automatically 6 months after a valid employee request is made or the employer has made a notification under regulation 11. The employer must have arranged for the election of I&C representatives before the end of this 6 month period, or will be liable to a penalty.
47. Where I&C representatives are elected before the end of the 6-month period in which they must be elected, the standard information and consultation provisions begin to apply straightaway.
48. ***Election of information and consultation representatives*** (regulation 19). I&C representatives must be elected in a ballot. They do not necessarily have to be the same people as negotiating representatives. The employer is responsible for organising the ballot, which must comply with the requirements in Schedule 2 to the Regulations. The number of I&C representatives is proportional to the number of employees in the undertaking—one per 50 employees or part thereof, subject to a minimum of 2 representatives and a maximum of 25. In other words, 2 representatives for undertakings with 50 to 100 employees, 3 for those with 101 to 150 employees, etc.

Further guidance on the election of Information and Consultation representatives under the standard provisions

- The requirements for ballots set out in Schedule 2 only apply to elections of I&C representatives where the standard provisions apply. Where a negotiated or a preexisting agree-

[41] that is, where a valid employee request has been made under regulation 7, or where employers notify an intention to begin neotiations on their own initiative under regulation 11. Initiating negotiations involves arranging the appointment or election of negotiating representatives, informing employees who these representatives are and inviting them to enter into negotiations.

ment provides for the election of I&C representatives, the legislation does not oblige employers to follow the requirements of Schedule 2, though they may wish to adopt similar arrangements.

- In outline, Schedule 2 requires as follows:
  - employers must draw up proposals for the ballot and consult representatives of the employees about them (eg the negotiating representatives or trade union representatives);
  - there can be separate ballots for separate parts of the workforce (eg different sites, business units, groups of employees), if that would better reflect the interests of employees as a whole;
  - all employees of the undertaking must be entitled to stand for election and vote in the ballot;
  - employers must appoint an independent person to supervise the ballot and ensure he/she carries out their functions without interference;
  - once employers have consulted about the proposed ballot arrangements, and made any modifications in the light of this consultation, they must publish the final ballot arrangements for employees and their representatives to see;
  - any complaints about the final ballot arrangements may be made to the CAC within 21 days of their publication by any employee or representative of employees (eg about any constituencies chosen by the employer, the identity of the ballot supervisor, or the adequacy of consultation about the proposals). The CAC may order changes to be made;
  - the supervisor must supervise the ballot in accordance with the final arrangements, and hold the ballot no earlier than 21 days after the arrangements have been published in case a complaint is brought. He/she must ensure that everyone entitled to stand as a candidate or vote can do so, and can vote in secret, and that votes are fairly and accurately counted;
  - the ballot supervisor must publish the ballot results for the employer, employees and candidates to see, and must publish an 'ineffective ballot report' where appropriate (eg where the ballot requirements were not met and this affected the outcome, or where the employer did not co-operate). Where an ineffective ballot report is published, the ballot is void, and must be reheld;
  - all costs are to be borne by the employer.
- If too few employees stand as candidates for election, the employer does not need to hold the ballot, and the candidates will become the I&C representatives.
- No 'long haul crew member' may be an I&C representative, unless allowed by the employer (see regulation 43). A long haul crew member is a member of a merchant navy crew other than a ferry worker or someone who normally works on voyages of less than 48 hours.[42] This exclusion recognises the difficulties and disruption shipping companies would face in arranging for crew members to be replaced on ships in order to attend information and consultation meetings.
- Where an employer fails to arrange to hold a ballot before the end of the 6-month period in which it must be held, a complaint may be brought to the CAC by an employee or a representative of employees. Where the CAC upholds a complaint it must order the employer to arrange and hold the ballot. The complainant may then apply to the Employment Appeal Tribunal for a penalty against the employer.

49. **Negotiated agreements after the standard provisions apply**. Employers and I&C representatives may come to a negotiated agreement at any time after

[42] it does not include airline staff

the standard information and consultation provisions apply (see regulation 18(2)). Such agreements must comply with the requirements in regulation 16(1), with the exception that the agreement is deemed approved where it is signed by a majority of the I&C representatives. Where an agreement is reached, the moratorium on employee requests or employer notifications under regulation 11 applies for 3 years from date of the agreement.

50. ***The standard I&C provisions*** (regulation 20). Where an employer is subject to the standard provisions, the obligation on employers to inform and consult in accordance with those provisions begins to apply once the I&C representatives have been elected. The requirements for informing and consulting I&C representatives in regulation 20 are based very closely on Article 4 of the EC directive, and are intended to be the same as the requirements in the directive. They are not intended to go beyond the requirements of Article 4 of the directive, and they cannot require less than Article 4 does.
51. What the requirements mean in practice for an individual organisation will vary depending on the circumstances of that organisation. For example, where there is a lot of change underway in the organisation such as a restructuring programme, more frequent information and consultation may be appropriate, I&C representatives should be given the opportunity to express their views on the information that ought to be provided, the subject matter, frequency, timing and method of consultation. It is good practice to seek to agree these things, although this is not a requirement of the legislation.
52. Ultimately it will be for the courts to interpret what these requirements might mean in practice in the particular circumstances of any specific complaint. It is possible the courts might take a wider, or a more restrictive, interpretation of the requirements than DTI. This guidance is intended to help firms think about such things as the subject-matter, frequency, timing and method of information and consultation. It is not intended to be either prescriptive or comprehensive.
53. ***Information***. There are three categories of information that employers who are subject to the standard provisions must provide to I&C representatives:
    (a) information on 'the recent and probable development of the undertaking's activities and economic situation.' Given that the two following categories of information are about employment within the undertaking, and changes to work organisation or employees' contractual relations, the purpose of this first category is best understood as helping I&C representatives understand the context in which decisions affecting employment, work organisation and employees' contractual relations are made;
    (b) information on 'the situation, structure and probable development of employment within the undertaking and on any anticipatory measures envisaged, in particular, where there is a threat to employment within the undertaking'. The emphasis here is on the overall number of employees within the undertaking;
    (c) information on 'decisions likely to lead to substantial changes in work organisation or in contractual relations'. This includes decisions covered by the legislation on collective redundancies and transfers of

undertakings. DTI believes 'contractual relations' means an employer's contractual relations with their employees.

54. What affects employment, work organisation and employees' contractual relations within an individual organisation will vary from one organisation to another, and it is therefore not possible to provide comprehensive guidance that would cover every organisation. It will depend on a variety of factors, for example, the nature and diversity of the organisation's activity, its size and financial position, the sector in which it operates, its position in the market and the strength of the competition.

55. To reduce the risk of a successful complaint being brought for breaching the legislation, it is advisable to seek the views of I&C representatives on the sort of information that should be provided, although this is not a requirement of the legislation.

Further guidance on information to be provided under categories (a), (b) and (c) of the standard I&C provisions

- ***Category (a) information.*** Taken in isolation, the phrase 'recent and probable development of the undertaking's activities and economic situation' might appear to cover a wide range of subjects. However, the quantity and scope of information provided should be limited both to avoid undue burdens on the employer, and so as not to overwhelm the I&C representatives. There is no requirement to consult I&C representatives about the matters on which category (a) information is provided.
- The information provided must be 'appropriate', in particular to enable the I&C representatives to study it adequately and where, necessary, prepare for consultation on the matters covered by categories (b) and (c). It should help provide the background, and inform the rationale, for subsequent decisions on which representatives are informed and consulted.
- Employers are therefore advised in effect to 'work backwards' from categories (b) and (c), by first considering what decisions are likely to lead to substantial changes in work organisation or employees' contractual relations in the specific circumstances of their undertaking, and what is likely to affect the situation, structure and development of employment within the undertaking. Having done so, they will be better able to decide what aspects of the recent and probable development of the undertaking's activities and economic situation they should provide information about under category (a).
- The phrase 'recent and probable development' implies both looking backwards and looking forwards. So, information should be provided on developments in the undertaking's activities and economic situation in the recent past, and on probable future developments. 'Probable' implies that a development is likely to take place. In particular, it implies something more than the mere possibility of a development in the undertaking's activities and economic situation, such as where discussions or negotiations with a third party were at a very preliminary or early stage.
- Bearing the above points in mind, the information to be provided under category (a) might include:

  information on the undertaking's activities:
  - the launch of new products or services, or significant changes to, or discontinuation of, existing products or services;
  - increase or reduction in production or sales as a result of, for example, under or overcapacity, increased or reduced demand, moving into a new market or exiting a market, cost-saving measures;

- takeovers/mergers (both by and of the undertaking)[43], acquisitions and disposals of subsidiary companies, businesses, parts of a business, or other assets, investment, opening or closure of establishments (eg plants, offices, factories, retail outlets, branches), restructuring plans;
- developments in technology, production processes or ways of working;
- a reorganisation within the undertaking, including a transfer of production or posts to different locations, or to different divisions or units within the undertaking;
- changes to the undertaking's aims, objectives, vision, mission statement, strategy, business plan etc;
- changes in senior management;

where these developments are likely to affect employment within the undertaking, or lead to substantial changes in work organisation or employees' contractual relations;
information on the undertaking's economic situation:

- the competitive environment in which the organisation operates, trading conditions, the outlook for the sector, the level of demand, and the state of the undertaking's order book; and
- the undertaking's financial situation based on its accounts;

where these developments are likely to affect employment within the undertaking, or lead to substantial changes in work organisation or employees' contractual relations.

- There is no specific requirement in the legislation to meet with I&C representatives in relation to category (a) information. Employers could simply send the information to them. However, they should consider the need to meet in order to explain the information, since it must be given in an 'appropriate' fashion, in particular to allow the representatives to conduct an adequate study of it.
- Some of the above information above must be made public by law, for example in a company's annual report and accounts. However, it may not be easily understood in this form, and employers should consider providing a separate report on such matters for the I&C representatives, or an explanation of the material.
- ***Category (b) information.*** This comprises information on the 'situation, structure and probable development of employment within the undertaking' and includes information on 'any anticipatory measures envisaged ... in particular, where there is a threat to employment'. In addition to providing I&C representatives with this information, employers must also consult them about these matters.
- The emphasis here is on the overall number of employees within the undertaking—both the present level of employment and future levels. It would therefore include recruitment of new employees and redundancies (both voluntary and compulsory), employee turnover, the possibility of moving to reduced hours working or the need for overtime, and could include changes in retirement policy or early retirement schemes.
- It also includes the 'structure' of employment, which can be understood to mean how employees are distributed within the undertaking, for example, geographically at different establishments (eg plants, offices, factories, retail outlets, branches), or organisationally within different divisions or units of the undertaking. It would therefore include a reorganisation of posts within the undertaking, redeployment of employees, or a transfer of posts to different locations.
- The reference to 'anticipatory measures envisaged, in particular, where there is a threat to employment' is clarified by recital 8 to the EC Directive, which refers to employee training and skill development so as to increase the 'employability and adaptability' of affected

[43] where initial discussions are being held with a possible bidder or target company, a company may legitimately take the view that there was only the possibility of a takeover etc, rather than a 'probable' development.

employees. This suggests the employer should consider whether the threat to employment can be offset through redeploying and perhaps retraining employees whose posts are under threat.

- ***Category (c) information.*** This comprises information on 'decisions likely to lead to substantial changes in work organisation or in contractual relations' and includes decisions covered by the legislation on collective redundancies and transfers of undertakings. In addition to providing I&C representatives with this information, employers must also consult them with a view to reaching agreement on these decisions.
- There is little indication within the EC Directive, or its recitals as to what the terms 'work organisation' and 'contractual relations' are meant to include other than collective redundancies and business transfers. However, the context of the directive is about employment within the undertaking, and it is reasonable to infer that 'contractual relations' means employers' contractual relations *with their employees*, rather than a business's contracts with third parties.
- In DTI's view, 'changes in work organisation' would include:
  - changes in the level, or distribution of employment within the undertaking, including redundancies and relocation of posts;
  - changes in policy on flexible working, part-time working, overtime;
  - a move to reduced hours or overtime working, changes in shift working or other work patterns;
  - introduction of significant new technology or equipment, and any training associated with it.
- In DTI's view, 'changes in contractual relations' would include:
  - a change of employer as a result of a transfer of the business, or part of the business;
  - changes in employees' terms and conditions (including hours of work, leave entitlement, rest breaks). This would not necessarily include any and every change in terms and conditions. It should be a substantial change that affected the overall contractual relations between the employer and employees;
  - introduction of, or a change to, compulsory retirement age;
  - changes to an occupational pension scheme but only where there was a contractual right to participate in the scheme as that right would form part of the contract;
  - changes in disciplinary or grievance procedures.
- In addition, any consideration of the phrase 'changes in contractual relations' must be consistent with the Treaty Base (Article 137) under which the Directive has been adopted, which states that matters such as pay are not covered by that Article. In DTI's view therefore, category (c) would not cover changes in pay or benefits that have a monetary value.
- It should be borne in mind that consulting over a change in contractual relations under the standard provisions of the I&C Regulations would not relieve employers of any obligation they may have to agree such changes with employees (since in general, any change to contractual terms must be agreed between the employer and employee).

Other points

- Category (b) concerns employment as a whole within the undertaking while category (c) concerns 'substantial changes' in work organisation or contractual relations. Neither are about individual posts or employees. They do not require information and consultation to take place on the recruitment, redundancy, dismissal, retirement, redeployment, training, development, transfer or terms and conditions of an individual employee or a small number of employees.
- It is not possible to specify a lower limit in terms of the number of employees who would have to be affected—this will depend on the circumstances of the individual case. Clearly, the more employees affected, and the greater the proportion of all the employees in the

undertaking, the more likely it is to be covered. A situation that was likely to lead on to collective redundancies as defined by statute (that is, 20 or more redundancies at one establishment) would be covered.

- There is no specific requirement in the legislation to provide information about the activities or economic situation of another undertaking. However, where they would have a significant impact on the undertaking itself, for example, in the case of the activities or economic situation of a parent or subsidiary company which might affect the prospects of the undertaking, then relevant information may need to be provided. The failure of a parent company to provide necessary information is not a valid reason for the employer failing to inform and consult under the standard provisions (see regulation 20(6)).
- Employers who are subject to the standard I&C provisions are free to go beyond their requirements by informing and consulting on other matters. ACAS guidance suggests a range of issues for information and consultation, although many of these are not required by the I&C Regulations. Employers can also inform and consult the workforce directly, as well as through I&C representatives, though they are not obliged to do so by the legislation.

56. ***Consultation under the standard I&C provisions.*** Employers who are subject to the standard I&C provisions must consult the I&C representatives on the matters referred to in categories (b) and (c) above. The timing, method and content of consultation must be 'appropriate', and relate to the information supplied by the employer. The I&C representatives must have the opportunity to give their opinion on the matters they are being consulted about, and to meet with the employer for a discussion. The employer should be represented at this meeting at a level of management relevant to the subject being discussed. Where the representatives give their opinion, the employer must give a reasoned response to it.
57. Consultation about the decisions referred to in category (c) above must be undertaken 'with a view to reaching agreement' if those decisions are within the scope of the employer's powers. The employer must therefore aim to reach agreement with the I&C representatives on such decisions, though sometimes agreement may not be possible.

Further guidance on consultation under the standard I&C provisions

- The legislation defines consultation as 'the exchange of views and establishment of dialogue' between the employer and the I&C representatives. There is caselaw in other contexts that helps clarify the meaning of the term.[44]
- Consultation is more than simply providing information. Consultees must be given a fair and proper opportunity to understand fully the matters about which they are being consulted, and to express their views on those subjects—that is, they must be given adequate information and time both to consider the matter, form a view on it, and express that view.
- There must be genuine and conscientious consideration by the employer of the consultees' views. The standard provisions in the I&C Regulations specifically require the employer to meet the I&C representatives at a level of management relevant to the

[44] For example, *R. v. British Coal Corporation and SoS for Trade and Industry ex parte Price and others* [1994] IRLR 72 where the judge adopted the tests set out in *R v Gwent CC, ex parte Bryant* (1988) COD 19

subject under discussion, and to give a reasoned response to any opinion the representatives may give.

- The purpose of consulting I&C representatives on the matters covered by categories (b) and (c) is to give them the opportunity to express their views on such things as the existing level and structure of employment within the undertaking, and its probable development, including possible recruitment, transfers or redundancies, and any plans to redeploy or retrain affected employees; and on decisions covered by category (c). I&C representatives may consider the existing level and structure of employment to be inappropriate, or may disagree with the employer's plans for changes or for redeployment or retraining. They may disagree with decisions or have suggestions for modifying them or alternative proposals. They may also have views on how decisions are to be announced to employees.
- However, employers are not obliged to follow the I&C representatives' opinion. Consultation is different from negotiation, collective bargaining or joint decision-making. Decision-making remains the responsibility of management.
- The requirement to consult with a view to reaching agreement is confined to decisions covered by category (c) that are within the scope of the employer's power. This would therefore exclude, for example, trying to reach agreement on decisions taken by a parent company that impacted on the undertaking, or decisions required by law or by a regulatory authority.[45] The requirement only applies to consultation about category (c) matters, not consultation about category (b) matters. This is because category (c) concerns *decisions*—something on which agreement may in principle be possible—whereas the 'situation, structure and probable development of employment' referred to in category (b) is of a more factual nature and therefore less appropriate for 'agreement'.
- The standard provisions require consultation to take place at the level of management relevant to the subject under discussion. In some cases this will mean the management of the undertaking itself, in other cases it may mean local management. In a group of companies it may include management from a parent company. It is for individual employers to decide what it may mean for them in practice. In DTI's view it implies a level of management with the authority to change the decision being consulted about.
- There is no specific obligation in the standard provisions for I&C representatives to report back to the employees they represent, or to obtain their views. Nevertheless, it is good practice to do so (subject to any confidentiality restrictions), so that the views of the workforce are fairly represented in meetings with employers.
- ACAS guidance provides good practice advice on how to carry out effective consultation.

58. ***Frequency and timing of information and consultation under the standard I&C provisions***. The legislation is not specific as to the frequency or timing of information and consultation. It requires information to be provided by the employer to the I&C representatives at an 'appropriate' time, in particular to enable the I&C representatives to conduct an adequate study and to prepare for consultation.

59. The EC Directive is aimed at strengthening dialogue and promoting mutual trust, improving risk anticipation and promoting employee involvement. The definition of 'consultation' also refers to the establishment of a dialogue. This, and the subjects to be covered, imply that information and consultation

[45] though there may still be a requirement to consult I&C representatives about those decisions.

should be on-going and regular, and not simply a one-off event when a problem arises.

60. As with the subject-matter of information and consultation, its frequency and timing will depend on the specific circumstances of individual organisations, and it is therefore not possible to provide comprehensive guidance that would cover every organisation.
61. To reduce the risk of a successful complaint being brought for breaching the legislation, it is advisable to seek the views of I&C representatives on the frequency and timing of information and consultation, although this is not a requirement of the legislation.

Further guidance on the timing and frequency of information and consultation

- ***Frequency***. Where there is a lot of change underway in a business, such as a restructuring, redundancies, or closures, more frequent information and consultation is likely to be needed. In any business though, at least one meeting per years would seem to be a minimum requirement—this may be an appropriate time to provide an overview of the undertaking's activities and economic situation, and of employment within the undertaking.
- The requirement to inform and consult the I&C representatives about the probable development of employment within the undertaking, may mean one or more additional meetings on this aspect are needed, because 'probable' implies the developments are likely to place, which could be difficult to predict a long way in advance. In addition, the requirement for the employer and I&C representatives to meet for consultation on the decisions referred to in category (c), implies that special or one-off meetings concerning these decisions will be needed.
- ***Timing***. The requirement to provide information on the probable development of the undertaking's activities and economic situation, and of employment, clearly means that some information must be provided in advance of these developments. The comments above concerning the frequency of information and consultation are relevant here—'probable' developments are those that are *likely* to take place, and so information and consultation on them could not take place a long way in advance when there was only a possibility of the development occurring.
- Genuine consultation implies seeking views *before* a final decision has been taken, when proposals are still at a formative stage, and when it is not too late to change a decision. If it is believed a final decision has already been taken, and the employer is simply 'going through the motions' of consultation, the outcome is likely to be mistrust and cynicism on the part of I&C representatives. However, there is a balance to be struck here—consultation too early in the decision-making process could be a waste of time and prove unsettling to employees and their representatives.
- Information must be provided early enough to allow I&C representatives to conduct an adequate study of the material, and where necessary, prepare for consultation. This implies that information must be provided in advance of a consultation meeting—how far in advance will depend on the quantity and complexity of the information, although practical considerations may make it difficult to produce the necessary information a long way in advance of the meeting.
- There may also be an issue of confidentiality to be considered. If confidential information is to be provided on a restricted basis, it may be appropriate to limit the period of time between it being provided to I&C representatives and it being made public, so as to reduce the risk of confidential information being misused.

62. **Overlap with legislation on collective redundancies and business transfers**. The decisions referred to in category (c) above include decisions on

collective redundancies and business transfers which are covered by existing legal obligations to consult representatives of employees[46]. These existing legal obligations continue to apply and are not affected by the Information & Consultation (I&C) Regulations. This could create a situation where an employer is subject to two different legal requirements to consult over the same decision.

63. To avoid this, the I&C Regulations relieve employers who are subject to the standard information and consultation provisions of the obligation to inform and consult under those provisions if they notify the I&C representatives in writing that they will be consulting under the legislation on collective redundancies or business transfers (see regulation 20(5)). This notification would need to be made on each occasion when a collective redundancy or business transfer situation arises. Employers and employees may wish to include a similar provision in negotiated agreements, or agree to exclude collective redundancy and business transfer situations altogether from negotiated agreements.

Further guidance on dealing with the overlap with collective redundancies and business transfers legislation.

- The exemption for decisions on collective redundancies and business transfers in the standard I&C provisions can be used on a case-by-case basis. Employers who are subject to the standard provisions may make use of the exemption as and when they become subject to the legislation covering those situations. So for example, they must continue to inform and consult the I&C representatives under the standard provisions over matters that may lead on to, but have not yet become, a collective redundancy or business transfer situation covered by the relevant legislation.
- Employers are not obliged to act in this way. 'Where they are required (or choose) to consult different representatives of employees under the collective redundancy or business transfers legislation, they may be quite happy to do so at the same time as consulting I&C representatives under the I&C Regulations, and will be free to do so.
- The legislation on collective redundancies and business transfers requires employers to consult representatives of employees. Where there is a recognised independent trade union representing employees who may be affected, the employer must inform and consult that union. Where there are affected employees who are not represented by a recognised union, the employer must inform and consult other appropriate representatives of those employees. These may be either new representatives specially elected for the purpose, or existing representatives provided that their remit and method of election or appointment gives them suitable authority from the employees concerned. I&C representatives elected or appointed under the I&C Regulations would be appropriate representatives for this purpose, although the employer would still be free to consult other appropriate representatives or arrange for new ones to be specially elected for the purpose.

DUTY OF COOPERATION

64. Regulation 21 requires the employer, the negotiating representatives, and I&C representatives to work together in a spirit of cooperation. In other words, cooperation must be two-way. They must also have due regard for

[46] For collective redundancies–sections 188 to 192 of the Trade Union and Labour Relations (Consolidation) Act 1992; for business transfers—regulations 10 to 12 of the Transfer of Undertakings (Protection of Employment) Regulations 1981.

one another's rights and obligations under the legislation, while taking account of the interests of the undertaking and its employees.

ENFORCEMENT OF NEGOTIATED AGREEMENTS AND THE STANDARD I&C PROVISIONS

65. The provisions on compliance and enforcement in Part VI of the Regulations apply where a negotiated agreement is in place, or where an employer is subject to the standard I&C provisions in regulation 20. They do not apply to pre-existing agreements. Any dispute about the operation of a pre-existing agreement must be resolved in the way provided for in that agreement. A pre-existing agreement would be enforceable through the courts only if that means of enforcement had been expressly agreed between the parties to the agreement, or it was shown there was an intention to create legal relations.
66. Where a negotiated agreement is in place, or where an employer is subject to the standard I&C provisions, any complaint that the employer has failed to abide by the agreement, or to comply with the standard provisions, must be brought to the CAC within 3 months of the alleged failure. However, before making a formal complaint to the CAC, employees are advised to consider discussing the matter with the employer to see if a solution can be found.

Further guidance on disputes about the operation of a negotiated agreement or the standard information and consultation provisions

- Complaints may be brought by one or more I&C representatives (where they exist), or where there are no I&C representatives, by one or more individual employees or an employees' representative. Complaints may not be brought against I&C representatives or individual employees.
- ***Breach of a negotiated agreement.*** In the case of a negotiated agreement, a complaint may be brought about failure to comply with any of the terms of the agreement. This might include:
  - a complaint that the employer has failed to establish the agreed consultation arrangements at all, or has not established them fully in accordance with the agreement. For example, an agreement might provide for the election or appointment of I&C representatives from different parts of the organisation, with the employer having agreed to make the necessary arrangements. If the employer failed to make these arrangements, or did so in a way that meant parts of the organisation were not represented as agreed, a complaint could be brought;
  - a complaint that the employer had not provided adequate information, or had provided it too late, or had not consulted in the way required by the agreement.
- Negotiated agreements may contain requirements that are different from the standard I&C provisions in regulation 20, for example, the employer may agree to inform and consult on different subjects or in a different way compared with the standard provisions. A complaint of failure to comply with a negotiated agreement may include failure to comply with any such requirements.
- ***Breach of the standard I&C provisions.*** In cases where there is no negotiated agreement in place and the employer is subject to the standard I&C provisions in regulation 20, a complaint may be brought about failure to arrange for the election of I&C representatives (see regulation 19(4)), or failure to comply with any of the standard provisions. Such complaints might include that the employer:
  - had not provided adequate information;
  - had provided information too late for the I&C representatives to study it adequately;

- had not met with the representatives at all, or had not been represented at a meeting by the level of management relevant to the subject under discussion;
- had not allowed the I&C representatives an opportunity to give their opinion;
- had not given a reasoned response to any opinion given by the representatives; or
- had not consulted with a view to reaching agreement with the representatives, in other words, that consultation had not been genuine.

67. ***CAC orders.*** Where a complaint of failure to abide by a negotiated agreement or the standard I&C provisions is upheld by the CAC, it is required to make a decision to that effect. It may also make an order requiring the employer to take the necessary steps to rectify the situation within a given period of time. However, no order of the CAC may have the effect of:
    - suspending any act done or any agreement made by an employer;
    - altering the effect of any such act or agreement; or
    - preventing or delaying any act which an employer proposes to do, or any agreement he/she proposes to make (see regulation 22(9)).
68. ***CAC proceedings*** (regulation 35). Any complaint or application to the CAC must be made in writing and in the form required by the CAC. The CAC will be publishing guidance on the procedures for handling cases concerning the Information and Consultation Regulations. The CAC must make appropriate enquiries and, as far as reasonably practicable, give a hearing to anyone it considers has a proper interest in the matter. The CAC may draw an adverse inference against someone if they fail to comply with any reasonable request to provide relevant information.
69. Any declaration or order by the CAC must be in writing and give reasons for the findings. Where necessary, enforcement of CAC orders may be pursued through the courts. Appeals against CAC declarations or orders on a point of law may be made to the Employment Appeal Tribunal (see paragraph 71 below). The CAC may refer questions of EC law to the European Court of Justice.
70. ***Conciliation by ACAS*** (regulation 38). Where the CAC considers that an application or complaint made to it is reasonably likely to be settled by conciliation or other assistance, it must refer it to the Advisory, Conciliation and Arbitration Service (ACAS) and ACAS may seek to promote a settlement. This applies to all applications or complaints, made under any provision in the Regulations. When referring cases to ACAS, the CAC must notify the applicant or complainant, as well as anyone it considers has a proper interest in the case. Where ACAS decides not to offer assistance, or is unable to resolve the dispute, and where the original application or complaint is not withdrawn, ACAS must inform the CAC, which will then be responsible for hearing and determining the dispute.
71. ***Appeals.*** Any question of law arising from a declaration or order of the CAC, or arising in any proceedings before the CAC, may be appealed to the Employment Appeal Tribunal (EAT). Appeals to the EAT are subject to requirements set out in Part II of the Employment Tribunals Act 1996 and the Employment Appeal Tribunal Rules 1993 (SI 1993/2854). An appeal must be brought within 42 days of the date on which written notification of the declaration or order was sent to the appellant. EAT decisions, including

decisions on penalties, may be appealed to the Court of Appeal on a point of law.

72. ***Penalties*** (regulation 23). Employers are liable to a penalty where the CAC upholds a complaint that they have failed to inform and consult as required by a negotiated agreement (if they have one)[47] or as required by the standard I&C provisions (if they are subject to them). They are also liable to a penalty if they are subject to the standard I&C provisions but fail to arrange a ballot to elect I&C representatives. The provisions on penalties do not apply to other complaints upheld by the CAC such as a failure to provide data on employee numbers, or complaints concerning ballots, the identity of negotiating representatives, or information restricted or withheld on confidentiality grounds.

73. Where the CAC upholds a complaint for which a penalty is liable, the person who brought it may apply to the Employment Appeal Tribunal (EAT) for a penalty. The EAT must impose a penalty unless satisfied by the employer that the reason for the failure was beyond his/her control or there was some other reasonable excuse.

74. The maximum amount of any penalty £75,000. In setting the amount the EAT must take account of all relevant factors, including: the gravity and duration of the failure, the reason for it, the number of employees affected by it, and the size (in terms of the number of employees) of the undertaking or group of undertakings where a negotiated agreement covers more than one. Penalties are payable to the Secretary of State. A penalty notice is suspended if an appeal against a CAC decision is made.

75. ***Exclusivity of remedy.*** Regulation 24 makes clear that where there is an infringement of any right conferred by Parts I to VI of the Regulations the remedy is by way of complaint to the CAC and not otherwise. This means that the rights cannot be pursued through the courts. However, a breach of a confidentiality restriction which is in Part VII of the Regulations, for example by an I&C representative, could be pursued in the civil courts, and the protections given to I&C representatives and others under Part VIII can be enforced through an employment tribunal.

CONFIDENTIAL INFORMATION

76. Employers who have a negotiated agreement[48], or who are subject to the standard provisions may, on confidentiality grounds:
    (1) restrict any information or document they provide to I&C representatives or others[49], so that it may not be passed on to anyone else (see regulation

[47] the penalty provisions do not apply to pre-existing agreements

[48] The confidentiality provisions in the legislation do not apply to pre-existing agreements. Employers and employees or their representatives are free to agree whatever confidentiality provisions they wish in a pre-existing agreement. Disputes would not be resolved by the CAC.

[49] This guidance refers to 'I&C representatives *or others*'. The reference to 'others' is intended to cover situations where the employer voluntarily chooses, whether under a negotiated agreement or under the standard provisions, to provide information to people other than I&C representatives. However, there is no obligation to do so.

25). They may do this where it is in the legitimate interest of the undertaking. It would include information that is share price sensitive;

(2) withhold information or documents altogether that they would otherwise be required to give I&C representatives (see regulation 26). They may do this where disclosing it to them would seriously harm the functioning of the undertaking, or be prejudicial to it.

77. Disputes about confidential information are to be resolved by the CAC.

Further guidance on confidential and price-sensitive information

- ***Information subject to a confidentiality restriction.*** Where employers impose a confidentiality restriction on information or documents, the recipients may not then disclose them to third parties, unless permitted by the employer.
- It is up to employers to make clear when providing information on a confidential basis what restrictions there are on it being passed to others. For example, an employer may allow the recipient to share the information with someone advising I&C representatives, or to other named employees of the undertaking or to other people with the express consent of the employer. In doing so, employers should make sure the original recipients are clear as to whether they can share the information or document with anyone else, if so, with whom, and for how long the restriction applies. The employer should also make clear that any person with whom the original recipient shared the information or document would themselves be bound by an obligation of confidentiality.
- A restriction could last for any length of time, although it should not be longer than is necessary in the legitimate interest of the undertaking. For example, it should cease if the information has been made public.
- Employers may only restrict information on confidentiality grounds where this is justified in the legitimate interest of the undertaking. Restricting information which is not genuinely confidential could hinder I&C representatives in carrying out their role. For example, they may need to consult the employees they represent or seek advice from an expert, about information they have been given.
- In deciding what information or documents to provide to I&C representatives or others, employers will need to bear in mind any confidentiality obligations they may themselves be subject to. For example, companies with securities listed on a stock exchange, will need to comply with their obligations regarding price-sensitive information[50]. Companies involved in a takeover or merger will need to comply with their obligations under relevant legislation or codes—in the UK, the City Code on Takeovers and Mergers. And companies that have entered into a contract, eg for the sale or purchase of plant or other assets, may be subject to contractual restrictions as to what information can be divulged to third parties (although no contract or other agreement could exclude or limit the information and consultation requirements in the Regulations, except in accordance with the confidentiality provisions—see paragraph 80 below).
- It is important to point out that neither the UK Listing Rules, nor the City Code on Takeovers and Mergers, nor US rules[51] prevent a company sharing price-sensitive information with representatives of employees before it is disclosed to the market, as long as those representatives are subject to an obligation of confidentiality. DTI does not believe there is any inconsistency between the obligations in the I&C Regulations and those in the Listing Rules or the Takeover Code, so there is no issue of one taking precedence over the other. However, the Listing Rules and the Takeover Code would limit the number of

[50] information which could affect the share price of a company listed on a stock market

[51] of the Securities Exchange Commission, the New York Stock Exchange and the National Association of Security Dealers

people who can be made privy to price-sensitive information, and restrict who those peoplecan be.

- ***Price-sensitive information.*** Chapter 9 of the Listing Rules imposes a general continuing obligation of public disclosure on listed companies (and in the future on companies with securities admitted to trading on a regulated market) in respect of matters which are not public knowledge and which may substantially affect their share price.
- When a company is preparing proposals, for example a restructuring, this does not have to be publicly disclosed during the planning stage provided the relevant information is kept confidential. Rule 9.4 provides that a company need not notify to a Regulatory Information Service information concerning impending developments or matters in the course of negotiation. However, the company may give such information *in confidence* to recipients within the categories described in Rule 9.5. The categories include 'representatives of employees or trades unions acting on their behalf'. The company must be satisfied that such recipients of information are aware that they must not deal in the company's securities before the relevant information has been made available to the public.
- Before it has been announced to the market, any price-sensitive information could not be shared with the wider workforce, but only with a limited number of named individuals[52]. For the purpose of regulation 25, it would therefore be legitimate to make price-sensitive information subject to a confidentiality restriction. Annex 2 of the guidance deals with making announcements to the wider workforce involving price-sensitive information within the requirements of the Listing Rules and Takeover Code.
- Investors who trade on Inside information are liable to prosecution under the Insider Dealing laws. Furthermore, if an employee in receipt of confidential information disclosed it in breach of a restriction, their employer could take disciplinary measures against them. Such action by a recipient of confidential information could also amount to market abuse. In addition, the employer could bring an action for damages in the civil courts, whether or not the person concerned was an employee.[53]
- Chapter 9 of the Listings Rules will be revised through the implementation of the EU's Market Abuse Directive in the course of 2005. The directive includes two significant provisions directed at protecting the confidentiality of inside information. First, the directive permits companies and their advisers to disclose inside information on a selective basis, but only where there is a legitimate reason for doing so and the person receiving the information owes a duty of confidentiality. This could include representatives of employees. Secondly the directive requires companies that issue shares, or their advisers, to keep a list of those who have access to inside information concerning the company. These lists are to be made available to financial regulatory authorities on request.
- ***Information withheld on confidentiality grounds.*** Employers may withhold any information or document altogether from I&C representatives or others if giving the information to them would seriously harm the functioning of the undertaking or be prejudicial to it.
- This exemption could apply where, for example, information was so sensitive that, if it were leaked to third parties, whether inadvertently or deliberately, it could cause serious harm or prejudice to the undertaking. Evidence of past leaks might be relevant here.
- The fact that information may be price-sensitive or confidential would not necessarily, by itself, justify withholding information because it can be provided on a restricted basis to I&C representatives under regulation 25.

[52] This means that price-sensitive information could not be given out under a negotiated agreement that provides only for direct information and consultation with employees, rather than through representatives.

[53] no action may be taken against a person if they reasonably believed a disclosure was protected under Part IVA of the Employment Rights Act 1996 (the so-called 'whistle-blower' protection).

- ***Disputes.*** Anyone to whom the employer has provided information or documents in confidence may apply to the CAC for a declaration as to whether it was reasonable for the employer to impose such a confidentiality restriction. Where the CAC considers that the employer's action was not justified in the legitimate interest of the undertaking, it may make a declaration to that effect, and the confidentiality restriction will not be regarded as valid.
- In the event of a dispute over information withheld on confidentiality grounds, an application may be made to the CAC for a declaration as to whether the employer is justified in withholding the information. Applications may be brought either by the employer, or by one or more I&C representatives, or where there are no such representatives, one or more individual employees or a representative on their behalf. Where the CAC considers that disclosing the information to the I&C representatives or to others would not prejudice or seriously harm the functioning of the undertaking, it may order the employer to disclose it by a specified date.
- Before making a formal application to the CAC, employers and employees or their representatives are advised to consider discussing the matter with one another to see if a solution can be found.

RIGHTS AND PROTECTIONS FOR I&C REPRESENTATIVES AND EMPLOYEES

78. *Right to paid time off.* Employees who act as negotiating representatives or I&C representatives are entitled to take reasonable time off during working hours to perform their functions as representatives, and to be paid for this time (see regulations 27 and 28). Employees may complain to an employment tribunal if their employer unreasonably refuses to let them take time off; or fails to pay them for it (see regulation 29).

Further guidance on the right to paid-time off for representatives

- The right to reasonable paid time off during working hours[54] applies to employees who are elected or appointed as negotiating representatives or as I&C representatives (whether under a negotiated agreement or because the employer is subject to the standard I&C provisions).
- A complaint may be made to an employment tribunal where an employer has unreasonably refused the time off, or failed to pay the employee. Complaints must be brought within 3 months[55] of the time taken off, or when it should have been taken off.
- Where a complaint is upheld, the tribunal must make a declaration to that effect and, if the time off had not been allowed, order the employer to pay the employee the remuneration they were entitled to (in addition to their normal pay), or if the employee had not been paid for the time off, order the employer to pay them what they were entitled to.

79. *Unfair dismissal and detriment.* Employees are protected against unfair dismissal or detriment by their employer when acting as representatives of employees under a negotiated agreement or under the standard information and consultation provisions. They are also protected when standing as candidates for election, or when seeking to enjoy rights given them by the Regulations, and in certain other circumstances. However, the protections do not apply where an employee has disclosed confidential information in breach of

[54] working hours are any time when employees are required by their employment contracts to be at work

[55] a tribunal can extend this 3 month deadline where it is satisfied it was not reasonably practicable to bring the complaint within that period

a restriction imposed by the employer. A claim for unfair dismissal, or a complaint of detriment, may be brought before an employment tribunal.

Further guidance on protection against unfair dismissal and detriment

- An employee who is:
  - an employees' representative[56]
  - a negotiating representative
  - an information and consultation representative (where these have been elected or appointed under a negotiated agreement or the employer is subject to the standard provisions)
  - or a candidate to be such a representative

  and who was dismissed for performing any function or activity as such, or for requesting paid time off to act as a representative, would be unfairly dismissed. Similarly, representatives and candidates are protected against detriment by their employer done on the same grounds.
- Protections against unfair dismissal or detriment do not apply where an employee breached a confidentiality restriction imposed under regulation 25[57].
- Any employee (whether or not a representative or candidate) is protected against unfair dismissal or detriment on a number of grounds including for:
  (1) taking proceedings before the CAC or an employment tribunal (whether or not there is a valid complaint, as long as it is made in good faith);
  (2) requesting data on employee numbers under regulation 5;
  (3) acting with a view to securing that an agreement was negotiated or the standard provisions apply;
  (4) indicating support or lack of support for a negotiated agreement or the application of the standard provisions;
  (5) seeking to influence by lawful means how votes were to be cast in a ballot, or voting in a ballot;
  (6) expressing doubts about whether a ballot had been properly conducted.
- The Dispute Resolution Regulations 2004[58] will apply to cases of unfair dismissal or detriment relating to the I&C Regulations. They do not apply to complaints made to the CAC. An employee would not be able to bring a complaint of detriment to an employment tribunal if they had not put the reasons for their grievance in writing to their employer at least 28 days before applying to the tribunal. Also, if an employee had not completed the statutory dispute resolution procedure in relation to unfair dismissal or detriment before bringing the complaint to the tribunal, even if they were successful at the tribunal, their compensation would normally be reduced by between 10 and 50%. An employer who had not set up and followed a procedure that meets the minimum requirements in the Dispute Resolution Regulations, and against whom a complaint was upheld by a Tribunal, would normally have an award against them increased by between 10 and 50%.

[56] that is, someone who may on behalf of employees, request data on employee numbers (see regulation 5), or who may bring a complaint to the CAC, ie concerning an endorsement ballot (see regulations 8(7) and 10(1) and (2)), concerning an employer notification (see regulation 13(2)), concerning the appointment or election of negotiating representatives (see regulation 15(1)), or concerning proposed ballot arrangements under Schedule 2 (see Schedule 2 paragraph 3); or who must be consulted about ballot arrangements under Schedule 2 (see Schedule 2 paragraph 2(f) and (g)).

[57] unless it was a 'protected disclosure' (the so-called 'whistle-blower' protection)

[58] The Employment Act 2002 (Dispute Resolution) Regulations 2004 (SI 2004/752)

RESTRICTIONS ON CONTRACTING OUT OF RIGHTS GIVEN BY THE LEGISLATION

80. Employers may not try to exclude or limit the rights and obligations in the Regulations by means of an agreement, for example, through an agreement or contract with a third party, or through employees' contracts. Any provision of an agreement or contract that sought to do so would be void (see regulation 39). Similarly, any provision that sought to prevent someone bringing a dispute or complaint before the CAC or the Employment Appeal Tribunal would generally also be void. Similar rules apply in the case of rights to time off for employee representatives, and protections against unfair dismissal and detriment (see regulation 40), except that a formal agreement can be made not to take proceedings before an employment tribunal.

Further guidance on contracting out of rights given by the legislation

- Employers may not try to exclude or limit the operation of any provision in the I&C Regulations, by means of any agreement. This would include by means of employees' contracts, an agreement or contract with a third party, or a pre-existing or negotiated agreement.
- The restriction on contracting out means, for example, that employees' contracts may not waive their rights to be informed and consulted as provided for by the I&C Regulations.[59] A contract for the sale of the undertaking, or part of it, could not prevent employers informing and consulting employees or their representatives about the sale if they were required to do so by the standard I&C provisions or by a negotiated agreement (although the provisions on confidential information may be relevant).
- A pre-existing agreement could not prevent employees making a request to negotiate a new I&C agreement (although if an employee request had been made that was not endorsed by the workforce in a ballot the 3-year moratorium on subsequent requests would be relevant).
- Regulation 39 is not intended to prevent negotiated or pre-existing agreements that differ from the standard provisions in regulation 20, for example by providing for information and consultation on different subjects, by different means, or with different timing, since this is expressly allowed by the legislation. However, Article 5 of the EC directive would only allow negotiated agreement to contain provisions that are different from the standard rules in regulation 20 (which transpose Article 4 of the directive), not provisions that differ from other requirements of the legislation. So for instance, negotiated agreements could not deal with confidentiality issues in a way that was contrary to the confidentiality provisions in regulations 25 and 26, and could not exclude the right to make an application or complaint to the CAC or to the Employment Appeal Tribunal (EAT).
- The restriction on contracting out does not apply to an agreement to stop proceedings before the CAC or the EAT, for example, because a dispute had been settled 'out of court'.
- Any provision in an agreement (including an employee's contract) which sought to exclude or limit employees' rights to paid time-off, or to prevent someone bring a complaint to an employment tribunal under Part VIII of the Regulations, would be void. There are special provisions concerning formal agreements to refrain from instituting or continuing proceedings before an employment tribunal under Part VIII.

OTHER POINTS

Changes in the undertaking

81. Where there is a significant increase or decrease in the number of employees,

[59] this does not mean that a pre-existing or negotiated agreement must follow the standard provisions in regulation 20

for example, as a result of an acquisition, divestment or merger, or simply through substantial recruitment or redundancies, the employer and employees or their representatives will need to consider the implications for existing consultation arrangements.

82. A pre-existing or negotiated agreement must cover all the employees in an undertaking, so it is advisable to word it in such a way that new employees would automatically be covered. It is also advisable to include a provision stating how a restructuring will be dealt with, for example, in terms of any changes in the number and identity of employee representatives, including if appropriate arranging for new, additional or fewer representatives to be appointed or elected, and the possibility of revising the agreement.

Crown employees

83. Employees of the Crown are covered by the Regulations if they work in an undertaking that carries out an économic activity.

Administrators and receivers

84. Where there is a negotiated agreement, or an employer is subject to the standard information and consultation provisions, the obligation to inform and consult in accordance with that agreement or the standard provisions will continue to apply where a company goes into administration or receivership. The administrator or receiver would be acting on behalf of the employer who will continue to be subject to the obligations in the agreement or the standard provisions. The administrator or receiver must fulfil the employer's obligations, but would not be personally liable for failing to do so. The requirement to inform and consult would also continue to be subject to the provisions allowing confidential information to be subject to a confidentiality restriction in the legitimate interest of the undertaking, or to be withheld where disclosure would seriously harm the functioning of the undertaking or be prejudicial to it.

GLOSSARY OF TERMS AND ABBREVIATIONS

ACAS	Advisory, Conciliation and Arbitration Service. ACAS provides up-to-date information, advice and training to help employers and employees solve problems and improve employment relations.
Anonymous request	An employee request to negotiate an I&C agreement sent via the CAC which will handle it on the employees' behalf if they do not want to divulge their identity to their employer.
CAC	Central Arbitration Committee. The CAC has the main enforcement role under the Regulations.
Confidentiality restriction	A restriction on information given by an employer to employee representatives preventing them passing it to anyone else except as permitted by the employer.
Contracting out	Agreeing to exclude or limit the operation of any

	right or obligation in the I&C Regulations, for example through an employment contract. This is not permitted by the legislation except in limited circumstances.
EAT	Employment Appeal Tribunal. The EAT hears appeals against CAC and employment tribunal decisions, and is responsible for imposing penalties.
Employee request	A request made by the employees to their employer under regulation 7 to negotiate an I&C agreement.
Employer notification	A notification by an employer to his/her employees under regulation 11 of an intention to negotiate an I&C agreement. This allows an employer to start the statutory process without waiting for an employee request.
Endorsement ballot	A ballot of all the employees in an undertaking to see if they support an employee request to negotiate an I&C agreement. The ballot is allowed where the employer already has a valid pre-existing agreement. At least 40% of the workforce and a majority of those who vote must support the employee request in order to require the employer to negotiate a new I&C agreement.
I&C representatives	Information and Consultation representatives who are informed and consulted under either a negotiated agreement or the standard I&C provisions.
Listing Rules	Rules drawn up and enforced by the Financial Services Authority. They apply to companies whose shares are 'listed', a requirement for admission to the main market of the London Stock Exchange.
Moratorium	A prohibition on émployee requests and employer notifications to negotiate an I&C agreement. The prohibition normally applies for 3 years from the date of a negotiated agreement; the date on which the standard I&C provisions apply; or the date of an employee request which was not endorsed by the workforce in a ballot where there is a valid pre-existing agreement.
Negotiated agreement	An agreement negotiated between the employer and negotiating representatives under regulation 14, following a valid employee request, or an employer notification, and that meets the requirements in regulation 16.
Negotiating representatives	Representatives of the employees elected or appointed by the employees under regulation 14 to negotiate an I&C agreement following an employee request or an employer notification.

Pre-existing agreement	An agreement approved by employees before an employee request is made, and that meets the four criteria in regulation 8(1).
Price-sensitive information	Information which would be expected to cause a movement in a listed company's share price.
Standard I&C provisions	The standard information and consultation provisions that apply where an employer fails to initiate negotiations for an I&C agreement when required to do so, or where negotiations have failed to lead to an agreement.
Undertaking	In the case of companies, a separately incorporated *legal* entity as distinct from an organisational entity such as an establishment (site) or business unit.

Annex 1: Suggestions for Contents of Pre-existing or Negotiated Agreements

This annex makes suggestions for the contents of pre-existing or negotiated agreements. It is not intended to be prescriptive. Employers and employees or their representatives are free to agree whatever arrangements they wish as to the method, frequency, timing and subject-matter of information and consultation, according to the specific circumstances of their own organisation. ACAS publishes good practice guidance on drawing up voluntary agreements for information and consultation.

Pre-existing or negotiated agreements may provide for separate and different arrangements in different parts of the undertaking, such as different establishments or business units.

Coverage

- The undertaking covered by the agreement (or group of undertakings in the case of agreements covering more than one)
- Which employees in the undertaking(s) are covered by the agreement. (A negotiated agreement must cover all employees in the undertaking, though it could consist of several parts each of which only covers some of the employees. In the case of a pre-existing agreement, if the agreement does not cover all employees in the undertaking, there must be one or more other agreements which cover the remaining employees.)
- Whether separate arrangements will exist in different parts of the undertaking (for example, in different establishments, organizational divisions, or sections of the workforce)
- Where the employer has one or more collective agreements with trade unions, what the relationship is between those collective agreements and this agreement

Methods of information and consultation

- The type of arrangements to be set up, including whether there will be representatives of employees, and/or direct information and consultation with the workforce

- Whether any 'hierarchy' of structures will be set up, eg at national, regional, local level
- How any representatives of employees are to be chosen or appointed, how many such representatives, how long they will serve, how they are to be replaced
- Any facilities and time off for employee representatives
- Any obligations there may be on any employee representatives, for example, to report back to the workforce or to seek their views
- The nature of any direct forms of information and consultation with the workforce

Frequency and timing of information and consultation

- How often information and consultation will take place
- When information and consultation will take place

Subject-matter

- Types of subjects to be covered
- How subjects will be chosen and how agendas of any meetings will be drawn up

Information and consultation

- The type and nature of information to be provided
- How views/opinions of employees can be given
- What the employer will do in response
- Who will represent management at any meeting

Statutory consultation requirements

- How other legal requirements to consult employees (eg on collective redundancies, business (TUPE) transfers, health and safety, European Works Councils, pensions) will be handled where relevant, and what the relationship will be with the consultation arrangements set up under this agreement
- Employers and employees may wish to agree either to expressly exclude from the scope of the agreement matters about which there is a separate statutory obligation, or to adopt a similar arrangement to that allowed by regulation 20(5) of the standard I&C provisions. This would be to avoid being subject to two different legal requirements to consult over the same issue.

Confidential information

- How confidential or price-sensitive information will be dealt with (in the case of a negotiated agreement, this must be consistent with the requirements in I&C regulations 25 and 26 concerning confidential information)
- Obligations on anyone in receipt of confidential information
- Disciplinary measures for breach of any confidentiality restriction

Disputes

- How disputes can be resolved, ie disputes about whether the employer has properly informed and consulted in accordance with the agreement. (A negotiated agreement is enforceable at the Central Arbitration Committee, but it is advisable to have a mechanism for trying to resolve disputes without the need for a formal complaint.)

- In the case of a pre-existing agreement, whether it is legally enforceable

Restructuring

- Implications of a company restructuring for I&C structures, for example, the implications for the number and identity of any employee representatives, or the possibility of revising the agreement

Duration of agreement

- Duration of the agreement and the circumstances in which it can be reviewed, revised or terminated. This could be important because a three year moratorium on employee requests for a new I&C agreement (and on employer notifications under regulation 11) may apply.

Annex 2: Announcements to Employees Involving Price-sensitive Information[60]

Introduction

1. One of the key drivers behind the Government's approach to the implementation of the Information and Consultation Directive is that employees deserve fair treatment at work. This is particularly so when there have been rumours of a company restructuring, or an announcement of proposed redundancies is to be made. Ultimately, the decision to undergo a restructuring is for management but a commitment to establish a clear process and to communicate in an open and timely way with employees and their representatives is vital.
2. Employees have a right to know when their jobs are at risk. It is not acceptable that such news is first heard through the media. The reason sometimes given by employers for this is that these types of announcements involve price sensitive information which is required to be disclosed to the financial markets before it is disclosed to the employees themselves. This is not the case. This annex is intended to clarify that the Listing Rules and other equivalent rules do allow disclosure of price-sensitive information simultaneously to the financial markets and to the employees. Many companies already do this, and the Government strongly support such good practice.

The Listing Rules

3. Companies whose securities are listed (a requirement for admission to the main market of the London Stock Exchange) are subject to rules drawn up and enforced by the Financial Services Authority. These rules are known as the Listing Rules. Following the implementation of the Market Abuse Directive, the rules relating to disclosure of price sensitive information will also apply to issuers whose securities are admitted to trading on a regulated market. Among the aims of the Listing Rules is the maintenance of an orderly market by seeking to ensure that all market participants have simultaneous

[60] DTI has consulted the Financial Services Authority, AIM Regulation, OFEX Plc, The Takeover Panel, Her Majesty's Treasury and the US Securities and Exchange Commission over the factual content of this annex.

access to accurate price-sensitive information. This too is a fundamental principle of the AIM and OFEX rules.

4. Chapter 9 of the Listing Rules requires issuers to announce price sensitive information without delay[61]. Equivalent standards are contained in the AIM and OFEX rules. A major restructuring operation will often be price-sensitive. In other words, the announcement of the proposed restructuring would be expected to cause a movement in the company's share price, reflecting the market's re-evaluation of the company's new prospects. If this is not the case the obligations in Chapter 9 of the Listing Rules will not be relevant.
5. As discussed at paragraph 76 of the guidance on confidential information, employee representatives may be privy to price sensitive information on a confidential basis before it is publicly announced. However, neither the Listing Rules, nor the AIM or OFEX rules or the City Code on Takeovers and Mergers allow companies to give price-sensitive information to *all* the employees during the pre-announcement phase. In order to give a reasonable guarantee that information will be kept confidential, the circle of people privy to price-sensitive information must necessarily be a restricted one[62]. To inform more widely before a public announcement would mean that a group of potential and perhaps actual shareholders (the employees) were given access to price-sensitive information before others, which might risk creating a disorderly market and might also lead to breaches of the insider dealing provisions and the market abuse regime.
6. The Listing Rules and its equivalents require announcements involving price-sensitive information to be made as soon as proposals are finalised. This is to reduce the possibility of leaks between the taking of a decision and its announcement. For some companies the practice appears to have developed that the board will approve decisions towards the end of the day, after trading in the Stock Exchange has ceased, and then notify them to a Regulatory Information Service for release at 7am the following day, before trading starts. A consequence of this is that in large-scale restructurings involving redundancies, the affected employees may first learn of the proposals through early morning news reports before they arrive at work, rather than directly from their employer. This is a deeply unsatisfactory situation for employees.

[61] Chapter 9 of the Listing Rules will be revised as part of the implementation of the EU's Market Abuse Directive. The changes will come into force in the course of 2005. They will not change the need for companies to release inside information in a timely fashion.

[62] The City Code on Takeovers and Mergers requires that in the period before the announcement of a bid only a very restricted number of people can be privy to this information. The Panel's Annual Report 2003 stated that a very restricted number of people would generally be interpreted to mean no more than six external persons or parties. The Panel generally regards employee representatives as constituting one 'person' for this purpose, but may take the view that this would not be appropriate if a large number of representatives were appointed.

Good practice

7. The Listing Rules and its equivalents do not prescribe the specific time of day at which announcements should be made, only that the announcement must be made without delay. With this in mind the Government considers it good practice for a company to take such decisions during working hours so that the details can be released directly at the same time both to the stock market and the employees. There are provisions in the Listing Rules for submitting announcements at any time of the day and they can be released to market at any point between 7am and 6.30pm (there are other arrangements for releasing market announcements outside of these hours). This would allow the company to make a simultaneous announcement in the workplace to the employees concerned.
8. Many companies already do this and announce a decision involving price sensitive information to its workforce at the same time as to the market, by making the simultaneous announcement more or less straight after the decision is taken. The Government strongly supports this approach. However, it should be noted that the announcement of a decision could not be delayed overnight until after the market had opened and employees were at work as that would constitute a breach of the Listing Rules.
9. Of course it may not always be possible to inform every single employee directly before they hear about the announcement through other channels. For example shift workers may not be at the workplace if an announcement there was made at say 3.00 pm. Also it may be difficult to control the timing of announcements made by multinational companies based in other countries and who are carrying out global restructuring operations.

Companies listed in the US

10. It has sometimes been said that companies whose shares are also listed on the New York Stock Exchange are prevented by US rules from either sharing price-sensitive information with employee representatives in advance of market disclosure, or of timing their announcement in the way advocated in this guidance. The Securities Exchange Commission's Regulation on Full Disclosure (FD) applies to disclosures outside the company and generally requires non-selective disclosure of price-sensitive information. However, a disclosure made to employees would *not* be outside the company, and so would not be subject to Regulation FD. Similarly, the New York Stock Exchange rules and the National Association of Security Dealers rules do not prevent disclosures of price-sensitive information to employees.
11. Some UK companies with a dual London and New York listing, time their announcements for the afternoon in the UK which would be the morning in New York

Conclusion

12. Employers sometimes have to make difficult decisions that impact upon their employees. But how they approach this is important both for the sake of the affected employees and also to allow the restructured company to move forward with good morale among the employees who remain. The Govern-

ment believes that it is not acceptable that employees should hear about these kinds of developments via the media. Nor is it a legitimate defence to cite rules covering market announcements, either in the UK or overseas, as the reason why this should happen. Companies should be able to ensure that most of the employees affected by important announcements learn about them directly via company channels, no later than the public announcement is made.

Glossary

ACAS	Advisory, Conciliation and Arbitration Service
ARD	Acquired Rights Directive (2001/23/EC)
CAC	Central Arbitration Committee
CBI	Confederation of British Industry
DELNI	Department of Employment and Learning Northern Ireland
DTI	Department of Trade and Industry
EAT	Employment Appeals Tribunal
ERA	Employment Rights Act 1996
ETUC	European Trade Union Confederation, one of the European-level social partners representing employee interests
EWC	European Works Council
EWC Directive	European Works Council Directive (1994/45/EC)
Fixed Term Employees Regulations 2002	Fixed Term Employees (Prevention of Less Favourable Treatment) Regulations 2002 (SI 2002/2034)
ICE Regulations	Information and Consultation of Employees Regulations 2004 (SI 2004/3426)
Information and Consultation Directive	EU Information and Consultation (European Parliament and Council) Directive (2002/14/EC)
SEC	Securities Exchange Commission
TICE	Transitional Information and Consultation of Employees Regulations 1999 (SI 1999/3323)
TUC	Trades Union Congress
TULRCA	Trade Union and Labour Relations (Consolidation) Act 1992
TUPE	Transfer of Undertakings (Protection of Employment) Regulations 1981 (SI 1981/1794)
UNICE	Union des Industries de la Communanté Européenne — one of the European-level social partners representing business interests

Index

Made in the USA
Monee, IL
13 September 2026

62977353R10201